UK vs. UofL

College Basketball's

No. 1 Rivalry

Enough Said!

By Paul Willman

BEARHEAD PUBLISHING
- BhP -
Brandenburg, Kentucky

BEARHEADPUBLISHING
- BhP -
Brandenburg, Kentucky
www.bearheadpublishing.com

UK vs. UofL
College Basketball's No. 1 Rivalry
Enough Said!
by Paul Willman

Cover Design Bearhead Publishing
UK Athletics/Chet for the 2013 Final Photo on Cover
UofL Assistant AD Kenny Klein Photo on Cover

First Printing - April 2014
ISBN: 978-1-937508-27-2

1 2 3 4 5 6 7 8 9

Proudly printed in the United States of America.

UK vs. UofL

College Basketball's

No. 1 Rivalry

Enough Said!

"Although this book is full of facts and figures, it's really about author Paul Willman's passion for basketball in Kentucky and his firm conviction that no rivalry in college hoops, including Duke-UNC, is better than UK-UofL. He documents his argument with a mother lode of anecdotes, trivia, and factoids gleaned from a lifetime of watching the games and getting to know the men who played and coached them. It's a fresh, fun read that won't sway anybody on Tobacco Road, but that will delight all those who live and die with the Cats and the Cards."

Veteran Sportswriter Billy Reed

Biography

Paul Willman, a native Louisvillian, is a graduate of Atherton High School and Brigham Young University. Entering the broadcasting profession in April of 1986, at the age of 36, he started at WXVW Radio in Jeffersonville, IN. He also worked at WAVG Radio in Louisville before joining the WHAS Radio staff in June of 1988, where he hosted the Sunday Sports Roundtable Talk Show, and was a member of the UK Network with Tom Leach, the current "Voice of the Wildcats" as co-host of the post game talk show from 1990-94.

He was the lead writer for two productions produced by AdCraft, "It Started With a Peach Basket, the First 100 years of College Basketball History and "Flight to Greatness," the history of UofL Men's Basketball. He also produced two tape documentaries on the life of Adolph Rupp.

He has done radio play-by-play for high schools, Bellarmine University and was with the Louisville Fire Arena Football team for six years. Married 37 years, to Janette (Raeber) Willman, Paul and his wife have six children and four grandchildren – with one more grandchild due shortly after the release of this book.

Acknowledgments

My sincerest gratitude goes out to the following people who helped to make this great book possible:

INTERVIEWS CONDUCTED FROM 1988-2014

MITCH BARNHART, RALPH BEARD, CHIP BOES, RICK BOLUS, PHIL BOND, BOB BORAH, JUNIOR BRIDGEMAN, GARY BRUCE, DWAYNE CASEY, GOV. ALBERT B. "HAPPY" CHANDLER, "PAPA" JOE CHEVALIER, DR. THOMAS CLARK, JOHN CLAY, JACK COLEMAN, GARY CONNELLY, OSCAR COMBS, SCOTT DAVENPORT, BRAD DAVIS, BOB DOTSON, PAT DOYLE, JOHN DROMO, CLARENCE "BIG HOUSE" GAINES, LLOYD GARDNER, LARRY GAY, JOHN GIBSON, GARY GUPTON, CLIFF HAGAN, JOE B. HALL, TOM HAMMOND, FRANK HARTLEY, VERNON HATTON, BASIL HAYDEN, BERNARD "PECK" HICKMAN, NAT HOLMAN, TERRY HOWARD, LEE HUBER, STEVE KIRSCHNER, JOE KITCHEN, KENNY KLEIN, BOB KNIGHT, JOE KOCH, MIKE KRZYZEWSKI, KAREN KUTZ, TEV LAUDEMAN, DAVE LAWRENCE, BOB LOCHMUELLER, PAUL McBRAYER, TIM McGINTY, DOUG McINTOSH, TONY NEELY, TL PLAIN, KEN PORCO, LELO PRADO, BILLY REED, JOHN REUTHER, GENE RHODES, RUSSELL RICE, PHIL ROLLINS, PAUL ROGERS, EARL RUBY, HERKY RUPP, GROVER SALES, DAN SCHAEFER, HOWARD SCHNELLENBERGER, MIKE SILLIMAN, HOWARD STACEY, LOUIS STOUT, GIL STURTZEL, JOHN TAYLOR, KENT TAYLOR, VINCE TAYLOR

PHOTOS

UNIVERSITY OF LOUISVILLE ATHLETICS
UK ATHLETICS/CHET   COURTESY UK SPECIAL COLLECTIONS
RUTH BRYAN DIRECTOR MATTHEW HARRIS
DEBORAH DUNN
ED WARREN PHOTOGRAPHY

WHAS TV-11 DOCUMENTARY
ADOLPH RUPP, 40 YEARS AND COUNTING

BYU SPEECHES OF THE YEAR 1958
CBS SPORTS
CBS SPORT.COM
ESPN.COM
ADOLPH RUPP INTERVIEWS RUSSELL RICE
ADOLPH RUPP INTERVIEWS TEV LAUDEMAN
BIG BLUE HISTORY.NET

UK ATHLETIC DEPARTMENT

MITCH BARNHART   AD
JOHN HAYDEN   MEDIA RELATIONS
TONY NEELY MEDIA RELATIONS
KELLI ELAM MARKETING ASSOCIATE DIRECTOR UK ALUMNI ASSOCIATION FOR
COMMUNICATIONS, MEMBERSHIP AND MARKETING

UofL ATHLETICS

TOM JURICH   AD
KENNY KLEIN SENIOR ASSOCIATE AD/SID
NANCY WORLEY ASSOCIATE SID
ROCCO GASPARRO ASSISTANT SID
IRA GREEN ASSISTANT SID
LORI KORTE ASSISTANT SID
KIM PEMBERTON ASSISTANT SID
GARETT WALL ASSISTANT SID
SEAN MOTH ASSISTANT SID
KATHY TRONZO PROGRAM ASSISTANT

BEARHEAD PUBLISHING LLC

GARY D. DRECHSEL
MARY C. DRECHSEL

BEST FRIEND STEPHEN E. WHITE

Dedication

I have my own sports pedigree that I am dedicating this book to. My grandfather, Edward James Willman Jr. had an uncle, Charles Hambrick (he switched his name to Hamburg when he played baseball) who played for Louisville in the 1890 World Championship against Brooklyn that ended in a 4 to 4 games tie in the best-of-five out-of-nine. The last game was snowed out.

On my first birthday, I was with my grandfather and grandmother Willman at Parkway Field to watch the Colonels. They would later take me to see the Colonels play baseball again, the annual Policemen vs. Firemen baseball game and the Louisville Rebels play ice hockey.

My father, Paul Frederick Willman Sr. was for a time, the batboy for the visiting team at Parkway Field. Later, he returned to work the scoreboard in the outfield. We had a collection of old-time equipment, gloves that looked like Ty Cobb had used them.

He put my first rim up in the basement when I was five and we attended the annual UK game in Louisville and went to watch the Cardinals play as well.

He told me stories of when he went to New York to watch the Giants play at the Polo Grounds, his trips to the State High School Championship and watching the Cats play in the SEC Tournament at the old Armory. And he loved to tell of Male High School's 1945 State Championship team with Ralph Beard and Gene Rhodes who he attended school with.

This love I have for sports, especially basketball, in a large part comes from my progenitors who I love with a passion. When my father was in his last days in March of 2005, he got to see the Cards advance to the Final Four and the Cats almost make it.

I was working on a book idea back then, but it didn't materialize. He was disappointed, he wanted it published and wanted to read it before he left. I told him: "Dad, I'll write you one and wherever you are you'll be able to read it." I believe he, my grandfather and Uncle Charlie are all engaged in that reading right now.

Table of Contents

Preface

I sincerely believe that the UK-UofL is the No. 1 rivalry in all of college basketball. How do I know that? Because I have lived it for 63 years.

It was a very "blue" Christmas for me in 1957. I was just seven-years old when Santa Claus brought me a UK uniform. Nobody was doing that back then, but I had an angel mother who was always doing that kind of stuff. I wore it and dribbled my basketball as I listened to the games on the radio with my father. The UK band played the fight song a bit differently than they do today. It had a real distinct staccato opening. When I heard it, I came running.

One of my close friends from Junior High School was David Sholis. His father Vic, was the president of WHAS Radio and TV. He started the Crusade for Children and we became friends. I remember distinctly the afternoon he took his wife, Dave and me to see Rupp's Runts play Vanderbilt in Memorial Coliseum. Walking up the Avenue of Champions towards the Coliseum the building seemed to change before my eyes. It appeared almost like a great cathedral. You felt as though you were on sacred ground.

Dave, his dad and I along with *Courier-Journal* sportswriter Dean Eagle had a Bob Uecker seat for the December 12, 1967 matchup with UK and North Carolina in Freedom Hall. Front row, smack dab in the middle. I had never seen the ball move so fast as the "Super Sophs," Mike Casey, Dan Issel and Mike Pratt made it spin.

My dad and I went to the annual game in Freedom Hall and I still remember Charlie Ishmael making the free throw that took the Cats to the century mark, beating Notre Dame 100-53.

I've never witnessed another game like the December 30, 1958 matchup with UK and Illinois in Freedom Hall. Kentucky had a nice lead, but Mannie Jackson really started to take control. With just a few seconds left in the game, and UK leading 76-75, he stole the ball and went up for a jumper from around the foul line and missed. Time ran out and Kentucky won, but it was like we were filming an episode for the Twilight Zone as we headed for the exits; no cheering, no clapping and no one was talking above a whisper. I remember saying to my father, "Why is it so quiet?" Kentucky won. We talked about it outside where it was safer.

My father and I also went to Louisville games as well. One of my favorite Cardinals was Joe Kitchen. I liked his name. It was a pleasure to interview him in 1989 about UofL's win over UK in the 1959 NCAA.

I was going to major in communications at BYU but for some reason changed my mind after my freshman year. One night years later when I was 34-years old, watching the movie "The Natural" I told my wife, Janette, that I was going to be the "Roy Hobbs" of broadcasting. Two years later, I was working at WXVX and WAVG Radio in Louisville. Then in June of 1988, I had my own Sunday night talk show on WHAS Radio and joined the UK Network for four years (1990-94), co-hosting a post game talk show, with my friend Tom Leach, the current "Voice" of the Kentucky Wildcats.

Tom and I met at the 2013 UK-UofL football game. One of the first things he mentioned was the opportunities he still has sharing our experience as we watched the UK-Duke 1992 NCAA regional championship game. We were in the meeting room in the WVLK studios preparing for our post game show, when Coach Pitino didn't place anyone on the baseline to guard the inbounds pass. Both of us simultaneously yelled out: "No! No!"

I recently asked Sean Woods if there was any disorganization coming out of the huddle. Every time I see the replay, which seems to be most every day, I thought I detected some surprise in the face of Deron Feldhaus as he returned to the court. Woods said, "There was no disorganization. Coach Pitino called the play to double team Laettner instead of having one man guard the inbounds pass. He did tell Feldhaus and Pelphrey to be careful and not foul him."

The late, great coach, Red Auerbach, of the Boston Celtics did a study that showed when you put pressure on the player throwing the ball inbounds, the advantage goes to the defensive team 78 percent of the time. With my two oldest sons, Rhett and Adam, we watched Pat Riley do the same thing when he was coaching the New York Knicks. He had no one guarding the player throwing the ball inbounds. I said to my sons "that Riley had a seven-footer (actually 6-10) on the bench, Herb Williams who should be guarding that man."

The pass came in to the Chicago Bull's Toni Kukoc who hit a jumper to win the game. Shortly after that game, we saw the Knicks in the same situation, but this time Riley had Williams guarding the inbounds pass, the player threw the ball away and the Knicks won the game. Of course, coaches don't have the luxury of sleeping on those split-second game decisions, but the Godfather, Vito Corleone would advise one to go with the percentages.

On my talk show, at press row and working on various projects and assignments, I have had the opportunity to meet the fans and learn their feelings firsthand, the coaches, who have taught me much about the game, administrators who have been insightful and my colleagues who cover the games by word; spoken and written. I have invested countless hours in the research of basketball, and not just the UK-UofL side of the issues.

Starting in the fall of 1988 I was able to interview many of the figures who belong to the great Kentucky tradition: Herky Rupp, son of Coach Adolph Rupp, Paul McBrayer, former Rupp assistant coach 1935-43, Ralph Beard, Alex Groza, Larry Conley, Louie Dampier, Tom Kron, Cliff Hagan, Lou Tsioropoulos, Basil Hayden (UK's first All-American), and Russell Rice, former UK Sports Information Director just to name a few. I was able to find a victory for Coach Rupp that had not been included in his official total moving him from 875 to 876.

And especially during my talk shows, I have become acquainted with much of the fans' banter about the Cards and the Cats.

In October of 1991, I was the lead writer and researcher for the video entitled: "It Started With A Peach Basket." It was a panorama of the first 100 years of college basketball produced locally by Roy Hamlin's company, AdCraft.

Among the coaches I interviewed were John Wooden, Denny Crum, Dean Smith, Mike Krzyzewski, Ray Meyer, Judd Heathcote, Bob Knight, Pete Newell, Nat Holman, Clarence "Big House" Gaines, John McLendon and Tex Winter (Phil Jackson's right-hand man, who developed the "Triangle Offense")

Following that video, I worked again with AdCraft on a UofL video entitled: "Flight to Greatness". I had the privilege of interviewing Coach Denny Crum again, Coach "Peck" Hickman, Assistant Coach Jerry Jones, A.D. Bill Olsen and former players Junior Bridgeman, Charlie Tyra, John Turner and many others, getting to know firsthand, the stories of the Cardinals' championship seasons.

From 1939 when the NCAA tournament first started, until 1969 when John Wooden won his fifth NCAA championship, the game of college basketball was dominated by one-Adolph Rupp and his University of Kentucky Wildcats. As he said in an address to the BYU student body in 1958:

"Kentucky did not make the greatest name in basketball by having a bunch of boys who wouldn't train."

Not too far behind was Bernard "Peck" Hickman, who took a struggling University of Louisville men's basketball team, and used the U.S. Navy's V-12 program to launch the Cardinals to a big-time status level on the college basketball stage.

At that time, until November 26, 1983, this rivalry continued to be played only on paper, except for four post-season contests, since the last regular season meeting between the two schools played out in January of 1922.

As important as football is to the financial well-being of college athletic programs, basketball still reigns supreme in the Bluegrass state. Many have said: "it is a religion," and so be it. This basketball passion, has created the greatest base of college basketball fans in the country. Fans that confirm this fact, by the many ways they reveal their "fanatical" support.

My desire was to produce a one-volume primer that would maintain the relevance of the rivalry's history, as it continues to annex greater levels of excellence with Calipari and Pitino.

Unfortunately, I believe after continuing research, that there is no one living today who knows why the two schools stopped playing each other in the major sports of basketball and football in the 1920s. However, the story of this rivalry's revival is fascinating. After establishing the meaning of this rivalry, I follow a time line of earlier history right up to the resumption of the regular season basketball game on November 26, 1983. I have written a capsule of all 33 games since that time. I include a heading of pertinent facts, a pre-game report, quotes, probable starters, game analysis, box score and points after. Unless I include interviews I have done in the present and the past, these quotes are from sportswriters who have covered the games originally. I give credit to these writers in the Acknowledgment part of the book. It would be cumbersome to always be citing the sources, but quotation marks reveal they came from the original contributors of these game stories.

Those who covered these games in the past, in many cases, collected the same quotes at different press conferences and other information they gathered on their own. I have either added my own ideas in the review of these games or have expanded on ideas from the original source.

In chapter ten, I have produced a model which I feel quantitatively establishes UK vs. UofL as college basketball's No. 1 rivalry—enough said!

The concluding chapters cover a short treatise on how the restoration of the football series in 1994 has added to the dimensions of this rivalry, defectors, near-misses, (games they might have played) interesting facts the future of the rivalry and final thoughts.

I express my heartfelt gratitude to all those who have contributed to the writing of this book with their time, information or photos that have been included. It is also my hope, that everyone who has the opportunity to read this work will find it informative, thought-provoking, entertaining and helpful in creating even more interest and enjoyment for this rivalry.

Paul Willman, Author

Chapter One
What's in a Rivalry?

Coach Adolph Rupp spoke to the 1958 Brigham Young University student body about the contribution he felt sports make to our world. And he made this point early in that speech, "Now, you may not agree with everything that I say, but if you would agree with everything that I say; then, there'd be no use in me coming here in the first place. So you take everything with a grain of salt, and possibly when we leave here today, you'll have some idea of what I think of the sports world."

Coach Denny Crum basically said the same thing, this way: "People don't see the same things the same way. They look at them differently." That gives persuasion an opportunity to help level the playing field, bringing more fans into agreement.

The intent of this book is to prove beyond a shadow of doubt; leaving a hung-jury as no option, that the University of Kentucky (UK) versus the University of Louisville (UofL) is indeed, college basketball's No. 1 rivalry. There are also secondary purposes layered between the lines: (1) to persuade more people to pull for the adversary, or arch rival in this case, because both teams represent the same state, (2) although you may never pull for the other team even with your teeth clinched, give credit where and when it is due, and last but not least, (3) healthy competition is good for fun and business.

Competition between the two cities officially began with the arrival of the 1790 U.S. Census. Lexington was the largest city in Kentucky at that time, and even bigger than Cincinnati and Pittsburgh. Louisville would seize the lead for the Bluegrass conglomerate, which it retains today, when the 1830 Census was completed.

The rivalry in basketball would not take birth for some 83 years until UofL came to Lexington on February 15, 1913 to play Kentucky State, as it was known at that time.

First, it is necessary to define rivalry. The Merriam-Webster Online Dictionary states: "Rivalry is an earnest effort for superiority or victory over another. It speaks of a healthy rivalry in sports between two schools" (If there is such an animal). Obviously, basketball takes center stage here, but all sports in which the two universities compete are included. However, these activities can be expanded to cover virtually anything such as academics, fundraising etc., when a state of competition exists between the two schools.

Let's examine rivalry's related terms. We have words coming off-the-bench to enter the fray with incendiary intensity-argument, words such as ball game, battle, clash, collision combat, competition, conflict, confrontation, contention, contest, controversy, debate, disagreement, discord, disputation, dispute, dissension, dogfight, duel, face-off, friction, grapple, horse race, match, nail-biter, quarrel, row, showdown, strife, struggle, sweepstakes and even war! Pretty much covers UK-UofL.

Now, a rival is one or two or more striving to reach or obtain something that only one can possess—victory—in this case, the national championship.

Yes, you want to win state bragging rights. Yes, you want to win your conference. Yes, you want to win your conference post season tournament. Yes, you want to go to the Final Four, but bringing home that championship hardware is the ultimate—Yes!

This desire at times seems to border on lust, even covetousness or unyielding passion. To stay in good graces with your religious leader, parents or mentor, better not go too far past that unyielding passionate level. Fans tend to forget this at times though. That's why each year, when Midnight Madness arrives, 351 Division I groups of basketball fans renew their quest by visualizing their team winning that national championship. But in reality, only a small fraction of those roundball fanatics have a legitimate hope of reaching that gloried destination.

Five schools have won 33, or 44 percent of the NCAA's 75 National Championships: UCLA (11), UK (8), IU (5) North Carolina (5) and Duke (4). Add three more schools, Louisville (3), Kansas (3) and Connecticut (3) and eight schools have won 42 or 56 percent of the championships!

Six more schools have won two each: Oklahoma State, (known as Oklahoma A&M when they won their titles) San Francisco, Cincinnati, North Carolina State, Michigan State and Florida. Fourteen of the 351 schools have won the NCAA 54 times or 72 percent of the national championships. Add the 21 schools that have won a single national championship, and only 10 percent of the 351 teams competing for the title in this 2013-14 season, can be repeat winners.

We are fortunate in Kentucky, to have two programs which are capable of going all the way, and have done so a combined 11 times. UK's eight titles and UofL's three represent almost 15 percent of the 75 championships.

Only one state, California has more with 15: UCLA (11), San Francisco (2), California (1) and Stanford (1). North Carolina also has 11, but it takes three teams to make its total: North Carolina (5), Duke (4), and North Carolina State (2).

Considering the population of our Commonwealth, no other state has more national championships per person than Kentucky. Many have described basketball in this state as a "religion." Back to the dictionary for one aspect of the meaning of the word: "An interest, a belief, or an activity that is very important to a person or group." That definition fits the many denominations found here in the Bluegrass State: Cardinals, Wildcats, Hilltoppers, Colonels, Racers, Eagles, Knights, Thoroughbreds, Panthers, Norse, Saints, Pioneers, Mountaineers, Bearcats, Tigers, Patriots, Blue Raiders, Cougars, Bears, Golden Eagles, and Bulldogs. Each fan has a "conversion" story to share, how they decided to "join-up" with one of these particular congregations.

Most fans will say: "That is the way I was raised, or I went to school there." But it's more than just upbringing or getting an education. It requires an experience or memorable moment that sticks with a person to brand one's loyalty to his or her beloved school. And it may have nothing to do with attending school there.

In my case, memory tells me that I loved the game first. I can remember my dad putting up my first goal in the basement when I was five years old. Then, in 1957 Santa Claus brought me a UK uniform. Hardly anybody was doing that back then, but I was blessed with an angel mother who had connections with that "Jolly Old Elf." I would listen to every UK game on the radio with my dad, wearing the uniform and often, dribbling my basketball.

Couple that with the fact that I went to church with three of Vernon Hatton's uncles (He was an All-American on UK's 1958 NCAA championship team) and I was a Wildcat fan, true blue through and through by the time I was seven. My dad and I went to the annual UK game in Freedom Hall, but we also went to UofL games too.

Each truly converted fan is vital to the life of the rivalry. The fans are the rivalry's foundation. Without the fans nothing happens. One may give credit to administrative leaders, coaches, community leaders, corporate sponsors etc. and rightly so because they're all vital to the overall operation, but it's the fans that really make things happen. They buy the tickets, purchase the merchandise, travel and talk the talk 24-7.

Almost everyone I have spoken to around Kentucky, and many outside the area, agree that the UK-UofL fans are the most passionate, knowledgeable and enthusiastic college basketball fans in the country.

UK fans are found everywhere in the state—border to border. Kentucky is the attendance leader and travels better than any other basketball fan base.

The Louisville metro area has led the nation for over a decade in watching college basketball, and UofL is the No. 1 college basketball revenue generator in the nation. WLKY-TV Sports Director Fred Cowgill confirms those metro Louisville stats: "Those are facts that cannot be disputed. The fans are why I have stayed here for 28 years. I get excited when I hear women talking about the game as they reach around the lettuce in the store. In fact, more women came up and talk to me about basketball than men do. The fans get the strategy of the game too."

Bellarmine University basketball coach Scott Davenport describes the UK-UofL fans this way: "From horn to horn, they'll bring it better on that day, than any other time of the year."

Chip Boes, former Pensacola State College basketball coach added: "If you go to a coffee shop in Raleigh, N.C., they're not talking about Duke-UNC, but go to any coffee shop in Kentucky and they'll be talking UK-UofL. Alabama-Auburn are the most passionate rivals in college football. They're at it 24-7, 365 days a year. Kentucky-Louisville does the same thing in college basketball."

Ground rules for rivalry bashing is a must and the first rule for rivalry bashing is—there are no rules, but some guidelines may be helpful, because unfiltered passion can evoke such words as hate, and cause fans to commit absurdities and obscenities that most would normally omit from their activities of daily living. Watching excited fans destroy property or become violent with each other turns a rivalry into something very different, something to be avoided. That's why it is imperative that we do not allow the emotion of the event to power the motion of our reactions to rivalry encounters.

The purpose of sports is to have fun. It's entertainment, but we can also be counted as benefited observers, if we are inspired by the players on the court to improve the level of performance in our own personal "arenas" of life. I'm not saying it's necessary that every fan became an ordained minister but using profanity, off-color stories, obscene hand-gestures, screaming or physical attacks to prove one's position, reveals in essence; that either you are defending a weak position, have no position at all, have been influenced by some environmental stimuli or need to enroll online for a social graces webinar.

I succumbed to the hate approach when I interviewed Coach John Wooden in his home back in December of 1991. I was writing the script for a video entitled: "It Started With a Peach Basket." It covered the first 100 years of college basketball and was produced by Roy Hamlin's company, AdCraft which was located here in Louisville. Roy had worked with Howard Schnellenberger in Miami and came to Louisville with him.

While my cameraman was getting everything ready to roll I told Coach Wooden that, "for 12 years I hated your guts because you were breaking all of Coach Rupp's records."

Then the man known as the "Wizard of Westwood" started doing what he did best—teach. His unassuming reply was, "That's alright son." Three simple words changed everything. He disarmed me, for in reality, I never hated the man; he knew that and now, I knew it.

In fact, he complimented Coach Rupp and smiled when he said, "There's only one man who has won more national championships."

He came on my radio show sometime after that and I enjoyed talking with him very much.

It's the way we say things. I have a lawyer friend named Drew White, naturally, he talks a lot about how we use words in conveying meaning. Here's a Drew White story to illustrate the point:

Jim: Hey John! Are you hungry?

John: Sure.

Jim: How would you like some bacon and eggs?

John: Sounds fine.

Now the wording and the story change just a little bit:

Jim: Hey John! Are you hungry?

John: Sure.

Jim: How would you like some chicken embryos and a few strips of swine flesh?

John: Oh, on second-thought, I ate last week.

Let's try that with "Little Brother," the phrase that UK Coach Eddie Sutton made so popular or unpopular back in the mid-1980s. Let's insert the phrase, "Younger Brother." How's that for soothing the meaning? It's much easier to comprehend that a younger brother's accomplishments do nothing to detract from the older brother's successes and vice-a-versa.

If anyone doesn't agree that UK and UofL are both college powerhouse elites, then there's really nothing that can be done to save them. Cardinal fans should take into account that their leader, Athletics Director Tom Jurich has no aversions about being called "little brother." He said: "It makes me want to work harder. I learned the value of hard work and what it can do growing-up." Not just words, but some actions show little constraint or class.

We're familiar with the 2012 Final Four sideshow in a Georgetown, Ky. kidney dialysis clinic, where a UK and UofL fan got into a fight.

I picked up this unusual tale from Karen Kutz of Louisville, who says she will never pull for Kentucky under any circumstances. Some ten years ago she and her mother went to Lexington for a football game. In a section occupied mostly by Cardinal fans, a few Wildcat backers were setting in front of Karen and her mother.

This one female Cat fan continued to stand-up during the action and was asked by Karen's mother and others if she would please sit down. The Wildcat fan turned around and said that she had bought her ticket and would do as she pleased. Karen's mother placed her hand on the lady not down in front, and asked again if she would please sit down. The UK fan responded by turning around and belted Karen's mother in the mouth, damaging her teeth. Security was called; the female Kentucky fan was escorted out of the stadium. But the drama was far from over.

The UK fan filed a criminal suit against Karen's mother but failed to make an appearance in court. The Cardinal side filed a civil suit for sustained damages and won the case.

Karen and her mother returned to Commonwealth Stadium this year, 2013 and were treated much better. No punches thrown this time. I told Karen there is the principle of repentance, but she preferred to think that the Cats have just been simply humbled in football. Although humility hadn't shut things down completely, there were some fans still slinging trash talk, even falling back on the old reliable "little brother" jab for what it's worth and what are you doing in our stadium?

Former UofL football player from 1955-57, Gil Sturtzel remembers a not so "magic" bus ride in Lexington. It was Coach Steve Kragthorpe's first year and the game was at Commonwealth Stadium. The Cats had lost four consecutive games in the series while Coach Bobby Petrino was on the Cards' sidelines.

There were 70,857 fans jammed-packed in the stadium. Excitement was high since Kentucky had beaten Clemson in the Music City Bowl the year before and Bobby Petrino was coaching elsewhere. UK won 40-34, snapping that four-game losing skid against Louisville.

Gil Sturtzel described the bus ride back to the Red Mile horse racing track where the Cardinal fans had parked their cars and tailgated before the game: "When we came to a stop close to the track, there were many Wildcat fans roaming the area. A wave of them came over to the bus while we were still inside and began to push on the bus, rocking it back-and-forth."

Some call that the "lunatic fringe." That doesn't mean those in this fraternity are crazy, but as the dictionary defines it, "they are members of a political or social group or movement who have the most extreme or foolish ideas."

One can have a foolish or extreme thought, but the problem arises as one of my friends Hartman Rector says: "When you feed it pie a la mode!"

Now let's go for some lighter fare. There's always a reason why someone does something and that includes changing sides in the rivalry. Kent Taylor, Sports Director at WLKY-TV might have been named; Adolph. His dad John Taylor, lived in Louisville and enrolled at UK in September of 1963. He quickly became one of the biggest Wildcat basketball fans on campus. He was a fraternity brother with Pat Riley, knew all the guys and this helped to seal the deal. He also was a huge admirer of Coach Adolph Rupp.

But a slight problem developed. He was very interested in a young lady named Ann Schmidt who still lived in the River City. Every weekend found him back in Louisville, dating the young lady, so he decided to transfer to UofL. He arrived on the Belknap campus in January of 1966, the year of "Rupp's Runts" and continued dating, but remained a staunch UK fan. He even attended the game when Coach Rupp became college basketball's all-time winningest coach. He married Ann and joked that when they had a son, they would name him Adolph, because of his love for UK basketball. Things fell in place this way: they bought a toy poodle and named it Adolph so that their first son could be named Kent.

Even after graduating from the University of Louisville Law School, John Taylor still sported Big Blue. But around 1980 after Denny Crum had won his first NCAA championship, the young lawyer could no longer understand why UK fans still looked down on Louisville as a second-class citizen in the basketball world. He also didn't understand why Coach Hall and the university wouldn't change the policy and allow the Wildcats to play the Cardinals.

He liked Denny Crum's style of play, and so, unlike the 186 men who declined to cross the line in the sand at the Alamo, and remained to fight, (some say Jim Bowie crossed over due to illness, but remained anyway) John Taylor became a Louisville Cardinal fan.

Kent became a ball boy for the Cards along with Allan Houston, and John Taylor, a successful lawyer in Denver, CO., still has Louisville season tickets for the 30th year and counting. Crossing that line in the sand occurs periodically from both sides.

Tim McGinty, former A.D. and current Steward for Development at St. Gabriel School in Fern Creek, and his wife Loretta were both UofL fans when they got married. But when Howard Schnellenberger left town for Oklahoma saying that he couldn't win a national championship here because of the conference affiliation, Tim made an exchange of Cardinal season tickets for the Wildcat brand. Now, they still are happily married, but this happiness exists in a "house divided" and divided it certainly is.

In 2012 Tim took his son Kyle to the Final Four and left Loretta at home, explaining that she wouldn't fit in listening to them talk about Kentucky's victory. In 2013 it was Loretta who wanted to follow the Cards to the championship. Tim resisted the first and second rounds and the regional, but promised he would take her to Atlanta for the national championship.

Upon arrival in Atlanta, Tim became sick, so sick, that he went to the hospital. After a battery of tests, he was told there was absolutely nothing wrong with him. He told the doctor why he was in town, and that he just couldn't force himself to watch Louisville play, and the doctor suddenly changed his prognosis to "Cardinalitis."

Loretta didn't get to see her Cardinals win their third national championship.

On October 18th, 2013 the McGinty home had a decision to make; UofL was playing UCF and Big Blue Madness was on TV as well. Loretta stayed upstairs to watch Cardinal football and Tim enjoyed Big Blue Madness in the basement.

Tim is hoping that Wildcat football will come around with Stoops, but he goes to all of the games because he wants to see teams like Alabama play.

Now it's time to devote our energies to "Handling Objections." Fans say I could get along better with the other side if they would only make some changes in their positions.

Many Cardinal fans wail, "Kentucky fans think they invented basketball! I just can't stand that!" For the record, Dr. James Naismith invented basketball and he was born in Almonte, Canada.

Abraham Lincoln was born in Kentucky but try to get someone from Illinois to concede that fact. Their automobile license plates proudly proclaim Illinois as the "Land of Lincoln." Even though Lincoln was born in Kentucky, he became so popular in Illinois that he was elected President of the United States.
Same result about basketball's origin can be applied here.

Let's play our word modification game. Instead of saying that Kentucky invented basketball, simply say that Kentucky has popularized basketball. I know that is an accurate portrayal, for I have seen even Coach Wooden's signature on a photograph proclaiming Coach Adolph Rupp as Mr. Basketball.

Louisville fans like to say that the SEC is a football conference and that Coach Rupp played a weak schedule. The truth is when Coach Rupp first arrived at Kentucky, many of his players also played football. If the SEC was so weak, he should have won all of his games.

From top to bottom, the SEC may not be as strong as some conferences, but four teams from the ACC Conference have won 12 NCAA titles and three teams from the SEC have won 11 titles. Not much difference where it really counts. In reality I think that Coach Rupp and Coach Crum had very similar philosophies when it came to scheduling.

Coach Rupp played a strong non-conference schedule taking his team to New York, challenging the Big Ten and playing in such tournaments as the Sugar Bowl that brought other good team to New Orleans to play. Then, there would always be three or four teams you had to battle in the SEC.

Coach Denny Crum played a strong non-conference schedule as well. As he told me: "I didn't back down from anyone."

In the Missouri Valley and Metro Conferences there would always be three to five teams that could really play.

Many said UCLA had the benefit all those years of playing weaker overall competition in the West and Midwest NCAA regionals. Again, Coach Crum said: "That may be true, but nobody was able to beat the Bruins." (Except for N.C. State in 1974)

When Kentucky went all the way, the schedule really didn't matter; they beat who they had to beat. Kentucky fans have felt the same way about UofL's schedule from time to time, which translates-continuously. Right now the Cardinal football staff, team and fans don't appreciate being in the "jaws of the vice" concerning playing a weak schedule.

One final thought to ponder, how long will fans on both sides of the issue be content to pay such prices for basketball tickets, while so many average teams at best, appear on their home games part of the schedule? UofL will be in a better position when they start playing in the ACC in 2014 schedule wise.

Another rivalry irritant that effects both sides deals with not allowing the other fan base to enjoy its bragging rights. For example, if the game is played on New Year's Eve, the next day the losing side will counter with: "Don't talk to me about that game, it was last year."

The extending no credit for winning list is endless; you had more time to rest, we were sick, our team was taking tests, I spilled my drink on the guy in front of me, the officials were crooks, we had too many injuries, the ball wasn't inflated properly, we were tired, your guys got away with hacking incessantly, we came close, so we won the game too or the ball boy spiked our water cooler. You get the idea.

December 29th, 2012 at the YUM Center, UK almost pulled it-off, but the Cards prevailed 80-77. The Cats were 11 of 23 from the foul line.

Bob Borah, one of the two Cardinals left from the 1948 team that played UK in the Olympic Trials game, the other is Kenny Reeves, told me that after that game, is 97-year-old sister called him and said: "Y'all cheated."

I called my brother and said, "If the Cats had hit some free throws, they might have won." I could still feel the word, won, reverberating on my lips when my brother Eric exclaimed: "The refs took us out of our game calling too many fouls."

Maybe Coach Pitino was telling his guys in the huddle that the best defense was to foul Kentucky. Are you guilty of creating problems discussing the game, when there is an opportunity to finally extend some credit?: "Hey, enjoy your win; it may be your last." Be pleasant in victory or defeat. It's only a game? Right?

Accusations of fans being obnoxious will uncover about the same percentage of adherents on both sides. Since there are more UK fans in the state, then logic begs that the Cats have an obnoxious edge in this rivalry.

Many Cardinal fans tell me they feel that there are still those UK fans and members of the administration that have a nasal condition that science has been unable to eradicate; dare I say It? Stuck-up! They have a conceited, condescending opinion concerning everything Red and Black. I have to agree in some cases that rings true, but there are many more who don't feel that way at all.

The insurance industry is a prime example of how competition should work. The top producers in the business are always trying to help their fellow agents improve. That's good for everybody. They congratulate one another, then go all out to beat the other guy by selling the most insurance possible to be No.1.

Another bashing technique often used by both sides is "back-and-forth." No! I'm not talking about a mid-court violation.

Here's how it works. Talking to a UK fan, he begins to thaw-out and agrees that UofL has accomplished a thing or two. Then, I proceed to add to his list and he will abruptly change his countenance and in a stern voice utter, "Hey! If you start talking nice about them I'll change my mind."

Talking to a UofL fan, he begins to thaw-out and agrees that UK has accomplished a thing or two. Then, I proceed to add to his list and he will abruptly change his countenance and in a stern voice utter, "Hey! If you start talking nice about them I'll change my mind."

During each of these conversations, I'm sure I've seen Pavlov's dog walking around somewhere in the room.

Another bashing technique that really grates on the nerves, like the scratching of chalk on the chalkboard is "if." It usually spins like this: If the officials had called all the fouls on your team, if the officials hadn't called so many fouls on us, if our best player hadn't fouled out, if my team hadn't practiced so much, if we didn't have so many injuries, if our fans had received more tickets, if that rebound shot had gone in, if we didn't play the game so early in the season, if we didn't play the game so late in the season, if the play-by-play man hadn't jinxed us, if a couple of our players hadn't been sick, if our one player hadn't broken-up with his girlfriend and if and if and if.
That makes it pretty "ify."

I played the "if" game with Coach Wooden. When I and my cameraman were in his home for an interview, when I said, "If Larry Conley had not been sick, and Pat Riley didn't have that infected toe, Kentucky would have beaten Texas Western. If Mike Casey hadn't severely broken his leg in the summer before his senior season, and Bob McCowan hadn't been kicked off the team for breaking rules, (Mike Pratt said Bob was the quickest player on the team) Kentucky would have beaten you in 1970 when we were ranked No. 1 as it was."

Coach Wooden then turned to my cameraman and said: "This boy likes to major in ifs. Son, I had a player that was injured in 1966 (Freddie Goss). If he had been able to play, I like to think I could have won another championship. Et tu, Johnny?

I interviewed Doug McIntosh, who played at Lilly High School in Laurel County. He was recruited by Tennessee, Kentucky and UCLA. When Tennessee Coach John Sines resigned, that eliminated the Volunteers, but Sines had played at Purdue, a few years after Coach Wooden and recommended Wooden sign McIntosh.

After UCLA had won back-to-back national championships, Doug's goal was to be a member of the first team to win three consecutive national championships. He said, "That Goss was out for the year and he believes like Wooden, that they could have won again if Goss had been in the line-up." Then he said, "There's that if again."

Another bashing measure is "the conference." Cat fans are frequently criticized for pulling for the SEC. They are constantly told they don't belong there in football. That's a tough one to respond to because the record usually reinforces the criticism. Get the 20th best recruiting class in the nation and your 10th in the SEC (2014 recruiting year). But pulling for the other conference team isn't a problem unless they play another state school. Then the debate heats up again.

Now, when I ask a Cardinal fan if they will pull for UK against Duke or North Carolina if they play for the national championship, about 45 percent say yes. Now that UofL is going to the ACC, some fans are using the Wildcat answer concerning their own ACC: "No we won't pull for the Cats because the Tar Heels and Blue Devils are in our conference. It works about the same for UK fans as well.

Last, but not least is the Silent Treatment (New techniques are constantly on the rise). I'll be discussing the rivalry with someone who has just seen the movie "Glory Road." My comment: "There are many inaccuracies in that movie." Well, he or she responds: "They need to include things like that to make the film more interesting." Didn't Billy Joel have a song about honesty?

Then, I proceed to inform them that the movie portrays the UK band playing Dixie, and a Kentucky person running while waving the Confederate flag.

First, the university president wouldn't provide the money for the band to travel with the team, so the band stayed home. Second, I have never seen a UK cheerleader use a Confederate flag at a game and I have never heard the band play Dixie.

Then, I do hear the "Sounds of Silence" from the fan, and find him, or her, clinging to some object, but saying nothing.

I did some research and found a review of football in the 1890s at UK and one sentence that mentioned the band did play Dixie. That is not prima facia evidence that it has always been so, for it has not.

The silent treatment reminds me of what Jim Watkins, former head of the Jefferson County Schools Activities and Athletics shared with me: "Paul, there have been several people who have come to me and said: 'I know so and so is cheating trying to get my son to come to their school.'" Jim continued: "But when I tell them to come with me and I'll let you testify to that, they don't come forward."

On my talk show I used to refer to that as a memory lapse, or a case of laryngitis. It's just the silent treatment manifesting itself in different forms. But they all fail to properly acknowledge something.

The ultimate rivalry bashing issue to wrestle with is the success of both programs.
Kentucky fans are accustomed to hearing how great they are: "The Roman Empire of College Basketball", from Coach Pitino, "We're everybody's Super Bowl" to quote Coach Calipari.

If they don't believe it, this kind of conditioning will help those weak in the faith.
Eight National Championships, winningest program of all-time, UK has been at or near the top of the college marquee for a long time.

Louisville's name has been on that elite marquee for sometime too, counting three national championships to their credit.

Robert Morris' win over Kentucky in the 2013 NIT, and Louisville's loss to Morehead State in the NCAA 2nd Round in 2011, did not implode these two great programs. But here's the dilemma that demands a solution: Since both teams are now at the top of the college basketball world, (some may not agree with this statement) how can one recognize UK's greater accomplishments without detracting from UofL and vice-a-versa?

Fred Cowgill of WLKY-TV in Louisville thinks it's simple: "Kentucky is the iconic program in this sport, just accept that fact and move on, don't let it bother you." Cowgill continues: "Competition is a wonderful thing. Enjoy what your team can do. I'm a Yankees' fan. It's driving me crazy what the Red Sox are doing this year, but we can take them next year."

Fred points out that, "Kent Taylor who is the sports director at WAVE-TV worked with me here. I love him. This business is tough, so when he breaks a story; I'm glad for him, but I'm out to get the next one."

Administrators and coaches are very important but fans are everything, and fans need somebody to cheer for and of course, that's the players.

Those who attend the two schools from outside the state, may not have a grasp on the rivalry when they first arrive here, but before they unpack their suitcases they are veterans. Players today, since both schools are signing top prospects, may be more familiar with each other than players of yesterday, because of social media, all-star games and the AAU competition. They may do things together off the court, but when game time arrives, they go at it with all they've got.

The number-one reason they want this rivalry win so bad—is the fans. They appreciate their support and want to present them bragging rights for the year.

The two men at the top, UK A.D., Mitch Barnhart, and UofL A.D., Tom Jurich, have been successful in their own right in moving their programs forward.

Tom Jurich told me there are three things that make a successful athletics director: (1) the ability to raise money, (2) the competitive spirit to win and (3) the ability to like people.
Both have scored well on points one and two, the third element calls for a closer examination based on the personalities of the two men.

I can speak for Tom Jurich as hundreds, or even thousands of other fans from both schools can. You feel he is a friend at your first meeting. You naturally, want to like him in return. He is outgoing. Mitch Barnhart is different.

John Clay of the Lexington-Herald Leader describes it this way: "If you are at a table in a restaurant and Mitch Barnhart walks by; he will smile and wave at you. If Tom Jurich walks by, he will stop, shake your hand, say a few words and then, go to his table." That's what's called providing accessibility. Tom has opened the doors not only to Louisville fans, but Kentucky as well.

Tom invited former Fabulous Five member Ralph Beard to games. He had him speak to the Cardinal athletes about avoiding gambling and similar situations that might jeopardize their careers and harm the university.

Those invited to his suite at Papa John's Cardinal Stadium, over the years, include Harry Jones, (who played for Bear Bryant but has been a mainstay in UofL leadership for years and actually hired Jurich), Rick Robey and many more, including most recently Joe Koch who also played for Bryant at UK. Harry Jones says he's neutral when the two teams play while Coach Schnellenberger thinks he leans Louisville's way. Joe Koch had been there just once when I met him and he still considers himself Big Blue.

I told Tom he's like the movie preacher Elmer Gantry (in a complimentary way) converting his own personal congregation. Tom's accessibility won't enable UofL to surpass Kentucky in popularity, but it sure isn't detrimental to the Cardinals for him to try. Again, Tom says he doesn't mind being like Avis, No. 2, it makes him work harder.

Although not as outgoing as Tom, or as his predecessor at UK, C.M. Newton, Clay continues, "Mitch knows everything about his student athletes, he really cares about them." I did get the opportunity to interview Mitch and when I did, it was like talking with a friend. I mentioned what John Clay had said and brought up that word, accessibility. You could tell in his voice that he has heard this line before, but I was impressed with his composure and self-confidence as he said, "I know who I am. I know what I want to accomplish. The student athletes are the most important. If someone needs help they'll get it. If someone needs access, they can get it. I don't turn people away."

Sure, both of these leaders have scored big and they both have made mistakes. No one is perfect, but I feel that both of these schools are fortunate to have these men leading their athletic programs.

Although after the aforementioned explanation, some fans have still been turned off by what they consider Barnhart's making accessibility to the program more difficult, but as Gary Gupton of the Red and Blue Review points out: "UK has not been in any trouble with the NCAA on Barnhart's watch."

Yes, both have done well, but Tom has received so many accolades, including the Street & Smith's Sports Business Journal/Sports Business Daily Athletic Director of the Year Award in 2007. Tom says: "You can only win it once." That doesn't make much sense in such a competitive business.

I talked with UK swimming and diving coach, Gary Connelly before his retirement this past season about the rivalry with UofL. I pointed out that beginning with the 1992-93 season, it was 14 straight wins for UK, but now UofL is in control. I asked him what caused the turnaround.

His reply was, "Simple. Two words, Tom Jurich. He has done so much for his school in building great facilities, hiring good coaches and they like him have a great desire to win. They have recruited well and competed hard."

Getting ready to go to press, fans and many in the media are questioning why Jurich made the decision to allow Clint Hurtt, football recruiting coordinator and defensive line coach (who has since left UofL for a career in the NFL), to remain on the team after the NCAA hit him with a two-year show cause penalty.

Jurich's overall performance record is excellent, and that's why, even though many are in the questioning mode, they'll trust their leader who has been adamant since he arrived in 1997, that the University of Louisville's athletic programs will always be in compliance with NCAA rules. Then some fans started spinning the same old broken record—Calipari is cheating. UK has always cheated. One even said that Louisville had never been on probation. It's human nature to cry out and point to someone else when the blame finger could be pointing at you.

Yes, UK has been on probation. When the SEC and other NCAA teams refused to play Kentucky, the Cats played intra-squad games. Some UK players were involved in the point-shaving scandal leading to that cancellation of the 1952-53 season.

Ralph Beard and UK historian Dr. Thomas Clark told me that Coach Rupp had nothing to do with the scandal. The Lexington gambler, Ed Curd, in a final interview before his death with the Lexington Herald-Leader, confirmed their statements.

Two of John Calipari's Final Four appearances have been vacated according to the NCAA, but he has never been implicated in these situations. Under Basketball coach Eddie Sutton and football coach Hal Mumme UK has suffered extensively.

Louisville Men's Basketball was on a two-year probation for recruiting violations from 1956 to 1958. Basketball and volleyball were cited for violations in the 1980s.

It's amazing how someone can go on a talk show and just blatantly accuse another of being a liar and a cheat, with no regard to any consequences. Cheating stories are much like forgotten or misplaced land mines. One may explode if just faintly agitated, causing severe damage. Current misdeeds need to be dealt with, but these old cheating stories true or untrue, need to be handled with care and are better off left to "rest in peace."

BOBBY WATSON
All-SEC guard

BILL SPIVEY
All-American center

FRANK RAMSEY
Third team All-American

SHELBY LINVILLE
Honorable Mention-All-American

CLIFF HAGAN
Heralded soph star

SKIPPY WHITAKER
Speedy guard

188

That goes as well with establishing the accuracy of any rivalry stories. I had always heard that Cliff Hagan, who was an excellent hook shot artist on UK's 1951 NCAA championship team, had experienced some trouble with a rim on a road trip.

The story went like this. During warm-ups Hagan took a shot and missed. He tried another hook shot and that rolled off the rim as well. He then tells Coach Rupp to get the janitor and examine the rim. He thinks it's bent. The janitor confirmed Hagan's assumption.

Cliff said no, never happened, and told the real story: "We were on the road playing in the Cincinnati Gardens. I believe the opponent was Xavier. During warm-ups as I was going in for a layup, I landed out of bounds. There wasn't enough room behind the backboard. We examined it from the free throw line and a change had to be made."

I got fearful and mentioned the story attributed to Rupp about determining how much killer instinct a boy had by how many bites it took him to eat a steak. "Now, that Hagan boy could eat a steak in two or three bites," Rupp bragged. Hagan chuckled and replied, "Growing up I didn't have the opportunity of eating much steak. So, when I did get one, I finished it pretty fast."

Killer instinct may have not been the primary motivating element of the steak debate; secondary in this case is alright. Hagan was a highly motivated player, steak or no steak.

Here's one more story telling aspect to take into consideration. Ask someone to relate a story and it varies, sometimes substantially by how many times they repeat it. Although some of the secondary details may not add-up, the core information remains the same.

Texas Tech, Assistant Coach Vince Taylor, who went to high school in Lexington, played for Duke and was an assistant coach at Louisville, agrees with me that the Kentucky-Louisville rivalry is the hottest one right now in all of college basketball and much of that has to do with the their coaches, John Calipari and Rick Pitino.

Vince said, "It wouldn't even come to mind for a Duke coach to go to North Carolina or vice-a-versa. UNC would never have a Duke player like me even be an assistant coach there." The fact that the former coach at Kentucky, Rick Pitino, now coaches at Louisville, certainly contributes to the intensity of the rivalry, but the fact that they are both charismatic, excellent recruiters, motivators, love their players, love coaching, know the game, are extremists when it comes to winning and maybe, just maybe have something between them that just doesn't quite fit, completes the formula for making UK vs. UofL college basketball's No.1 rivalry.

Having been unable to talk to either one of the coaches for this book, former Wildcat great and current color commentator on the radio broadcast team, Mike Pratt gives an assist in trying to help us, understand this situation: "On the professional level both coaches respect each other, on the personal level it's not as easy."

I mentioned to Mike that Coach Rupp and Coach Henry Iba of Oklohoma A&M (now Oklohoma State) were good friends. When they were at a meeting together, they would stay up late into the night diagramming plays and discussing strategy. But on the court, they desperately wanted to beat each other. They met in the 1949 NCAA Championship Game in Seattle, Washington. UK was ranked No.1 and A&M No. 2. Coach Rupp had won the NCAA title the year before and was asked before this game how he thought it would turn out?

Rupp replied, "We are going to let the points do the talking." That's sound advice for coaches and players today.

Mike told me basically that Rupp and Iba were at one on both levels. But Coach Rupp wasn't at one on both levels with another coaching competitor, Ray Mears of Tennessee: "Adolph respected Mears on the professional level, but personally couldn't stand him. It was pretty rough back in those days when Kentucky went to Tennessee. It was the big rivalry game and the Vols would place their football team behind the UK bench. Obscenities, spitting and more came our way. Coach Rupp would place the freshmen down front, as a shield to protect the varsity."

Pratt played on the varsity from 1967-70. Tennessee had beaten Rupp's Runts in Knoxville on March 5, 1966, 69-62. It was UK's first defeat of the year in 24 games. I'm sure Coach Rupp hadn't forgotten that one, straining the Mear's relationship a hundred-fold or more.

Duke Coach Mike Krzyzewski told me in a 1991 interview that he would like to be on the same basis as Rupp and Iba with those in his coaching fraternity, but today there is so much "stich" in the game between coaches, that kind of relationship is almost impossible to establish.

Having had the privilege of setting on press row for almost 20 years, the two worst road games I attended as far as obscenity and low-brow trash talk were concerned were (1) in Knoxville at the Thompson-Boling Arena UK vs. Tennessee and (2) in Birmingham, Al. where it was BYU vs. UAB.

My childhood friend Steve White and I got to Knoxville about an hour early. Almost all we heard before the game started was obscenities directed towards the Wildcats. The words used were big, small and hyphenated. In Birmingham, Steve and I were together again. If BYU had won that game, the Cougars would have been ranked No.1 in the nation for the first time in their history. BYU is my alma mater. The best I can say for the fans sitting behind us on press row, is atrocious. I told Steve I felt like going into the stands and letting them have a piece of my mind.

But now, years later and writing this book, I hope some of this kind of talk diminishes when the Cards and the Cats are the focal point of the discussion.

The rivalry is the best right now with Calipari and Pitino pacing the sidelines. Cal has beaten Rick ten times. Rick has beaten Calipari nine times. Calipari is 5-1 in the UK-UofL rivalry. The other games occurred when Cal was at UMass and Memphis and Rick was Kentucky and Louisville.

UK Mens Basketball Coach John Calipari (L) and UofL Mens Basketball Coach Rick Pitino (R)

Each has won a national championship in the past two years, both have been to back-to-back Final Fours since they have been involved in the rivalry, but Pitino's streak is current. In fact, Coach

Pitino claims that if his team makes its third consecutive Final Four in this 2013-14 season, it will be a "mini-dynasty."

Pitino prevented Calipari from becoming the first coach in the rivalry to win five consecutive games with UofL's 80-77 win last season at the YUM Center. Calipari does have a victory over Pitino in the 2012 Final Four, 69-61. UK prefers the one-and-done approach, UofL the traditional way mingled with a one-and-done, here and there.

John Hayden, a member of UK's media relations staff who handles men's basketball told me: "That Coach Calipari doesn't like to talk about the rivalry. He prepares for that game just like any other game. The preparation is the same for Louisville as it would be for Northern Kentucky."

While still gasping for air, Mike Pratt came to the rescue: "Paul, I basically agree with that statement. In my day you could look over the schedule and find the teams you could beat. Not anymore, teams have improved; you have to prepare for every game one at a time." Coach Crum said the same thing about his days when he was with Coach Wooden at UCLA. I shot back to Mike: "Like Robert Morris?" Pratt replied, "You got it."

I understand that as far as I can. But on December 28, 2013, when Louisville comes to Rupp Arena, Northern Kentucky will be residing in oblivion. December 28, 2013 will be the most anticipated game in this rivalry's history, all basketball eyes will be on Lexington, with state bragging and national bragging rights on the line, because UK vs. UofL is college basketball's No. 1 rivalry. (This paragraph was written previous to this game. I will cover the actual game in Chapter Twelve.)

Chapter Two
The Game

I feel a brief history of basketball is appropriate to understanding the passion the people of Kentucky have for this game.

It was just before Christmas; on December 21, 1891 that Santa received an assist, not from one of his elves, but from a Canadian student who had moved to America. It was a new game, but this first Christmas it would not be found under any tree or hanging in any stocking, nor would it be available in stores or appear in any mail-order catalog, but discoverable only in a gym at the International Y.M.C.A. Training Center in Springfield, Massachusetts.

James Naismith, a native Canadian, who wanted to be a minister, changed his mind when a friend told him he thought he could accomplish great good by working with young men in athletics, had gone to that training center in Springfield for instruction.

The school's director, Dr.Luther Gulick, was mired in a quandary trying to figure out a game between the football and baseball seasons. Individual or team gymnastics weren't meeting the needs of his students in the down-period. Dr. Gulick said a new game was needed and "That there was nothing new under the sun. All so called new things are simply recombinations of the factors of things that are now in existence."

Naismith remarked: "Doctor, if that is so, we can invent a new game that will meet our needs. All that we have to do is to take the factors of our known games and recombine them, and we will have the game we are looking for." The next week no one had any ideas. It would take many weeks before Dr. Naismith game up with the right combination.

No one knows for sure, but Lee Williams, the director of the Naismith Memorial Basketball Hall of Fame in October of 1991 told me that they believe it was on December 21, 1891.

Naismith came into the building that morning with the idea for his game firmly in place. He gave the original 13 rules for the game, (no name at this time) to the school's stenographer Miss Lyons, who typed them and they were placed on the bulletin board. Naismith asked the building superintendent, Mr. Stebbins if he had two boxes about 18 inches square. Stebbins replied: "No, I haven't any boxes, but I have two old peach baskets down in the store room, if they will do you any good." The baskets were round and somewhat larger at the top than at the bottom.

Then, Dr. Naismith got a ladder and nailed the baskets to the lower end of the balcony in the gym (a running track was located above the gym floor) which just happened to be ten-feet from the top to the floor down below.

He saw two balls, one a football and the other a soccer ball. Wanting to eliminate the roughness in the new game, he preferred the soccer variety to the football.

He was the first official in basketball; there were nine men on each side, playing on a court that was some 25' by 50'. It was a huge success. The school's official newspaper the Triangle did a piece in January on the "New Game with No Name." That was solved shortly thereafter, when Dr. Naismith asked his class for suggestions in naming his new invention.

One said: "Naismith-Ball." The doctor replied: "that will kill any game." Then, Frank Mahan from North Carolina said: "We have a basket and we have a ball so let's call it basket ball!"

With missionary zeal, the converts to this new game went home for Christmas and began to spread the word and play the game as they first saw it. Upon graduation from the training school, these new instructors would take the message across the U.S. and around the world. Basketball originally was played indoors or outdoors, where there could be as many as fifty on a side.

It made the 1904 games held in St. Louis, and the 1936 and 1948 Olympic Games.

1948 Olympic Runners-Up

Time Magazine stated in 1946 that basketball was the No. 1 participant sport in high schools with more students playing basketball than football and baseball combined.

Famous Long Island University coach, Clair Bee, in the introduction to Basketball It's Origin and Development by James Naismith, along with a 1991 interview with former coach John McLendon, are the sources for much of the information cited here, says: "The fiftieth anniversary (1891-1941) of the invention of basketball finds the game recognized as the world's most popular sport. More spectators attend and more players participate in basketball than any other game. There has been no accurate account taken of participants, but whenever a ball and a hoop are available, it is certain that basketball in some form is being played.

That was so true here in Kentucky. All over the state youth were playing basketball. The high school tournament started in 1917. UK won its first conference championship in 1921. When the depression hit, the game was something they could still hang on to because the cost of playing was so much less than football and baseball. You could play with a lot fewer players too. When UK games began to be broadcast on radio stations, there was now a constant in a poor stricken area that people could count on.

Then, Adolph Rupp became the Baron of the Basketball World, and no matter what else transpired, nobody was better than Kentucky in college basketball. Kentuckians had something they could take great pride in.

The crescendo nationally was in the late 40s and very early 50s at Madison Square Garden. The NCAA and NIT were playing tournament games there. Huge crowds were attending, that sadly included the gamblers and those using the game for what Dr. Naismith never intended. The point-shaving scandals rocked college basketball.

The NCAA pulled out of New York along with Kentucky and other prominent teams.

UK started its own tournament, the UKIT in December of 1953 beating Duke in its first game and Tom Gola and LaSalle in it's second.

The Baron, Adolph Rupp, continued to ride at the top of the college basketball world, winning his fourth NCAA national championship in 1958 in Louisville.

In 1964, fans witnessed the arrival of a new star in the West, named John Wooden and his UCLA Bruins. Wooden's teams won 10 of the next 12 NCAA tournament titles between 1964 and 1975.

On January 20, 1968, the matchup between No. 1 UCLA and No. 2 Houston was billed as the "Game of the Century." It was the first time that basketball was played in the Astrodome. A crowd of 52,693 came out to the dome, but it also marked the first time that a college basketball game was broadcast nationally other than in the NCAA tournament.

According to Wikipedia, Eddie Einhorn's TVS Company paid some $27,000 dollars for the broadcast rights. Each team received $125,000 for the game compared to the NCAA 1968 tournament payout of $31,781.

Houston had lost the previous year to UCLA 73-58 in the NCAA tournament. The Bruins entered this game with a 47-game winning streak and Lew Alcindor (later known as Kareem Abdul-Jabbar) with an eye injury. Houston won 71-69. It was one of only two times that Alcindor shot less than 50 percent in his UCLA career, and Elvin Hayes blocked three of his shots. But UCLA had the last laugh when it won the rematch in that year's NCAA tournament 101-69.

When I interviewed Bob Knight, then the coach of Indiana in early 1991, this was a game that we locked down on. I interviewed so many great coaches for the video AdCraft produced, entitled: "It Started With a Peach Basket."

Knight didn't want to participate, but Joe Vancisin, the president of the National Association of Basketball Coaches at that time, pleaded with Knight, telling him he just had to be included in the documentary. He finally agreed and my cameraman and I arrived on the IU campus. I told him, that we were not going to be intimidated, but we would not be rude either. My cameraman had played some basketball and I told him we were not novices going in for this take with Knight.

When inside, an assistant A.D. called to Coach Knight who was down the hall and said: Coach! "These are the two fellows that are going to conduct the interview." Knight smiled and waived at us. I told the cameraman that this wasn't the same man that we saw on TV and heard on the radio.

When the coach entered our room, he said he only had 30 minutes to give us. Knight is 6-ft 5-ins. tall and my cameraman was the same. I'm about 5-ft 9-ins. tall. They had their backs turned to me as the microphone was being adjusted properly to the coach's lapel.

When we sat down, I said, "Coach we really do appreciate your taking time to do this interview with us." Knight snarled, "Let's get on with this." Remember, I told my cameraman I was going to challenge Bobby Knight with knowledge. As we started he seemed satisfied. I continued to probe and he continued to be interested. I said back 50 or 60 years ago anybody could beat anybody on a given night. He bellowed out: "Not the case!"

I proceeded to tell him that in 1934 Kentucky was 16-0 and lost to a nothing Florida team in the first round of the SEC tournament. I guess he didn't mind hearing about Kentucky losing as it proved my point. He said Kentucky didn't win the 1946 NIT. I knew they did, but I didn't feel impressed to tell him that.

I followed with there are really only eight or 12 teams that can win the tournament. He said that wasn't true, but I reminded him that he had helped make that so by winning three of the last 11 NCAA tournaments. Then, he said: "Yeah! Let's go back to something that you said earlier."

You must always remain humble because as I felt things sliding my way, the interview took an abrupt 180 degree turn when we switched courses to that first game in the Astrodome. I said: "Coach must people agree that the game in the Astrodome, January 20, 1968 when No. 1 UCLA and No. 2 Houston played, was the benchmark, for taking basketball to the next level of success."

Bob Knight replied: "It was a lousy game. I'll tell you a better game. The 1954 Holiday Festival Tournament. Tom Gola and LaSalle. I remember where I was, I remember who I was with; it was a great game." I didn't think it was time to make a response. We went on for some time more; then he leaned forward and said, "I think you have enough."

I looked at the clock. He had told us we had 30 minutes when we first began, but now the scoreboard read, "43 Minutes." We had gone into overtime for 13 whole minutes. I felt that we had earned those 13 minutes by being professional and I certainly enjoyed my time with this basketball legend. But I wasn't through!

Once again, the coach and the cameraman had their backs turned to me when I made this statement: "Coach! I do want to thank you for your time and I realize that history can be viewed by the same people, different ways, but coach! January 1968, No. 1 UCLA vs. No. 2 Houston. I remember where I was, I remember who I was with, it was a great game!" Coach Knight turned around and said, while winking with one eye and smiling, "It was a lousy game."

John Wooden had made the same comment a few weeks earlier that, "It was a lousy game." Those two are the only ones who thought that way, I do believe.

However, this demonstrates the difficultly in determining how hard it is to decide what or who is the greatest? Maybe we shouldn't try to monopolize the "Greatest Categories." There are so many good candidates available.

In my interview with Coach Wooden in December of 1991, he said "he wasn't the greatest." Most others will say it for him.

That game in the Astrodome fueled the rise for what we have today.

Here I go again. We host the two greatest minutes in sports in the Kentucky Derby and our teams play in the NCAA tournament which is known today as the "Three Greatest Weeks in Sports!"

Coach Wooden described the elements that make basketball the best game to watch, "The crowd is the closest to the players, (domes have doomed that statement to some degree but we can for the most part still agree with it) the ball is so easily seen, the movement, the action is quick, it's back and forth, the players athleticism and there is plenty of scoring."

I interviewed Earl Ruby, sports editor for the *Courier-Journal* for 30 years some 25 years ago. He was a freshman on the Manual football team that lost to Male 81-0 in 1919. I asked him if there were any eligibility rules back then and he laughed and said: "Hell Paul! Half the guys playing were bald-headed!"

He had a popular column called "Ruby's Report." In the March 16, 1966 column he pointed out one of the other elements that makes the game of basketball so compelling; is officiating. In that column he claimed the role of basketball referee is the toughest in all of athletics.

I was at a high school game in the Louisville Gardens when an official counted a basket good, when the ball never went through the net. His partner did not consult with him and correct the missed call.

I was sitting at press row and when I said the ball never went through the basket (my voice carries deep into three-point range). Chris Renner, who was coaching his Ballard team, looked at me and raised his hands as if I was able to help him nullify the blown call. What made matters worse, a foul had also been called and the other team was trying to complete an old-fashioned three-point play on a basket that was no good.

These kinds of things do happen. I'll share a few stories I've gleaned from some of the coaches and players who have participated in the rivalry. I'll start with Coach Wooden since Coach Crum worked with him.

Coach Wooden was new on the West Coast at UCLA. He was on the road and said this particular referee wasn't very good. Wooden then continued: "This official made a bad call near our bench. 'I told him I thought he had made a bad call.' The play goes the other way and when they come back down the floor, he runs over by me and says: 'I don't know about that coach. They kinda liked that call down at the other end."

Bud Olsen who played for Louisville coach, "Peck" Hickman, from 1959-62 shared this story about back-to-back nights against my all-time favorite pro player, Wilt Chamberlain.

When Bud started in the NBA there were only eight teams. It grew slowly to nine and then 10 when he was with the San Francisco Warriors. Many times, teams would play games back-to-back when a visiting team from the East arrived.

The first night playing the 76ers, teammate Nate Thurmond was injured. Coach Alex Hannum sent Bud into the game and told him to foul Wilt Chamberlain. Bud followed orders, pushing, shoving, hanging on and striking Chamberlain on the body. No foul was called.

Coach Hannum continued to tell Bud to foul Chamberlain. Olsen replied: "I am. I am." Returning to play, he fouled Chamberlain again. No Call. So when play stops, Bud tells official Earl Strom: "Call the foul, Earl. Call the foul! Strom delivered the final answer, "Wilt told me not to Bud."

After the game Wilt was waiting outside with Bud's wife and said: "Bud! Don't do that tomorrow night." The next night Wilt stayed under the basket and Bud stayed outside hitting jumpers, scoring a career high 24 points.

Grover Sales, Coach Rupp's last driver tells of a night down in Georgia. UK won the contest but Coach Rupp didn't like the way the two officials worked the game. So he waited for them outside their locker room. The two officials completed their showers and were carrying their bags ready to leave, when the coach asked them to come over and sit down beside him. The officials accommodated the coach, with one sitting down on his left-side and the other on the right.

Then Rupp started talking about how tired he was, how sick he was and he was concerned that he might not make it out alive that night. He remained silent for a few moments and then said: "Boys! I thought I might keel over tonight, so I wanted to be ready and go out like Jesus—between two thieves."

Coach Crum related this story when he was coaching at Pierce Junior College. Phoenix Junior College had joined the league and Coach Crum's team was on the road to play back-to-back games on successive nights.

Denny said there was this one little guy who was doing all of the officiating. "We had hit five straight baskets and were down 10-0. This guy had called three-seconds in the lane, foul away from the ball, traveling and anything else he could come up with and we got beat by 25-points.

The next night this same little guy was back again, when we had this big guy walk in there who was about 6-ft 3-inches and weighed 300 pounds.

23

I never said a word to anybody. After about five or six times up and down the floor this big guy said: 'Coach, it looks like I'm working this one alone. I'll do the best job I can.' Coach Crum continued: "He started making calls clear across the floor that the little guy wouldn't make. We went from losing by 25 to winning by 25 in one night.

That's the nature of the game of basketball, what happened last night really doesn't necessarily determine what's going to happen tonight. You're going to win some and you're going to lose some, especially when you're playing good competition."

In 1975 UK played UCLA for the national championship. Wooden was retiring after this game. Late in the game Wooden stormed out on the court complaining about UK's style of play. UK fans thought a technical foul should have been called on the legendary coach.

Coach Hall comes on to the floor and official Bob Wortman yells at him to get back on the bench. Then, turns to Coach Wooden, takes him gently by the arm and said, "Coach Wooden. Will you please comeback and sit down on your bench?" Ball game over.

Chapter Three
The Early Years

All of this talk about up and down transition play, slam dunks and the "Three Greatest Weeks in Sports," is fun, but it was the women who first played basketball at UK. Caption in the picture below says Girls' Basketball Team 1902 Champions.

Girls' Basket Ball Team, 1902. Champions.

In those early years, there were only mythical champions designated each season. The teams would simply calculate wins vs. losses to other teams in the state and the school with the best record would claim themselves "State Champions."

In these early years in Kentucky, Centre College in Danville was a power house in football and strong in basketball and baseball too. Transylvania College was known in the early 1900s as Kentucky University and the Wildcats were called Kentucky State, or sometimes just State.

UK men started playing basketball in 1903. Many early games were against local Y.M.C.A. teams. We laugh now, but remember these are our early missionaries and graduated instructors who took the game across the country. These teams were pretty good, at least from the experience standpoint. Church teams would also be found on the schedule.

In Louisville the Y.M.C.A. ran ads in the newspaper that they had the best court in town. Just like in Springfield, MA, there was the running track with the balcony above the floor. No backboard-Back then, fans would stick their hands through the balcony railing to bat the opponent's shot away or help guide their team's shots into the basket. Chicken wire would be used for the first backboards, thus the term "cagers" as the nickname for early participants. The study of the game's rules and equipment evolution is simply fascinating.

Interior View Gymnasium 1903

UK Gym

One can read of one-handers from the corner in the newspaper in the 1900-1910 decade. Primitive, yes, but the game was in the developmental stage.

The Cardinals took to the court on January 28, 1912 against none other than the Louisville Y.M.C.A. losing 35-3. Those young Christian men were tough in those days. The Wildcats and Cardinals met for the first time in Lexington on February 15, 1913 with UK winning the game 34-10.

There was no fanfare in the paper about this being the inaugural meeting between the schools from the state's largest two cities. Kentucky won the first four in basketball, outscoring the Cardinals 100-54.

The two teams actually hooked-up for football first with UK beating UofL 41-0 in Lexington on October 28, 1912. UK won all six games against Louisville piling up a points margin of 210-0, the last game being played in 1924. Interesting that the two schools played four of those first six football games between 1912-1915, alternating home and home games with the first contested in Lexington.

Louisville would not field another team until 1921 and traveled to Lexington for the fifth game in 1922. Then, in 1924, they played the sixth game of the early era and it too was at Kentucky, Louisville having lost the alternating home games advantage.

The Cardinals notched their first win in the basketball series by defeating the Cats 26-15 in Louisville on February 27, 1915. The year 1916 would prove to be interesting and may supply a clue to the discontinuance of the series in the future.

In basketball, UofL was afforded a contract on a home and home basis, starting in Lexington in 1915 and ending there in 1922, with a split of five total games at UK and four at UofL. On February 12, 1916 the Cards upset the Cats in Lexington 28-22 but UK turned the table in Louisville 10 days later winning 32-24.

Maybe all the games should be played on President's Day since Lincoln's and Washington's birthdays held sway that year to rivalry action.

Coach Scott Davenport of Bellarmine University said, "Coach Tubby Smith thought the game should be played sometime other than around Christmas Day, because it makes it tougher for the losing team to enjoy the holiday season."

I thought this game was just like any other game? So losing to Northern Kentucky, Michigan State, North Carolina etc. should make celebrating Christmas like getting a lump of coal in your stocking, shouldn't it?

This December 28, 2013 takes Christmas celebrating off-the hook, but endangers welcoming the New Year to town. The national networks want the game right where it is and that's where it will stay.

With no tournament being held, the Cards and the Cats would have to opt for the conventional method, totaling the wins and loses against state teams and declare the team with the most wins, the winner.

In 1916 Louisville was 7-1 against state competition and Kentucky 5-1, but that year the Cards and Cats politicked for a third game to determine the State Championship and the headline in the Lexington newspaper read: "WILDCATS TIE UP STATE TITLE IN EXCITING, GAME.

In one of the hardest fought contests of the season, featured by fouling on the part of both teams, the Wildcats took the measure of the University of Louisville basketball team here tonight, 32 to 24. There were forty-four fouls called altogether, State being penalized twenty-five times and Louisville nineteen times. Out of 19 attempts from foul, (Derrill) Hart threw twelve (UK) and (Harding) McCaleb, of Louisville threw 14. This pair made the greatest number of points for their respective teams. Hart getting twenty and McCaleb fourteen, the Wildcats keeping him from scoring a single goal from the field. (Jim) Server (UK) led in goals from field, making a total of ten points. The crowd was with the Cardinals throughout, even to the extent of hissing the work of referee Golde. (Edward Golde was from Cincinnati).

The Y.M.C.A. floor, on which the game was played, suited the Wildcats, who were determined to settle up past scores exactly. (UK had lost in Lexington 10 days before 28 to 22). They completely outplayed the Cardinals all the way.

The state championship is now in doubt, inasmuch as State and the Cardinals are tied for first place. Dr. Tigert (UK A.D.) said tonight he would be willing for the Wildcats to meet the Cardinals on any floor that might be selected for the state title." Louisville gladly accepted his challenge.

But this game would be played only on paper. Both sides went back and forth in the newspapers and then after its last game against Marietta on March the fourth, Tigert disbanded the UK team for the season, without meeting UofL for that championship game. The Cardinal camp wasn't happy about this decision. They thought that a third game would become a reality. Sound familiar? If you don't play the only losers are the fans.

The following year the Cardinals had no team. It would be six years later when the two got together for the last time in the regular season until November 26, 1983.

They played two games in four days in January of 1922, UK winning the first 38 to 14 in Louisville and 29-22 in Lexington. Did bad blood surface between the two after they failed to play for that championship in 1916?

The freshmen teams would still play one or two games most every year, even during the first two seasons of Coach Rupp's tenure, then that ended too. Robert Frost wrote about "the two roads that diverged in a yellow wood, and he took the one less traveled and that has made all the difference."

Kentucky took a different turn. They joined the SIAA conference in 1911 and won the championship in 1921 over Georgia 20-19.

Basil Hayden UK's first All-American was the team captain. He told me in a 1988 interview, "The floor down in Atlanta was a make-shift project that was propped up on saw horses. One of the Wildcats jumped and came down and went right through the floor."

Near the end of the game, a foul was called and Hayden as the captain, selected Bill King to take the shot. He made it and UK won 20-19, marking the first time they had won a conference tournament championship.

Wildcat fans were delirious back home. Messages had been sent during the four games the Cats played in the championship keeping the fans in Lexington well-informed of the team's progress. A nice group of loyal fans awaited them at the railroad station when the champions returned home.

A new facility, Alumni Gym, which seated 2,500 opened in 1924. UK won the Southern Conference regular season championships in 1926 and 1932. It would win its second post-season conference tournament in 1933, the SEC's first year.

The rule of selecting a player to take the foul shot was in vogue in the previous mentioned game between the Cards and the Cats, and in this 1921 SIAA tournament championship game.

1921 Champions

For years, rule makers have been tinkering with different methods to stop this incessant fouling in the final minutes of a college basketball game. Maybe we should go back to this designated free throw shooter rule that was abandoned in 1924.

Instead of free-choice for the entire game, make it legal in the final two minutes to allow the team captain to select a player on the floor who will shoot the free throws. Having a player that is shooting 82 percent from the line, instead of the fouled player that shoots 58.9 percent, should certainly curtail the number of fouls late in the game. The other team still has some hope existent that the better player will miss the shot or shots. Remember, Dr. Naismith always thought the responsibility rested on the defensive player to speed up the pace of the game. And fouling is not the remedy.

With that win in Atlanta, basketball had a more secure place at UK, but things could have been different. In 1922 a young assistant coach from Vanderbilt, William Wallace Wade was interviewing at Kentucky and Alabama for a football head coaching position. He decided to become a Wildcat. He wanted to bring some others with him to be his assistants. He was told to wait outside the meeting room. The hiring committee would consider it and then let him know.

About an hour later, with no word from the group, Wade banged on the door and said: "I'm going to take the Alabama job and I will guarantee you one thing. You'll never beat me." UK played Wade eight times when he was at Alabama and three when he was at Duke and never beat him.

He became one of the greatest football coaches of all-time. At Alabama he went to three Rose Bowls, winning two, and tying one. His record was 61-13-3. At Duke, he went to two Rose Bowls losing both and finishing with a record of 110-36-10.

In 1925 UK led their football series with Tennessee 10-8-3. General Neyland came to UT in 1926 and the rest is history. Neyland never lost to Kentucky either. Even the "Bear" couldn't beat him.

Would UK have been a powerhouse under Wade? We'll never know. Sure would like to know what that committee that kept him waiting was talking about.

Louisville hired Tom King, the coach from Male, who brought his entire starting team with him that had won the mythical state championship as told to me by sportswriter Earl Ruby. It was the best hire of the rivalry until UK brought Adolph Rupp on board.

In basketball, King was 44-31 in five years and won UofLs only KIAC championships in 1928 and 1929.

In his first season in football in 1925, his team was 8-0, scoring 133 points and allowing only two, a safety by Marshall in the final game. In 1926, one of his players from Male, Fred Koster led the nation in scoring with 134 points. His overall six-year winning record was 27-21.

In 1930 the university cut his ever so meager budget and he left to go to Michigan State where he became the Dean of Men.

When Kentucky started playing basketball in 1903 through the 1929-30 season, the Cats won 205 games of the 351 they played. That's a winning percentage of 58.4 percent. John Maurer who coached for three seasons from 1927-1930, pushed the program forward, winning 40 and losing 14 to finish with a 74.1 winning percentage.

His style wasn't the fast-break type that fans love here, but his slower paced game did give Coach Rupp some trouble when Maurer took over the coaching duties at Tennessee.

Louisville took to the hardwood in 1912, missed the 1916-17 and 1922-23 seasons completely. In the seasons they did play they had 94 wins and 105 losses for a percentage of 47.2 percent.

Louisville had its troubles back then. They had lost their best coach, did not have a place of their own to play, and maybe, just maybe had only two basketballs on campus. And more trouble was heading their way as one of the greatest coaches in basketball history was about to take over at Louisville's rival, non-rival, Kentucky. A guy who liked to wear brown suits.

Chapter Four
The Rupp and Hickman Years

Adolph Frederick Rupp was hired in May of 1930 to be the new head basketball coach at the University of Kentucky. He was only 29 years old at the time and had been coaching for the previous four years at Freeport High School in Illinois where his record was 66-21, for 75.9 percent. He wore a khaki uniform to practice and was known as the "Colonel" by his players.

Coach Rupp beat out dozens of other candidates for the UK job. When he was asked the question of why the university should hire him, he is said to have answered the question this way, "Because I am the best damn coach in the country." Former governor Albert B. "Happy" Chandler, who was one of Rupp's closest friends told me this story, "Rupp was given a two year contract at the time he signed, paying him $2500 a year, the same pay he received at Freeport High School.

He came to me after he had lost on a last second, half-court shot to Maryland in the finals of the 1931 Southern Conference tournament 29-27, (UK had not been to the finals of the conference tournament since they won the SIAA tournament in 1921) and said the university would not extend his contract.

I replied: 'Adolph what if you have a losing season?' I didn't know him well enough at that time, to ever imagine that he would never have a losing season in his career. I went on further to assure him that if the board didn't extend his contract after next season, when it expired, I would get him a job with me in politics."

Rupp also was an assistant football coach his first two years at UK on the offensive line. After that, he concentrated strictly on his most cherished game-basketball. He got and continued to receive some criticism that the SEC was a football conference, and didn't care a thing about the roundball game.

Many of Rupp's players also played both sports in those early days. Even Wallace "Wah Wah" Jones, a member of Adolph's Fabulous Five was a standout in both sports in the late forties. But Adolf Rupp wanted to concentrate on basketball. Was the campus big enough for both the major sports to be successful? One can answer that with a resounding, YES! When Rupp and Paul "Bear" Bryant were together at Kentucky articles were written about Lexington being the sports capital of the U.S.

MILLER   RUPP   PRIBBLE   OILS   GAMAGE   SHIVELY   DRURY

Varsity Football

Before the Southeastern Conference there was the Southern Conference. In 1933 the Southern Conference had grown so large that a major split was necessary. Thirteen schools departed and formed the Southeastern Conference or SEC. The other teams, including Duke and North Carolina remained in the Southern Conference until seven teams separated in 1953 and formed the ACC.

From 1921 when UK technically won the Southern Conference tournament, until the split in 1933, six tournaments were won by the teams that formed the SEC and six by the teams that eventually would start the ACC in 1953. There were six different SEC teams that were winners in the old conference; UK, Mississippi State, Vanderbilt, Mississippi, Alabama and Georgia. But only three different teams from the future ACC, North Carolina with four and North Carolina State and Maryland one each.

The SEC was on par with the ACC schools when the split was made as both conferences were dominated by just a few teams and Kentucky was one of them. In his only two years in the Southern Conference, Rupp was 11-2 vs. future SEC teams, 8-3 against future ACC teams, beating Clemson three times, Georgia Tech and Duke twice, and N.C. State once. Rupp lost to Clemson, North Carolina and Maryland once each. His winning percentage vs. the SEC teams was 84.6 percent, ACC teams, 72.7 percent and the 11 others 100 percent making his overall winning percentage 85.7 percent.

In my opinion, this was basically the programming structure for his future scheduling, because 27 years later, his winning percentage was almost identical—610 wins, 106 losses for a percentage of 85.2%. That is a remarkable record by any standard.

Play your conference teams, schedule some strong teams in other areas that will provide your national bona fides and then round up the other games with the usual weaker suspects. That is what Denny Crum did as the Louisville head coach. Your conference will supply some tough games, but from top to bottom you'll have an advantage.

This is exactly what Coach Rupp did, playing tougher schools from other areas that would give him national publicity and make his teams better. The SEC got stronger thanks to Rupp. The other schools eventually saw the game of basketball was profitable and the conference continued to improve.

When I told longtime national broadcaster Tom Hammond, a native of Lexington, who did the SEC TV broadcast for 30 years, that after all is said and done, the ACC has won 12 national championships and the SEC 11, (not counting the teams coming into the conference) he responded: "Sometimes perception is reality. I can tell you the SEC has greatly improved over the years. Maybe they're not the best from top to bottom, but they'll always have several teams that can play, and when you stand the athletes on their own, they're very talented."

On the football side Alabama dominated, winning three mythical national championships and Georgia Tech one. William Wallace Wade, who wanted to come to Kentucky, started the Tide rolling with a Rose Bowl victory over Washington in 1925.

Wade helped to make southern football exciting and changed the way other areas of the country viewed the South. In other words, he brought class and respectability to the South.

Rupp did the same for basketball, showed the South itself that basketball could make money for the schools, and helped take basketball to the national level. His first game however, would be against a state school; Georgetown on December 18, 1930 which he won 67-19. Georgetown's team captain was Harry Lancaster, who would later become Rupp's full-time assistant coach from 1947-68.

While at UK, Rupp played Georgetown seven times, Berea eight and Kentucky Wesleyan once, in 1938. His record in those games was 16-0. The record clearly shows that he played some state schools while coaching at UK. A few hair-splitters have arisen saying those teams weren't part of the state school system. But neither was Louisville until 1970.

In my research and observation all these years, many violate my rivalry bashing guidelines by not wanting to give any credit to Adolph Rupp, while on the other hand; some blame him for everything that goes wrong. This kind of thinking would make him responsible for the 1929 Stock Market crash because he was hired just a short period after it occurred.

Rupp was far from perfect, but none are who currently reside on the planet. Perfect is not humanly possible. I mentioned to Lee Williams, the Director for the Naismith Memorial Basketball Hall of Fame, back in 1991 that perhaps Coach Rupp would have won more championships if he had been a little friendlier with his players? Lee countered, "Paul, his system produced four national championships, what more could you want?"

I didn't give him an answer.

UK had stopped playing Louisville in basketball in 1922 and football in 1924. This precedent had been established in basketball eight years before Rupp arrived. So it's false to say this was originally Rupp's policy. John Maurer played Eastern Kentucky on December 15, 1928 winning 35-10 marking the first time the Wildcats had played them. But that was it, one-and-done. The UK and UofL freshmen competed during Rupp's first two years, then that came to a close as well. Yet he continued to play state schools until 1938, when UK beat Kentucky Wesleyan 57-18.

The 1934-35 season marked the first time that Adolph Rupp failed to play a state school since his arrival. He played two Big Ten teams for the first time, Chicago at home, whom he beat and Michigan State, which beat him on the road. The Cats also went to New York for the first time losing to NYU 23-22.

George Keegan the coach at Notre Dame warned Rupp that he had no chance of winning there because his team was an outsider. After the game, the "Baron of Basketball," as Rupp was known, used that "if" word when he told the press, "If I can't beat these fellows by 10 in Lexington, I'll buy all you boys a new suit of clothes." This was the beginning of his national campaign. Here we can mark the birth of "Big Brother" or in a more kindly fashion, the older brother in the rivalry race. I believe in these first few years on the job, that Rupp had already raised the bar for basketball excellence.

There were other great basketball coaches in the state. Ed Diddle, the outstanding coach at Western, who played at Centre College in Danville, started coaching the Hilltoppers in 1922. From that point until Coach Rupp arrived at UK, Diddle's record was 73-57, a winning percentage of 56.2 percent. But he matched Rupp's first five years at UK, when Diddle improved to 83-28 for a 74.8 percent winning percentage. Then, through the 1948 season, he was 296 and 74, with a winning percentage 80.3 percent. I am sure there are many other factors for Coach Diddle's success, but the bar had been raised in the state, even though Rupp refused to play the other teams.

Some of the reasons stated by critics for Rupp refusing to play other state schools included fear of losing. Why did he go play some of the tougher teams around the nation then? Yeah, but losing to a state school would hurt his recruiting in the state. I've never bought into that point of view, even when it was used by Coach Hall in the 70s and early 80s; because Rupp was losing some recruiting battles without playing the state schools.

I interviewed Jack Coleman in 1988, I asked if Kentucky had recruited him in the early 40s, and he said, "Yes." Then I followed with, "What was Rupp's presentation?" Coleman replied: "He told me he had one scholarship left and he would like to have my answer by the end of the week." Wow! What if all recruiting was done in that fashion? He went on to say, "But I thought he was too egotistical so I committed to Duke." Coleman went into the military and when his service period ended, he came to play at Louisville.

Rupp lost Charlie Tyra of Louisville, who played for my high school, Atherton. Charlie recounted the recruiting process, "Rupp told me I would be another All-American, but I wasn't comfortable with the pressure atmosphere, so I stayed home and played for the Cardinals. I thought it would be the best for me." It was for Charlie and UofL.

Phil Rollins, originally signed a letter of intent with Kentucky, where his brother, Kenny, was a member of the Fabulous Five. He failed to receive continuing information except for one letter stating that the school looked forward to him having four glorious years at UK. After seeing Assistant Coach Harry Lancaster drive by one day and nothing other than a greeting was mentioned about his coming to play, Phil started rethinking things.

Then, before school was to start, Phil was playing in an all-star game in Lexington. The players were sleeping in the furnace room in Memorial Coliseum and when the game was completed, assistant UK Coach Harry Lancaster came in, called out the names of several players to follow him, and then he turned to Phil and said: "Phil are you coming?" Rollins said: "No," and he went to UofL.

He had a wonderful career there and was known in the media guide as "Phil the Gem" Rollins and was the captain of Louisville's 1956 NIT champions. I asked Phil how his parents felt when his team, Louisville, played his brother's team UK, Phil responded: "They say they couldn't lose."

John Turner was another recruiting casualty. UK had beaten UofL twice in the post-season, so shouldn't that have helped in the signing of Turner? Recruiting is just not that simple. John was from northern Kentucky and an outstanding athlete. He related his story to me this way, "I was interested in playing some football too, Kentucky said no, Louisville was at least open to the idea."

He didn't play football for the Cardinals, but he was one of the keys in UofL's NCAA Regional victory over the Cats in 1959.

Another reason suggested for not playing other state schools is whether of not it will decrease your fan base, by giving them more publicity. Losing games will be even more damaging. This has some merit, but the Kentucky fan base is so large, that the Big Blue Nation is in no danger of falling like the Roman Empire. Rupp is to have said on occasion, "Let's don't beat up on each other, one can go to the NCAA and one to the NIT."

After UK beat UofL in the NCAA East Regional in 1951, 79 to 68, a suggestion was made by James G. Stewart, campaign chairman of the Louisville Red Cross, that the two teams play a charity game to benefit the organization in the post-season. He sent this proposal to the presidents of both universities.

The response by UK President Herman Lee Donovan as to why he opposed the game, which appeared in the *Courier-Journal*, "He was greatly in sympathy with the Red Cross, but was opposed for two reasons:

1. Several years ago, we got so many requests for charity games—six or eight a year—that the Athletic Board finally decided we were not going to play any of them. The board would have to reverse that decision.

2. As long as I'm president, I'm never going to consent personally to playing a game with any other state institution, because I know the antagonism they create between undergraduates and, particularly the alumni."

What about the "Agony and No Ecstasy" created when they fail to play? Fans need the opportunity to let the vented-up feelings of not playing, dissipate through the rigor of real competition as former Lexington Herald-Leader sports columnist Chuck Culpepper advocated, "It was easy to state your case on paper. But to rely on the prowess of young men on the court to help you fend off a potential year's worth of barbs from a program next door, that's real-life stuff. With so much pride tangled with basketball, this outcome has a high misery index for someone." I think that is called a rivalry.

When the two teams are playing, Chuck saw it this way: "Pardon me for being naive, but there is no way to anticipate this year's game in the same way you would an attempted burglary of the family jewels. You may relax. The reason: in an unusual circumstance given the events of recent years, this comes as a game between upbeat programs. They will be upbeat after tonight as well, no matter what." (December 28, 1991)

UK President Donovan went on to say that UK has "nice relations" with all the other institutions in the state and that he felt UK had "far more to lose than to gain" by such a game. This is close as it gets to having a non-playing policy in force, his policy not the school's in general. Donovan's career ended at UK in 1956.

When C.M. Newton became the Kentucky Athletic Director in April of 1989, he said, "There were still those belonging to the "old school" of thinking, like football coach, Jerry Claiborne, who didn't want the two schools to play." I believe C. M. felt the same way in his earlier days among his contemporaries. He said, "Coach Rupp didn't play the other state schools, because he didn't want to help them build-up their programs." That explains having more to lose.

One thing he did want for football "was to start the series according to the two schools' desires, instead of being forced to play as it occurred with basketball."

Later when Coach Newton was UK's AD, he "felt it better to give games to state schools so they could receive a split of the game revenue that was going to such teams as East Tennessee State." Very few will change sides because of a win or a loss, the schools will have no residual negatives from losing to a state school. If that was so, recent back-to-back losses in football to Western Kentucky would have caused a mass exodus by UK fans.

Don't get me wrong, they're not happy either, but they'd rather fight than switch. When a coach is in trouble, first, an assistant goes, and then if he's still in trouble, he goes. That's how losing to teams you're not supposed to on a regular basis works itself out. What about other reasons, such as snubbing your opponent or failing to recognize they're human and on the same playing field as your team, are more likely to cause the loss of some fans.

When Kentucky lost in the first round of the 2013 NIT to Robert Morris 59-57, the school didn't drop to Division 2 status. When Louisville lost to Morehead State, 62-61 in the second round of the 2011 NCAA tournament, the school didn't close its doors, neither was there a mad rush of fans joining the Wildcat ranks.

Still there was no Mt. Sinai experience to this policy of not playing state schools. Nothing was carved in stone like the tablets Moses received there saying: "Thou shall not play state schools!" Donovan also pointed out that the state of Kentucky now has five outstanding basketball teams and that if they all scheduled one another, "there would only have been one outstanding one" at the end of the season.

That resembles Rupp's advice since in the early days of the NCAA and NIT tournaments, only a limited number of teams were invited to play. Why knock each other off? The NCAA expanded from eight invitees to 16 in 1951, and has continued throughout its history to do so, where now, even 68 teams are not enough for some. The expansion helps eliminate concerns that you might not make the tournament. I have one other reason that may help us find a partial answer to this Blue and Red dichotomy.

I had John Dromo, the former UofL assistant coach under Hickman who would go on to become the head coach from 1967-71, on my talk show one night. Off the air I told him that I had grown up a Kentucky fan. He said, "There's nothing wrong with that! I was friends with Adolph."

Then, he proceeded to share with me a story, "While Adolph was over in Europe conducting a basketball clinic for the Army, I called Joe Hall, who was now his assistant coach, and told him I wanted to schedule a game with the freshmen teams to play in the Armory" (now the Gardens).

I contacted Marlowe Cook, the Jefferson County Judge and he was willing to provide the Armory for us at no charge. We were to receive the ticket money, the concession money and the revenues from parking. No cost to us. I figured the amount raised would be $25,000 to divide equally between the two schools—big money for the time, but when Adolph returned he said, 'No'. I asked him why he was willingly to cost the universities this money and the fans the opportunity to see them play.

Rupp's response was to the point, 'When I first came to Kentucky I played some state schools. Well, we started to get good real fast and were going to New York. I called a couple of these fellows and asked them for a game and they turned me down. I vowed right there, they can get as good as me or they can get better than me—I will never play them."

That's one man's story. No other witnesses available, but why should he lie?

There is one other witness—Joe B. Hall. I asked him if he remembered the event, his response was, "I do remember talking to John about that, but I didn't know the details of what he was working on."

As the line from the old police show, "The Naked City" goes, "There are eight million stories in the Naked City, you have just seen (or in those case, read) one of them."

I believe this story has merit and is one more piece of evidence aiding in the understanding of the "no play policy". If Coach Hall had remembered nothing concerning the event, it would have been hard to share it with others. Why would Coach Dromo share this with me and possibly a few others?

He had to retire as UofL head coach at the end of the 1971 season when he suffered a heart attack. He complimented me after the show for doing my homework and later sent me a book on the Final Four and some magazines. In the book he wrote, "Paul, you are the first one to have me on a program like this in 17 years. If I can be of help in the future let me know."

One asset UK possessed in greater measure than any other school in the state was publicity, newspaper coverage state-wide and radio broadcasts as Joe B. Hall remembers, "My brother Bill and I would listen to the Kentucky games on radio as religiously as any Big Blue fan ever." We kept our own score sheets, which included shot attempts, baskets made, and rebounds to the best of our ability…

We also included free throws, personal fouls and we kept a running chart of what was happening.

Sometimes we would sit on the opposite ends of the bed, and toss paper wads into a tin can, preferably a coffee can and be our own Wildcat players. In the kitchen we'd place our papers on the table which had an oil cloth draped over it. When we would remove our papers, sometimes the stats were still visible on that oil cloth and we would pop it up and put it back down to clear it.

I would usher football games as a Boy Scout. UK basketball and football were guiding lights for me through my high school years growing up in Cynthiana, Ky."

Oscar Combs discovered on his trip, to New York to watch UK in the 1976 NIT (where they won their second NIT championship), just how valuable the 50,000 watt clear channel radio station, WHAS, had been to Kentucky in building its in-state as well as national fan base, "While in New York I'd meet a fan from Philadelphia, one from Boston and one from New York City who were Big Blue all the way. They had become such, by listening to the games broadcast on WHAS radio." Oscar started his famous Cats' Pause magazine as a by-product from these most insightful meetings and observations at that NIT.

Garry Gupton, who is the owner of the popular TV show, The Red and Blue Review explains, "When we put this concept together of discussing the rivalry weekly on TV, we quickly sold out the advertising. We expanded the show, the advertisers stepped forward again, another sellout and it is a great success and fun to do. It is the only show of its kind in the country as far as I know."

After the departure of Coach and A.D. Tom King, UofL would remain in the wilderness for quite some time.

When Kentucky played Notre Dame on January 5, 1937 *Courier-Journal* Sports Editor Bruce Dudley wrote about the 6,352 enthusiastic fans, which was the biggest crowd ever to attend a game in the state, "Big time basketball, for which Louisville long has hungered, was served to the city by Notre Dame and Kentucky last night at the Jefferson County Armory and the feast was relished to a gay glow by the greatest gathering ever to see a game in the State." Rupp started three players from Louisville that night, Warfield Donahue, Jim Goforth and Joe "Red" Hagan. He also started Homer "Tubby" Thompson from across the river in Jeffersonville, Indiana.

Dudley continued, "There was our own beloved University of Kentucky, which since the coming of Adolph Rupp in 1931 (should be 1930) always has had a sparkling team." Notre Dame won the game 41-28, but UK had a stronghold here in Louisville and would continue to build on that foundation when the SEC tournament was brought to the Armory in 1941.

The Cardinals could offer no competitive resistance at the time and the Baron didn't need a rivalry game to accomplish his goal of making the Wildcats the best in the nation. Thus, the "older" brother was continuing to mature. Meanwhile, the University of Louisville continued to be mired in the athletic wilderness after the departure of Tom King.

In 1939, the Cards hit rock bottom when they lost to Hanover College at home 56-39 and finished 1-15 for the season. Frank Hartley, who played on that Hanover team and later became the Sports Editor for the Louisville-Times, the city's evening newspaper, remembered the celebration after that game, "We were so happy, thinking we had really done something beating the big city team that we had taken the basketball with us as a momento. When the Louisville coach, Laurie Apitz, entered the room and said: 'Look! I only have two basketballs in the entire school,' he walked away taking our trophy with him."

From 1938 until Bernard "Peck" Hickman arrived in 1943, the Cards were 21-67 for a 23.9 percent winning percentage. Mercifully they had no team for the 1942-43 campaign.

"Peck" was a nickname an uncle gave him from a book entitled, "Peck, the bad boy". Hickman was coaching at Valley High School in Louisville and told me in an interview in 1992 how he got the Louisville job. "My Valley team was playing the highly favored Anchorage team in the high school regional tournament. We beat them. The referee who was John Heldman, A.D. at the University of Louisville came over to me and said, 'How would you like to be the coach at UofL?' I accepted his invitation."

Coach Hickman, like some 131 other schools around the country, was able to use the Navy's V-12 training program to launch his team. George Hauptfuhrer played just two seasons at Louisville, 1944-1946, then transferred to Harvard and became a lawyer, turning down an opportunity to play professionally.

Former UofL A.D., Bill Olsen said, "George was the one player that helped Coach Hickman build the program. He was a good player and a good man. Just the type of athlete you wanted in your system and just the kind who could attract others like him to come join the program." In 1948, Hickman won his first national championship, winning the N.A.I.B. tournament beating Johnny Wooden and Indiana State 82-70.

In five years Bernard Hickman's teams had won 84 while losing only 21, which is an 80 percent winning percentage and a national tournament championship. It had been 26 years since the Cards and Cats had played each other in basketball, now both teams would advance to New York for a chance to go to the Olympics.

In these Olympic Trials, both teams from the Bluegrass were slated by game officials to meet in the first round. UK had won the right to participate in the games by beating Baylor 58-42 for the NCAA championship. Alex Groza, the All-American center was ailing from the flu, without him, UK was only an 8-point favorite, but he was able to play, and that made the wildcats favored by 12.

Louisville's Bob Borah, only one of two surviving UofL players from that game recalls, "We thought we had a chance. We were going to play hard, and we did. When we lost Jack Coleman on fouls, that really made it difficult, but they were pretty good. As the Lexington Herald paper recounted, 'Louisville was the capital of Kentucky for two minutes. The Cards had jumped to a five to nothing lead, with former UK player Deward Compton scoring all of the points.'

The Wildcats called timeout. On the way to the bench, Cardinal John Knopf made an unscheduled pit stop by the Kentucky bench and paused. He put both hands around his neck and while looking at Ralph Beard, made the infamous "choke sign". There's an old TV commercial that goes like this: "It's not nice to fool Mother Nature." And you can add to that slogan: "Or, fool with The Fabulous Five".

Borah told me he didn't see John do that, but it wouldn't have surprised him, since Knopf was kind of a prankster. Beard told me, "He noticed it." Kentucky reacted with 14 unanswered points and led by nine. After 12 minutes of play the Cats were on top 31-12. The Combs brothers, Roy and Glenn were able to score a dozen points between them near the end of the half to cut UK's intermission margin to 14, at 43-29.

Kentucky started quickly again in the second half and with 12 minutes remaining led 51-33. Jack Coleman scored seven unanswered points for the Cards to slice the UK lead to 51-40. But each time Louisville made a run, Kentucky came right back.

The Cats lost Kenny Rollins on fouls three and a half minutes into the second half, and Jack Coleman went to the Cardinal bench five minutes later. UK led at that time 63-47, and without Coleman, UofL was outscored 28-10 to finish the game at 91-57. Kentucky had been favored by 12 points.

Ralph Beard led all scorers with 22 points and three Cardinal players, Jack Coleman, Roy Combs and Glen Combs were tied with 10 points a piece to lead their team in scoring. Kentucky advanced to the Olympic Trials title game losing to the semi-pro team the Phillips Oilers 53-49.

Cliff Barker broke his nose in the first half and did not play in the second half. Alex Groza went two of 19 from the field, but Kentucky only lost to the seven-footer and former college great Bob Kurland and his teammates by four points. The headline in the New York Times read, "Greatest Game Ever Played." And Bud Browning, the coach of the Oilers said, "Ralph Beard is the best basketball player in America."

Years later in an article in Earl Ruby's Report in the *Courier-Journal*, Coach Browning told the story that wherever he travels, the fans asked about Coach Rupp. They have his book, Rupp's Championship Basketball and they run his plays. Just another example of Rupp's reputation as, "Mr. Basketball."

By losing to the Oilers however, Rupp became the assistant coach instead of head coach of the Olympic team, which made him very unhappy and he let the players know it.

On a tape given to me recorded by former C- J. sportswriter, Tev Laudeman, the coach said this, "My greatest moment in all of coaching was to see my boys standing on those platforms as they received their Olympic Gold Medals." At the end of that championship season, 37 percent of the 44,000 fans who voted in a poll to determine the best college basketball coach in the country, declared Adolph Rupp the winner. The second place finisher, Nat Holman of CCNY was a distant second. (1948 UK Yearbook)

In the March 24, 1948 edition of the *Courier-Journal*'s Ruby Report, it states that Coach Rupp was complaining about a story that appeared in the NIT program that Rupp had pushed a bill through the Kentucky State Legislature absolutely "prohibitin' and preventin' any basketball activities whatsoever and under no account between his Wildcat teams and a passel of varmints known as Western Kentucky. Coach Ed Diddle admits as how this is true, sho' nuff for try as he and the other authorities might, Col. Rupp steadfastly refuses to meet Western Kentucky on the basketball court, all of which, considering what the Hilltoppers do to their opponents, redounds to the credit of the otherwise fearless Kentucky colonel.

As one Hilltopper adherent put it, "Can you imagine that Rupp, giving examinations as the reason his team couldn't go to the invitation tourney this year! Whoever heard of exams at Kentucky!"

Rupp demanded explanations from everybody but Albert B. Nixon of NYU, President of the Metropolitan Intercollegiate Basketball Association which sponsored the Invitational Tournament.

Every basketball follower in Kentucky knows that Rupp did not have the legislature do what the story says. Every cage fan, and Mr. Rupp should know that Mr. Diddle did not say what the article said he said. The Metropolitan Association did the University of Kentucky and Western a great injustice by printing it. That's the truth. (Really? Uncle Ed Diddle was a Character.)

COACH ADOLPH RUPP

Basketball

"The greatest collegiate basketball team in the history of the game" is the title acclaimed Kentucky's Wildcats at the finish of the 1947-48 season. Behind the tremendous success of the Lexington Lynxmen is the incomparable Coach Adolph Rupp, who is recognized as the best in the country. Last March, the 47-year-old mentor was voted as the No. 1 basketball coach in a poll of over 44,000 fans from all sections of the nation. Rupp finished far in front of the runner-up, College of the City of New York's Nat Holman, as he garnered approximately 37% of all the ballots.

In 18 seasons with the Wildcats, "The Man in the Brown Suit" has directed his team to a record of 353 wins, only 70 losses for an average of .834, certainly one of the foremost records in the sport. Six times in this period the UK Ocelots ended the season with a percentage over .900, including the last three campaigns.

Coach Rupp came to the University in 1930. He is a native of Halstead, Kansas. In his youth, he attended Kansas University, graduating from there in 1923. In 1944 he was elected to the Basketball Hall of Fame. He will serve as the Assistant Basketball Coach of the U. S. Olympic Team this summer in London, England. Around the South, the Baron is known as Mr. Basketball himself. And he will try to keep it that way with his ever-winning Kentucky basketball teams.

190

I inserted this piece because Russell Rice, former UK Sports Information Director, who has done so much valuable research, said, "The first team Kentucky was getting pressure to play was

Western, because they were better than Louisville at that time." That's before Coach Hickman, who played for Coach Diddle at Western, had turned the Cardinal program around.

So in 1948, UK had the Fabulous Five, Western was at its pinnacle under Diddle, and UofL was well on the way with Hickman. And Eastern, Morehead and Murray had good teams. The state of basketball at this time in the Bluegrass was "Big Time."

Although articles like this promote the thought that a mandate existed to persuade UK to play other state schools, when talking to former players at Louisville, Western and Morehead, their respective coaching staffs weren't talking very much about it with their players.

Former UofL forward Bob Lochmueller said, "They weren't talking about it all the time, but it was mentioned and the importance of it." From Bob's standpoint, he can understand why UK wouldn't play the other state schools, "If I had been in their place (UK's) I probably would have done the same. They really only had something to lose at that time."

But some tension must have existed between the schools, as evidenced by a story Coach Lloyd Gardner, the manager/trainer at Western during the 1963-64 season related to me.

Western travelled to play Middle Tennessee on 2/18/1964. Earlier in the season Western had beaten the Blue Raiders at home 90-54. Middle Tennessee beat Western that night 93-84 and the Hilltoppers were riding the bus back to Bowling Green.

Coach Diddle told the team he did not want to hear one word spoken on the way back, and if guilty, he would kick the offender off the team the next morning.

The heater on the bus wasn't very effective. When on, it was extremely hot and when off, extremely cold. There was no happy medium.

Glenn Marcum, Western's 6' 9" center was frustrated by these conditions. He leaned his head up against the window, making it appear he was asleep. Here's the play-by-play account by the center turned broadcaster:

When too hot he would yell: "heat-off!"

When too cold he would yell: "heat-on!"

Coach Ed Diddle would jump and say to Assistant Coach Ted Hornback: "Who's that talking!" Heat off, heat on, was the clarion or not so clear call on the way back home.

Back in Bowling Green Coach Gardner said, "Assistant Coach Ted Hornback related the Marcum incident to head coach Ed Diddle."

The next morning Diddle called Marcum into his office and told him, "I'm kicking you off the team." Marcum in dismay replied: "Why Coach? What did I do?" "I was told by Coach Hornback that all the way back home on the bus you kept yelling, Adolph! Adolph! Adolph!"
Marcum told Coach Diddle the rest of the story and he was re-instated.

Kentucky won the 1949 NCAA title and in 1951 was back for the third time in four years, with the first round being held in Raleigh, N.C. where Louisville was the opponent once again. (Back then, this was the only way the two teams were going to play each other.)

The Wildcats were favored by 15 points, but they would find this second encounter with the Cards in the postseason, a much tougher ballgame. In fact, this match was a slugfest with 48 total fouls called, 34 coming in the first half of play. 20 fouls whistled against the Cards and 14 against the Cats. With 9:23 remaining in the first half, UK's Bill Spivey went to the bench with four personal fouls.

His teammate, Shelby Linville who had kept the Cats on top, scoring 17 points in the first half, also had four fouls and Cliff Hagan, three.

On the Cardinal side of the ledger things were even worse. Dick Robinson and Bob Naber who had scored 25 points between them, both fouled out of the game in the last two minutes of the first half. Bob Brown and Bob Lochmueller each had three personals and Wayne Larrabee had two. After this 20 minute, 10-man "Royal Rumble" UK led 44-40 at the half.

Five minutes into the second half, the Cats had increased their lead by just one-point, 54-49. Then Louisville got hot. Lochmueller hit a couple of long shots, Roy Rubin scored on a tip-in and Brown cashed in on a layup to make it 57-54 UofL. Brown went under the basket to score again and even with UK's Spivey back in the game, Louisville was leading 59-54.

The Cards slowed the pace and were trying to work it inside to Lochmueller, since Spivey had fouled out with 9:35 left in the game. They were hoping to also foul out Linville who still was playing with the four fouls he picked up in the first half. Skippy Whitaker came in and gave UK a lift hitting two outside shots to make it 64-64, marking the ninth tie of the game.

Whitaker tallied ten big points in the last half, and Lou Tsioropoulos's speed and rebounding helped down the stretch. UK had more depth; UofL tired, and went cold from the field, scoring only four points in the last nine minutes, none in the final five, as Kentucky won 79-68.

In an interview with Bob Lochmueller he commented, "We had stopped practicing, but when the NCAA tournament bid was issued, we resumed practicing. In that practice, I went to the floor and a teammate fell on my leg, injuring my knee. I was wrapped from ankle to knee, which gave it some support, but my movements were limited. I was only about 50 percent that day.

In those final nine minutes, our guards were content just to shoot from the outside. We might not have won, but had they worked the ball inside like the article says, we may have been able to win that game. We had a guard do the same thing to us in the NIT the following year when we lost to Western." (62-59)

Louisville outscored UK on field goals, 31 to 29 but connected on only six of 19 free throws, a terrible 31.8 percent compared to UK's 21 of 28 for 75 percent from the free throw line. The referees whistled 27 fouls on the Cards and 21 on the Cats. Bob does remember that Coach Rupp came into the Louisville dressing room and said a few words, (the context he doesn't remember) congratulating the team on its performance.

C-J sportswriter Larry Beck commented, "Neither team lost in prestige in this tilt. Louisville proved it can be difficult when hot as it was tonight. And UK, under terrific pressure each time it plays, once again showed it is a team of raw courage and can bounce from behind." UK went on to win its third national championship, beating Kansas 68-58.

In 1956 UofL won the NIT beating Dayton for the third time that season 93-80. Many looked at the NIT as a bigger game than the NCAA back then. The NCAA did not draw as many fans in the early years as the NIT which was played in New York City.

The NIT started in 1938, a year before the NCAA, and was sponsored by the Metropolitan Basketball Writer's Association. They were highlighting the strong local teams there, Long Island, CCNY, St. John's and NYU, to name a few.

The National Association of Basketball Coaches started the tournament in 1939, but found themselves in the red by over $2,500. That can happen when you play your games at Northwestern University and the NIT plays in Madison Square Garden. When the NCAA came to New York, it drew the larger crowds as well.

One reason both tournaments could draw these crowds was due to the limited number of teams that were participating in each tournament.

The NIT invited six teams in 1938, expanded to eight in 1941 and 12 in 1949.

The NCAA started with eight in 1939, choosing only one team from each of the eight regional districts which left many fine teams available to play in the NIT. It expanded to 16 in 1951 and continued to increase in size to the tournament's current 68 team field today.

A major change occurred in 1975 when the NCAA allowed more than one team from a conference to participate. Prior to 1975, If you did not win the automatic qualifier, either your conference regular season or conference tournament championship, you stayed home.

It's always tough to compare eras because many variables are included, but if coaches today were held to the same standards before 1975, their records would be different. For example; Duke's Mike Krzyzewski would have three championships and six Final Fours instead of his present four and 11. However, for those Cat fans that live by the prior 1975 standards for Duke must "die" by the same, because UK would lose two titles, 1996 and 2012 when they failed to win the SEC conference tournament to gain the automatic qualifier.

From 1943-45 the NCAA winner beat the NIT winner all three times they played in the Red Cross benefit game:

1943 Wyoming (NCAA)	52	St. John's (NIT)	47
1944 Utah (NCAA)	43	St. John's (NIT)	36
1945 OK. A&M* (NCAA)	52	DePaul (NIT)	44

*(OK A&M is now Oklahoma State.)

In a conversation with Ralph Beard, he told me that in 1946 when UK won the NIT 46-45 over Rhode Island, that Coach Rupp believed the NCAA was like playing in a Y.M.C.A. tournament. The Cats went to the NIT the following year, 1947 losing to Utah, and then it was back to the NCAA in 1948 and both tournaments in 1949. I wonder if that sentiment from Coach Rupp had anything to do with his friend, Hank Iba winning back-to-back NCAA tournaments with his big man, seven-footer Bob Kurland, in 1945 and '46. In 1949, a New York Times article stated that Kentucky was bringing the national championship back home to the Bluegrass. And that was the NCAA championship.

The Helms Foundation, which retroactively named their national champion in basketball from 1901 until its founding in 1936, continued naming national champions until 1982. Only four times in its history did it chose another national champion over the NCAA winner.

YEAR	NCAA	NIT	HELMS
1939	OREGON	LONG ISLAND	LONG ISLAND
1940	INDIANA	COLORADO	USC
1944	UTAH	ST. JOHN'S	ARMY
1954	LaSALLE	HOLY CROSS	KENTUCKY

In 1954 UK finished 25-0, which was their only undefeated season. The Cats had defeated LaSalle in Lexington 73-60, and were ranked No. 1 most of the season. But when the NCAA ruled Cliff Hagan, Frank Ramsey and Lou Tsioropoulos ineligible for post season play because they were graduate students, the Wildcats declined to play in the NCAA tournament. Kentucky was the AP National Champion of the Year. The Helms Foundation also awarded Kentucky their 1933 crown.

Some attempt to discredit the Helms selection committee, but if that's so, North Carolina and Kentucky need to remove the information from their media guides. I don't believe they need to worry, the media guides aren't changing.

When the AP Poll originated for basketball in 1949, the final regular season poll was the AP Poll Champion. The postseason national champion was the NCAA winner.

In football, the final regular season poll winner was the national champion. The bowl games were not included in the national championship equation. That changed permanently in the 1968 season, when the champion was named after the bowl games.

With the onset of the 1949 AP Poll, many of the top 20 teams would be divided between the NCAA and NIT since they were just 20 spots available in both tournaments combined.

However, the NCAA had more of the top five teams in its tournament:

YEAR	NCAA TOP 5	NIT TOP 5
1949	1,2,4	1,3,5
1950	1,2,4,5	1,3
1951	1,2,3,4,5	NONE
1952	1,2,4,5	4,5
1953	1,3,4,5	2
1954	2,4 No. 1 UK declined bid	3,5
1955	1,2,3,5	NONE
1956	1,2,4	3
1957	1,2,3,4	5
1958	1,2,3,4,5	NONE
TOTAL	38	12

After 1950 a team could not play in the NCAA and the NIT, although a few did.

Kentucky was No. 1 in both tournaments in 1949, winning the NCAA over No. 2 Oklahoma A&M and losing to Loyola of Chicago in the NIT. In 1950 CCNY became the first and only team to win both tournaments in the same year beating No. 1 Bradley in both games.

The higher ranked teams chose the NCAA when a choice of tournaments was mandated.

Over that 10-year period from 1949-1958, The NCAA had 58 Top Ten Teams, the NIT 30. The NCAA's total number of TOP 20 teams during this period was 89, The NIT had 56. The percentage of Top 20 teams from the number of participants for both was virtually a deadheat. The NCAA 89 of 192 for 46.4 percent and the NIT was 56 of 120 for 46.7 percent. This paper trail is easily substantiated after my discussion with former Cardinal Phil Rollins, who said, "I'm not saying that the NIT we won in 1956 was greater than the NCAA tournament, but it was still a prestigious event.

I agree with Phil.

And I believe the majority of coaches and writers felt the NCAA was the national championship, while the NIT was a national title.

Growing up in Cynthiana, Coach Hall really didn't know anything about University of Louisville basketball. He went with his high coach to watch Eastern Kentucky play because his coach went there. Coach Hall said, "Kentucky dominated the big news, but the Eastern vs. Western game was next in line."

When he got his first coaching job at Shepherdsville High School in Bullitt County, he got to learn about the UofL program first hand, "I took my team and scrimmaged the Cardinal freshmen team. I watched the varsity play and became good friends with Assistant Coach John Dromo. I became a Louisville fan back in those days."

The Cardinals had been placed on NCAA probation for two years so they were unable to defend their 1956 NIT title. But they were back in the 1959 NCAA tournament as an at-large-selection, and their first stop was to play Eastern Kentucky on the Wildcats home floor.

The Cardinals had beaten Eastern during the regular season in Freedom Hall 86-75 and beat them again in Lexington 77-63, earning the right to play the Wildcats in the Mideast Regional in Evanston, Illinois.

UK was the defending national champion and ranked No. 2, but got the NCAA bid when Mississippi State, the regular season SEC champion declined to participate because of its policy of refusing to play against teams with black players. Louisville finished the regular season 16-10, but had won 12 of their last 15 games.

'You And The Boys Knock Down Number Five, Johnny'

1959 All-American Johnny Cox

I wrote an article for the ScoreCard, a Cardinal fan paper, which appeared in the March 18, 1989 edition that I am bringing off the bench to cover this UK vs. UofL rivalry game on Friday, 13 1959. I had interviewed Joe Kitchen about the game. I used his recollection of the event along with my childhood memory of the game.

The title of the article is: Friday the 13th Part 1: 1959. "It appeared to be a typical March evening that 14th back in 1959 (30 years ago this week) as the old cedar trees swayed with the brisk night wind.

Inside the house, supper dishes were drying as the sound of bath water running signaled little ones that play time had ended. As usual, mother was in the bedroom organizing Sunday's attire while Dad devoured the Saturday edition of The Louisville Evening Times. But to the astute observer, one could detect a sense of foreboding as an anxious eight-year-old slid into TV position for the evening sportscast.

Jubilant Redbirds "Whoop it up" after long awaited victory over Kentucky.

An inspired band of Louisville Cardinals roared back from a 15-point deficit to upset defending NCAA champion Kentucky by 76-61 in the first round of the Mideast-regional at Evanston.

The Wildcats were razor sharp in building up a 15-point lead with 9:07 left in the first half. Then Coach Peck Hickman's charges began to apply their hawking defense that completely befuddled the Bluegrasser's, and the Cardinal gunners were beginning to find the range.

Down by eight at the half, ten fired-up Redbirds continued their pressing defensive tactics and forced the Wildcats to take

NCAA Mideast–Regional

The uneasiness had all started the night before—Friday the 13th—when in Orson Welles-fashion, the man on the radio revealed that the University of Louisville Cardinals had defeated the Kentucky Wildcats in NCAA tournament play by a 76-61 score. Memories of monsters paled in comparison as this bewildered eight-year-old spent a restless night tossing and turning.

Still the light of day brought no relief as the morning paper was even more disturbing. There it was! A second witness in bold print: LOUISVILLE 76, KENTUCKY 61. Even the Baron was quoted as saying that the Cardinals had kicked the tar out of his Wildcats.

Now on this anything but typical Saturday night, only one hope remained. Maybe, just maybe the same television screen that faithfully delivered "Howdy Doody" could free the eight-year-old from this Friday the 13th madness. But the ballgame was over. There it was once again in black and white—Kentucky's Billy Ray Lickert driving in for a meaningless layup. Final score: Louisville 76,

Kentucky 61. With mouth still wide open from shock, the eight-year-old kept thinking, 'Billy Ray, how could you do this to me? How could you lose to those guys?'

Billy Ray Lickert with the ball

Sure, this eight-year-old was a Wildcat fan. He lived out in the state, didn't he? OK, Brentlinger Lane was only three miles past Fern Creek, but in the mid-1950s, Bashford Manor Mall was just a cornfield, so he lived out-in-the-state.

There was no battle for broadcast rights back in those days on WHAS. All of the stations's 50,000 watts belonged to the Cats, and the eight-year-old listened to every game.

Sure, he wasn't even on the drawing board when UK destroyed Louisville in the Olympic Trials (91-57) and he was still in the crib when Kentucky beat the Cardinals 79-68 enroute to the Wildcats' third NCAA title (in four years) in 1951.

But he knew the names Hagan and Ramsey, and went to church with three of Vernon Hatton's uncles. So what else could one expect but a true-blue Wildcat fan, formed by the time the lad was eight. But that night in March he wanted some answers, who were those guys Billy Ray? Just who were Goldstein, Turner, Sawyer, Tieman, Andrews, Kitchen and Leathers? Wasn't this the same Louisville bunch who had lost earlier in the season to Georgetown—not Alonzo Mourning's Georgetown, but Georgetown College right here in Kentucky.

This bunch had lost seven of their first 12 games, but they were competitors. They had bounced back and were on a roll as they finished the 1958-59 regular season with a record of 16-10. Although not in the top 20, UofL received an at-large bid to the NCAA tournament where it was placed in the Mideast Regional along with the Wildcats and Eastern Kentucky.

So the 1959 Bluegrass battle was on. The Cards eliminated Eastern Kentucky 77-63, but the eight-year-old wasn't concerned. Still, in the back of his mind, he knew the Cardinals had a proud tradition of their own. Since Coach Bernard "Peck" Hickman had arrived at UofL, the Cards had won almost 74 percent of their games. Hickman's team had won the N.A.I.B. title back in 1948, and even more recently had taken the NIT crown in 1956.

That night before the game, Assistant Coach John Dromo would tell them he was tired of typical recruiting trips. Often when introducing himself from Louisville, Ky., prospects would ask him how Coach Rupp was doing.

So that night before the big game in Evanston, IL., Dromo asked this bunch to help him with recruiting. On the bus ride to the game, Joe Kitchen remembered the silence: 'It was kind of eerie. You knew something was going to happen.'

Under Coach Hickman, the Cardinals were building a national reputation. But a victory over the University of Kentucky Wildcats would solidify Louisville's position on the national scene. And finally, the Louisville coaches and players felt the second-ranked Wildcats had weaknesses the Cardinals could exploit.

However with 9:07 remaining in the first half, the Cats looked anything but weak as they blew out to a 29-14 advantage. Kitchen remembers the Cards were 'worried but not scared.' The UofL contingent felt the Kentucky guards couldn't handle pressure defense, so they went to work and trimmed that 15-point deficit to eight by halftime. During the break, Coach Hickman told his squad he didn't want to see any daylight between them and the men they were guarding.

Starting the second half, the Cardinals picked up their men at midcourt. Roger Tieman stole the ball twice, and five unanswered points from the guard from northern Kentucky helped tie the game at 42 with 15:35 remaining to be played. UofL never looked back, outscoring the Wildcats 25-8 over the next eight minutes, going on to win 76-61.

The Louisville Cardinals simply played a great second half, one of their greatest in history. They scored 48 points while shooting 57 percent from the field. They outrebounded the Wildcats after intermission 27-14, losing the battle of the boards 23-19 in the first half. UK hit just 10 of 37 shots from the field in the final 20 minutes for a dismal, dull 27 percent.

UK All-American Johnny Cox, who normally shot almost 41 percent from the field, was held to just 20 percent shooting, making only three of 15 attempts. That night in Evanston, Louisville proved there was more than just one team in the Bluegrass state. And the University of Kentucky's reputation wasn't tarnished by the loss. In fact, Coach Adolph Rupp rooted for the Cardinals the next night against Michigan State, just as Coach Hickman and Coach Dromo had rooted for the Wildcats after Louisville lost to Kentucky in the East Regional of the 1951 NCAA tournament.

Coach Rupp congratulates Cardinal Coach Peck Hickman.

Since that game in 1959, UK has been to 10 Final Fours and has won four national champion-ships for a total of eight NCAA crowns.

During the same time, the Cardinals have appeared in 10 Final Fours and have brought home three national championships for a total of three. The state's total of eleven NCAA crowns outshines our basketball conscious neighbors both in Indiana and North Carolina.

No matter what happens on and off the hardwood, die-hard Card and Cat fans will always uphold the tradition of their outstanding teams. But the groundwork for two national powers within the same state was formed that night in March back in 1959.

Oh, and to Billy Ray Lickert, that eight-year-old was a little rough on the Cats that Friday the 13th. Thirty years later, he now understands it wasn't your fault that night in Evanston. The Cats just got beat by a better team."

The Kentucky coaching staff, players and cheerleaders had seats behind the Louisville bench and pulled for the Cardinals against Michigan State. There is a picture of Rupp and Hickman shaking hands. Bud Olsen was there and said, "Coach Rupp did shake hands with Coach Hickman, but it didn't take place on the court where more people could see it."

In the March 14, 1959 *Courier-Journal*, Coach Hickman responded to the question if this win over Kentucky was sweeter than UofL's 1956 National Invitation championship? Hickman pro-tested: "Why no. That was for a national title, and, anyhow, that might have happened a lot sooner if Kentucky played us during the season."

Louisville was able to contain No. 7 Michigan State's "Jumping" Johnny Green and beat the Spartans 88-81 to win its first trip ever to the Final Four on its home court in Freedom Hall. This is where my rivalry bashing guidelines need to be activated; giving credit where credit is due.

In the 1957 NCAA Midwest Regional held in UK's Memorial Coliseum, the Cats beat Pitts-burgh and then lost to Michigan State for the right to go to the Final Four. The Cats led at the half 47-35 but were outscored 24 points by the Spartans in the second half and lost the game and another Final Four trip 80-68.

I asked John Crigler, a member of that team what happened, and he said: "I don't know."

I followed up with one of his teammates who is a personal friend of mine, Vernon Hatton. I asked the same question, his answer was different: "I'll tell you, it's easy "Jumping" Johnny Green."

In the March 15, 1961 *Courier-Journal* one of the headlines on the sport page read: "Kentucky, Rupp Leading Nation with Victories." The story reads, "Ohio State currently is the king pin of college basketball, but you have to dip down into the Blue Grass country to find the modern career champion—the University of Kentucky. Just as Adolph Rupp is the most successful of the coaches, so his Kentucky Wildcats own the best winning record in the nation—not only for the last ten years (83.5 percent), but also for the last 20 (86.2 percent)."

And to demonstrate that Coach "Peck" Hickman built the winning foundation for Cardinal basketball, UofL was tenth (71.8 percent) in the last ten years and eighth in the past 20 years. (71.3 percent) And Ed Diddle's Western Kentucky Hilltoppers were fourth, for the past 20 years (73.3 percent). Duke and North Carolina were not listed in either category.

In that 20 year-year period, Adolph Rupp had gone to five NCAA Final Fours, won four national championships and made three NIT Finals winning one championship.

"Peck" Hickman had won the N.A.I.B 1948 national title, the 1956 NIT and had taken Louisville to its first Final Four.

The Cards were gaining in the local and national recognition race, but needed a quality run in the NCAA to complete Hickman's building process. The future looked bright indeed for Cardinal fans. They had arrived.

Chapter Five
The Cold War Years

Even though Rupp and Hickman were still coaching, I've entitled this chapter the Cold War Years, because after playing three times in the post-season in 12 years, ('48, '51, '59) it would be another 24 before the two teams would meet again in the 1983 "Dream Game" in Knoxville. However, there was much happening during this stalemate period of time.

The NCAA tournament was the great equalizer. A near-miss occurred in the 1961 NCAA Mideast Regional played in Louisville's Freedom Hall.

On March the 14th the Cards beat Ohio University 76-70 sitting up a match with defending national champion Ohio State in one of the regional semifinal contests and Kentucky was to play another state rival Morehead, for the first time, in the other semifinal game. Louisville lost a heartbreaker to the Buckeyes 56-55 while UK beat the Eagles 71-64.

Those results sent UofL to the regional consolation game, where they beat Morehead 83-61 and the Cats to the title game where they lost to Ohio State 87-74.

When Ohio State is fortunate to beat the Cards by one, and takes Kentucky by 13, one might say Louisville is getting better. But it's the 1962-63 season where Louisville made a distinct separation from UK that benefited the Cardinals' future and helped secure the foundation that Hickman built. Seven words sum it up; Wade Houston, Eddie Whitehead and Sam Smith.

Frank Camp had integrated the UofL football team in the 1950s, which made him a pioneer in the South. The former white football players of that time still bristle at the way their African-American teammates were treated when they played against teams in this state, and it's no different with assistant basketball Coach John Dromo in 1962. He told me he had a cross burned in his yard and that the players were treated very shabbily while on road trips.

Coach Rick Pitino has been quoted as saying, "That the rivalry was built on racial hatred." That's absolutely not true.

T.L. Plain was an assistant coach for UK from 1963-64, and 1969-71 and for UofL from 1967-1969, he said, "There was no racial prejudice by anyone on either staff."

Now amongst the fans, that was a different issue. Certainly racial remarks, inferences and even physical actions occurred more frequently back in the 60s and 70s. Some UK fans used the term "blackbirds" when referring to the Cardinals and characterized Crum's style of play as "streetball" or "alley ball" and the "n" word was in play as well.

Former UofL Assistant Coach and A.D. Bill Olsen said, "When Coach Crum arrived and started making changes in the starting line-up, using more African-American players I was incensed by those Louisville fans who came to me and said he shouldn't be playing that many black players. Racial actions by fans and other citizens may have added fuel to the rivalry fire, but was absolutely not the foundation upon which it was built.

No doubt, successfully recruiting black players before Kentucky did was an advantage for UofL in the integration phase of the rivalry. Sam Smith would leave for Kentucky Wesleyan, but many others would come to take his place, like Wes Unseld. Rupp wanted Unseld. I have a letter he wrote to a fan, stating that he and his staff had made 13 recruiting visits either to watch or visit with Wes in his home.

John McClendon the first African-American coach in Division I history at Cleveland State saw Rupp coming out of the Unseld home as he was going in. McClendon told me, "Adolph Rupp was not a racist, but I wish he would have tried to do more with his powerful influence to help the situation."

I believe a quick look at some of the things Coach Rupp did that Coach McLendon may have been unaware of is warranted. Years ago, I interviewed Dan Schaefer, who played for Coach Rupp at Freeport high school in Illinois. I asked him what he thought about accusations that Coach Rupp was a racist? He shrieked: "A racist! No way. When he would take William Mosely (Rupp's first black player) out of the game because of racial slurs, he would build him back-up and send him into the game again. On a bus ride back from a Christmas tournament in Chicago, Coach Rupp praised this player who went on to be an All-American in track at Marquette. Coach Rupp told us that the Negro athletes would greatly change the face of sports as we knew it back in the late 1920s. If the "Colonel" (He always came to practice dressed in khakis) as they called him, was a racist, he became one after he left Freeport."

Dr. Charles Hurt, childhood friend of "Herky" Rupp spent quite a bit of time not only with Herky but with Mr. and Mrs. Rupp as well. He rode to the basketball games with the family, and waited after the game while Coach Rupp conducted business with Cattlemen. (The coach loved to see his stock win Blue Ribbons almost as much as his boys win a basketball game). Dr. Hurt has fond memories of going to Reds' game with the family and the coach helping him get autographs. Dr. Hurt made this comment about his days with the Baron. I never heard Coach Rupp tell an off-color story about blacks. I never heard him use the "n" word, but I sure heard him use son-of-a-bitch!"

When we were filming our video "It Started With a Peach Basket" we visited Clarence "Big House" Gaines, a native Kentuckian born in Paducah who became the coach of Winston-Salem State University in North Carolina. He won the 1967 NCAA Division II National Championship with standout player Earl Monroe.

In one book, The Golden Game by Billy Packer and Roland Lazenby, Gaines is quoted on page 241 as saying this about Rupp. "I've met him, but I have never talked with him. I don't think, Rupp was too interested in talking to anybody black." However Gaines told me unsolicited that as a young 22-year-old head coach, "You could learn more about basketball by talking to Adolph Rupp for 20 minutes than anybody else."

I had the late Louis Stout on my talk show back in the 1990s. He was the first African-American to be the head of a high school athletic association in America. Off the air I asked him if Coach Rupp had ever recruited him, He answerd, "He sure did. He came to an all-star game that I and Tom Thacker, who went on to an outstanding career at Cincinnati, winning two national championships, were attending. Rupp's approach was, "Things are getting better in the state and the SEC for you to play for me."

Louis Stout saw it this way, "Paul, I could not have handled it psychologically to be the first black to play in the SEC in 1959."

But Rupp was losing some key recruiting battles for white players too. Jeff Mullins did not grow up in Kentucky but went to high school in Lexington and signed with Duke. Tom Hagan, whose father "Red" Hagan played for Rupp (they didn't get along all the time) went to Vanderbilt. And Mike Silliman, the standout on Louisville St. X's 1962 state championship team, went to Army after being recruited by a young Cadet assistant coach, named Bobby Knight.

I had Mike on my show before he passed away and he said he should have gone to Kentucky. Most everyone thought he was going to UK back in 1962. He would have been a senior with Pat Riley and Louie Dampier. That would have been quite a team.

I don't believe UK ever really had a shot with Wes Unseld, who was the best rebounding, outlet passing center in college basketball, even though the NAACP and Kentucky Governor Ned Breathitt encouraged Unseld to sign with UK and break the color barrier. That was 1964.

Nat Northington was the first black player to sign with UK in 1965. He played football for Coach Charlie Bradshaw.

Butch Beard's situation was a little different. Rupp told the family that he could not guarantee Butch's safety, but UK would do everything possible to make sure nothing happened.

The team was having problems as Coach Rupp told Russell Rice. A dead skunk was put under Rupp's seat at Mississippi State. The fans there with those deafening cow bells running up the noise decibels were ultimately outlawed.

Herky Rupp described the atmosphere in the old Quansot Hut at Auburn, seating capacity about 3,500: "The locker room door would be locked when the team arrived and that took time to find someone to open it. The football team was placed behind our bench and they would lean over and pluck the hair off your leg.

At Alabama, I think in 1955, Earl Adkins was going in for a lay-up when behind the backboard some kind of explosion, occurred."

At a track meet on the UK campus, Wildcat player Randy Embry watched as Butch Beard shook hands with Coach Rupp and told him he was coming to Kentucky. Then, Beard proceeded to sign a letter of intent with John Dromo to play at Louisville. I believe safety issues played a part in that decision.

The March 26, 1967 edition of the *Courier-Journal* stated that Rupp was recruiting five black (Negro at that time) players. I know from interviews with former UK Sports Information Director Russell Rice and former UK Coach Joe B. Hall that Jim McDaniels of Allen County High School, Jim Rose of Hazard, and Jerome Perry of Louisville Manual, were all recruited by the Wildcats but all three went to Western Kentucky.

Rose had visited Coach Rupp with the mayor of Hazard, saying he was coming to UK but then went to Western. Then, there was Felix Thruston of Owensboro High School who played for Bobby Watson, a former Rupp player.

He stood 6-5, averaged 19.1 points a game and was a member of the *Courier-Journal*'s First-Team 1967 All-State team. Russell Rice heard him tell Rupp and Watson that he was coming to UK. Russell can't remember if he signed anything but said he may have. Rice took a picture of Rupp, Thruston and Watson, and then Felix went to an out-of-state school.

UK did sign it's first black player Tom Payne in 1969. Coach T.L. Plain said they knew someone who was friends with Payne's mother and that helped in the recruiting process. When Payne made the All-UKIT team in December of 1970, some fans booed in Memorial Coliseum. The next day on his coach's show, Herky Rupp said, "My father took the fans to task for booing Payne."

Phil Bond, former standout guard for the Cardinals when they played UCLA in the 1975 Final Four shared some thoughts about this period of time in the rivalry's history. He played for Coach Mike Pollio at Louisville Manual High School. Bill Olsen, assistant coach at that time had mentioned him to Coach Denny Crum who replaced John Dromo as the Cardinal's head coach in 1971.

Coach Crum was going to a game to scout Bond, but Bond was in Frankfort helping some students, meeting at the Kentucky High School Athletic Association offices. Denny thought another player he was observing was Bond, and told Olsen he wasn't impressed. "Quit recruiting him." Bond became interested in Vanderbilt when he thought the Cards had forgotten him. He was also recruited by Kentucky. He had two visits with then Assistant Coach Joe Hall and Phil really liked him. He met with Coach Rupp and said "it was a nice visit."

Coaches Crum and Olsen got back on the "Bond Trail" when they watched Manual and Ballard play in the regional tournament. Crum sees the real Bond for the first time and tells Olsen, "Why aren't you recruiting him!" Olsen replied, "You told me not to."

Of all the schools that had sent him letters, his grandmother told Phil: "You can go anywhere you want but Mississippi." In the final analysis, Bond said "that if you grew up in Louisville and the Cardinals wanted you, that's the place to go."

Bond did go on to say that watching the 2005 documentary produced by Lexington TV station WKYT: "Adolph Rupp: Myth, Legend and Fact" has opened his eyes to other information about Coach Rupp's recruitment of black players and has caused him to look at the issue a little differently.

Coach Denny's Crum's first year at UofL would be Coach's Rupp's last at Kentucky. Coach Crum was not like his predecessors, he began right away to press for an annual game with Kentucky and when he talked basketball, he talked about Wooden instead of Rupp. That was natural for him, having played and coached with John Wooden, but seemed blasphemous here.

However in the March 16, 1972, Dean Eagle Column, in the *Louisville Courier-Journal*, Adolph Rupp said, "Johnny Wooden is the greatest coach this nation has ever produced." Crum continued to make statements like: "I wouldn't trade Ricky Gallon for Rick Robey and Mike Phillips."

Former Crum Assistant Coach Jerry Jones said, "Denny really believed what he was saying, he wasn't trying to start trouble."

Former C-J Sports Editor Billy Reed commented, "That may be so but in my opinion he was taking real jabs at the opponent."

UK fans laughed about the Gallon comparison, but Ricky got the last laugh. Jerry Jones pointed out that Gallon made a lot of money and all-star teams playing in Europe.

UofL would add to its fan base because of Crum's exciting style of play and lose some because of his tactics to make UK change its non-playing policy.

In 1975, the first UK-UofL game since the 1959 NCAA Mideast Regional was on a collision course heading for San Diego, CA. and the Final Four. Kentucky beat Syracuse in the first game 95-79 but UCLA edged Louisville by one in an overtime thriller 75-74. There would be no UK-UofL NCAA championship game that year as so many fans had hoped. Wooden announced his retirement before the championship game against Kentucky, which he won 92-85.

In 1976, a possible match-up was taking shape again, this time in the NIT, but Providence beat Louisville dashing those hopes for the second consecutive year, and Kentucky went on to win their second NIT.

Former Louisville guard Phil Bond recalls "that the team just wasn't playing good basketball at the time."

These "Cold War" years, when the skirmishes and close encounters occurred off of the court, ended in the most intense manner at the Stokely Athletic Center, the home of the Tennessee Volunteers.

Card and Cat fans, were packed like sardines among a crowd of 12,489, assembled for the first UK-UofL game in 24 years. This matchup was for the NCAA Mideast Regional title and the right to go to the 1983 Final Four.

The last time they played, March 13, 1959 Louisville upset the No. 2 and defending national champion Wildcats 76-61 in the Mideast Regional semifinals, then dispatched Michigan State 88-81 going to it's first ever Final Four on its home court, Freedom Hall.

CBS's preview of the "Dream Game" included a segment from November 1981 in which John Tesh interviewed the coaches. He asked Coach Hall why the two schools didn't play each either, the coach responded: "I can't answer that, I don't know." Then he had the interview stopped regarding that subject.

Tesh followed that abbreviated meeting with Hall by talking with Coach Crum. "They won't play," Coach Crum said. Tesh asked: "They're afraid of you?" "Well, did you ask them that?" Crum said. Tesh replied: "Well, we asked Coach Hall," and Denny quickly interrupted, saying, "And he wouldn't give you an answer, would he?" Tesh Said: "Well he tried to walk out on the interview actually." Crum's response: "That's typical."

The day before the game, March 25, 1983 Coach Crum had this response regarding the issue of not playing: "We wanted to play Kentucky cause it was close, inexpensive and we'd be playing a good school and that's how you learn. You get better playing good teams. But they didn't ever want to play, so after a while I got to the point where it didn't make any difference, we didn't need them."

The Cats had beaten IU 64-59 and Louisville made a furious comeback to beat Arkansas by a Scooter McCray last second tip 65-63. The table was set for the "Dream Game" to become a reality.

Tennessee Coach Don DeVoe gave a scouting report for the game. His team split games with UK that season, winning 65-63 in Knoxville but losing 69-61 in Rupp arena. He lost to Louisville in the first game of the Mideast Regional 70-57.

He believed that the edge for this game clearly belonged to the Cardinals. He said: "For Kentucky to win, there are two really important areas. They've got to be able to handle Louisville's various full-court presses, and they're going to have to do a good job of playing zone defense. Those two areas are critical.

Nobody can match up man-to-man with Louisville. Only fools like me try that. Louisville's guards are just NBA guards. They post up, and I don't care how good you are defensively, when you don't have the height, it's impossible." Turpin inside would be a key for the Cats on offense.

UofL was ranked No. 2 and UK No. 12. UK controlled the tap and Dirk Minnefield scored the first points on a layup on the left side. His driving to the basket on the left side would impact this game tremendously. In the first half he was two of three on these drives, failing to score when Jones and Rodney McCray blocked the shot.

Milt Wagner #20 UofL, Jim Master #20 UK, Dirk Minnefield #10 UK, Lancaster Gordon #4 UofL

Kentucky was in control for much of the first half. The Cards were not playing intense, aggressive defense and the Cats offense moved like a machine, making the pass to the open player. Derrick Hord who had been struggling before this game, scored on three consecutive trips down the floor.

All of Kentucky's starters were in the scoring column in that first half and the Cardinals were struggling with their shooting. Kentucky was 11 for 17 from the field and UofL only four of 14 as the Wildcats took a 23-10 lead. Louisville called a timeout. The Cardinals got more aggressive on defense; they began using a trapping defense which made it harder for the Cats to get into their offense.

Still, with 4:14 remaining in the first half, UK led 33-21.

CBS color commentator Billy Packer commented that UofL's press would eventually pay-off with a two or three minute run that could be devastating.

That would surely be the case in the first five minutes of the second half, but it also paid dividends in the closing minutes of the first half.

UK made only four turnovers in that first half, but the third and fourth mistakes, turned into four Cardinal points, trimming UofL's 12-point deficit to seven, 37-30, with just over four minutes left in the half.

The good news for Kentucky was they shot 62 percent. The bad news was that that would be hard to duplicate in the second half. Kentucky had balanced scoring too, both inside and outside. Meanwhile, UofL didn't make one outside shot. All of their points had come underneath. Their guards were trying to post–up the smaller UK guards.

The UK guards were seven of 12 at the half. The UofL guards were only three of 11. Louisville had increased its field goal percentage to 41 percent, after shooting only 20 percent earlier in the first half. Rodney MeCray was leading the way for UofL with nine points on four of five shooting. Each team had committed only four turnovers in the first half of play. If the Cats could do that again, they win the game.

However, Coach Denny Crum and his fighting Cardinals had other ideas. They changed to a denial press and the Cats couldn't handle the intense pressure of getting the ball inbounds.

Earlier in the second half, Charles Jones missed two free throws and UK's Turpin would get a rebound and stuff it in for a 39-30 lead. UofL trimmed that to 39-32 and then came up with a steal, but Rodney McCray was called for a charge nullifying the basket he had made in the process.

Kentucky would turn the ball over two more times, but the Cards couldn't take advantage of those miscues.

Charles Jones changed his defensive positioning by moving in front of Turpin instead of playing behind him. The press heated up and UK was having trouble getting into its offence, but stayed patient, and Turpin had two more inside scores. Just like that Kentucky led 43-32.

UofL answered with a lob pass to Rodney McCray which he slammed home cutting the lead to 43-34. The Cats threw the ball away but UofL couldn't score. UK ran an instant replay turnover and this time Milt Wagner hit the first outside shot of the game for the Cards, making a 13 foot leaning jumper—43-36.

Turpin stretched the lead to 45-36, but the Cards got another easy inside dunk by Rodney McCray making it 45-38.

Dirk Minniefield picked up his third personal foul and went to the bench with around 16 minutes left. The Cards came right back, scoring on a jumper by Gordon. Now that 11-point lead had shrunk to five at 45-40.

Louisville stole it again, scored and trailed by only three, 45-42. The press was working. The Cats had only been able to get the ball over the mid-court line only once in its last five possessions.

UofL had all five men in the backcourt and the Cats had been very accommodating, not once having tried to break the press by going long over the top. The first time they tried it, it worked. Turpin would continue to be the workhorse on Offence and Jim Master would start hitting from the outside.

Melvin Turpin - #54-UK, Charles Hurt - #44-UK, Charles Jones #33 UofL, Lancaster Gordon - #4 - UofL, Dirk Minnifield - #10 UK.

The Cards were now scoring inside and out, something they didn't do in the first half. Lobs to Rodney McCray or a guard inside and jumpers by Gordon, Wagner and McCray from the outside.

UofL claimed its first lead at 50-49, but Turpin put UK back on top 51-50. With the Cats breaking the full-court press, Coach Crum changed to half-court pressure, making UK work harder on their half-court offense.

UK was still shooting 62 percent, but Louisville was shooting a phenomenal 86 percent. Lancaster Gordon was hot and the Cards now lead 56-53. With 4:23 remaining, the Cards cooled off a bit, now shooting 71 percent, but were still leading by three at 60-57.

Kentucky was playing a chase game and forced the Cards to turn it over with 3:59 on the clock. Derrick Hord missed a jumper but was fouled. He made the first free throw but missed the second. Charles Hurt followed with a put back shot and the score was tied at 60.

The Cats went back to playing a zone as the Cards looked to take the lead again when UK changed to a man-to-man defense. Milt Wagner threw a low pass to Gordon, who couldn't reach it and the ball went out of bounds—possession, Kentucky.

With 2:26 left, and Turpin back in the game the men in blue looked to work the ball and the clock. They called a timeout with 1:46 to go. They used another timeout with 49 seconds remaining. Then, 26 seconds later, Minniefield found himself on the left wing with Gordon playing defense for UofL. Lancaster seemed to pause for just a split second and Minniefield saw the separation and accelerated around him and made a cut for home.

Denny Crum talking to Charles Jones

Charles Jones was not fronting Turpin who was at the high post on the left side, but was playing a step or so behind the Kentucky center. When he saw Dirk make his move, he turned and on an angle made his move to catch up with Minniefield, who had opted for a lay-up high off the glass instead of a dunk. Jones told me in a recent interview, "I can jump, but I am pretty quick too, I don't think he thought I could catch him, but I did. The angle I had to the basket gave me room to make the block. If he had tried to dunk the ball, I think the angle would have caused me to foul him."

Gordon hit a sweet jumper off the right side to give Louisville the lead at 62-60 with eight seconds left in the game when UK used its last timeout. Master got the ball deep on the left side and hit a jumper making it 62 all. That shot made Master five for five in the second half.

Neither team had lost in overtime during the season. UK was 2-0 and UofL 1-0.

The Cards controlled the tip to start the overtime but nothing happened in the first minute of play. Then Gordon started the scoring with a 12 foot jumper off the left baseline. Turnover UK and Gordon scores again, 66-62, Cards lead.

The Cats got the ball over the timeline but a steal from behind and back the other way. The Cats foul and Jones makes two free throws and its 68-62 with the Cards taking full control.

UK had one timeout left but didn't use it until 46 seconds remained. But there was nothing to discuss, this race was virtually over with three minutes left in the overtime. Turnover, then three shots at the basket, none would fall. When the Wildcats finally scored with 34 seconds left they trailed 76-64, losing by the final score of 80-68.

"To dunk or not to dunk," by Minniefield will always be debated. Dirk is on record as saying he should have dunked the ball, but he made a different choice when the game called for an immediate decision.

In the overtime UofL played as close to perfection as you can get in this life. In the end, they may not have been as fatigued as UK. But down deep inside the psyche of the athletes that motors those individuals and their collective drive, I believe they had the edge. Maybe of the slightest variety, but an edge it was as Charles Jones said, "I really wanted to beat Kentucky because I still didn't think they, the administration and certainly the fans gave us that much respect."

This game would be avenged by UK at Rupp Arena in November of the same year when the two teams would meet again resulting in a 21-point blowout as the modern series began. But this, the "Dream Game" was the motivation for the renewing of the greatest rivalry in College basketball.

Cardinals celebrate "Dream Game" victory

Chapter Six
The Rivalry Games

GAME 14

NOVEMBER 26, 1983

	UK	UofL
Record	0-0	0-0
Ranking	#2	#6
Series	9	4
Favored	KENTUCKY BY 10	
Location	RUPP ARENA	
TV	WTBS (ATLANTA)	

THE PRE-GAME REPORT

The "Dream Game" was already eight notches back on the 1983 calendar when the Cards and Cats reassembled in Rupp Arena to clash for their first regular season game in sixty-one years. The game was legislature motivated, athletics board negotiated and publicized simultaneously from their respective corners of the state, since the two universities could not agree on a mutual meeting place to reveal the new four game deal to their fans.

UK Athletics Director Cliff Hagan and his counterpart at UofL, Bill Olsen, negotiated the negotiations; that is where to meet to sign the deal. Cliff did not want to meet in Frankfort because he was disgusted that politics were involved. He thought it was best for the coaches to decide who they wanted to play. So he and Bill agreed to meet at a Long John Silver's in Shelbyville. Bill Olsen told me that Mr. Hagan informed him that he would be driving a red Thunderbird. There they met, signed the contract and Hagan bought lunch.

Today, some recoil in disbelief that the first regular season rivalry game was aired on WTBS instead of a national outlet like CBS. Bill Olsen explained the reason: "Ted Turner's company offered the two schools the highest broadcast rights for a game at that time." *Courier-Journal* sports editor Billy Reed called it the "most celebrated non-rivalry in the game, and hoped it would be the beginning of a series that would be a continuing source of pride for Kentuckians and of interest to the nation's fans."

Even when they were not playing-UK vs. UofL was number one. The NCAA, campus publications, newspapers, state government, television networks and thousands of fans clamored for the game to be played in the arena, instead of on paper. True "bragging rights" could not be secured by merely talking or arguing the opponent into submission. Visions of the "Dream Game" still ran up and down the court in the heads of the Louisville fans, but there would only be some 100 tickets available for them in Lexington when the team got off the bus. Ticket distribution is one of the many components that make this rivalry hot.

Louisville came to town minus the two McCray brothers, Rodney and Scooter who were now in the NBA. But they had what could be considered the best backcourt in college hoops, in the form of senior Lancaster Gordon and junior Milt Wagner who was part of the famous "Camden Connection." Billy Thompson, considered the best high school player when he came to Louisville last season, would be looking to improve and the steady 6' 8" Charles Jones anchors down the center position. Local product Manuel Forrest from Moore High School rounded out the starting lineup.

Kentucky's strength was on the frontline with three returning starters. Senior Melvin Turpin was the big, strong 6' 11" senior center from Lexington, and sophomore Kenny Walker would be back at small forward. However, to gauge the future success of this team, one would have to depend on a pair of legs. Sam Bowie had not played since the 1980-81 season when he fractured his left tibia, now he was back not to play center, but the power forward spot. Senior Jim Master would be the long-range bomber and sophomore Roger Hardin was starting at the point instead of the injured Dicky Beal.

Kentucky was to have the advantage off the bench which included two talented freshmen, Winston Bennett and James Blackmon. Winston Bennett was a recruiting coup for UK. Since the graduation of Ted Deeken in 1964, the Cats had only signed two players from the city of Louisville, Tom Payne (UK's first black player) and Ernie Whitus, neither of whom stayed four years.

The Cardinals had won the recruiting battle the year before when they plucked Jeff Hall out of the Cat's backyard from the Ashland area. Coach Denny Crum told me he was looking for a shooter and gave his staff orders to find one. They received an assist from Chip Boes, the head coach at Pensacola Junior College, who was working the Dave Bones/Rick Bolus Cage Scope/High Potential Basketball Camp. He knew Louisville Assistant Coach Bobby Dotson when he was on the staff at Florida State and gave him a call, telling him he needed to come and see Hall, Jeff Hall. Dotson made the visit and Hall became a Cardinal. Then, UK went after Jeff, but they entered a race that had already been run.

Coach Dotson described his first visit with Jeff this way: "I asked him which school was his favorite when he was growing up and he replied, 'Cincinnati.' I got a big smile on my face. I was afraid he was going to say Kentucky. If UK really wanted a boy from the eastern part of the state, they usually got him. Jeff had even gone to their camp-but they hadn't showed any genuine interest."

A game within the game was the personal contest of Billy Thompson vs. Kenny Walker. Both had been highly recruited out of high school and Thompson was considered the best in the class. They had played against each other in their pre-college days, but the summer before school began, Billy hurt his knee while trail-biking on Coach Crum's farm. He had to miss the National Sports Festival and heard that Kenny was sorry because they were unable to settle the score regarding which player was the best. Thompson's reply was: "I don't talk that way about players, and I give him less respect because of it."

QUOTES

"We got them in size and they got us in quickness, noting that even on a down night Bowie's passing inside will aid him and the offense. . . That evens things out. But last year is in the back of my mind. We're not going to rush ourselves as much."
UK CENTER MELVIN TURPIN

"The press and the media have got a job to do to build expectations. This game is not as important as last year's."
UK FORWARD SAM BOWIE

"Anytime you're in a running game with Louisville, you are going to lose."
DON DeVOE HEAD COACH TENNESSEE

"Who's gonna win? If I knew, I wouldn't even play. I'm serious. That'd take away the spirit of competition, and competition's what America was built on. Right?"
UofL GUARD LANCASTER GORDON

PROBABLE STARTERS

Kentucky

POS.	PLAYER	HT.	WT.	CLS.	PT.	RB.
F	KENNY WALKER	6-8	190	SO.	7.3	4.9
F	SAM BOWIE	7-1	235	SR.	17.4	9.1
C	MELVIN TURPIN	6-11	240	SR.	15.1	6.3
G	JIM MASTER	6-5	180	SR.	12.5	2.1
G	ROGER HARDEN	6-1	165	SO.	0.8	0.7

Bowie's stats are from the '80-'81 season.

Louisville

POS.	PLAYER	HT.	WT.	CLS.	PT.	RB.
F	BILLY THOMPSON	6-8	195	SO.	7.3	3.9
F	MANUEL FORREST	6-7	200	JR.	3.3	3.0
C	CHARLES JONES	6-8	215	SR.	10.9	6.9
G	LANCASTER GORDON	6-3	185	SR.	13.7	2.8
G	MILT WAGNER	6-5	185	JR.	14.4	2.6

"UK's Killer D's spelled doom"
LEXINGTON Herald-Leader

"UofL nightmare, UK romps 65-44"
LOUISVILLE Courier-Journal

Louisville was supposed to have the advantage at guard, but it was one of those nights when both Gordon and Wagner struggled from the field connecting on only six of 21 shots for a paltry 28.6 percent.

On the other hand, UK was playing a three-guard attack with 7-1 forward Sam Bowie helping out at the point-guard position. Bowie was 0-3 from the field, but was seven of eight from the foul line, pulled down 10 rebounds and dished out five assists for the evening and made the cover of Sports Illustrated.

UK did not lead from wire-to-wire in this race, but took the lead for good at 13-12 on a Master 18' jumper with twelve minutes left in the first half. Next, Master would add a free throw as the result of an seldom called technical foul. Freshman Mark McSwain checked into the game, but was wearing the wrong numeral on his jersey. This was Kenny Klein's, Louisville's Sports Information Director's first game. No pressure right? He had checked all the numbers but somehow McSwain was wearing number 32 instead of 52. Now, in 2013 it is a little easier to speak of that night's numbers game: "I had checked the scorebook and so did the coaches but it happened- a technical foul. I was thinking to myself, what if we lose by one point, what will happen to me? But the coaches were very gracious about it and obviously we were not sweating over that one point as the game went on."

McSwain turned out to be a bright spot off the bench for the Cards going five for five from the field.

The real key to UK's win was its swarming defense. Bowie had doubts about his ability to play defense from the forward position. Coach Hall had given Assistant Coach Lake Kelly control of the Cats' defensive attack, and Bowie gained confidence that he could deny the pass. In fact, he recorded three steals in the game. This pressure defense installed by Kelly may have settled an old score he had with UK.

He wanted to play for Kentucky but wasn't recruited and ended up playing for Georgia Tech and Coach "Whack" Hyder. He told the Yellow Jacket mentor that he knew all of Coach Rupp's plays, and that he would help his teammates prepare for the game. Kelly asked his father if he was going to come and watch him play, but his father's rebuttal was, "I'm going hunting, I don't want to see you get embarrassed."

UK had won a record 129 consecutive home games, one which still stands today, but they were stung by the Yellow Jackets that night 59-58. It had been twelve years since anyone watching a game in Lexington had seen the Wildcats lose. Fans remained in their seats -stunned at the outcome.

Coach Kelly called his father and told him that Georgia Tech had beaten Kentucky! His dad said, "I don't believe you." He needed the Sunday morning newspaper to confirm the results.

STATS

Kentucky

Player	Min	FG	FGA	FT	FTA	Reb	PF	Ast	St	BS	TO	Pts
Sam Bowie	33	0	3	7	8	10	2	5	3	5	3	7
Kenny Walker	24	6	9	1	4	3	0	0	3	0	0	13
Melvin Turpin	33	5	11	6	8	9	2	1	1	1	2	16
Jim Master	37	5	13	9	9	2	3	2	1	0	3	19
Roger Harden	25	0	0	0	0	1	2	2	0	0	1	0

Player	Min	FG	FGA	FT	FTA	Reb	PF	Ast	St	BS	TO	Pts
James Blackmon	16	3	5	0	1	2	3	4	3	0	2	6
Dicky Beal	4	0	0	2	2	0	0	0	0	0	0	2
Paul Andrews	1	0	0	0	0	0	0	0	0	0	0	0
Bret Bearup	2	0	1	0	0	1	0	0	0	0	0	0
Winston Bennett	23	0	6	2	4	7	4	1	1	1	3	2
Tom Heitz	1	0	0	0	0	0	0	0	0	0	0	0
Troy McKinley	1	0	0	0	0	0	0	0	0	0	0	0
Team						1						
Totals	200	19	48	27	36	36	16	15	12	7	14	65

Louisville

Player	Min	FG	FGA	FT	FTA	Reb	PF	Ast	St	BS	TO	Pts
Manual Forrest	24	3	8	0	0	5	3	0	0	0	3	6
Billy Thompson	25	2	6	0	0	6	4	2	1	1	5	4
Charles Jones	36	2	8	2	2	8	2	1	1	0	2	6
Lancaster Gordon	35	4	12	0	1	6	1	2	2	0	2	8
Milt Wagner	22	2	9	0	0	3	5	3	0	1	2	4
Robbie Valentine	1	0	0	0	0	0	0	1	0	0	0	0
James Jeter	1	0	0	0	0	0	1	0	0	0	0	0
Barry Sumpter	15	0	2	0	2	5	3	1	0	0	1	0
Jeff Hall	25	3	9	0	0	1	2	1	1	1	2	6
Danny Mitchell	4	0	0	0	0	1	0	0	0	0	1	0
Mark McSwain	12	5	5	0	0	2	4	0	0	0	2	10
Team						4						
Totals	200	21	59	2	5	41	25	11	5	3	20	44

POINTS AFTER

"How can you be discouraged tonight? We've been giving this kind of effort in practice. Tonight, we transferred it onto the floor. That really pleases a coach?"
UK COACH JOE B. HALL (responding to the fact that Louisville out rebounded his team 41-36)

"I think they got rattled a little bit. We'd watched film on 'em, and we knew exactly what they'd try to do. Milt was going to post me up, and to be honest, I just beat him to his spots."
UK GUARD JIM MASTER

"Kentucky is in mid-season form already."
UofL COACH DENNY CRUM

"When you play a good team, they're gonna try to take your strength away from you. Kentucky made that known early. They put constant defensive pressure on us, good hard-nosed man-to-man pressure."
UofL GUARD JEFF HALL

Sam Bowie was quoted as saying that last year's game meant more. Yes, the Final Four was on the line, but for Bowie, who was still recovering from his injury at that time, and his teammates who played hard, but were annihilated in overtime, this game was very important to them personally in my estimation. They played like it.

GAME 15

MARCH 22, 1984

	UK	UofL
Record	27-4	24-10
Ranking	#3	unranked
Series	10	4
Favored	KENTUCKY BY 9.5	
Location	RUPP ARENA	
TV	CBS	

PRE-GAME REPORT

This rivalry game, as a game, was the first and only "triple-double" in the history of the series. The Cards and Cats had not played for twenty-four years when they clashed in the "Dream Game" in Knoxville on March 26, 1983 and now, tonight's game would be their third meeting in a single year, with both additional games being played in Lexington's Rupp Arena. Two of those three games were in NCAA play, resulting in each school going to a Final Four.

Coming into the "Dream Game" UofL was ranked No. 2 and had won fifteen consecutive games, UK was No. 12 but had lost its first game in the SEC Tournament to Alabama. Yet a monumental battle occurred before UofL took complete control in the overtime to win 80-68. Now a year later, the Cats were No. 3, had won the SEC Tournament and were "fat" from their earlier season blowout over the Cards 65-44. UofL was unranked and went 7-4 in February, and lost the Metro Conference Championship to Virginia Tech. But you knew they were going to be better now, in the tournament than they were back in November.

In these battles you can't always go according to form and that's why Coach Crum was feeling no pressure for the upcoming rematch, "David was at a disadvantage against Goliath, too. Anything can happen in a contest. The pressure is not on us because we're not expected to win. We're not in that position often, and it's kinda fun. I'm more relaxed. If we don't win, it's because we're not good enough."

All the players were back from the earlier game and they expected the final score to be a lot closer.

Kentucky's Dicky Beal only played four minutes in November, but now, he was physically able to stay in the game; he would be indispensable to the Cats' attack. This was vital since there was no guarantee that Gordon and Wagner would repeat their earlier game combined performance, going six of 21 from the field.

UK still had the advantages of size and depth on the frontline, plus injuries to Billy Thompson's knee and Manuel Forrest's ankle, would render them less than 100 percent but should not affect the outcome of the game.

Then, there was the question of playing on Kentucky's home court in the NCAA. Coach Crum was quoted as saying: "I've never felt that it was fair in a game so important, but I certainly understand the problem the NCAA has, if you're going to remove somebody from their home floor in a year when their hosting a regional, then nobody is going to want to host them."

He continued, "I'd like to see something done about it eventually, and not because we're playing at Kentucky in this particular year. It's not the first time it's happened. I can remember two or three times when UCLA was the host in Pauley Pavillion. Those UCLA teams probably would have beaten anybody on any court, but it was still an unfair situation."

QUOTES

"I think this (the third meeting) takes some of the mystique out of it. It' not who we're playing, but what we're playing for. It's more important than the earlier game because of what is at stake."
UK GUARD JIM MASTER

"Pressure exists on our program all the time. The home court does exert some pressure but I'd rather have that pressure and play at home."
UK COACH JOE B. HALL

BULLETIN BOARD MATERIAL

Responding to a Sports Illustrated story that had Jim Master saying he thought Gordon and Wagner had been "out to lunch" in the November 26 game.

"Maybe we'll have prime rib this time."
UofL LANCASTER GORDON

"All the pressure is on them. We're the underdogs and that's kind of a new feeling. I'm a bit more relaxed, because we're not supposed to win, anyway."
UofL COACH DENNY CRUM

PROBABLE STARTERS

Kentucky

POS.	PLAYER	HT.	WT.	CLS.	PT/G
F	KENNY WALKER	6-8	190	SO.	13.0
F	SAM BOWIE	7-1	230	SR.	10.6
C	MELVIN TURPIN	6-11	250	SR.	15.7
G	JIM MASTER	6-5	180	SR.	9.7
G	DICKY BEAL	5-11	170	SR.	5.9

Louisville

POS.	PLAYER	HT.	WT.	CLS.	PT/G
F	BILLY THOMPSON	6-8	195	SO.	9.2
F	MANUEL FORREST	6-7	200	JR.	8.2
C	CHARLES JONES	6-8	215	SR.	11.5
G	LANCASTER GORDON	6-3	185	SR.	14.7
G	MILT WAGNER	6-5	182	JR.	16.6

"Cats out duel Cards to reach Mideast finals"
LEXINGTON Herald-Leader

"UK and Beal, deal Cards out of tourney"
LOUISVILLE Courier-Journal

Lancaster Gordon wasn't out to lunch this time around, in fact, he and his running mate Milt Wagner appeared to be on course for that "prime rib dinner."

Jim Master's 14-ft jumper with 12:36 to go in the first half put the Cats on top 16-11, matching their biggest lead of the game at five, but the next 146 seconds belonged to the Cards as they mounted an 11-0 run led by Lancaster Gordon's seven points.

With ten seconds remaining, UofL was up by six and working for the last shot of the half, hoping to stretch their lead to eight when Wagner took a quick look at the bench for the play, and just like that, in the twinkling of an eye, Beal stole the ball and went in for a lay-up to cut the lead to four at intermission, 36-32.

In the second half, Kentucky wanted to put more defensive pressure on Louisville's perimeter game, which they did, but the keys to victory were stopping UofL inside while Dicky Beal kept the UK offense in motion.

In the final 14:53 the guards scored 21 of UofL's final 27 points. Lancaster Gordon had a game-high 25 points, but netted 18 of those in the first half. Wagner however, made-up for this reduction in production by scoring 14 of his 21 points in the second act of this nail-biting drama before 23,525 delirious fans.

Wagner's outside shot put UofL on top again, 49-47 with just over 11 minutes remaining in the game. Then, UK would steal the momentum by crafting a balanced 10-0 run of its own over a 3 1/2 minute span.

UK regained the lead, 51-49 after Sam Bowie's two free throws and Jim Master's outside shot. Back on the attack, the Cards' Milt Wagner at 6-5, was backing down on 5-11 Dicky Beal when he slipped. Beal scooped up the ball, one of his six steals, went the other way and laid it in, 53-49.

When the run was over, it was 57-49 but there was no surrender found in the Cardinals this night. With 2:49 to go, Manuel Forrest was headed to the foul line to shoot the front-end of a one-and-one. Here was UofL's chance to tie the game at 63, but Forrest missed the first shot and Gordon, after snaring the rebound, missed his jumper in the lane.

Master and Walker didn't miss from the line, and their combined four free throws extended UK's lead to six, 67-61. But the fireworks weren't over. Wagner would connect from long-distance twice; 22-ft and 24-ft to be precise. Winston Bennett sandwiched a free throw in-between and with 21-seconds left, Kentucky was clinging to a three-point advantage, 68-65. Fouled five seconds later,

Master hit his first free throw but missed the second when Winston Bennett, the freshman from Louisville scored on a tip-in and was fouled. He made the free throw and UK was out of reach at 72-65 when Gordon hit the last shot of the game and Kentucky prevailed 72-67.

STATS

Kentucky

Player	Min	FG	FGA	FT	FTA	Reb	PF	Ast	St	BS	TO	Pts
Sam Bowie	38	3	9	2	2	12	3	2	1	3	5	8
Kenny Walker	35	2	7	4	4	6	3	3	2	1	0	8
Melvin Turpin	32	6	10	2	2	5	3	2	0	2	5	14
Dicky Beal	39	6	9	3	4	2	3	9	6	0	6	15
Jim Master	30	6	10	3	4	4	3	0	0	0	2	15
James Blackmon	10	1	1	0	0	1	0	0	0	0	1	2
Roger Harden	1	0	0	0	0	0	1	0	0	0	0	0
Winston Bennett	15	4	9	2	4	5	3	0	0	0	1	10
Team						1						
Totals	**200**	**28**	**55**	**16**	**20**	**36**	**19**	**16**	**9**	**6**	**20**	**72**

Louisville

Player	Min	FG	FGA	FT	FTA	Reb	PF	Ast	St	BS	TO	Pts
Manual Forrest	35	3	4	0	1	4	5	2	2	1	1	6
Billy Thompson	26	2	8	0	3	5	4	1	0	0	4	4
Charles Jones	37	2	9	4	4	9	1	0	3	0	0	8
Lancaster Gordon	34	10	18	5	6	3	2	2	1	0	6	25
Milt Wagner	36	10	17	2	2	2	2	5	1	0	4	22
Barry Sumpter	5	0	0	0	0	0	2	0	0	0	1	0
Jeff Hall	11	1	4	0	0	0	3	0	1	0	0	2
Mark McSwain	15	0	1	0	0	0	1	1	0	0	0	0
James Jeter	1	0	0	0	0	0	0	0	0	0	0	0
Team						6						
Totals	**200**	**28**	**61**	**11**	**16**	**29**	**20**	**11**	**8**	**1**	**16**	**67**

POINTS AFTER

"Beal did a super job down the stretch orchestrating for us, both offensively and defensively. He fired them up. He just did a great job."
COACH JOE B. HALL

"This was the true Louisville team. They came to play, and Gordon and Wagner were just phenomenal. They were looking for their shots, and it seemed we couldn't shut them down."
UK GUARD DICKY BEAL

"It was a tough game—a real tough game. But more than anything, it was a tough loss. I'll never forget this one. Never."
UofL FORWARD BILLY THOMPSON

"Maybe on a neutral floor it might have been different. We'll never know."
COACH DENNY CRUM

In a speech delivered at Brigham Young University Adolph Rupp responded this way to criticism that his team won the 1958 NCAA National Championship by being at home in Louisville's Freedom Hall. Incidentally, the Mideast Regional games that year, as well as in 1957, were held in UK's Memorial Coliseum.

"We got a little criticism by winning the national championship in Louisville. Louisville's not our home floor, the first time we had seen the place is when we walked in, Seattle had already played three games there.

Of course, we won it one time in New York City and that's a suburb of Ashland, Kentucky. We won it in Minneapolis and that's a suburb of Covington. We've won it in Seattle and that's a suburb of Paducah. We've won it in all four of the districts. We can win it anywhere they play it. That's the way we feel about it."

Even though the NCAA has made changes that have improved the situation Coach Crum referred to back in 1984, some still complain about where teams are placed, but one thing is sure—you can't please all the people, all the time.

In this game free throw shooting made the difference. Each team made 28 field goals, but Kentucky shot 75 percent from the line on 16 of 20, while Louisville hit 11 of 16 for 68.7 percent. There were twenty fouls called on the Cards and nineteen on UK. Not like in November when UK took thirty-six charity tosses and UofL only five. No room for complaints here. This game like so many others in the series, reveals the heart and soul, the passion of competition that exists between these two schools, the players, coaches, administrators and of course, the fans.

Fan can be seen as the abbreviated form of fanatic. Merriam Webster's Online Dictionary defines fanatic as one marked by excessive enthusiasm, and often intense, uncritical devotion. In the majority of cases, fans are good for the game. However, in this contest nothing can justify the action of the fan, who after UofL's Barry Sumpter had knocked a fast-breaking Dicky Beal to the floor, threw a quarter from the stands which hit Coach Crum in the forehead. That is the most despicable, unsportsmanlike action that has surfaced in the rivalry.

One final point, Charles Jones told me: "We kept the fans on the edge of their seats. We we're proud of our effort."

No argument there. Even the most die-hard UK fans must admit that, just as the most die-hard UofL fans are required to give the same response for the Cats' effort in the "Dream Game."

GAME 16

DECEMBER 15, 1984

	UofL	UK
Record	1-3	3-1
Ranking	#14	unranked
Series	4	11
Favored	LOUISVILLE BY 6	
Location	FREEDOM HALL	
TV	LORIMAR	

PRE-GAME REPORT

Not much was happening out of the ordinary before the tip-off of the 16th game in the nation's No.1 rivalry. However, one must remember that there is nothing ordinary when it comes to these two. The Cards say they play better later in the season, but on November 24th with Milt Wagner leading the way, they beat IU on the road 75-64. Never had they played UK this early. But in the next game against VCU at home, Wagner breaks his foot and is out for the season. And their highly recruited freshman guard, Kevin Walls, joined Wagner on the injured redshirt list with knee problems.

The coaches, Crum and Hall teamed up with their shoe company, Converse for a promotional poster featuring the two in a locker room ready to square-off in an arm- wrestling match. Designed to promote good will, the poster was entitled: "EITHER WAY, YOU CAN'T LOSE!" That was a given for Converse. Coach Crum was quoted in a Billy Reed article as saying, "The idea is to show that we are foes and we compete, but we're not enemies."

Joe Dean Sr. an executive with Converse, and national basketball color commentator said, "This will have national appeal because everybody knows about the UK-UofL rivalry and kids love this kind of stuff." On the other hand, UK basketball graduate assistant Wayne Breeden detected what he thought was a distinct grip advantage for Coach Joe B. Hall, demonstrating once again the unparalleled, incessant striving by the Blue and Red to get one up on the other.

The last time the Cats dropped in to the River city to play the Cards in a regular season game was January 17, 1922 at the old St. Xavier Gym, defeating UofL 38-14.

Starting in 1937 against Notre Dame in the Armory, followed by the SEC Tournament from 1941-52 and the opening of Freedom Hall in 1957, UK would only miss playing at least one annual game in Louisville on four occasions.

In Freedom Hall, UK would start a game day morning workout for the public before they took the floor that night. It was a big draw for thousands of Cat fans, especially those who did not have a ticket for that night's game. But on December 15th, 1984 the Cats would be the visiting team in a newly renovated Freedom Hall. Naturally this would create some stir according to C-J sportswriter Earl Cox: "A UK spokesman said the 10:00 am workout before that night's Louisville game would be sponsored by radio station WHAS." But WHAS sales director Bob Scherer denied the report saying: "We are not sponsoring anything."

A UK source who asked not to be identified because of the sensitivity of relations involving the two schools and WHAS, which carries football and basketball broadcasts for both schools said that a WHAS representative did call and asked to withdraw WHAS' participation from the Saturday workout. Don Russell, UofL's associate director of athletics said, "UK fans were upset when WHAS sponsored our (preseason) workout, and I'm sure that UofL fans will be upset when WHAS sponsors UK's."

There would be some limited representation by WHAS planned, passing out programs and having a station announcer there. At that time UK had top billing on WHAS with Cawood Ledford doing the play-by-play and when schedules conflicted, Van Vance handled the play-by-play for UofL on WHAS' sister station, WAMZ. The "radio wars" would continue in the future, when Louisville found a loophole in the contract and took WHAS' top billing away from UK for a period of time.

Kentucky came into this game with a record of 1-3. That was certainly out of the ordinary, the last time UK lost four of their first five games was back in 1927.

QUOTES

"You have the fear of losing now. Playing in Freedom Hall I would hate to lose. I've got a lot of friends in Kentucky and I don't want to put up with hearing their mouths for a whole 'nother year."
UofL FORWARD MANUEL FORREST

"As long as we play as hard as we can play, I'll be pleased with them even if we don't win."
UofL COACH DENNY CRUM

"We would not have to win to be happy with our improvement."
UK COACH JOE B. HALL

"Thompson is a potentially explosive player who can beat you on the boards, with his passing or with his scoring."
UK COACH JOE. B. HALL

PROBABLE STARTERS

Louisville

POS.	PLAYER	HT.	WT.	CLS.	PT/G
F	BILLY THOMPSON	6-8	195	JR.	16.8
F	MANUEL FORREST	6-7	200	SR.	13.3
C	BARRY SUMPTER	6-11	235	SO.	7.8
G	CHRIS WEST	6-3	175	SO.	5.5
G	JEFF HALL	6-4	180	JR.	12.0

Kentucky

POS.	PLAYER	HT.	WT.	CLS.	PT/G
F	KENNY WALKER	6-8	195	JR.	17.0
F	WINSTON BENNETT	6-7	210	SO.	7.7
C	BRET BEARUP	6-9	230	SR.	6.8
G	ROGER HARDIN	6-1	165	JR.	4.3
G	ED DAVENDER	6-2	165	FR.	3.5

"UofL walks line, UK walks plank   71-64"
LOUISVILLE Courier-Journal

"UofL tops UK despite Walker's 32"
LEXINGTON HERALD-LEADER

Louisville's 71-64 victory over Kentucky in this, the third game since the rivalry's renewal a little over a year ago, solidifies the game's importance for all concerned. Neither team is expected to be a serious contender for this season's national championship, but they battled as if the title was on the line. Both teams were led by their super juniors. UofL's Billy Thompson had 17 points, 12 rebounds, and game highs in assists and steals with six and four respectively. UK's Kenny Walker was the game's top scorer with 32, and rebounder with 15. He also had two assists and a steal.

Louisville had the more balanced attack with five players scoring in double figures while Kentucky had three make the double digit scoring column.

UK had changed the offense to feature Walker coming off screens to get open shots within twelve feet of the basket. Musing sometime later, Bret Bearup told me, "Me and Winston Bennet both made the First Team, All-American Pick-Setters Squad for our work with Kenny Walker."

The first half was a real slugfest with ten lead changes and six ties. Walker's lay-up with four seconds left gave UK a 30-28 halftime lead. The see-saw battle continued until the 8:31 mark of the second half, when Thompson's 12-ft put back of a missed shot, gave the Cards the lead for good at 43-42. The score however remained close. Jeff Hall's 22-ft. baseline jumper with 2:49 to go, made it 58-53, the second time they had led by five in the half. Three seconds later, Hall stole an in-bounds pass from Roger Harden that was intended for Bret Bearup and a foul followed. Hall's two free throws started a string of 13 out of 15 down the stretch that sealed the deal 71-64 for the Red and Black.

STATS

Louisville

Player	Min	FG	FGA	FT	FTA	Reb	PF	Ast	St	BS	TO	Pts
Manual Forrest	28	5	10	2	3	0	2	3	0	0	2	12
Billy Thompson	39	7	13	3	7	12	1	6	1	4	3	17
Barry Sumpter	30	4	8	2	3	7	4	1	0	2	0	10
Chris West	33	1	6	3	4	3	1	4	2	1	1	5

Player	Min	FG	FGA	FT	FTA	Reb	PF	Ast	St	BS	TO	Pts
Jeff Hall	33	3	8	4	4	2	2	1	1	0	5	10
Mark McSwain	23	2	5	9	10	4	3	0	1	0	0	13
Mike Abram	3	0	0	0	0	1	0	0	0	0	0	0
James Jeter	11	0	0	4	4	2	0	2	1	0	2	4
Team						1						
Totals	**200**	**22**	**50**	**27**	**35**	**32**	**13**	**17**	**6**	**7**	**13**	**71**

Kentucky

Player	Min	FG	FGA	FT	FTA	Reb	PF	Ast	St	BS	TO	Pts
Winston Bennett	34	6	14	2	4	9	5	0	0	0	4	14
Kenny Walker	40	14	25	4	5	15	2	2	1	0	1	32
Bret Bearup	36	3	8	0	0	9	4	1	1	0	4	6
Paul Andrews	18	0	0	0	0	0	4	1	0	0	2	0
Roger Harden	33	6	9	0	0	2	1	2	1	0	2	12
Richard Madison	6	0	2	0	0	2	5	0	0	0	1	0
James Blackmon	23	0	1	0	0	0	2	1	1	0	1	0
Robert Lock	2	0	0	0	0	0	2	0	0	0	0	0
Ed Davender	8	0	4	0	0	0	2	1	0	0	2	0
Team						2						
Totals	**200**	**29**	**63**	**6**	**9**	**39**	**27**	**8**	**4**	**0**	**17**	**64**

POINTS AFTER

"Billy didn't make as many mistakes handling the ball. I've been on him about that, but his attitude has been good. He played like an All-American is supposed to play."
UofL COACH DENNY CRUM

"It's tough for one guy to beat you."
UofL COACH DENNY CRUM (referring to Kenny Walker's 32 Points)

"Coach Hall opened it up a little more for the guards."
UK GUARD ROGER HARDIN (scored a career-high 12 points)

"Tell him I dedicated this game to him."
UK FORWARD KENNY WALKER (Referring to the young man he had visited the day before at Kosair Children's Hospital).

This was the only game carried by the Lorimar Network. They covered seventy-two markets nationally, which included thirty-four of the top fifty market areas. However, three of the nation's largest TV market areas were excluded; Los Angeles, (#2) Chicago, (#3) and San Francisco (#5). Too bad in this case, this was a very good game with Thompson vs. Walker, Bennett making good on his first starting assignment and Roger Hardin scoring a career-high 12 points.

Eric Crawford of WDRB Sports in Louisville said, "What if they had played all those years before 1983, the national audience could have been like Duke and North Carolina with all the great players the two teams had."

Billy Thompson

GAME 17

December 28, 1985

	UK	UofL
Record	7-1	6-2
Ranking	#13	#15
Series	11	5
Favored	KENTUCKY BY 7	
Location	RUPP ARENA	
TV	CBS	

PRE-GAME REPORT

Kentucky may have had a new coach in Eddie Sutton, but he was no stranger to Louisville Coach Denny Crum, as the two had met four times in NCAA competition. The first was in the consolation game of the 1974 Midwest Regional in Tulsa, Oklahoma, Sutton's Creighton team winning 80-71. Next, the two would meet three times while Sutton coached at Arkansas. The Razorbacks beat the Cards in the 1979 Midwest Regional in Cincinnati 73-62, which loss was a blessing in disguise. This game was a major factor in motivating Darrell Griffith to prepare for his senior season, which would result in Louisville's first NCAA National Championship. And who could forget the Midwest Regional in Austin, Texas in 1981 when the Cardinals, the defending national champions, had turned their season around, winning 15 straight and 19 of their last 20 games, only to be eliminated in the first game of that regional by Arkansas' U.S. Reed whose prayer from some 50 feet with time running out was answered with a swish, final 74-73, Hogs.

 Scooter McCray was the hero for the Cards in the 1983 Mideast Regional in Knoxville, as his tip-in beat the buzzer and Arkansas 65-63, sending UofL to a "Dream Game" against the Cats. After that win, Coach Crum was quoted as saying this to Coach Sutton, "If you'd have gotten me this time, you'd have owned me."

The redeemable value of the rivalry was still being debated by the sportswriters. Billy Reed went to the archives and found these comments from UK's president Otis Singeltary, given during negotiations for the game's contract: "(1) there was little interest in the game outside of the state, and (2) it would be just another game after the novelty wore off." But for this game, Reed pointed out that after CBS discovered that its rival NBC was going to air the NFL Wild-Card playoff game between the Patriots and Jets at 4:00 pm, CBS switched its line-up and moved UK-UofL from 12:30 pm slot to 4:00 pm, believing it would provide stiffer competition for the pro game.

Billy Reed went on to say that Singeltary was right to the extent that-mercifully—the hype, hoopla and hysteria have been reduced to at least tolerable levels. "Never again will there be a repeat of the feeling generated by the UK-UofL game in the final of the Mideast Regional on Saturday March 26, 1983 in Knoxville, TN., their first meeting in twenty-four years.

That 80-68 overtime victory by UofL was the one and only "Dream Game," which is why it's silly for writers and broadcasters to keep applying that tag to every UK-UofL meeting."

That game was something special indeed, and it may be redundant to make every contest a "Dream Game," but you must be careful when using those retributory exclamations—never and always! Billy, like the rest of us are not handicapped with an infallible repertoire of predictability. But, I understand why he would make such a statement. Even hindsight, which some say is 20/20, cannot be relied on as a "perfect science" if some of the story's key elements remain at-large, while others view the same history through a jaded prism.

Here's one of the many "missing parts" capers. While broadcasting a Miami-Florida football game, Brent Musberger said something to this effect: "that former Miami Coach Howard Schnellenberger's running-up the score in a previous game was one reason their was so much "bad blood" in this rivalry." On November the 29th, 1980 in Gainesville with time running out and Miami leading 28-7, Coach Schnellenberger did call a timeout, the Canes would tack-on another field goal, making the final 31-7 causing the Gator fans to lose their minds.

Schnellenberger wasn't running up the score for the sake of a larger winning margin, but merely responding to the conduct of the Gator students, who were hurling oranges onto the field from the upper part of the stadium. Those students according to Coach Schnellenberger had prepared their oranges the night before by coring the center, and filling them with their favorite beverage, then putting them on ice.

Miami was running out the clock when several of these now missile like objects were directed towards the Miami sideline. Florida fans were not exempt from possible injury by this most unsportsmanlike conduct. One struck Howard's son Steve, one got a cheerleader, and another struck Assistant Coach Chris Vagotis in the head while he and Coach Schnellenberger were shaking hands on the victory. Howard said, "Vagotis was struck in the head, hit the ground and we were still shaking hands. It appeared he was knocked out; when he rose to his feet, he was still groggy!"

Schnellenberger's offensive coordinator Kim Helton urged him not to go for the field goal, but he called timeout and opted for Danny Miller to kick a twenty-five yard field goal which made the final score 31-3.

Howard didn't know it at the time, but the play-by-play color commentator, Frank Broyles, former Arkansas coach, was going wild in the broadcast booth about Schellenberger's despicable act. Coach Schnellenberger told me that even though the University of Florida president wrote him a letter apologizing for the students' behavior, and saying he would take corrective measures; looking back today maybe the better part of valor would have been to kick the ball into the stands.

The jaded look usually occurs when a fan of one school is attempting to minimize the glory attributed to his hated rival. One evening on my Sunday Sports Roundtable Show, we were discussing UK being the all-time college basketball wins leader, when a caller joined the conversation and said, "They may be the all-time leader, but its an unfair comparison because Kentucky has been playing basketball eight years longer than North Carolina, and should have more wins!" My reply was yes, Kentucky had been playing basketball eight years longer than UNC, but in that period of time the Tar Heels had played more games. UK is still the all-time wins leader today, (at the end of the 2012-13 season) and has 21 more victories than third place North Carolina, while playing sixty-three fewer games.

I think the Final Four game in 2012 topped the "Dream Game" for anticipation and excitement. It had been 28 years since the two teams had played each other during the regular season and in the NCAA tournament. But in 1984, it was the first game of the Mideast Regional in Lexington, while this trip to the NCAA in 2012, would cover uncharted territory—never before had they battled each other in a Final Four game.

Not to long ago Coach Pitino said, "Cal and I could toss horseshoes and 5,000 would show-up!" The hoopla and hysteria is trending well above the DOW and could pay its biggest rivalry dividend on December 28, 2013 when the Cards and Cats clash in Rupp Arena. Both teams will be near the top in the 2013-14 pre-season poll. It's the "One-and-Dones" vs. the "Hold Overs". Up for grabs as usual is a slightly better seeding position for the NCAA tournament, state bragging rights and this time around, national bragging rights as well.

These national bragging rights stem from the momentum created by each team winning a national championship in the past two seasons, the two high profile coaches with Pitino now leading Calipari in championships two to one, UK's incoming recruiting class rated No.1 again for the third time in the past four years, the outstanding talent on both squads and of course, the mild-mannered fans (laugh out loud) have all transformed this shindig beyond its impact zenith.

Looking at the personnel for this game, the Cards had a size advantage, the best freshman in the country in Pervis Ellision, their outstanding guard Milt Wagner returning from a red-shirt season in which he broke his foot and a deeper bench.

Courier-Journal reporter Russ Brown had interviewed Kansas Coach Larry Brown, whose team had beaten both UK and UofL that season and sizing up the game he said, "Shooting, ball-handling and defense should be a virtual standoff…I would worry about the boards if I was Kentucky." On that point of rebounding, UK watched lots of game film and detected what they believed was a weakness in UofL's rebounding technique. The Sutton staff felt that the Cards were relying to much on their jumping ability to snare rebounds and that the Cats might gain an advantage by getting inside.

QUOTES

"(Pervis) Ellison isn't a youngster. Nobody plays like that as a rookie. He doesn't make freshman mistakes. He probably played in his other lifetime and was a guard. Now, he is a center and he's got all that guard smarts."
UK COACH EDDIE SUTTON

"Louisville has the type of squad, if they continue to improve and I have to believe they will, may very well be in Dallas (for the NCAA Final Four)."
UK COACH EDDIE SUTTON

"Last year (UofL won 71-64)…We weren't a real good team. Maybe they weren't, either, but we won and that's probably the way it will go most of the time. Occasionally, somebody will beat somebody on the road, but for the most part, good teams don't lose too many at home."
UofL COACH DENNY CRUM

"I don't care where they play it. Let them play it on an aircraft carrier, there is no way UK is going to win this game."
UofL RADIO COLOR COMMENTATOR JOCK SUTHERLAND

"Rupp is a nice place to play, but in a way it kind of scares you. You never know how young guys are going to react under these kinds of circumstances."
UofL GUARD JEFF HALL

PROBABLE STARTERS

Kentucky

POS.	PLAYER	HT.	WT.	CLS.	PT/G
F	KENNY WALKER	6-8	210	SR.	20.3
F	WINSTON BENNETT	6-7	210	JR.	10.6
C	JAMES BLACKMON	6-3	180	JR.	9.9
G	ROGER HARDIN	6-1	175	SR.	4.1
G	ED DAVENDER	6-2	170	SO.	14.8

Louisville

POS.	PLAYER	HT.	WT.	CLS.	PT/G
F	BILLY THOMPSON	6-7	195	SR.	14.6
F	HERBERT CROOK	6-7	190	SO.	10.8
C	PERVIS ELLISON	6-10	195	FR.	13.0
G	MILT WAGNER	6-5	185	SR.	13.0
G	JEFF HALL	6-4	180	SR.	9.6

"Cardinals lost but learned fact of life on road"
Lexington Herald-Leader

"Hammering the Boards, UK nails UofL"
Louisville Courier-Journal

In this version of the "biggest loser," predictability often takes center stage. Rebounding and bench play were the Card's biggest advantages heading into this game, but the Cats soundly won the rebounding battle 36-24, with an astounding 20-5 edge on the offensive glass. And from the bench, UK freshman Richard Madison outscored four UofL players 10-4, and out rebounded them 5-1.

Regarding rebounds, Kenny Walker said, "We looked at films of Louisville and saw that they don't block out that much. They rely on their jumping ability. So if you get guys like ourselves who were pretty active, spinning around and getting in there…well, we can jump also and that showed today." Walker had 14 rebounds and Bennett seven.

UofL's Billy Thompson saw it this way, "It was definitely a numbers game. We rely on Pervis and me to get the rebounds. With a team that sends all players to the boards, that creates a problem."

Even from the free throw line, UK grabbed three rebounds on missed shots. With the score tied 46-46 and 9:31 remaining in the game, Bennett made his first foul shot then missed, but Blackmon got the rebound and was fouled by Billy Thompson, giving the Cardinal star four fouls with over nine minutes left to play. Blackmon made his first shot, but missed the second and Bennett got the board and made a lay-up.

Jeff Hall thought the Cards did a good job on Kenny Walker, limiting him to 11 points after he had scored 32 the previous year, "But the other guys he said took up the slack." And Winston Bennett was the biggest "slacker". Kentucky had made a change on offense, bringing Walker outside and leaving Bennett in the low post to roam the lane with his physical prowess. He scored 23 points and grabbed seven rebounds, had three steals, two assists, a blocked shot and only one turnover while playing the entire 40 minutes.

STATS

Kentucky

Player	Min	FG	FGA	FT	FTA	Reb	PF	Ast	St	BS	TO	Pts
Winston Bennett	40	8	13	7	8	7	3	2	3	1	1	23
Kenny Walker	36	5	13	1	5	14	3	0	0	0	0	11
James Blackmon	28	3	12	3	4	4	1	1	0	0	1	9
Ed Davender	38	1	9	4	4	2	0	2	1	0	2	6
Roger Harden	28	3	6	4	4	2	2	4	2	0	3	10
Richard Madison	26	5	7	0	0	5	2	1	0	0	0	10
Cedric Jenkins	4	0	0	0	0	0	1	0	0	1	0	0
Team						2						
Totals	**200**	**25**	**60**	**19**	**25**	**36**	**12**	**10**	**6**	**2**	**7**	**69**

Louisville

Player	Min	FG	FGA	FT	FTA	Reb	PF	Ast	St	BS	TO	Pts
Herbert Crook	30	7	9	0	0	1	4	4	1	1	1	14
Billy Thompson	33	3	6	2	2	8	4	3	0	2	4	8
Pervis Ellison	38	5	10	3	3	7	2	3	13	4	4	13
Milt Wagner	37	9	13	1	2	2	2	4	0	1	2	19
Jeff Hall	32	3	5	0	0	3	3	3	0	0	2	6
Kenny Payne	2	0	2	0	0	0	1	1	0	0	1	0
Chris West	10	1	2	0	0	0	3	1	0	0	0	2
Tony Kimbro	10	1	3	0	0	1	1	0	0	0	2	2
Mark McSwain	8	0	0	0	0	0	2	0	0	1	0	0
Team						2						
Totals	**200**	**29**	**50**	**6**	**7**	**24**	**20**	**19**	**64**	**9**	**16**	**64**

POINTS AFTER

"There are some great rivalries, but most of them are within a conference. All week my players kept telling me, 'Coach, this is a big one, for braggin' rights.' Now, I know why."
COACH EDDIE SUTTON

"Roger Hardin is the most underrated basketball player in America."
UK FORWARD WINSTON BENNETT

"We just weren't aggressive enough."
UofL FORWARD BILLY THOMPSON

"We need to get more consistent play off the bench to be a great team. Especially on the road."
UofL COACH DENNY CRUM

Jock Sutherland's aircraft carrier docked in Dallas (no small feat) in March as the Cardinals won their second NCAA National Championship beating Duke 72-69. Pervis may have been the MVP of the Final Four, but without Jeff Hall smothering Johnny Dawkins defensively in the second half, the Cardinals don't win. In retrospect, that surprise recruiting windfall, snatching Jeff Hall out of traditional Big Blue territory in 1982, and Milt Wagner's broken foot in 1984 that kept him around for an extra year, benefited the Cards immensely on their road to the 1986 national crown.

If you are a Cat fan and could go back in time, would you trade the regular season win that year over Louisville for the Cardinals national championship trophy? Those who say no, may need to see a "shrink." But let's save the co-pay and put this in perspective. If you only play once a season, it's paramount that your team wins that game. Now, rollover on the doctor's couch. If you play twice, and can only win once that year, and the one game is the national championship, you take that game and lose in the regular season, because as rivals, the national championship is the ultimate prize.

One more shot on that '86 season. I think the NCAA Selection Committee has on several occasions geographically mistreated the Commonwealth of Kentucky when it comes to seeding the tournament. In 1986, Kentucky played Western Kentucky in the second game, that's fine, but in 2012 they played each other in the first game at the YUM Center in Louisville. In 2011, UofL had to play Morehead State in the first game.

These other teams from the state work hard to get to the tournament, and I believe it should be at least the second game before the in-state teams play each other. The flip-side to that is those teams really don't have a great chance, because of their seeding, to get very far down that "Glory Road."

In 1986, the committee placed three SEC teams in the same Southeast Regional. It takes a Herculean effort to beat a good team twice in the same year. But three times? And don't stop there, why not four? When UK beat Alabama in the regional 68-63, it was for the fourth time that season and I remember watching Billy Packer almost come out of his seat when he learned that UK had won the game

Then, in the regional title game with the Final Four berth on the line, and a chance to meet UofL again, the Cats, who had already defeated LSU three times that season, lost to the Bengal Tigers by two, 59-57. Louisville won its second national championship with Denny Crum beating Duke 72-69.

GAME 18

December 27, 1986

	UofL	UK
Record	4-5	5-1
Ranking	unranked	#18
Series	5	12
Favored	LOUISVILLE BY 2	
Location	FREEDOM HALL	
TV	CBS	

PRE-GAME REPORT

To all aspiring comedic writers, using such material as defending national champions may instantly land you a spot on the Tonight Show or Dave Letterman's staff. Yes, Louisville was the defending national champions, but like so many other returning winners, they weren't defending their title with the same players. Gone are Billy Thompson, Milt Wagner, Jeff Hall and forty points per game. The frontline is the Card's strength with senior Mark McSwain, junior Herb Crook and sophomore center Pervis Ellison returning. Coach Crum will need steady development from sophomores Tony Kimbro and Kenny Payne, plus help from the bench to fill the vacuum left by the departing seniors. The Cards found themselves ranked No. 2 in the 1986-87 pre-season poll, but quickly fell from the rankings after losing all three of their games in the Great Alaskan Shootout.

Kentucky also lost three seniors from last year's team that beat Louisville 69-64. While Kenny Walker and Roger Harden were seniors on that team, current senior, Winston Bennett was lost for the season due to a knee injury. UK's strength would be the three guard offense once again. This time around, senior James Blackmon and junior Ed Davender would be on the attack with freshman standout Rex Chapman. Chapman had scored 26 points in UK's only loss of the season at IU, setting up his coronation as "King Rex" on a story in *Sports Illustrated*. And the timing was perfect for the arrival of Chapman and another freshman shooting guard Derrick Miller, with the three-point shot now in vogue for all of college basketball.

The Cards were averaging 71.1 ppg. on 47.1 percent shooting from two-point range and the Cats 71.7 ppg. and 54.2 percent. But from the new three-point distance of 19-feet-9-inches, UK was 25 of 64 for 39.1 percent and UofL was three of seventeen for 17.6 percent. This would be a telling statistic.

The *Courier-Journal* was also experiencing some roster changes. Their long-time writer and current sports editor Billy Reed was transferring to the *Lexington-Herald Leader* in January.

Meanwhile, negotiations were still in motion for a new contract between the two schools, since this was the last year of the current four-game series, and the NCAA was conducting and investigation of the UK program. But the biggest pre-game uproar was UK Coach Eddie Sutton's comment concerning UofL's role as the Cats' "little brother!"

Paul Willman

QUOTES

"We're stronger inside than we are at guard, but I don't know if we are stronger than Kentucky. Our guards are going to have to play better if we're going to have a chance, but our inside guys will have to play awfully well too."
COACH DENNY CRUM

"Everybody is looking for the reason we're not playing good. It's not only the guards, it's the whole team, but I think it's starting to click."
MIKE ABRAM

"Put our guards and their frontline together and we'll play the Celtics. If Chapman was playing for Louisville, I'd take a sabbatical."
COACH EDDIE SUTTON

"We want to pressure their guards, apply a lot of heat, make them make some turnovers."
REX CHAPMAN

PROBABLE STARTERS

Kentucky

POS.	PLAYER	HT.	WT.	CLS.	PT/G
F	IRV THOMAS	6-7	210	SO.	7.3
F	ROB LOCK	6-11	230	JR.	8.7
C	ED DAVENDER	6-3	165	JR.	16.8
G	JAMES BLACKMON	6-3	170	SR.	6.8
G	REX CHAPMAN	6-5	170	FR.	16.3

Louisville

POS.	PLAYER	HT.	WT.	CLS.	PT/G
F	MARK MCSWAIN	6-9	205	SR.	6.2
F	HERBERT CROOK	6-7	190	JR.	17.4
C	PERVIS ELLISON	6-9	195	SO.	18.3
G	TONY KIMBRO	6-7	190	SO.	10.1
G	CRAIG HAWLEY	6-7	175	FR.	5.0

"Cats destroy Cards 85-51"
Lexington Herald-Leader

"UK 'Rex' UofL 85-51 as Rockets, Records Fall"
Louisville Courier-Journal

Some twists on well-known phrases appropriately sums up the UK blowout: "It's the three-point shooting-stupid!" "Elementary my dear Chapman." "We'll always have the three." "Frankly, my dear-I don't shoot the three!" "Remember the three! "Three! Three! Comeback three!"

	2-PT FG/A	3-PT FG/A
Chapman	10/20	5/8
Davender	5/13	1/3
Blackmon	4/7	3/3
Miller	3/4	2/3
Total	22/44 (50%)	11/17 (64.7%)

Overall UK shot 54.2 percent from the field and UofL 38 percent. The Cards were only one of eight from three-point land for a dismal 12.5 percent. And the rebounding in this game did a complete 180 from regular season play. Louisville was averaging just over 40 rebounds a game and UK 32, but the final margin here went to Kentucky 41-33, due in large part to Richard Madison coming off the bench and snaring 17 boards in twenty-nine minutes of play.

C-J writer Jim Terhune examined the record book in regards to Coach Crum's tenure at the university. "Never in the 15 year seasons of Denny Crum's reign has anything happened like this…UofL's worst previous loss under Crum was 22 points (North Carolina in 1980). Its worst loss under Crum at home was 20 (Virginia Tech 1985). Its worst loss to UK was by the same margin, 34 (in an Olympic Trials match in 1948). Never had it lost by this margin in its 30 seasons at Freedom Hall. Never had it lost on any of its home courts by this margin since Evansville beat them 80-43 in 1940. One has to go back to a 99-59 pasting at Xavier on Feb. 13, 1956 to find a worse defeat anywhere."

That loss to Xavier has a "Rest of the Story" segment to explore. Sixteen days later at home, the Cardinals defeated that same Xavier team 83-70, and took a giant leap in its basketball history in that "leap year," by going to New York City and winning the 1956 NIT Championship over No. 3 Dayton 93-80. UofL was ranked No. 6.

STATS

Kentucky

Player	Min	FG	FG A	3PT FG	3 PT FGA	FT	FT A	Reb	PF	Ast	St	BS	TO	Pts
Rex Chapman	35	10	20	5	8	1	3	0	2	4	2	0	2	26
James Blackmon	24	4	7	3	3	0	2	1	2	2	2	0	1	11
Ed Davender	35	5	13	1	3	5	7	8	1	5	0	0	1	16
Robert Lock	25	4	5	0	0	1	1	7	4	0	1	1	2	9
Irving Thomas	24	2	3	0	0	2	2	5	4	0	1	1	2	6
Derrick Miller	24	3	4	2	3	0	0	3	3	1	0	0	1	8

Player	Min	FG	FG A	3PT FG	3 PT FGA	FT	FT A	Reb	PF	Ast	St	BS	TO	Pts
Steve Bruce	1	0	0	0	0	0	0	0	0	0	0	0	0	0
Terry Shigg	2	0	0	0	0	0	0	0	0	0	0	0	0	0
Richard Madison	29	4	7	0	0	1	1	17	3	2	1	0	2	9
Cedric Jenkins	1	0	0	0	0	0	0	0	0	0	0	0	0	0
Team								0						
Totals	**200**	**32**	**59**	**11**	**17**	**10**	**16**	**41**	**19**	**14**	**7**	**2**	**11**	**85**

Louisville

Player	Min	FG	FG A	3PT FG	3 PT FGA	FT	FT A	Reb	PF	Ast	St	BS	TO	Pts
Kenny Payne	17	3	8	1	4	0	0	1	2	1	0	0	3	7
Herbert Crook	27	1	5	0	0	4	6	7	2	1	1	0	1	6
Pervis Ellison	26	2	8	0	0	0	0	4	0	1	0	3	3	4
Craig Hawley	17	1	3	0	1	0	0	2	1	2	0	0	2	2
Tony Kimbro	28	4	9	0	0	2	2	3	3	1	1	0	0	10
Keith Williams	22	0	2	0	2	0	0	0	0	4	0	0	0	0
Mark McSwain	11	1	2	0	0	0	1	4	0	1	0	0	0	2
Chris West	8	0	2	0	1	0	0	2	2	1	0	0	1	0
Avery Marshall	4	1	2	0	0	0	0	1	1	0	1	0	0	2
Mike Abram	25	4	10	0	0	0	0	3	2	1	1	1	1	8
Felton Spencer	15	4	7	0	0	2	6	5	0	0	0	0	1	10
Team								1						
Totals	**200**	**21**	**58**	**1**	**8**	**8**	**15**	**33**	**13**	**13**	**4**	**4**	**12**	**51**

POINTS AFTER

"Things snowball. A team gets such momentum up that whatever you try fails to work."
COACH DENNY CRUM

"They're not that good and we're not that bad."
HERBERT CROOK

"If anything, I think this makes our fans believers. They've been talking about waiting until next year. I like this year."
COACH EDDIE SUTTON

"It's such an awesome feeling because some are saying it's the greatest victory in UK basketball ever. That's because no one expected it. They expected it with teams like the Twin Towers and others. I can't describe how I felt when we were up 20 with 15 minutes to go. The full effect won't sink in until later."
ROB LOCK

UK was going to be the home team the following Monday night in Freedom Hall against the Georgia Bulldogs. The euphoria continued through the weekend, bringing 20,000 people to Freedom Hall Monday for the game day shoot around. I was there with my two oldest sons Rhett and Adam and gave them this bit of advice, "If your ever good enough, you want to play for Kentucky!"

Then Monday night, the Cats went out and of all things lost to Georgia 69-65. UK would finish the season 18-11, losing the first game in both the SEC and NCAA tournaments. Louisville was 18-14, losing their second game in the Metro Conference Tournament to Memphis State.

GAME 19

December 12, 1987

	UK	UofL
Record	3-0	0-1
Ranking	#1	unranked
Series	13	5
Favored	KENTUCKY BY 8	
Location	RUPP ARENA	
TV	CBS	

PRE-GAME REPORT

This marked the first time that either team entered this contest ranked No. 1 since the series renewal in November of 1983. The Cats were 3-0 with a win over IU (82-76) in overtime in the Big Four Classic in Indianapolis, while the Cards were 0-1 losing in the same location to Notre Dame 69-54.

Winston Bennett was back from his knee injury for his senior season, and two outstanding freshmen, Eric Manuel and Leron Ellis had joined the team. But the NCAA investigation of the Kentucky program continued to hover over the campus and would prove to be the toughest opponent at the end of the season.

Louisville had Pervis Ellison and Herbert Crook back on the frontline and an outstanding freshman of their own in LaBradford Smith. Two other local products, seven-foot center Felton Spencer and 6-4 guard Keith Williams along with junior Kenny Payne, created an interchangeable starting five that desperately wanted to prove the Notre Dame game a fluke, and of course, they still had the 85-51 drubbing they took from UK last year at home on their minds. One player they could use, but would not be available till the following season, was 6-7 junior Tony Kimbro, sitting out due to academic problems.

QUOTES

"Louisville is always an outstanding rebounding team. We can't give them to many shots."
COACH EDDIE SUTTON

"He's trying to psych us out. (Coach Crum's gloomy outlook) We won't fall for any of that."
ROB LOCK

"Playing the No. 1 team on their floor, we're not supposed to win."
COACH DENNY CRUM

"If we don't play any better than we did against Notre Dame, we'll get beat by 60."
FELTON SPENCER

PROBABLE STARTERS

Kentucky

POS.	PLAYER	HT.	WT.	CLS.	PT/G
F	WINSTON BENNETT	6-7	215	SR.	12.7
F	CEDRIC JENKINS	6-9	205	SR.	7.3
C	ROB LOCK	6-11	225	SR.	16.7
G	ED DAVENDER	6-2	165	SR.	16.7
G	REX CHAPMAN	6-4	185	SO.	13.3

Louisville

POS.	PLAYER	HT.	WT.	CLS.	PT/G
F	HERBERT CROOK	6-7	195	SR.	10.0
F	PERVIS ELLISON	6-9	205	JR.	23.0
C	FELTON SPENCER	7-0	250	SO.	0.0
G	KEITH WILLIAMS	6-4	180	SO.	4.0
G	LaBRADFORD SMITH	6-4	180	FR.	2.0

"Cats tip Cards on Jenkins tip-in"
Lexington Herald-Leader

"Kentucky wins 76-75, UofL wins 75-76"
Louisville Courier-Journal

Kentucky led at halftime 45-32, due in part to a 12-0 run that received a technical boost. It was UofL's ball, when Felton Spencer came in for Kenny Payne, but Payne didn't leave the game and the Cards were whistled for a technical foul, too many men on the floor. Ed Davender hit the free throw and followed that with a three-pointer.

The Cats would see the same red and black Cardinal uniforms when they returned to the court, but the players were anything but the same.

Undaunted, Louisville came to play the second half. Putting extreme pressure on UK, the Cats hurried their passes, making turnovers and watching their shooting percentage drop drastically to 35.7 percent while UofL was hitting 64.3 percent.

Even when the UK guards got past the perimeter defenders, UofL clogged the middle with a zone, complicating UK offensively. Couple that with Winston Bennett's mere six minutes in the second half due to foul trouble; and No.1 ranked UK was in trouble. The lead would change three times during the final 8:01 of the game. With 39 seconds left, UofL's Pervis Ellison hit a ten foot baseline jumper that put the Cards on top 75-74.

UK called timeout with 11 seconds remaining. Ed Davender got the ball and was double-teamed, so he worked his way to the baseline. What transpired from that position in the final, razor-thin six seconds, would determine the outcome of this "royal rumble."

Davender let fly an eight-foot jumper with six seconds to go that bounced off the right side of the basket. A three-man configuration, consisting of two Cats, Cedric Jenkins and Rob Lock, and a single Cardinal, Herb Crook, touched the ball at the same time, sending it back on the rim with just 0:04 on the clock.

Crook was the Lone Ranger underneath for the Cards since Ellison had gone outside to cover Chapman, and Felton Spencer, who hadn't had a rebound all season, was screened away from the basket.

Once again, the ball bounced off to the right, and there was Jenkins, known as "Swoop" for his 39-inch sleeve, scoreless, who nudged the ball toward the basket. Herb Crook said, "It was dancing around up there." An eternity seemed to flash by at warp speed as the ball finally goes in, giving No. 1 UK an exhausting, but exhilarating 76-75 victory over its arch rival, who was nothing but gallant in defeat.

STATS

Kentucky

Player	Min	FG	FG A	3PT FG	3 PT FGA	FT	FT A	Reb	PF	Ast	St	BS	TO	Pts
Cedric Jenkins	32	1	4	0	0	0	0	11	0	3	0	1	0	2
Winston Bennett	24	6	11	0	0	2	4	6	5	2	0	0	2	14
Robert Lock	32	1	7	0	0	4	6	6	4	2	3	1	0	6
Rex Chapman	37	8	15	2	7	3	4	3	1	2	1	0	3	21
Ed Davender	34	7	14	2	3	4	4	2	3	3	2	0	2	20
Eric Manuel	18	2	7	0	0	4	4	5	1	2	0	0	0	8
Derrick Miller	9	1	5	0	3	0	0	1	0	0	0	0	0	2
Richard Madison	8	0	1	0	0	0	0	1	1	1	0	0	3	0
LeRon Ellis	6	1	1	0	0	1	2	1	2	0	1	0	1	3
Team								1						
Totals	**200**	**27**	**65**	**4**	**13**	**18**	**24**	**37**	**17**	**15**	**7**	**2**	**11**	**76**

GAME 20

December 31, 1988

	UofL	UK
Record	6-2	5-6
Ranking	unranked	#14
Series	5	14
Favored	LOUISVILLE BY 18.5	
Location	FREEDOM HALL	
TV	NO LIVE TV	

PRE-GAME REPORT

Sam Bowie had made the front cover of *Sports Illustrated* since the rivalry had resumed, but now, the UK program's *SI* front cover page read, "Kentucky's Shame." The Cats were banned from post-season play and live televised games for two seasons. But the rivalry would be uninterrupted and Louisville fans were clamoring for a slice of revenge. There was no memory problem from two years ago when they witnessed a Big Blue blowout, 85-51 on their home court. Everywhere Cardinal players went they heard the same thing, "A blowout victory over Kentucky!"

Not only were the fans eager to party in the New Year with a win over UK, but Pervis Ellison was 0-3 against the Cats, "Bragging rights is what it boils down to."

The longest win streak in the series' history stood at five, by UK. The Cats won the last three games the two teams played back when Wilson and Harding roamed the White House; 02/22/1916, 32-24, 01/17/1922, 38-14 and 01/21/1922, 29-22. Twenty-six years later with Harry Truman in the Oval Office, UK won 91-57 in the Olympic Trials played in New York City and 79-68 in the first round of the NCAA Tournament in Raleigh, NC. 79-68.

On paper the Cardinals were in control, starting two seniors, two juniors and a sophomore and they had a much deeper bench available. The Wildcats would start one junior, three sophomores and a one freshman. However, Coach Crum was leaving no stone unturned, closing practice for the week and putting his players off limits to the media.

QUOTES

"I'd at least like to beat them once before I leave here."
PERVIS ELLISON

"In the end many in the crowd of 19,153 were cheering for UK, and the Cards walked off the court with chants of "Go Big Blue" ringing in their ears. And that wasn't the end of the ridicule."
CJ WRITER RUSS BROWN on the UK 85-51 win two years ago.

93

"We heard a lot of stuff about it. Everywhere you went it was like, 'What happened to you guys?'"
TONY KIMBRO

"I think the time off will be good for us in the long run, but I don't know how it will affect us in this one game."
COACH DENNY CRUM (UofL hadn't played in 12 days).

"I think Louisville is kind of underestimating us as a team. Their coaching staff is probably telling them not to overlook us. But if they are thinking about overlooking us, they've got another think coming."
UK FORWARD CHRIS MILLS

"That's the only shot we have of winning at Freedom Hall. Slow it down and keep the score in the 60s."
UK GUARD SEAN SUTTON

PROBABLE STARTERS

Louisville

POS.	PLAYER	HT.	WT.	CLS.	PT/G
F	KENNY PAYNE	6-8	195	SR.	11.0
F	TONY KIMBRO	6-7	215	JR.	10.0
C	PERVIS ELLISON	6-9	205	SR.	15.9
G	KEITH WILLIAMS	6-4	185	JR.	10.0
G	LaBRADFORD SMITH	6-3	200	SO.	14.0

Kentucky

POS.	PLAYER	HT.	WT.	CLS.	PT/G
F	REGGIE HANSON	6-7	200	SO.	10.2
F	CHRIS MILLS	6-7	200	FR.	13.9
C	LeRON ELLIS	6-10	235	SO.	20.4
G	DERRICK MILLER	6-5	170	JR.	9.2
G	SEAN SUTTON	6-1	175	SO.	13.3

"UofL bash becomes 97-75 bashing of UK"
Louisville Courier-Journal

"Swarming Cards sting Cats 97-75"
Lexington Herald-Leader

UK surprisingly jumped out to a 10-3 lead with Sutton and Miller each hitting a three, while UofL was limited to taking seven of its first eight shots from three-point territory, hitting only one of those seven treys (three-point shots). But the Cards would quickly redeem themselves making three consecutive threes in 1:34. In fact, UofL made more threes than UK for the first time in the rivalry, 7-6.

There wasn't a statistically category the Cardinals didn't win, but with 6:49 to play, UofL led by 12, 75-63, not exactly the blowout proportion their fans had imagined. From here to the end, however, the Cards outscored the Cats 22-12 for a final 22-point margin of victory 97-75.

STATS

Louisville

Player	Min	FG	FG A	3PT FG	3 PT FGA	FT	FT A	Reb	PF	Ast	St	BS	TO	Pts
Kenny Payne	33	5	8	1	3	5	6	5	2	2	0	1	2	16
Tony Kimbro	27	4	7	3	4	0	0	3	0	1	2	0	0	11
Pervis Ellison	31	8	16	0	1	4	5	7	0	3	1	2	1	20
Keith Williams	28	2	7	0	3	0	0	1	2	5	1	0	2	4
LaBradford Smith	29	3	5	1	3	8	8	2	4	8	1	0	3	15
Everick Sullivan	19	5	10	2	4	3	4	6	1	4	0	0	1	15
Cornelius Holden	15	1	1	0	0	2	2	4	0	0	0	1	1	4
Felton Spencer	10	1	1	0	0	4	4	1	5	0	0	1	1	6
James Brewer	7	2	4	0	2	0	1	5	3	1	0	0	1	4
Craig Hawley	1	1	1	0	0	0	0	1	0	0	0	0	0	2
Team								0						
Totals	**200**	**32**	**60**	**7**	**20**	**26**	**30**	**35**	**17**	**24**	**5**	**5**	**12**	**97**

Kentucky

Player	Min	FG	FG A	3PT FG	3 PT FGA	FT	FT A	Reb	PF	Ast	St	BS	TO	Pts
Reggie Hanson	30	4	6	0	0	3	3	4	4	4	1	0	2	11
Chris Mills	34	4	9	0	1	5	7	10	4	4	2	0	3	13
LeRon Ellis	36	3	7	0	0	1	4	5	5	1	1	2	3	7
Derrick Miller	39	13	26	5	14	3	3	4	4	1	1	0	4	34

Player	Min	FG	FG A	3PT FG	3 PT FGA	FT	FT A	Reb	PF	Ast	St	BS	TO	Pts
Sean Sutton	38	3	6	1	2	0	0	3	3	3	0	0	4	7
Mike Scott	12	0	3	0	0	3	4	2	4	2	0	0	0	3
Deron Feldhaus	9	0	1	0	0	0	0	1	1	0	0	0	0	0
Richie Farmer	2	0	0	0	0	0	0	0	0	0	0	0	1	0
Team								2						
Totals	200	27	58	6	17	15	21	31	25	15	5	2	17	75

POINTS AFTER

"All week the seniors had been talking about how much they wanted to beat Kentucky. They said they had never beaten them (in three tries) and they were tired of losing. They wanted to win. They wanted to win big".
UofL GUARD EVERICK SULLIVAN

"Our press had been a yo-yo, Mickey Mouse jockey for position type thing. But we changed it, forced a bunch of turnovers, got the lead and pretty well maintained it."
COACH DENNY CRUM

"We started denying the ball and making them throw long, then we'd get the steal."
LaBRADFORD SMITH

"We never could really get control of the game once they got ahead. I thought our team competed very hard, but Louisville just has a fantastic team."
COACH EDDIE SUTTON

GAME 21

December 30, 1989

	UK	UofL
Record	5-4	8-1
Ranking	unranked	#8
Series	14	6
Favored	LOUISVILLE BY 10	
Location	RUPP ARENA	
TV	CLOSED CIRCUIT (LOUISVILLE)	

PRE-GAME REPORT

Coach Rick Pitino was elected to The Basketball Hall of Fame in 2013, and if his body of work had been confined only to his eight years at UK, he still deserved it. Many UofL fans (don't discount a number of UK fans too) and a fair share in the press, thought it would take Kentucky years to get back in winning form to compete for championships. A friend of mine, Butch Troutman (Now passed away), who worked the Rick Bolus basketball camps, extended a challenge, "Paul, I don't see more than four wins for UK out there, and I'll bet you a steak dinner on that!"

In fan mode, I exclaimed, "They'll win 10!"

Upon relating this story to my father he inquired, "Son, why didn't you just say five." I replied, "I've got my pride, dad."

Upon further review, I went on my Sunday Night Sports Roundtable Show and predicted that Rick Pitino would win 14 games that year, and he did, going 14-14 in his first season. There were many who thought that prediction was silly, but there was precedent for my living on the edge.

I started my show on WHAS-Radio in June of '88. Without ever speaking to him, I predicted that Howard Schnellenberger's team would finish 7-4 that season. Immediately, challengers came out of the woodwork with green stuff in their hands, eager to prove I didn't know what I was talking about. In his first three years at UofL, Howard was 8-24-1, with three wins, the most in any one season. My boss, program director Gary Bruce was leading the charge. When UofL lost its first two games, I could hear Bruce and others snickering in the halls. However, the noise soon dissipated as the football Cardinals finished strong, with an overall record of 8-3.

Many times I was criticized for being a Big Blue Fan, thinking nothing of Louisville. Sometimes that may have rung true, but overall I think I was fair and behind the scenes, was even a very strong Cardinal supporter. I predicted Schnellenberger's Cards would finish 11-1 in 1990. Well, they did only lose one game, but tied San Jose State 10-10, thanks to Ted Washington blocking a kick. The Cardinals went to the Fiesta Bowl to battle Alabama. The Tide quit rolling in Arizona as UofL crushed them 34-7.

Now, back in the studio here in Louisville, as I was witnessing on TV what the Cards were doing, nothing was planned for a post-game show. I called up the station's program director Skip

Essick and told him, "We have to do something for UofL! This is a BIG win!" He paused, and then said: "Okay, go ahead."

I came on the air after the game playing Lionel Ritchie's song, "All Night Long:"

And a good time was had by all. Oh, some tried to take the starch out of the win by complaining Alabama really didn't want to be there, and didn't take the game seriously. If that's the case, decline the invitation to play. No matter how you twist it, it was huge for UofL. I guess Florida approached the BCS Sugar Bowl game in 2013 the same way. But that's another reason the rivalry is the best, so many prefer to painstakingly agonize, wail and gnash their teeth or fly into contortions, rather than acknowledge that the opponent deserves a morsel of credit.

The Cards had never beaten the Cats in Rupp, so they had motivation, sensing this was a great opportunity to do so. Their fans and some writers were conjuring up ideas for a "dunk" competition, since UofL was averaging six a game, and were more athletic and deeper than the Wildcats.

Players like Feldhaus, Farmer and Pelphrey were complimentary players to the team that UK had, and then lost. As a result, they were in their second year of probation, which included no "live" TV.

In fact, originally, John Pelphrey was not found on the Cats' recruiting wish list. After landing Jeff Hall in 1982, UofL Assistant Coach Bobby Dotson was told that he would never get another player out of the mountains. But here was Louisville going after another by the name of John Pelphrey. It was late in the recruiting season when Pelphrey made a visit to Louisville.

Dotson received a phone call from John's father wanting to know why UofL was recruiting his son. Yes, the Cards had Pelphrey on their list from the beginning as one who could help them, but not at the top of that list. Now, Coach Dotson was having thoughts, maybe UK was trying to recruit him, so he asked Mr. Pelphrey, "What about, UK?" Mr. Pelphrey replied, "It's too late for Kentucky!" Somewhere between Louisville and Paintsville things changed and John Pelphrey became one of those branded "Unforgettable" Wildcats.

In the other locker room, Coach Pitino was taking his team to the movies. He showed them a film of his first Providence team, an energetic bunch, who gave everything they had, including various body parts in an effort to get loose balls. Coach Pitino said, "It just showed a team so phenomenal with back-tipping and diving that it showed what average players can do collectively. They can do great things." Derrick Miller responded: "It was unbelievable, showing us how they hustled…I believe that got to some of the guys. We just said, 'Hey, we've just got to go out and be like those guys."

QUOTES

"Nothing this great or with this many people involved."
UK COACH RICK PITINO responding to whether he had ever encountered a rivalry quite like this one.

"I really don't know if he (Pitino) has a feel for how big this game is to everyone or not, but I know how much it means to me and all of us."
UK GUARD RICHIE FARMER

"We just want to beat them, I don't care if it's here (Rupp), there or anywhere."
UofL GUARD KEITH WILLIAMS

"We've been pretty darn good on the defensive end. Out team isn't that easy to score on. They're going to have to hit a real good percentage of those three-pointers to score 100."
COACH DENNY CRUM

PROBABLE STARTERS

Kentucky

POS.	PLAYER	HT.	WT.	CLS.	PT/G
F	DERON FELDHAUS	6-7	199	SO.	13.2
F	JOHN PELPHREY	6-7	185	SO.	13.1
C	REGGIE HANSON	6-7	200	JR.	14.2
G	DERRICK MILLER	6-5	170	SR.	21.9
G	SEAN WOODS	6-2	175	SO.	10.7

Louisville

POS.	PLAYER	HT.	WT.	CLS.	PT/G
F	EVERICK SULLIVAN	6-5	190	SO.	16.0
F	TONY KIMBRO	6-7	215	SR.	5.2
C	FELTON SPENCER	7-0	265	SR.	14.7
G	LaBRADFORD SMITH	6-3	200	JR.	13.8
G	KEITH WILLIAMS	6-4	185	SR.	7.9

"Cat's loss seems like Cat's gain"
Louisville Courier-Journal

"Cats Lose Prettily 86-79"
Lexington Herald-Leader

Before the Wildcats bolted from the locker room to the Rupp Arena Floor, Rick Pitino reminded his smaller, slower players of one final thing, "Don't back down!" And they didn't. The Wildcats used their press to register 15 steals and forced UofL to commit 24 turnovers. Louisville had the overall rebounding edge 35-33, but on the offensive glass, the Cats dominated the Cards 20-8, led by Deron Feldhaus' dozen.

Aggressive play showed early in the game, within the first three minutes, UK's Derrick Miller and UofL's LaBradford Smith got into a shoving match near the Cardinal bench. Both benches emptied but order was soon restored. Smith for the Cards, and Sean Woods for the Cats were whistled for dead ball technical fouls. Felton Spencer picked up two personal fouls in the game's first 4:30 and his fourth with 12:30 left to play. He had only seven points, but 6-7 reserve sophomore forward Cornelius Holden filled-in the gap, playing 23 minutes while scoring eight and snagging seven rebounds.

UofL led throughout the first half, twice, by as many as 11 and had a seven-point margin at the half, 42-35. But Kentucky opened strong to start the second half, outscoring the Cards 11-4 in the first 2 ½ minutes of play to tie the score at 46-46. After that, the lead changed seven times before Keith Williams broke through UK's pressure defense, scoring on a lay-up that gave UofL the lead for good, 61-60 with 10:43 to play.

Ultimately, Louisville survived the Kentucky pressure by shooting the ball well, 59.6 percent to 38.5 percent. UK hit nine of 29 three-point shots for the game, but were just three of 16 in the second half. Without much of an inside game, most of UofL's offense came from LaBradford Smith,

Everick Sullivan, Keith Williams and Jerome Harmon. They accounted for 24 of the Cardinals 31 field goals and 69 of their 88 points.

UofL scored two firsts in the rivalry with this victory. Its first win in Rupp and the first time it had won back-to-back games since the series was renewed.

For the Cats, they would have to settle for "shapes of things to come," translated six wins in their next seven games.

STATS

Kentucky

Player	Min	FG	FG A	3PT FG	3 PT FGA	FT	FT A	Reb	PF	Ast	St	BS	TO	Pts
John Pelphrey	22	4	8	0	2	3	4	4	4	0	1	0	1	11
Deron Feldhaus	37	3	13	1	3	2	2	16	5	2	3	0	4	9
Reggie Hanson	39	8	21	4	11	4	6	6	3	2	3	1	5	24
Derrick Miller	36	5	14	2	8	1	2	2	2	0	0	0	0	13
Sean Woods	25	3	7	0	0	0	1	1	1	7	4	0	3	6
Richie Farmer	20	4	7	2	4	0	0	1	2	9	3	0	2	10
Jeff Brassow	19	3	7	0	1	0	0	2	4	1	1	0	1	6
Johnathon Davis	1	0	1	0	0	0	0	0	0	0	0	0	0	0
Skip McGaw	1	0	0	0	0	0	0	0	0	0	0	0	0	0
Team								1						
Totals	**200**	**30**	**78**	**9**	**29**	**10**	**15**	**33**	**21**	**21**	**15**	**1**	**16**	**79**

Louisville

Player	Min	FG	FG A	3PT FG	3 PT FGA	FT	FT A	Reb	PF	Ast	St	BS	TO	Pts
Tony Kimbro	13	1	2	0	0	0	0	2	1	0	0	0	5	2
Everick Sullivan	37	4	11	2	5	6	8	6	2	2	0	0	2	16
Felton Spencer	26	3	4	0	0	1	2	6	4	3	0	4	3	7
LaBradford Smith	38	6	9	0	1	10	11	0	3	4	2	0	4	22

Player	Min	FG	FG A	3PT FG	3 PT FGA	FT	FT A	Reb	PF	Ast	St	BS	TO	Pts
Keith Williams	33	7	8	1	2	0	0	5	4	2	3	0	4	15
Jerome Harmon	29	7	14	0	1	2	2	6	0	3	3	0	3	16
Cornelius Holden	23	3	4	0	0	2	4	7	1	0	0	1	3	8
Troy Smith	3	0	0	0	0	0	0	1	0	0	0	0	0	0
Team								2						
Totals	**200**	**31**	**52**	**3**	**9**	**21**	**27**	**35**	**15**	**14**	**8**	**5**	**24**	**86**

POINTS AFTER

"Every coach hates to lose, but I can't tell you how proud I am."
UK COACH RICK PITINO

"Right now, we're shocking people. People expect us to get blown out, to see a dunk festival, and I think coach's attitude is carrying over to the players."
UK GUARD DERRICK MILLER

"I was never expecting a blowout. This isn't an easy place to play in, and I knew Kentucky would come out and make it rough on us as possible. And that's what they did."
UofL GUARD KEITH WILLIAMS

"It kind of took our mind out of the game. But after a while you have to forget about things like that and just play."
FELTON SPENCER referring to the shoving match that started with LaBradford Smith, Derrick Miller and Sean Woods, followed by both benches emptying on to the court.

GAME 22

December 29, 1990

	UofL	UK
Record	5-1	7-2
Ranking	unranked	#18
Favored	LOUISVILLE BY 1.5	
Series	7	14
Location	FREEDOM HALL	
TV	NO LIVE BROADCAST	

PRE-GAME

It would have been fitting to have found Charles Dickens (still hanging around, he visited Louisville in 1842) along press row in Freedom Hall for this game giving his famous line from his *Tale of Two Cities,* "It was the best of times, it was the worst of times." Well, maybe not the worst or the best, but at this moment in time these two teams were headed in perceivably different directions.

UK was in its second year of NCAA probation, and not eligible either for a conference championship or post-season tournament and again, no "live" TV. But the sanctioned "Doomsday Effect" that many predicted would keep the Cats out of the college basketball limelight for years was turning furiously in a 180 degree direction.

The Cats were back in Freedom Hall for the second time in eight days after being the home team on the 21st, beating Western Kentucky 84-70. That game marked the first time the Cats had played the Hilltoppers in a regular season game. Coach Pitino, also added the Colonels to the schedule beating them in Rupp 74-60, making the rivalry game even more of a "state championship" in 1990, since the Cards had beaten Western on the road 76-69.

The sun was now shinning with a brighter hue on "My Old Kentucky Home" since Coach Pitino had expanded UK's schedule to include other teams from the Bluegrass. Former UK athletics director C.M. Newton told me in a recent interview, "He thought the money that was going to teams like East Tennessee State to come and play at Rupp, should go to other in-state teams."

In this day and age of such phenomenal technological advances in personal, business and entertainment communications, making information available on an almost instant basis and providing fans, coaches and players alike with the opportunity to make their feelings known, it makes no sense to cling to the "old line" of not playing other state schools because it will hurt your fan support and/or recruiting. You may lose or gain a few fans here and there and possibly a recruit in a generation, allowing for a plus or minus margin of error from one to 100 percent. And Coach Pitino's system of using the three to score and disrupt the opponent, made this team a "Cinderella" type fit for the "oh so soft" rims of Freedom Hall.

UK vs. UofL College Basketball's No. 1 Rivalry - Enough Said!

Richie Farmer had scored fifty-one points here for Clay County in the 1988 State Championship Game won by Ballard and their superstar Allan Houston. The Cards would be much stronger now and in love with the "three" if Houston had remained with Louisville after signing, but the NCAA released him to play for his father Wade, a UofL assistant coach who had moved back to his home state of Tennessee after being named the head coach of the Volunteers.

Farmer had his UK career high of 21 points here last season against North Carolina and beat that mark last week in the "Hall" with 22 against Western Kentucky.

As happens so often in this rivalry, activities off the court may have a profound affect on how the players and coaches handle the atmosphere that hovers over the arena come game time. Morley Saffer of CBS' 60 Minutes had signaled UofL out on a story they aired about academic problems in the world of college sports that necessitated a response from Coach Crum. He believed the Cardinals were better than the report portrayed, others did not, but again here was another distraction to deal with. Away from the television set UofL had lost four of six promising recruits to academic eligibility issues, and Jerome Harmon, an outstanding talent who was the second leading scorer on the '89-'90 team at (14.7) was dismissed from school because of grades.

The previous year in Lexington, UofL was ranked No. 8, but had lost in an upset to Ball State 62-60 in the second game of the NCAA West Regional. And with the departure of senior seven-foot center Felton Spencer, the leading scorer (14.9) and rebounder (8.5) plus Harmon, the Cards would land at the 25th position in the '90-'91 pre-season poll. Then, they promptly dropped out of the poll with a 21-point opening season loss to Indiana in the Big Four Classic in Indianapolis. But now they were on a roll, winning their last five games. Yet these wins were not against top teams and Coach Crum said that UK had played a tougher schedule, making this an important game not only from the rivalry standpoint, but for the rest of the season as well.

Herald-Leader sports columnist Billy Reed made some comparisons between this UofL team and the '79-'80 squad that Darrell Griffith led to Louisville's first NCAA National Championship. He did not say this team was title bound but used a writer's exercise in responding to inquiries, "Fans were wanting to know if this current squad was too small, too young and too laid-back to handle Coach Rick Pitino's Wildcats. At the beginning of that season, UofL Coach Denny Crum was under fire, just as he has been recently because of his program's academic troubles. Back then, Crum was accused of being too lax, too uninvolved and too undemanding to win an NCAA title. This unrest stemmed from the fact that UofL was 0-2 in the Final Four of late. In addition, the previous season's team had been embarrassed by Arkansas in the NCAA Midwest Regional."

Turnovers are not limited to players, but can plague fans and coaches as equal opportunists. The problem in Denny's first two Final Fours was not his laid-back style, but his old mentor, Coach John Wooden of UCLA who from '64-'75 won 10 of 12 NCAA titles including seven straight, and was 44-1 in tournament games. I would add three other records to Wooden's list that will never be broken—and I mean never: (1) Cy Young's career 530 wins, (2) The Reds' Johnny Vander Meer's back-to-back no hitters and (3) UK's record 108 rebounds in a single game against Mississippi in 1961.

The loss to Arkansas helped inspire Griffith's summer preparation that enhanced his all-around play and provided the catalyst for that championship season.

Reed went on to say: "The Griffith role on the current team belongs to LaBradford Smith, the marvelously athletic senior guard who needs to take his game to a higher level if this Cardinal team is to have even a remote chance of making an impact in post-season play."

Comparing different teams and player's roles can be fun and is understandably not a sin, nor in this case a virtue, for even though Smith is UofL's all-time assist leader with 713, it strains the ink to compare him with Darrell Griffith and others from this 90-91 squad, with Griffith's teammates Rodney McCray, and Derek Smith.

Something else that was up in the air before tip-off was who would be favored? John Pelphrey thought it funny that the Cats could be favored in Freedom Hall. But that was viewed differently by Coach Pitino, "It's terrific for the program after one year. We're very happy to be in that role at this point because it can only help us next season."

In actuality there was one service that did favor the Cards by a point-and-a-half.

QUOTES

"Our biggest question is that when we substitute we don't know what to expect."
COACH DENNY CRUM

"I'm not going to say that we are better than UK. From a player's point of view, you're supposed to say your better than the next team. You're confidence is supposed to be there. Our team has that confidence. But they're thinking the same thing at UK."
LaBRADFORD SMITH

"The Cats are taking good shots"
COACH RICK PITINO, responding to the fact that UK was 14 of 66 (21.2 percent) from three-point range in their last two games

"It was time to shut down the old answering machine and go on to the next game."
JOHN PELPHREY, comments regarding his one for 11 three-point shooting performance against Eastern Kentucky.

PROBABLE STARTERS

Louisville

POS.	PLAYER	HT.	WT.	CLS.	PT/G
F	CORNELIUS HOLDEN	6-7	210	JR.	11.7
F	EVERICK SULLIVAN	6-5	190	JR.	15.3
C	TROY SMITH	6-8	205	SO.	10.5
G	LaBRADFORD SMITH	6-3	200	SR.	17.8
G	JAMES BREWER	6-2	190	S0.	14.2

Kentucky

POS.	PLAYER	HT.	WT.	CLS.	PT/G
F	JOHN PELPHREY	6-7	195	JR.	15.1
F	JAMAL MASHBURN	6-9	240	FR.	12.9
C	REGGIE HANSON	6-8	200	SR.	15.2
G	JEFF BRASSOW	6-5	195	SO.	8.9
G	SEAN WOODS	6-3	180	JR.	9.9

"Cats cruise to 93-85 win"
Lexington Herald-Leader

"Cats settle this argument outside, 93-85"
Louisville Courier-Journal

LaBradford Smith would give UofL its first lead 2-0 on a fourteen-foot jumper with 18:10 to go in the first half, and Cornelius Holden their last at 15-13 with 11:49 remaining in the half from eleven-feet. UK's Reggie Hanson tied it at 15, then Deron Feldhaus hit a three-pointer and Kentucky would never trail again going on to beat the Cards 93-85.

In their three previous games UK hit only 29 of their 92 three-point shots, but after missing 11 of their first 13 shots including three threes, the Cats straightened things out and finished shooting 50 percent on 13 of 26 from three-point range. Farmer, who came off the bench and scored all of his points in the first half, had the best percentage hitting four of five, but Jeff Brassow scored the most threes connecting on six of 11.

When Louisville played good defense against UK's perimeter game, the Cats took the show inside. Sean Woods lead the attack in the second half, scoring all of his UK high, 20 points.

UofL's point guard James Brewer said, "When they're doing that, you can't beat them. They're unstoppable." The Wildcat harassing press and switches from a man to zone and back to man defense kept the Cards off balance. Coach Crum responded: "Kentucky did a good job taking away the initial part of our offense. We didn't have the confidence or whatever it is to go to the second and third options, which is what you have to do versus good teams. A good team takes certain things away. We didn't adjust to that well."

Louisville, which had been averaging 53 percent from the field entering this rivalry game, was held to its lowest shooting percentage of the season, 44.6 percent and connected only on three of 15 from beyond the arc.

LaBradford Smith led the way for the Cards with 26 points and 11 rebounds. Bench play, Coach Crum's biggest uncertain pre-game expectation turned out not so bad, with three of the four players scoring, led by Kip Stone who pitched in 11 points, pulled down five rebounds and handed out four assists.

The final score of 93-85 was somewhat deceiving when considering UK's control of the game. The Cats led 39-28 at the half and held their biggest margin of 22 points with 6:42 to play, and were still up 17 with 2:03 remaining. The Cards hit two of their three pointers in the final 17 seconds, and UK's Junior Braddy added a last second free throw to determine the final margin.

STATS

Louisville

Player	Min	FG	FG A	3PT FG	3 PT FGA	FT	FT A	Reb	PF	Ast	St	BS	TO	Pts
Cornelius Holden	26	9	12	0	0	4	5	8	4	0	0	1	1	22
Everick Sullivan	30	2	13	1	6	2	2	5	3	3	0	1	4	7
Troy Smith	28	2	3	0	0	0	0	3	2	0	1	1	3	4
James Brewer	19	2	7	1	3	1	2	2	1	2	0	1	2	6
LaBradford Smith	38	9	19	1	4	7	9	11	2	3	4	0	2	26

Paul Willman

Player	Min	FG	FG A	3PT FG	3 PT FGA	FT	FT A	Reb	PF	Ast	St	BS	TO	Pts
Kip Stone	21	1	4	0	0	9	10	5	2	4	0	0	1	11
Tremaine Wingfield	15	1	2	0	0	1	2	3	0	1	0	1	1	3
Derwin Webb	13	3	3	0	0	0	1	2	2	0	1	0	1	6
Mike Case	10	0	2	0	2	0	0	1	1	0	1	1	1	0
Team								2						
Totals	**200**	**29**	**65**	**3**	**15**	**24**	**31**	**42**	**17**	**13**	**7**	**6**	**16**	**85**

Kentucky

Player	Min	FG	FG A	3PT FG	3 PT FGA	FT	FT A	Reb	PF	Ast	St	BS	TO	Pts
Jamal Mashburn	21	1	5	0	0	4	4	10	4	1	0	0	2	6
John Pelphrey	32	3	10	1	5	0	0	7	3	5	1	0	3	7
Reggie Hanson	29	7	13	1	2	2	4	8	4	2	0	2	3	17
Sean Woods	32	7	13	0	0	6	6	2	3	4	1	0	4	20
Jeff Brassow	24	6	12	6	11	0	0	2	3	0	4	0	1	18
Richie Farmer	20	5	8	4	5	0	0	3	3	3	0	0	0	14
Deron Feldhaus	24	2	5	1	2	1	1	2	3	1	0	0	0	6
Gimel Martinez	6	0	0	0	0	0	0	0	0	0	0	0	0	0
Nehemiah Braddy	11	2	4	0	1	1	2	0	1	2	1	0	0	5
Todd Bearup	1	0	0	0	0	0	0	0	0	0	0	0	0	0
Carlos Toomer	1	0	0	0	0	0	0	0	0	0	0	0	0	0
Team								1						
Totals	**200**	**33**	**70**	**13**	**26**	**14**	**17**	**35**	**24**	**18**	**7**	**2**	**13**	**93**

POINTS AFTER

"I am more excited about the way we played. We were fundamentally sound in all phases."
UK COACH RICK PITINO

"I let the game come to me. My job is to penetrate, draw the defense and kick it out. They stayed with their men, so I was able to go to the basket."
UK Guard Sean Woods

"The biggest problem we had, was our inability to go to our options."
UofL Coach Denny Crum

"Give them credit. They did an excellent job of what they wanted to do."
UofL Coach Denny Crum

In speaking of two teams going in different directions, all top coaches have a period of time we can highlight as their "run." In that context, Coach Crum is really no different than all the coaches who have won two or more NCAA Men's Basketball Championships. Only five have won more than Denny, John Wooden (10), Adolph Rupp (4), Mike Kryszewski (4), Bobby Knight (3) and Jim Calhoun (3).

When you're winning, fans make an amazing transformation, the laid-back style of coaching takes on the "Cool Hand Luke" monogram, flying chairs are tolerated and so are other quirks in the course of daily life. But no Final Fours and no national championships—and you'll soon find yourself dressing at the Big K Store. No one is immune from this malady. After winning seven consecutive national championships, Wooden's '74 UCLA team lost in overtime to North Carolina State in the semifinals. He confirmed to me the story about the fan who came up to him after beating Kentucky in the '75 title game and said, "Well, that makes up for the one you blew last year!"

Even the legendary sports broadcaster Curt Gowdy chimed in on my Sunday Night Sports Roundtable Show which aired on 84 WHAS Radio from 1988-1995, "Wooden blew that game in regulation by not slowing down the pace of the game."

After spending forty-two years on what he called the "Glory Road," Coach Rupp exclaimed, "It wasn't age that caused the University of Kentucky to retire him—it was illness, the Board of Trustees just got sick and tired of me." That's the kind of stuff that makes great rivalries. This one has been blessed with so many outstanding coaches: Adolph Rupp, "Peck" Hickman, Denny Crum, Joe Hall, Rick Pitino (UK), Tubby Smith, Rick Pitino (UofL) and John Calipari.

GAME 23

December 28, 1991

	UK	UofL
Record	7-2	6-0
Ranking	#17	#21
Series	15	7
Favored	KENTUCKY BY 9.5	
Location	RUPP ARENA	
TV	ESPN	

PREGAME REPORT

UofL was coming to Rupp with three first year players, sophomores Dwayne Morton and Greg Minor plus freshman guard Keith LeGree.

UK was playing a 4+1 game with Richie Farmer, Deron Feldhaus, John Pelphrey and Sean Woods all seniors, and oh; the one super sophomore, Jamal Mashburn.

Louisville again, was noted as the quicker team with a different twist this year—improved three-point shooting. In fact, they were coming off a sensational road victory against LSU, who still had "Shaq" engulfing the lane, when Keith LeGree hit a last second three-pointer to give the Cards a 93-92 reason to come to Rupp with increased confidence.

Naturally, there were quotes about how important winning this game is, like Cornelius Holden: "It seems like you see at least a little change in Coach Crum. He's more serious, and he tries to explain stuff and direct us a lot more. I think the Kentucky game is on Coach Crum's mind the whole year. It's the biggest game of the year for him and the fans."

Jamal Mashburn: "In New York you have a lot of schools you want to beat, but nothing of this caliber. I think nothing in America's as big as the Kentucky-Louisville game."

Players don't need heightened incentives to get ready for this game, Richie Farmer said, "You have to almost be a dead man not to be ready to play."

However, motivational tidbits were available. Some of the players were tired of hearing that the Cards were better athletes, but the real pre-game boost came from a UofL student newspaper writer who said, "UK was the lowest form of life."

QUOTES

"When you look at the game and break it down, that's the one obvious (advantage) you want to take away."

UK COACH RICK PITINO referring to rebounding. (UofL had a 9.5 rebound advantage over its opponents).

"A lot came in transition. Our press was a factor. We were making steals and getting open."
UK FORWARD JOHN PELPHREY on last year's game when UK got so many open three-pointers.

"We've got guys who can make it, (Three-pointer) so we'll shoot it a lot more."
 UofL COACH DENNY CRUM

"Everyone was like, if you win any game, please let it be this one; don't lose this."
 UofL FORWARD DWAYNE MORTON

PROBABLE STARTERS

Kentucky

POS.	PLAYER	HT.	WT.	CLS.	PT/G
F	JOHN PELPHREY	6-7	200	SR.	13.2
F	JAMAL MASHBURN	6-8	240	SO.	20.8
C	GIMEL MARTINEZ	6-9	220	SO.	8.4
G	DALE BROWN	6-3	200	JR.	7.9
G	SEAN WOODS	6-2	180	SR.	7.2

Louisville

POS.	PLAYER	HT.	WT.	CLS.	PT/G
F	CORNELIUS HOLDEN	6-7	205	SR.	10.8
F	GREG MINOR	6-6	200	SO.	10.0
C	DWAYNE MORTON	6-6	195	SO.	18.3
G	KEITH LeGREE	6-1	180	FR.	9.5
G	EVERICK SULLIVAN	6-5	190	SR.	15.7

"Three-point shooting keeps Kentucky out of danger"
Lexington Herald-Leader

"Blue skies open up on Cards yet again"
Louisville Courier-Journal

UK came out hitting six of its first seven three-pointers, then clanked five of its next six, but finished the half seven for 13 to take a 54-45 intermission lead.

"The big key was getting behind early," Everick Sullivan said. Keith LeGree concurred, "We were playing catch-up and fighting the crowd and them." Cornelius Holden echoed, "Every time we got close, it seemed like they'd hit a three." As many of these rivalry games reveal, there was a greater struggle than the final scores sometime indicate.

UK led 9-4, and then it was tied, 11-11, 13-13 and for the last time at 15-15 before Kentucky reeled-off four threes in the next 2:26, led by John Pelphrey with three.

At the 6:19 mark, the Cats led 47-33 when the Cards went on a 10-0 run of their own, narrowing the lead to just four points. Richie Farmer's ensuing three ended a 4:26 span in which UK had failed to score.

Coming into the second half trailing 54-45, UofL continued for the most part to trade baskets with the Cats, but a Dale Brown lay up pushed UK ahead 77-63, with 11:23 left to play. About two-minutes later Greg Minor scored inside, bringing UofL within seven at 78-71. Cats' point-guard, Sean Woods, who missed most of the first half due to early foul trouble, drove around Kip Stone on the right side of the lane, then into Cards' guard James Brewer underneath the basket. Brewer, known as "Boo" caught Woods in the air, threw him over his right shoulder, and was called for both a personal and technical foul.

Woods, earlier in the game had exchanged some "trash talk" with UofL's Dwayne Morton and now said about the Brewer incident, "I thought he was just holding me up, then he dropped me. I didn't think, I just reacted. Luckily, Rock Oliver, (UK's strength coach) grabbed me and kept me from getting kicked out." Woods hit one of two free throws. Travis Ford again came off the bench to make the two technical shots, followed by a Mashburn baseline jumper, and just like that Kentucky led by a dozen 83-71.

Cardinal Coach Denny Crum thought this was really a key play: "We never seemed to recover from that point. If something good had happened to us instead of something bad, it could have turned the game around." Louisville did trim the lead to six at 84-78 with 6:40 remaining, but turnovers and missed shots allowed UK to take control on its way to a 103-89 victory.

UK's biggest advantage was from the three-point line once again, outscoring UofL by 24, hitting on 11 of 21 while the Cards were anemic from beyond the arc, managing only three of 17 treys.

Jamal Mashburn's stat line was impressive here in Lexington, his hometown of New York City, or anywhere else the game is played. He was on the floor for almost the entire game, 39 minutes and 10 seconds, scoring 25 points, grabbing seven rebounds, recording a block and a steal, and dishing out three assists. His three in the first half made him the only UK player to make a three in all ten games played this season.

Oh, and Pelphrey got the final word in on the quality of "life" at Kentucky. The UofL student newspaper article that called Kentucky "low life," had been locker room fodder for four or five days previous to the game. Pelphrey, who was one of 10 from three-point range in his previous two games, was four of five in this game, seven of 11 overall, eight of 10 from the foul line, with five rebounds, two blocks, two steals and three assists and a game-high 26 points.

STATS

Kentucky

Player	Min	FG	FG A	3PT FG	3 PT FGA	FT	FTA	Reb	PF	Ast	St	BS	TO	Pts
Jamal Mashburn	39	9	17	1	4	6	7	7	4	3	1	1	6	25
John Pelphrey	26	7	11	4	5	8	10	5	3	3	2	2	1	26
Gimel Martinez	12	1	3	1	1	2	2	1	5	0	0	3	1	5
Dale Brown	30	5	10	3	7	3	6	9	4	2	2	0	4	16
Sean Woods	20	2	3	0	0	5	8	0	3	5	2	0	3	9

Player	Min	FG	FG A	3PT FG	3 PT FGA	FT	FTA	Reb	PF	Ast	St	BS	TO	Pts
Deron Feldhaus	31	1	4	0	2	0	0	3	2	5	0	0	2	2
Richie Farmer	17	4	6	2	2	0	1	1	4	1	3	0	0	10
Carlos Toomer	4	0	0	0	0	0	0	2	0	0	0	0	1	0
Aminu Timberlake	11	2	3	0	0	0	0	3	1	0	0	0	0	4
Chris Hanson	3	0	0	0	0	0	0	0	0	0	0	0	0	0
Nehemiah Braddy	4	1	2	0	0	0	0	0	0	0	1	0	0	2
Travis Ford	1	0	0	0	0	4	4	0	0	0	1	0	0	4
Andre Riddick	1	0	0	0	0	0	0	0	0	0	0	0	0	0
Team								3						
Totals	**200**	**32**	**59**	**11**	**21**	**28**	**38**	**34**	**26**	**19**	**12**	**6**	**18**	**103**

Louisville

Player	Min	FG	FG A	3PT FG	3 PT FGA	FT	FTA	Reb	PF	Ast	St	BS	TO	Pts
Greg Minor	34	6	17	0	3	6	6	6	2	2	2	2	3	18
Dwayne Morton	23	4	6	0	0	5	6	4	3	0	1	0	0	13
Cornelius Holden	25	2	8	0	0	3	6	8	4	0	0	1	1	7
Keith LeGree	27	3	7	0	1	2	4	3	3	0	2	0	4	8
Everick Sullivan	30	5	13	2	8	2	3	5	4	0	0	0	5	14
Troy Smith	18	4	12	0	0	3	4	8	1	2	0	1	1	11
James Brewer	10	1	3	1	3	2	2	1	5	3	0	1	0	5
Derwin Webb	14	3	3	0	0	1	2	3	2	0	1	0	1	7
Brian Hopgood	8	0	1	0	0	0	0	1	2	0	0	0	0	0
Kip Stone	11	3	7	0	2	0	0	2	1	1	3	1	3	6
Team								7						
Totals	**200**	**31**	**77**	**3**	**17**	**24**	**33**	**48**	**27**	**8**	**9**	**6**	**18**	**89**

UK #11 Seans Woods and UofL #21 Greg Minor

POINTS AFTER

"We wanted to see if they could keep up with us. They want to be a running team and shoot a lot of threes nowadays, so we wanted to see if they could keep up with us stamina-wise."
UK GUARD SEAN WOODS

"I really didn't get tired while the game was going on. We meant business tonight. This game means so much to everybody in this room that I would have played every second if that's what Coach Pitino wanted me to do."
UK FORWARD JAMAL MASHBURN

"It was either (equipment manager) Bill Keightley or Travis Ford"
COACH RICK PITINO responding to a question about Travis Ford coming off the bench only to shoot four free throws.

"I think "Boo" made a mistake. Sometimes you get caught in the emotion of the game. It wasn't intentional or premeditated; it just happened in the heat of the battle."
UofL COACH DENNY CRUM

"We didn't want to give them open three-pointers, and that's what they got. All we had to do was switch out and pick somebody up and it would have been a different story."
UofL GUARD EVERICK SULLIVAN

Today, Sean Woods says, "James and I laugh about that incident now, but when playing, the rivalry makes things like that happen because you want to win so bad."

GAME 24

December 12, 1992

	UofL	UK
Record	1-1	3-0
Ranking	#9	#3
Series	7	16
Favored	KENTUCKY BY 3	
Location	FREEDOM HALL	
TV	ESPN	

PRE-GAME REPORT

Kentucky was coming to Freedom Hall to claim a "three-peat," that phrase coined and registered by former Wildcat great, Pat Riley.

The Cats won two years ago 93-85, and last year in Rupp, 103-89. The M. O. for these victories is becoming readily more familiar in all circles. UK struggles shooting the three-pointer before the UofL game, then slams the shot in reverse and scorches the nets against the Cards. Louisville, if they shoot the three before the Kentucky game, make some improvement, but against the Cats, they can't spell the word three.

Somewhere during the forty minutes, UofL will have a lead, but can't maintain their advantage due to poor shooting from the field or free throw line or both. Turnovers increase, the opponent's trapping defense and full-court press induces fatigue, rebounding suffers at times especially on the offensive end, and one team plays loose, while the other plays the antonym.

QUOTES

"I think I can take him. (Travis Ford) I think I'm quicker and stronger than he is. I think I can handle him because he's slow and my defense is good. I'm ready for that matchup, myself. If Coach (Denny) Crum lets me, I can take him inside and post him up."
UofL GUARD KEITH LeGREE (Lexington Herald-Leader writer Jerry Tipton noted LeGree was grinning when he began this quote.)

"You can't do anything tricky with Mashburn because he's never in the same place. He's everywhere. He can go inside or outside."
UofL COACH DENNY CRUM

"I love (playing) on the road. Fans who boo make you come together as a team. That shows who has heart and who doesn't."
UK FORWARD RODRICK RHODES

"The young man who gives them an added dimension is Clifford Rozier. He's active and can handle the ball."
UK COACH RICK PITINO

"Because they try to pound it inside, if we get the rebound we can get open shots in transition. If we get the defensive rebounds, we'll have another good shooting night."
UK GUARD JEFF BRASSOW

PROBABLE STARTERS

Louisville

POS.	PLAYER	HT.	WT.	CLS.	PT/G
F	DWAYNE MORTON	6-6	190	JR.	13.0
F	TROY SMITH	6-8	240	SR.	3.5
C	CLIFFORD ROZIER	6-9	235	SO.	15.5
G	KEITH LeGREE	6-0	200	SO.	9.0
G	GREG MINOR	6-6	210	JR.	16.0

Kentucky

POS.	PLAYER	HT.	WT.	CLS.	PT/G
F	JAMAL MASHBURN	6-8	231	JR.	25.0
F	RODRICK RHODES	6-8	200	FR.	16.7
C	RODNEY DENT	6-10	240	JR.	9.7
G	TRAVIS FORD	5-9	160	JR.	10.0
G	DALE BROWN	6-2	200	SR.	8.3

"CATS: Wildcats' bombs throttle Louisville 88-68"
Lexington Herald-Leader

"No sweet dream for Cards: UK 88-68"
Louisville Courier-Journal

The Lexington Herald-Leader's John Clay wrote this headline: "Loserville faces reality of Wildcats:Threes hurt." Chuck Culpepper, same paper; headline was of a kinder, gentler persuasion, but the meaning was the same: "Cats remove all doubt with this one."

Louisville's transition game was working well early, four fast-break baskets helping the Cards take a 30-20 lead with ten minutes left in the first half, and with a record Freedom Hall crowd of 19,663 cheering them on. Then, it happened: "We played well the first ten minutes, and then we started making mistakes and they took advantage of them. They played good defense, and it seemed they hit everything they threw up," said forward Troy Smith.

UK, led by Jamal Mashburn's 11 points, nine by way of the three, ignited a 22-5 run, and by time the half ended, the Cats had outscored the Cards 28-10 and led 48-40.

free throw shooting woes added to Louisville's trouble. They managed just nine of 20 in the first half, and were 16 of 36 for the game, just 44.4 percent. Kentucky wasn't much better from the charity, or in this case; uncharitable stripe, shooting just 50 percent (11 for 22). It was the three-pointer that fueled the Cats' takeover. They attempted just four in the first 11 minutes of play, then made five during that 22-5 run.

Mashburn, who was only three of 15 before the rivalry matchup, managed five of seven against the Cards. The real surprise was Gimel Martinez, who wasn't expected to play much, since he was still trying to get in game shape from a hairline fracture of the foot he suffered in the pre-season. Martinez came off the bench to score 14 points, on six of eight shooting from the field, and made both of his three-pointers with a little help from his friends; Rick Pitino: "He passed up a wide-open three-pointer and traveled. I told him if he didn't want to shoot, then transfer, because at Kentucky we take that shot."

In the second half, it was another five-minute UK run that put the game out of reach. At the 15:21 mark, the Cats lead had been trimmed to 53-46, after Greg Minor made back-to-back baskets. Rhodes started the 18-4 run with an old fashion three. He was fouled on a layup attempt, but the Cards' Cliff Rozier was called for goaltending, and Rhodes made the free throw. Rodrick added a three-pointer, a slam dunk and layup to account for 10 of the 18 points UK scored.

Rozier had met Rhodes earlier in the first half at a block party. After Rozier had rejected an awkward, leaning shot by Rhodes, that sailed some twenty-five feet out of bounds, he stood over him like a boxer, throwing out his right arm several times over the prone Rhodes. A technical foul was called and Travis Ford made one of two free throws.

Shooting only 32 percent from three-point range coming into the game, UK improved to 52.3 percent by hitting 11 of 21 against Louisville. Coach Crum said: "That's the way it goes some nights."

Louisville only shot 33 percent in the second half. UK guard Dale Brown commented, "We got up in their faces and they got fatigued. When we're pressing and executing in the half-court, I'm never surprised by how well we play."

How about 88-68! Fourth worst defeat for the Cards in Freedom Hall history.

STATS

Louisville

Player	Min	FG	FG A	3PT FG	3 PT FGA	FT	FT A	Reb	PF	Ast	ST	BS	TO	Pts
Troy Smith	25	6	9	0	0	3	8	7	4	2	0	0	1	15
Dwayne Morton	17	1	5	1	1	1	5	6	4	1	0	1	5	4
Clifford Rozier	30	3	8	0	0	2	6	14	0	3	1	4	0	8
Keith LeGree	35	2	5	0	0	2	5	2	4	4	0	0	5	6
James Brewer	20	3	9	0	2	2	2	2	3	0	1	0	4	8
Derwin Webb	9	1	1	0	0	0	0	0	3	1	0	0	1	2
Brian Hopgood	10	3	5	0	0	3	4	4	1	0	0	2	2	9
Brian Kiser	10	1	3	0	2	0	0	2	0	1	1	0	0	2

Player	Min	FG	FG A	3PT FG	3 PT FGA	FT	FT A	Reb	PF	Ast	ST	BS	TO	Pts
Tick Rogers	4	0	1	0	0	0	2	1	0	1	1	0	0	0
Mike Case	2	0	1	0	1	0	0	0	0	0	0	0	0	0
Greg Minor	38	5	11	1	4	3	4	4	2	2	0	0	1	14
Team								1						
Totals	200	25	58	2	10	16	36	43	21	15	4	7	19	68

Kentucky

Player	Min	FG	FG A	3PT FG	3 PT FGA	FT	FT A	Reb	PF	Ast	ST	BS	TO	Pts
Rodrick Rhodes	34	8	16	2	5	2	4	7	2	3	2	0	2	20
Jamal Mashburn	31	10	15	5	7	2	4	7	5	4	1	1	1	27
Rodney Dent	14	2	4	0	0	0	1	3	4	0	0	0	1	4
Travis Ford	25	1	4	1	3	3	4	2	4	7	4	0	2	6
Dale Brown	29	2	5	1	2	3	6	3	2	3	2	0	2	8
Andre Riddick	3	0	0	0	0	0	0	0	0	0	1	0	0	0
Tony Delk	8	1	2	0	1	0	0	0	1	0	0	0	3	2
Gimel Martinez	20	6	8	2	2	0	1	1	3	0	0	1	1	14
Jeff Brassow	17	0	1	0	1	0	0	3	1	1	0	0	0	0
Jared Prickett	13	2	4	0	0	1	2	5	4	1	1	1	2	5
Aminu Timberlake	2	1	1	0	0	0	0	0	0	0	0	0	0	2
Nehemiah Braddy	1	0	0	0	0	0	0	0	0	0	0	0	0	0
Chris Harrison	3	0	0	0	0	0	0	0	0	1	0	0	0	0
Team								4						
Totals	200	33	60	11	21	11	22	35	26	20	11	3	14	88

POINTS AFTER

"We were very fortunate to come here and play great basketball. That's as good as we've zoned in on a game since Duke (in last year's East Regional final)."
UK COACH RICK PITINO

"Go-Big-Blue!"
UK fans in Freedom Hall with 8:42 left in the game.

"Right now it's very frustrating. This is my senior year and I wanted to go and play hard and get a win against Kentucky."
UofL GUARD JAMES "BOO" BREWER

"I don't feel like talking. I don't mean to be rude. But I don't want to talk."
UofL FORWARD DWAYNE MORTON

Clifford Rozier - #44 - UofL

GAME 25

December 27, 1993

	UK	UofL
Record	0-0	0-0
Ranking	#2	#7
Series	17	7
Favored	KENTUCKY BY 8.5	
Location	RUPP ARENA	
TV	CBS	

PRE-GAME REPORT

This rivalry game could be considered a skewed, variation of a "Final Four." UK had three consecutive wins, looking for four, and Cardinal fans wanted to know if finally; they could win, just one. The Cardinals had three returning starters in Dwayne Morton, Greg Minor and the big man in the middle, Clifford Rozier. Two local products, both freshmen, DeJuan Wheat from Louisville Ballard and Jason Osborne from Louisville Male High, rounded out the starting line-up.

Kentucky had lost Jamal Mashburn to the pros and steady two-guard Dale Brown had moved on, but the Cats had five starters, three of them sophomores, who were back from last year's team that went to the Final Four. The Wildcat's mainstay in the three previous victories was the three-point shot. UofL center Cliff Rozier talked about that: "I hope they go to Dent and inside. Outside you can't do anything but watch and hope they miss."

UofL forward Dwayne Morton injured his right (shooting) wrist in the preseason and has it heavily taped. UK Coach Rick Pitino said that didn't matter, really: "He may not be 100%, but an 85% Dwayne Morton is better than most players in the country."

QUOTES

"Talked to him a couple of weeks ago. (Jamal Mashburn) His only advice was (that) we all had to be ourselves, stay positive and everything would work out. He said there was plenty of talent here."
UK FORWARD RODRICK RHODES

"I totally disagree. The players in our system have been better than their players in their system. It all depends on whose players play better."
UK COACH RICK PITINO commenting on the statement that his system is better than Denny Crum's system.

"We want to win so bad. We need to settle down and play Louisville basketball. We'll be OK."
UofL CENTER CLIFF ROZIER

Paul Willman

"We ended up taking a lot of bad shots. We were our own undoing. We didn't have patience. UofL COACH DENNY CRUM commenting on last year's 88-68 loss

PROBABLE STARTERS

Kentucky

POS.	PLAYER	HT.	WT.	CLS.	PT/G
F	JARED PRICKETT	6-9	235	SO.	5.5
F	RODRICK RHODES	6-7	200	SO.	9.1
C	RODNEY DENT	6-11	245	SR.	6.4
G	TONY DELK	6-1	193	SO.	4.5
G	TRAVIS FORD	5-9	165	SR.	13.6

Louisville

POS.	PLAYER	HT.	WT.	CLS.	PT/G
F	JASON OSBORNE	6-8	200	FR.	26.9
F	DWAYNE MORTON	6-6	190	SR.	16.1
C	CLIFFORD ROZIER	6-9	235	JR.	15.7
G	GREG MINOR	6-6	210	SR.	14.1
G	DeJUAN WHEAT	6-0	165	FR.	22.8

*Scoring averages for upperclassmen are from last season, and for the freshmen, their senior high school season.

"Cats deal Cards 78-70 loss"
Lexington Herald-Leader

"Cats have Card's number again"
Louisville Courier-Journal

Clifford Rozier said before the game that Louisville would be OK. Well, at least he was OK, scoring a game and career high 29 points, grabbing 13 rebounds and blocking three shots. However, the Cats won their fourth consecutive game in the series by a score of 78-70.

Kentucky made 11 threes, but it took 30 shots to get there. The Cards improved from three-point range over past performances, making five of 11, but did themselves in at the free throw line again, hitting only 17 of 31 for 54.8 percent.

UofL's biggest lead was in the first half at 11-5, but when Andre Riddick made a six foot shot with 10:11 remaining in the half, the Cards would never lead again.

Louisville's freshmen struggled, but Rozier, Minor and Morton took up the slack, scoring 56 of the team's 70 points.

With Dent in foul trouble and Martinez outmatched against Rozier, junior center Andre Riddick came to the rescue. He had 15 points, eight rebounds, a block and an assist.

Louisville forward Dwayne Morton said the Cardinals were surprised by Riddick: "I can't remember him even coming up, (UofL's scouting report) but he was a big-time player today." The

120

Cats led at the half 39-28, but stretched that to 18 in the first three minutes after intermission, 49-31. Then, the Cards had a three minute burst of their own, scoring 11 straight to narrow the Cats' margin to 49-42. But over the next 11 minutes, UK wrapped four threes in their scoring package to go up 74-56 with just under three minutes to play.

The 78-70 final, gave the Cats their fourth consecutive win over the Cards, and made Gimel Martinez the first player in series history to finish undefeated, 4-0 in the series. The attendance of 24,327 was the second-largest crowd in Rupp Arena history.

Gimel Martinez - #44 - UK, Jeff Brassow #14 - UK, DeJuan Wheat - # 32 UofL
Jared Pricket - #32 - UK

STATS

Kentucky

Player	Min	FG	FG A	3PT FG	3 PT FGA	FT	FT A	Reb	PF	Ast	St	BS	TO	Pts
Rodrick Rhodes	23	3	8	1	6	2	3	0	3	1	2	1	4	9
Jared Prickett	33	2	5	0	1	0	0	2	2	4	0	0	2	4
Rodney Dent	14	3	5	0	0	0	0	4	4	0	0	1	0	6
Tony Delk	34	6	14	5	11	2	5	10	1	5	2	2	0	19
Travis Ford	39	4	11	2	5	4	4	2	2	5	0	0	2	14
Jeff Brassow	17	2	3	2	3	0	0	1	2	2	1	0	0	6
Andre Riddick	21	7	10	0	1	1	2	8	5	1	0	1	0	15
Gimel Martinez	9	0	5	0	1	0	0	2	2	0	1	0	0	0
Anthony Epps	1	0	1	0	1	0	0	1	1	0	0	0	0	0
Jeff Sheppard	6	0	0	0	0	0	0	1	1	1	1	0	0	0
Walter McCarthy	3	2	3	1	1	0	2	1	0	0	0	0	1	5
Team								2						
Totals	**200**	**29**	**65**	**11**	**30**	**9**	**16**	**34**	**23**	**19**	**7**	**5**	**9**	**78**

Louisville

Player	Min	FG	FG A	3PT FG	3 PT FGA	FT	FT A	Reb	PF	Ast	St	BS	TO	Pts
Jason Osborne	33	0	6	0	2	1	2	7	3	1	1	0	6	1
Dwayne Morton	35	5	10	2	2	2	5	6	2	1	0	0	2	14
Clifford Rozier	38	11	15	0	0	7	12	13	4	0	0	3	3	29
DeJuan Wheat	29	1	8	1	3	3	5	2	1	1	0	0	1	6
Greg Minor	37	4	12	1	3	4	5	5	2	4	2	0	2	13

Player	Min	FG	FG A	3PT FG	3 PT FGA	FT	FT A	Reb	PF	Ast	St	BS	TO	Pts
Matt Simons	2	0	0	0	0	0	0	0	0	0	0	0	0	0
Tick Rogers	17	1	2	1	1	0	2	2	1	2	3	0	0	3
Brian Kiser	8	2	3	0	0	0	0	2	0	1	0	0	1	4
Alvin Sims	2	0	0	0	0	0	0	1	2	0	0	0	0	0
Team								2						
Totals	**200**	**24**	**56**	**5**	**11**	**17**	**31**	**40**	**15**	**10**	**6**	**3**	**15**	**70**

POINTS AFTER

"Andre gave us a big boost."
UK COACH RICK PITINO

"It feels great to go undefeated over them."
UK FORWARD GIMEL MARTINEZ

"Riddick really hurt us. It's a wonder he didn't do a cartwheel on his way to the basket."
UofL CENTER CLIFF ROZIER

"If someone had told me before the game we'd only lose by eight, I'd have been tickled to death. I thought we'd get beat a lot worse than that."
UofL COACH DENNY CRUM

GAME 26

January 1, 1995

	UofL	UK
Record	6-3	7-1
Ranking	unranked	#4
Series	7	18
Favored	KENTUCKY BY 4.5	
Location	FREEDOM HALL	
TV	CBS	

PRE-GAME REPORT

Neither team in series' history had won five consecutive games in the same number of years with the same coach. The Cats patched worked five straight, winning in the regular season in 1916, twice in 1922, the Olympic Trial game in 1948 and the first game in the NCAA East Region contest in 1951. But, the Million Dollar Question (it was $64,000 when I was young, but we must allow for inflation, and the current TV game show craze of the day) was, do I hear five?

The Cardinal team was hearing about losing from their fans and the press: "It's time to face facts people. You once had to accept the grim truth about Santa Claus, and so now you must do the same with the Kentucky-Louisville basketball series: The "Dream Game" has become a routine game," said C-J writer Pat Forde.

In the UK locker room, a new player was suiting up---complacency: "I really don't look at Louisville as a rivalry," said Tony Delk back in October. "I think Arkansas is a much bigger rival." Rodrick Rhodes seconded that emotion in the current tense, "I'd probably say Arkansas is the big rivalry. There's a lot on the line when we play them. Louisville, to me, is not like a rivalry. It's more for the students and fans. I haven't seen it where everyone (on the team) has been hyping it up."

Opposing coaches will utter phrases like that from time to time for the press, but when players chime in; a rude awakening is right around the corner. And on that corner, like a traffic cop, UK Coach Rick Pitino, was trying to re-direct that traffic: "I think this is one of the best Louisville teams, potentially. The word 'team' is the most important thing. Last year they had three NBA draft picks…but I think this team has more potential than last year's. You watch them on film and they definitely look like a team."

QUOTES

"He's played really well for us. (Samaki Walker) He's got a pretty good knack for the game and he loves to play and practices hard. He's certainly gotten better since the beginning of the year."
UofL COACH DENNY CRUM

"I think we can hold our own with anybody. I don't think anybody is scared or nervous. We have great confidence in what we can do, and if we play the way we're capable of playing, we have a great chance to beat Kentucky."

UofL GUARD TICK ROGERS (led the nation in steals at this time averaging 4.5 per/game)

"I take a little offense with people who say Coach Crum doesn't know how to play the three-point shot because you could say the same thing about Bob Knight and none of you ever did. Knight gives up just as many three-pointers. It has nothing to do with coaching…We just play well in this big game. That's the only answer to it. It's not any offensive design by me or any defensive lapse by him."

UK COACH RICK PITINO

"When I came out of high school, Kentucky was the place to play. That is no longer true. In the past twenty years, Louisville and Indiana have had more success than Kentucky as far as national championships go. (his son B.J. Flynn decided to walk-on at UofL because Coach Crum first expressed interest and UK seemed to offer little opportunity to play))

Former UK GUARD MIKE FLYNN

PROBABLE STARTERS

Louisville

POS.	PLAYER	HT.	WT.	CLS.	PT/G
F	JASON OSBORNE	6-8	200	SO.	11.6
F	ERIC JOHNSON	6-3	200	FR.	5.4
C	SAMAKI WALKER	6-9	220	FR.	13.4
G	DeJUAN WHEAT	6-0	180	SO.	19.3
G	TICK ROGERS	6-5	180	JR.	13.1

Kentucky

POS.	PLAYER	HT.	WT.	CLS.	PT/G
F	RODRICK RHODES	6-7	217	JR.	13.1
F	WALTER McCARTY	6-9	223	JR.	11.1
C	ANDRE RIDDICK	6-9	227	SR.	4.7
G	JEFF SHEPPARD	6-4	183	SO.	9.6
G	TONY DELK	6-1	194	JR.	13.3

"Call it a noisemaker: UofL 88 - UK 86"
Louisville Courier-Journal

"Cards slap Cats 88-86"
Lexington-Herald Leader

Samaki Walker - #52 - UL

Samaki Walker, symbolizing a new Cardinal "Dream Game" attitude, scored the first basket of the game, and sealed-off the inside down the stretch, to lead Louisville to an 88-86 upset of UK, erasing the Wildcat's bid to become the first team to win five consecutive games in the series.

In the process, Walker's triple-double of 14 points, 10 rebounds and 11 blocked shots, also scored a double play; the first in the rivalry and in Denny Crum's coaching career. Walker said, "This is only my first year here, but I heard all the talk about what Kentucky was going to do to us and how we were too weak to stop them. So, early in the game I wanted to go out and make a statement. I wanted them to know this was our house and nobody comes into our house and beats us." Walker blocked three shots in the game's first five minutes, and when Eric Johnson scored on a four-footer with 15:12 left in the first half, UofLled 14-7.

Louisville would lead by as many as 10, but that margin had dwindled to four at the half, 40-36. Not only was the Cardinal defense spectacular inside with the play of Walker, UofL used it's quickness to harass the Cats from the perimeter. The result; the Cats shot a season low 34.1 percent from the field, making only 28 baskets in 82 attempts. They still won the three-point shooting contest in the number made, but it wasn't pretty. UK made only nine of 27 for 33.3 percent while the Cards hit five of 11 for 45.5 percent.

However, UK scored on two three's to start the second half, and took its first lead of the game at 42-40. Walter McCarty added two free throws and with almost three minutes gone in the half, Kentucky led 44-40. Louisville had failed to score. UofL fans may have been wondering if the Cards would let another one get away like the previous years.

In 1993 Howard Schnellenberger took his UofL football team to the Liberty Bowl. Michigan State returned the opening kick-off for a touchdown but the Cards went on to win 18-7. When he returned home I had him on my show and asked if he was worried when the Spartans scored the first time they touched the ball, he replied, "No! There was plenty of time left."

And so it was here. Four ties, and three lead changes later, UK was clinging to a one-point lead, 56-55. Then, DeJuan Wheat's three-pointer at the top of the key, coming off a high pick-and-roll, registered the fourth and final lead change of the game with the Cards on top 58-56. Wheat came right back with a fall away three over 6-9 Walter McCarty and Alvin Sims added a dunk. Louisville's lead had stretched to 63-56, but still, it would be tight the rest of the way.

Jason Osborne's two free throws had the Cards on top at the 5:23 mark, 73-68. UK Coach Rick Pitino talked about those final minutes of play: "Kentucky needs to throw out the "I and my" in team. It wasn't until the last five minutes that we started passing the ball, working it and getting good shots." From that point, UK outscored the Cards 18 to 15, but it wasn't enough with Samaki Walker down inside.

Wheat's long two-point jump shot with UK's Tony Delk flying right at him, was key in keeping the Cards on top 82-77. DeJuan would also hit three of four from the foul line in the last 25 seconds to preserve the game offensively. The preserver defensively was again, Walker who blocked Jeff Sheppard's leaner with 30 seconds to go and UofL only ahead 84-81. Five seconds later, Walker was fouled in the scramble for a loose ball and banked in a free throw on the way to the Cardinals' 88-86 victory.

UofL had a total of 17 blocks for the day. UK's rebounding advantage of 52-38, with a season high 34 offensive rebounds kept them in the game.

STATS

Louisville

Player	Min	FG	FG A	3PT FG	3 PT FGA	FT	FT A	Reb	PF	Ast	St	BS	TO	Pts
Eric Johnson	14	4	8	0	0	0	0	2	4	0	0	0	1	8
Jason Osborne	32	3	7	1	4	5	6	6	3	2	2	3	6	12
Samaki Walker	33	5	8	0	0	4	7	10	3	1	2	11	0	14
Tick Rogers	31	2	9	0	1	7	8	3	3	2	2	1	3	11

Paul Willman

Player	Min	FG	FG A	3PT FG	3 PT FGA	FT	FT A	Reb	PF	Ast	St	BS	TO	Pts
DeJuan Wheat	32	7	9	3	4	6	8	4	1	5	3	0	1	23
Alvin Sims	19	2	4	0	0	0	0	5	2	3	0	1	2	4
B.J. Flynn	17	3	9	0	0	3	4	5	0	2	1	0	4	9
Beau Zach Smith	8	2	3	0	0	0	0	0	3	0	1	1	0	4
Brian Kiser	15	1	3	1	2	0	0	2	3	1	0	0	0	3
Team								1						
Totals	200	29	60	5	11	25	33	38	22	16	11	17	17	88

Kentucky

Player	Min	FG	FG A	3PT FG	3 PT FGA	FT	FT A	Reb	PF	Ast	St	BS	TO	Pts
Rodrick Rhodes	29	1	9	1	3	2	2	1	5	0	0	1	3	5
Walter McCarty	23	5	11	3	5	4	5	9	1	1	0	0	1	17
Andre Riddick	16	1	3	0	0	0	0	4	2	1	0	1	0	2
Tony Delk	37	9	19	3	8	2	3	8	3	1	1	0	2	23
Jeff Sheppard	33	6	17	2	4	5	6	4	4	3	0	1	3	19
Anthony Epps	8	0	2	0	0	2	2	0	3	0	0	0	1	2
Jared Prickett	17	0	1	0	0	3	4	4	2	0	0	0	2	3
Antoine Walker	17	2	9	0	3	2	2	6	4	2	0	0	1	6
Mark Pope	24	4	10	0	3	1	3	10	2	1	1	0	2	9
Allen Edwards	4	0	1	0	1	0	0	1	1	1	0	0	1	0
Chris Harrison	2	0	0	0	0	0	0	0	0	0	0	0	0	0
Team								5						
Totals	200	28	82	9	27	21	27	52	27	10	2	3	16	86

POINTS AFTER

"I like this team. They play really hard and get after people. They're not very big, but they don't know that."
FORMER UofL GREAT DARRELL GRIFFITH

"We didn't lose our poise when we lost our lead. That's a hard thing for a young team. Usually, things get worse."
UofL COACH DENNY CRUM

"It was non-existent today. (Cats'signature full-court pressure) DeJuan Wheat went right through it. We couldn't get it rolling like we usually do."
UK GUARD JEFF SHEPPARD

"During the week we didn't think of him as an intimidator. (Samaki Walker) He turned out to be one."
UK FORWARD ANTOINE WALKER

GAME 27

December 23, 1995

	UK	UofL
Record	6-1	7-3
Ranking	#4	unranked
Series	18	8
Favored	KENTUCKY BY 18	
Location	RUPP ARENA	
TV	CBS	

PRE-GAME REPORT

UK enjoyed a three-in-one victory celebration on this rivalry game day. First, Santa made a slam dunk appearance announcing that Tim Couch, the nation's No. 1 high school quarterback prospect was staying home to play football for the Cats. At least Kentucky had beaten Tennessee with pen and ink. (At the end of the 1925 football season, the Cats had a 10-8-3 series lead over the Volunteers. Oh, that's another book; call it "The Trojan Wildcat." A Mark Stoops chapter just might change the aforementioned title).

Second, a new Rupp Arena attendance record was set, with 24,340* eager, salivating Cat fans ready to feast on a "revenge" win, compensating for the loss the previous year in Freedom Hall, 88-86.

That would be 24,198 Cat fans, I forgot the opposing team gets 142 tickets.

That is, if they don't sell them.

*Sometimes when the visiting fans' hopes have aged well, they'll dabble innovatively, finding more than the standard amount of tickets available; of course at popular prices. This entrepreneurial approach can work both ways, creating another rivalry dimension which fan base can slip more of its color inside the opposing arena.

And third, it was the third double digit victory of Rick Pitino's five wins over Louisville.

UofL had a "three" situation of its own, that would make it even more difficult to win in Rupp Arena. Eric Johnson was out due to injury, and Jason Osborne and Alex Sanders for academic issues. Good news however, Samaki Walker, who registered the only triple-double in Louisville history last year against the Cats, had been under investigation for rules violations and was cleared to play.

The biggest mismatch to overcome for the Cards is inside, where Brian Kaiser, normally a substitute, would have to fight for position against Antoine Walker.

QUOTES

"This is probably the biggest game of the season for me, being from Kentucky. It's a very emotional game for me. Last year when we lost, I got it from a lot of people back home. A lot of my

friends were getting on me. They still do. We even heard it the other night when we went to the Galleria before the Marshall game (in Louisville). Their fans were telling us, 'Whatever happens this year, we beat you last year."
UK GUARD ANTHONY EPPS

"Walking towards the court at Freedom Hall to play Marshall on Tuesday everybody was tapping me on the head and shoulders and they're screaming at me to beat UofL. And we're coming out for the Marshall game."
UK COACH RICK PITINO

"I think it helps. (having players on the team from KY) Over the years you're able to watch them play and know what it's like. Last year I was really excited about the game and wanted to do well."
UofL GUARD DeJUAN WHEAT

"I don't remember a better Kentucky team. They can physically dominate you. It's hard for us to physically hold up when we play a team of that caliber. No matter if we had them, (the three players unable to play) it'd be tough for us to beat that team."
UofL COACH DENNY CRUM

PROBABLE STARTERS

Kentucky

POS.	PLAYER	HT.	WT.	CLS.	PT/G
F	ANTOINE WALKER	6-8	224	SO.	6.3
F	RON MERCER	6-7	208	FR.	7.7
C	MARK POPE	6-10	235	SR.	10.0
G	TONY DELK	6-1	193	SR.	15.3
G	ANTHONY EPPS	6-2	180	JR.	5.6

Louisville

POS.	PLAYER	HT.	WT.	CLS.	PT/G
F	BRIAN KISER	6-7	205	SR.	7.8
F	ALVIN SIMS	6-4	220	JR.	14.9
C	SAMAKI WALKER	6-9	240	SO.	16.1
G	DeJUAN WHEAT	6-0	165	JR.	18.1
G	TICK ROGERS	6-5	205	SR.	9.3

"Cat's glass act a winner"
Lexington Herald-Leader

"Wildcats find tidings of great joy"
Louisville Courier-Journal

These are the winning numbers; 44-24-20-21. No, I am not talking about the lottery, but the more important rebounding game, from the UK perspective. The Cats out rebounded the Cards 44-24, the 20 offensive rebounds resulting in 21 second chance points. Ball game over, 89-66.

It was the Wildcats' defensive pressure and rebounding superiority that kept them in the game while they looked for their powerball outside. UK struggled early hitting only two of 18 shots, missing all nine of their three-point attempts, finding themselves down 10-4 with 11:33 remaining in the first half. But from that point, they shot 59 percent from the field and 50 percent from three-point range.

Tony Delk, who missed his first six shots, got hot in the final three minutes of the half, scoring 12 of his game high 30 points to give Kentucky a 36-24 halftime lead.

The Cats stretched that lead to 60-41 with 10:43 to play, but as it happens so often in this rivalry, the team behind doesn't quit. DeJuan Wheat led a Cardinal run, hitting two three-point shots in that span, and just like that, UK's lead had been trimmed to seven, 61-54.

Then, it was UK's turn for another run. Except for a Delk three-point shot, they went inside and regained momentum, 73-58, with just over four minutes to play, and went on to win 89-66.

STATS

Kentucky

Player	Min	FG	FG A	3PT FG	3 PT FGA	FT	FT A	Reb	PF	Ast	St	BS	TO	Pts
Antoine Walker	32	8	17	0	2	4	6	12	2	2	0	1	4	20
Ron Mercer	20	1	5	0	3	2	2	2	2	3	1	1	0	4
Walter McCarty	30	6	9	0	1	0	0	9	3	2	2	1	3	12
Tony Delk	28	10	17	4	8	6	6	6	1	2	2	2	3	30
Anthony Epps	31	5	9	1	2	3	4	5	1	3	4	0	3	14
Wayne Turner	9	0	1	0	0	0	0	0	0	1	0	0	1	0
Derek Anderson	13	2	6	0	2	0	0	3	2	3	2	0	2	4
Mark Pope	18	1	3	0	1	0	0	3	3	1	0	1	1	2
Jeff Sheppard	12	0	3	0	0	0	0	1	2	1	0	0	0	0
Allen Edwards	7	1	2	1	2	0	0	1	0	0	1	0	1	3
Team								2						
Totals	**200**	**34**	**72**	**6**	**21**	**15**	**18**	**44**	**16**	**18**	**12**	**6**	**18**	**89**

Louisville

Player	Min	FG	FG A	3PT FG	3 PT FGA	FT	FT A	Reb	PF	Ast	St	BS	TO	Pts
Brian Kiser	31	2	6	1	3	0	0	2	0	1	1	0	6	5
Alvin Sims	34	9	14	0	1	5	9	2	4	1	3	0	2	23
Samaki Walker	35	7	12	0	0	3	5	8	4	2	1	4	6	17
Tick Rogers	31	0	4	0	2	0	0	3	4	4	1	0	2	0
DeJuan Wheat	37	5	13	3	10	4	4	3	4	2	1	0	3	17
Damion Dantzler	10	0	2	0	1	2	2	1	1	0	0	1	1	2
Beau Zach Smith	7	1	1	0	0	0	0	2	2	0	0	0	1	2
B.J. Flynn	7	0	0	0	0	0	0	0	1	2	1	0	1	0
Charlie Taylor	8	0	1	0	1	0	0	1	1	2	1	0	1	0
Team								2						
Totals	**200**	**24**	**53**	**4**	**18**	**14**	**20**	**24**	**21**	**14**	**9**	**5**	**23**	**66**

POINTS AFTER

"Everybody was cold. Me and Tony (Delk) usually hit those shots. If we did, this game would have been over a long time ago."
UK GUARD DEREK ANDERSON

"Our double downs were great. The key was the way we got out of the double downs (to also cover the perimeter)." (The 24,340 in attendance established a new Rupp Arena).
UK COACH RICK PITINO

"Kentucky just dominated the offensive boards, and that was the big difference in the game."
UofL COACH DENNY CRUM

"I've got to give it to them."
UofL CENTER SAMAKI WALKER

Kentucky would go on to win its sixth National Championship, Rick Pitino's first, 76-67 over Pitino's former boss Jim Boeheim's Syracuse Orangemen.

The speculation mongers were distributing stuff at a feverish pace; the main thing was, "Pitino's gone." Of course, according to these so-called information specialists, he had left before he arrived.

I made a call to the late Bill Keightley and asked: "Is coach gone?" His reply: "PauuuuuuuuuL" in his famous drawl, "I'm making shirts for his basketball camp. I'll say he's coming back this year ('96-'97) but that's as far as I can go."

I called my friend Tom Leach, (now the play-by-play broadcaster for the Cats) we had been together for four years as co-hosts of the UK network's post-game call-in show, and I shared with him my information. He said, he agreed.

I believe Tom and I might have been the only ones in broadcasting (those that publicly had expressed an opinion) that had Coach Pitino coming back following that championship season.

GAME 28

December 31, 1996

	UofL	UK
Record	10-0	10-1
Ranking	#14	#3
Series	8	19
Favored	KENTUCKY BY 6	
Location	FREEDOM HALL	
TV	ESPN 2	

PRE-GAME REPORT

XXVIII is a special number, marking the most successful entry for both schools in the history of the regular season matchup. They're a combined 20-1, both boast current ten game winning streaks with UK ranked No. 3, and UofL No. 14 nationally. In game 25, UK was ranked No. 2 and UofL No. 7, but neither had played a game.

Coach Pitino said, "This is the best Louisville team we've played against. It's the deepest, quickest, most explosive. There may have been some bigger names the first year (1989), but this is by far the deepest, most talented team."

Coach Crum was also very gracious, "I'm impressed with their talent, I'm impressed with they way they're coached. I'm impressed with their rebounding and I'm impressed with the way they shoot it. They do everything well, and they don't have any apparent weaknesses."

It was also the second time in the series that one of the two rivals came in as the defending national champion, with both of those games being played in Freedom Hall. UofL had beaten Duke for the title 72-69 in 1986, but with the "Camden Connection" of Billy Thompson and Milt Wagner gone, plus Jeff Hall, UK with three juniors, a senior and a freshman named Chapman, did as it pleased, even with Pervis Ellison, belting the Cardinals at home, 85-51.

This time in Freedom Hall, Kentucky was the defending champion, having beaten future UK Coach John Calipari and his UMASS squad in the semifinals, and Syracuse for the title 76-67. Nine players who appear in the team picture from that 1996 championship season, played or play in the NBA. (Nazr Mohammed is still hanging around) Wayne Turner only played three games in the "League," but the phrase reads, played. Myself, and some seven billion other occupants on this planet, have not. This fact expands the mind to a celestial level of understanding of just how hard it is to play alongside James, Durrant, Bryant and company in the NBA.

Gone were Tony Delk, Antoine Walker, Walter McCarty and Mark Pope. Also, Jeff Sheppard was sitting out the season. Back however, were future NBA players Derek Anderson and Ron Mercer, along with Anthony Epps and Allen Edwards, who had played in the championship game. Future pros Nazr Muhammed, Scott Padgett, Wayne Turner and Jamaal Magloire would also see action.

UofL's DeJaun Wheat and Alvin Sims were the only two players from the Cardinal squad to play in the NBA, but this is still a college game, and the best rivalry; which on the vast majority of occasions generates the greatest effort from the players. Even with the bulk of its championship team no longer on the roster, UK still had advantages in terms of size and depth. But, both teams were loaded with a pair of senior guards, and Rick Pitino's plan was to contain UofL's, especially DeJuan Wheat, "Our goal was to keep them out of the open court. They tend to have a shark mentality when they get into the open court."

Although, UK had won 10 straight games after losing its opener to Clemson, Pitino made two lineup changes designed to give his team an offensive transfusion. Nazr Muhammed replaced Jamaal Magliore and Scott Padgett, with his penchant for shooting threes, replaced Jared Prickett.

QUOTES

"I don't want my friends to tease me that I was 1-3 against Kentucky in my career."
UofL GUARD DeJUAN WHEAT

"It would prove a lot if we could win, because I don' think we've gotten enough respect."
UofL GUARD ALVIN SIMS

"Wheat's versatility makes him tougher to contain than say, Wake Forest All-American center Tim Duncan."
UK COACH RICK PITINO

"We won't let them get easy baskets."
UK GUARD DEREK ANDERSON

PROBABLE STARTERS

Louisville

POS.	PLAYER	HT.	WT.	CLS.	PT/G
F	NATE JOHNSON	6-6	205	FR.	9.3
F	DAMION DANTZLER	6-7	225	JR.	6.4
F/C	ALEX SANDERS	6-7	260	SO.	11.9
G/F	ALVIN SIMS	6-4	235	SR.	11.7
G	DeJUAN WHEAT	6-0	165	SR.	20.1

Kentucky

POS.	PLAYER	HT.	WT.	CLS.	PT/G
F	RON MERCER	6-7	210	SO.	20.3
F	SCOTT PADGETT	6-9	227	SO.	6.7
C	NAZR MOHAMMED	6-10	238	SO.	8.3
G	DEREK ANDERSON	6-5	194	SR.	20.8
G	ANTHONY EPPS	6-2	182	SR.	8.11

"The fittest survive"
Lexington Herald-Leader

"Ring in the blue
Kentucky 74-Louisville 54"
Louisville Courier-Journal

Earlier in the year, UK had won the national championship and now, would celebrate the New Year with a victory party after beating its arch rival, UofL 74-54. The game plan was to contain UofL superstar DeJuan Wheat mission accomplished.

DeJuan, in his previous two outings against Kentucky averaged 20 points, making 12 of 22 shots and six of 14 three-point attempts. Today, Wheat finished with season lows of eight shots and eight points. When he scored, using a crossover dribble to make a driving layup with 13:47 left in the game, UofL led 42-39. But those were his last points of the day.

Wheat wasn't the only one taken off stride, Alvin Sims was limited to just three baskets in 14 attempts. In fact, the team registered season-lows in points (54), baskets (19), shooting percentage (34.5), and assists (11), while committing a season high 25 turnovers. The Cats' game plan was not necessarily to wear the Cards down, instead they used an alternating man-to-man and 1-3-1 zone defense in the first half, and switched defenders on Wheat in the second half. UK point-guard Anthony Epps concurred, "The secret was team defense. All five players really concentrated on him."

Kentucky wasn't the only team playing hard, playing defense as Coach Crum pointed out, "Both teams played so well defensively, neither team gave up anything."

The Wildcats missed all six of their three-pointers in the first half, and shot just 40.7 percent from the field, but only trailed at the half by a point, 28-27.

With Louisville leading 42-39 and about 10:30 left in the game, forward Damion Dantzler was called for walking while trying to get the ball in-bounds. UK went to work on a 12-0 run that put them up 51-42 with seven minutes to go.

Inside that run with 8:27 left, and Kentucky ahead 45-42, UK's Allen Edwards missed a free throw and UofL forward Damion Dantzler got the rebound, but Derek Anderson stole the ball and made a reverse layup giving the Cats a 47-42 lead.

Cardinal guard, B.J. Flynn looked back, "That was the turning point. We got tired and they didn't. I expected us to be tired, but that's not the reason we got beat."

From the time they held that 42-39 lead until the finish, Louisville connected on just four of 24 shots, losing 74-54.

STATS

Louisville

Player	Min	FG	FG A	3PT FG	3 PT FGA	FT	FT A	Reb	PF	Ast	St	BS	TO	Pts
Nate Johnson	25	2	6	0	0	0	0	4	2	1	0	0	1	4
Damion Dantzler	29	1	2	0	1	4	4	7	3	2	1	1	6	6
Alex Sanders	26	4	7	0	2	0	0	5	5	2	0	0	5	8
Alvin Sims	32	3	14	2	4	1	3	8	4	4	3	1	5	9
DeJuan Wheat	31	3	8	1	5	1	2	1	2	2	0	0	4	8

Paul Willman

Player	Min	FG	FG A	3PT FG	3 PT FGA	FT	FT A	Reb	PF	Ast	St	BS	TO	Pts
B.J. Flynn	28	3	8	1	3	5	5	3	4	0	2	0	2	12
Eric Johnson	16	1	4	0	1	0	0	3	4	0	0	0	1	2
Beau Zach Smith	8	0	3	0	0	1	2	2	1	0	0	0	1	1
Tony Williams	4	2	3	0	1	0	0	3	0	0	0	0	0	4
Matt Akridge	1	0	0	0	0	0	0	0	1	0	0	0	0	0
Team								1						
Totals	200	19	55	4	17	12	16	37	26	11	6	2	25	54

Kentucky

Player	Min	FG	FG A	3PT FG	3 PT FGA	FT	FT A	Reb	PF	Ast	St	BS	TO	Pts
Ron Mercer	36	5	13	2	4	4	5	2	2	1	3	0	2	16
Scott Padgett	33	3	6	1	4	8	8	6	3	3	2	0	5	15
Nazr Mohammed	22	5	8	0	0	0	0	5	1	0	1	1	3	10
Derek Anderson	34	8	13	1	3	2	4	6	3	2	2	1	1	19
Anthony Epps	32	0	6	0	4	3	4	4	1	4	1	1	1	3
Wayne Turner	8	0	1	0	0	0	0	0	2	0	1	0	2	0
Allen Edwards	12	0	1	0	0	1	2	2	2	2	1	0	3	1
Jared Prickett	20	2	4	0	0	6	8	9	3	1	0	1	0	10
Jamaal Magloire	3	0	0	0	0	0	0	0	1	0	1	1	1	0
Team								1						
Totals	200	23	52	4	15	24	31	35	18	13	12	5	18	74

POINTS AFTER

"I didn't think anybody could do that to DeJuan. They just shut him down."
UofL GUARD B.J. FLYNN

"They just kept running people in and out on me. I couldn't find a real good look at the basket, so I tried to get the ball to my teammates. And the ball just didn't go in the basket for them."
UofL GUARD DeJUAN WHEAT

"We played a spectacular defensive game, and we knew it would take that kind of effort to beat a Louisville team like that."
UK COACH RICK PITINO

"Coach told us to go out and play like champions. And that's what we did."
UK GUARD DEREK ANDERSON

'We just got tired. I'd like to play them again under different circumstances. But I want you to know they are a great team. I know they are a better basketball team than we are right now, but having played them I know we can do a lot of things better."
UofL COACH DENNY CRUM

The Lexington Herald-Leader's John Clay wrote: "The hoop junkie was watching 14th-ranked Louisville get down and dirty with third-ranked Kentucky for 30 or so minutes, before ultimately, talent and coaching and fatigue all took their inexorable tolls and the Cats rolled to a 74-54 victory at Freedom Hall. But the hoop junkie knows the final score. Misleading your honor. Hoop heads know that with 11:34 to go, Louisville actually led 42-39, before the roof caved in…But now the hoop junkie wants to know just how good Louisville is?"

Louisville would lose eight more games that year, finishing 26-9. They didn't win the C-USA Conference Tournament, but did make it to the NCAA East Regional final, losing to North Carolina 97-74, almost the exact margin of loss to UK in the rivalry game. DeJuan Wheat was hurt in that game, but played hard, courageous basketball. I'm sure Coach Crum and others would like to play that game again, but it will never happen. It's "One and Done!" I've got a few games I would like to rerun live, but in the final analysis, the University of Louisville had a great year.

UK lost four more games that season, won the SEC Tournament and was runner-up in the NCAA Championship Game, losing to Arizona in overtime, finishing 30-5.

That championship game, play it again "Sam" with Derek Anderson in there; and Ron Mercer not fatigued at the end, and UK repeats as national champion. Remember, "One and Done" is an equal opportunity employer.

In my interview with Coach Wooden in his home, I was telling him that if Mike Casey had not broken his leg, and if Larry Conley had not been sick when UK played Texas Western, and remember Pat Riley had an infected toe in that game too, Kentucky would have at least two more national championships.

He turned to my cameraman and said: "This boy likes to major in ifs!" Then, turning back to me said, "I had a player injured in 1966, if he had been able to play, I would like to think I'd have won another championship!"

This matter concerning time; UofL still led after 30 minutes. Not taking anything away from the Cardinal effort, because the Wildcats have been in that same situation as well—so what?

I saw Kentucky in person against Vanderbilt in 1966, and listened to Rupp's Runts play on the radio, and it happened time after time. The game was close and before you could swallow your A & W…Bingo! The game was over. Kentucky would go on a run, and it was over. The other team might have been close, right in there and Bingo, it was over.

Coach Pitino is known for his three-point emphasis, but his defense works real well too. I have always likened it to Rocky Marciano's style. Jack Dempsey's manager said that Rocky had the greatest one-punch knockout power of any heavyweight champion. But he also liked that steady, hammering to the opponent's body.

No, Rocky wasn't the greatest boxer, but his style would get you just the same. He worked the body. You could hit him twice, he just wanted his one. It took its toll. (49-0, 43 by knockout). I had Marty Weil on my show a couple of times. He was the son of Rocky's manager, Al Weil. I asked him why they didn't fight the up and coming Floyd Patterson and make it 50-0? He said, "Floyd's manager wasn't that dumb."

Back to basketball. You might last 30 or 35 minutes, but the run is going to get you, most of the time. It might be a short burst here and there, or one of the sustained variety for several minutes. It can happen at any time. The same happens to Kentucky in football. They hang in for three-quarters, but the game consists of four.

And of course, there is that variety of defeat which reminds me of the comedy team of Allen and Rossi. Rossi was the straight man, like Dean Martin was for Jerry Lewis. In one routine on the Ed Sullivan Show, Marty Allen was portraying a fighter.

Rossi: "In your last fight, when did you know you were in trouble?"

Allen: "Right after the National Anthem!"

In a recent interview I mentioned to John Clay that I was including this piece. He responded: "I agree about Pitino's style of play and what it can do to a team."

GAME 29

December 27, 1997

	UK	UofL
Record	10-1	3-6
Ranking	#4	unranked
Series	20	8
Favored	KENTUCKY BY 16.5	
Location	RUPP ARENA	
TV	CBS	

PRE-GAME REPORT

Kentucky had a new head coach, Orlando "Tubby" Smith. He had been an assistant and associate coach at UK from 1989-91 under head coach Rick Pitino. Now, he had inherited from his former boss, who had left Lexington for the Celtics, an unparalleled run in college basketball's best rivalry. The Wildcats had won six of the past seven games, outscoring the Cardinals in those six wins by a total of ninety-three points.

Coach Denny Crum was on the short-end of that run, and was taking heat from fans and the press alike. Complaints included various subjects; NCAA probation, recruiting, losing control of his team and the "feel" for the way the game is played, as in the three-point shot. As Coach Rupp often said on his post-game show with Cawood Ledford, "Let's take a look at the facts of the case."

The facts show that UK embraced the three-point shot from day one, but now, the Cards were closing the gap. In fact, the current season marks the first time since Rick Pitino's arrival at UK in 1989 that UofL is averaging both more three-pointers taken, and made than UK per game in a single season; 20.8 to 15.9 taken and 6.9 to 5.7 made per game. The Wildcats were shooting a better percentage from beyond the arc than the Cardinals, 36 percent to 33.2 percent.

The perception from the early days continued to blur the vision of Red and Black fans, for it seemed that Kentucky never missed a three-pointer when the "Dream Game" rolled around, while Louisville either didn't shoot one, or couldn't make one, even if a washtub was found attached to the backboard.

I used the washtub analogy, remembering what my father told me at one of the Louisville games we attended. Judd Rothman was a 6-8 center, but man, he was huge, a Goliath in those days. However, he struggled from the free throw line as many big men do today. After missing another one, my father leaned over and said, "Son, he couldn't make one if they had a washtub up there."

This time around however, the three-pointer would receive proper emphasis on both offense and defense as then, UofL Assistant Coach Scott Davenport remembers, "We had some under-sized players, like Eric Johnson, Troy Williams and Alex Sanders, but they were versatile, and athletic, able to step outside and shoot. We didn't want to 'grind-it' in down inside against their big players. Tubby Smith teams are oriented to play a tough, ball line defense. Our objective was to stretch them out, make them come outside so we could open up the middle. On defense, we wanted to challenge their shooters. We wanted to force Scott Padgett to put the ball on the floor before he could take a shot. If you didn't, he was going to make it."

QUOTES

"They're a very dangerous team. Coming into the game, they really have nothing to lose."
UK JUNIOR SCOTT PADGETT

"I think there a very good team. It's a team that has played a tough schedule.
UK COACH TUBBY SMITH

"We're working hard at trying to jell. It's been like that for a bout a week. Everybody's starting to come together a little more, and Nate (Johnson) and I are starting to get in top the flow."
UofL FORWARD DAMION DANTZLER

I think this team will get better. Can it improve enough to beat a team like Kentucky? I don't know."
UofL COACH DENNY CRUM

PROBABLE STARTERS

Kentucky

POS.	PLAYER	HT.	WT.	CLS.	PT/G
F	SCOTT PADGETT	6-9	229	JR.	8.6
F	ALLEN EDWARDS	6-5	200	SR.	11.4
C	JAMAAL MAGLOIRE	6-10	240	SO.	7.2
G	JEFF SHEPPARD	6-3	190	SR.	11.6
G	WAYNE TURNER	6-2	187	JR.	9.0

Louisville

POS.	PLAYER	HT.	WT.	CLS.	PT/G
F	NATE JOHNSON	6-6	205	SO.	8.8
F	DAMION DANTZLER	6-6	225	SR.	6.6
F/C	ALEX SANDERS	6-7	260	JR.	11.9
G	MARQUES MAYBIN	6-3	180	FR.	9.3
G	CAMERON MURRAY	6-0	180	JR.	11.1

"It was in the Cards"
Louisville Courier-Journal

"Rivalry revival: Cards stun Cats"
Lexington Herald-Leader

Marques Maybin hit a three-point shot to give Louisville the first lead of the game, but the Cards struggled early, missing eight of their first 12 shots and committed six turnovers.

Kentucky wasn't shooting that well either. Jeff Sheppard hit two three's in the first half, but most of the other points came on dunks, tip-ins and short-jumpers. When Padgett made a free throw with 2:33 remaining, UK was on top 32-23, but UofL managed one critical run in each half that would make all the difference in the end. It was all Eric Johnson for the next 31 seconds, as his six points cut the Cat lead to three, at 32-29. The final two minutes of the half ended with UK on top 35-31.

The second half was one of those grand see-saw battles. UofL took a 38-37 lead on Tony William's three-pointer with 17:33 left in the game. Five lead changes and three ties later, with UK leading 61-59, Eric Johnson ignited the Cardinal's second half, 11-0 run with a three, followed by Murray and Sanders both making threes and a Dantzler lay up, and the Rupp Arena crowd was stunned, as UofL led 70-59 with 4:23 left in the game.

Louisville gained this advantageous position by making threes. They had already canned 12 by this time, but their three-point attack was done for the day. Leading 74-66 with 3:00 to go, UofL would have to seal the deal from the foul line. They struggled to protect their lead, shooting only 50 percent from the charity stripe, making just five of 10 shots. Nate Johnson's last free throw with 0:15 remaining, pushed the UofL lead to a one possession game, 79-76.

Louisville stuck to its game plan and was all over the Cats beyond the arc. Scott Padgett forced up a three-pointer that missed badly, Alex Sanders caught it, then threw the ball toward the rafters as time ran out for the Cats.

The Cardinals, at 3-6, given no chance to beat the No. 4 team on its home floor, had done just that, 79-76.

STATS

Kentucky

Player	Min	FG	FG A	3PT FG	3 PT FGA	FT	FT A	Reb	PF	Ast	St	BS	TO	Pts
Allen Edwards	34	4	10	1	4	4	4	4	2	1	4	0	0	13
Scott Padgett	25	3	13	0	5	1	2	6	4	4	3	2	1	7
Jamaal Magloire	16	1	6	0	0	4	6	8	2	0	1	0	2	6
Wayne Turner	21	4	6	1	1	3	6	2	3	2	0	0	2	12
Jeff Sheppard	33	7	14	3	5	1	5	6	4	2	1	0	3	18
Nazr Mohammed	15	5	6	0	0	2	2	9	2	2	0	3	1	12
Heshimu Evans	19	1	5	0	2	0	0	6	3	1	1	0	3	2
Cameron Mills	7	1	4	0	2	0	0	1	2	0	0	0	0	2
Saul Smith	18	1	6	0	4	0	0	0	2	2	2	0	1	2
Myron Anthony	10	0	1	0	0	2	2	1	0	0	0	0	0	2

Player	Min	FG	FG A	3PT FG	3 PT FGA	FT	FT A	Reb	PF	Ast	St	BS	TO	Pts
Michael Bradley	2	0	1	0	0	0	0	0	1	0	0	0	0	0
Team													1	
Totals	200	27	72	5	23	17	27	43	25	14	12	5	14	76

Louisville

Player	Min	FG	FG A	3PT FG	3 PT FGA	FT	FT A	Reb	PF	Ast	St	BS	TO	Pts
Marques Maybin	22	3	5	2	4	0	1	1	2	2	2	0	1	8
Cameron Murray	33	4	9	2	4	5	6	3	4	6	0	0	4	15
Nate Johnson	21	1	3	0	0	2	4	3	2	0	0	0	1	4
Damion Dantzler	27	3	8	0	0	0	2	6	3	2	1	1	2	6
Alex Sanders	30	4	9	2	4	0	1	10	1	1	0	1	3	10
Eric Johnson	22	8	10	3	3	1	1	1	5	2	0	0	3	20
Tony Williams	26	5	9	3	7	3	6	6	2	0	0	0	2	16
Travis Best	9	0	1	0	0	0	0	1	0	2	0	0	1	0
Troy Jackson	9	0	1	0	0	0	0	2	2	1	1	0	0	0
Jerry Johnson	1	0	0	0	0	0	0	0	0	0	0	0	1	0
Team								4					1	
Totals	200	28	55	12	22	11	21	37	21	16	4	2	19	79

POINTS AFTER

UofL had allowed its first nine opponents to make 62 of 152 three-point shots. That's 40.8 percent. But, UK made only five of their 23 three-point attempts, for a measly 21.7 percent. Louisville on the other hand, connected on 12 of 22 three-pointers for an outstanding 54.5 percent, and overall they shot 50.9 percent compared to UK's 37.5 percent.

In an recent interview, Coach Scott Davenport of Bellarmine University talked about the two major factors that determine the outcome of a basketball game, "Shooting percentage. That's still the number-one factor, and the three-point shot is the great equalizer. We make all those three's, make a great percentage of our total shots, and it still comes down to a one possession game, that's amazing."

He continued, "It just goes to show you how hard it is to win a national championship in college basketball. It's one game and your done. It's not like the regional in college baseball where it is two out of three, or in college football, where so much is based on the body of conference work you've done all year long. In basketball, it's one and done."

Kentucky recovered to become the "Comeback Cats" and won the national championship, while the Cards missed post-season play that year finishing 12-20, making this perhaps the biggest upset in the rivalry.

GAME 30

December 26, 1998

	UofL	UK
Record	4-2	10-2
Ranking	unranked	#3
Series	9	20
Favored	KENTUCKY BY 4	
Location	FREEDOM HALL	
TV	CBS	

PRE-GAME REPORT

Kentucky entered this game with three senior starters. Normally, that's a recipe for success, but this is the "Dream Game" and normal doesn't count. However, these seniors may have been suffering from a hangover, not from some chemical, but from something contested—last year's fluky 79-76 loss in Rupp to these same Cardinals.

The Cats were ranked No. 4 before that game and now arrived in Freedom Hall ranked No. 3, with wins over UCLA, Kansas, Indiana and Maryland. Although they had just lost to Duke earlier in the week 71-60, shooting a season-low from the field, 34.9 percent.

Scott Padgett was irritated by things he was hearing in Louisville, his hometown: "I got a ring and they sat home during the (NCAA) tournament and the only game the Louisville fans talk to me about is Louisville beating us. I don't know how many times I hear the joke that we were No. 1 in the nation and No. 2 in the state last year, and that's what a lot of these people think about this rivalry." On the other hand, the Cardinals wanted to prove that last year's game was anything but a fluke.

They wanted to use the same game plan, stretch the floor, opening up the middle, contest all three-point shots and force UK point guard Wayne Turner to go to his right, according to Coach Scott Davenport, "There are legendary stories of Coach Crum having basketball discussions with Coach Wooden. Well, he and I had one about Wayne Turner. He liked to shoot from his left side, and I told Coach Crum we needed to make him shoot from his right. If he shoots from the right, he will be looking straight into our defense, while shooting from the left, he has a clearer shot at the basket."

The point guard battle between Wayne Turner and Louisville's Cameron Murray would be a major key in this rivalry battle. Last year, Murray got the upper hand, but was surprised that Tubby's son Saul, got so much playing time, 18 minutes, Wayne Turner 21. Coach Smith's substitution patterns, was a sore spot with many UK fans that never quite seemed to heal.

For this encounter however, Murray had a little more incentive for his confrontation with Turner, "I heard him say on ESPN he was the best point guard in the country, so I'm looking forward to it."

QUOTES

"Everybody thought last year was a fluke and it probably was. I told our players before the game that this was the same as playing anybody else, except both teams are going to play a little harder. That's the nature of rivalries."
COACH DENNY CRUM

"It's not even close. (UCLA vs. USC rivalry) Even though we had a bad year, a lot of our fans were happy because we beat Kentucky."
CAMERON MURRAY (Who transferred from UCLA)

"I think we'll be better prepared this year. That's one thing we learned from last year, that Coach Crum and his staff are great coaches. That's why they have won national championships, why he's been Coach of the Year, why he's a Hall of Famer. He's as good of a game coach as there is in getting his team ready to play."
COACH TUBBY SMITH

"This is their national championship game."
UK's SCOTT PADGETT

PROBABLE STARTERS

Louisville

POS.	PLAYER	HT.	WT.	CLS.	PT/G
F	TONY WILLIAMS	6-7	205	JR.	10.3
F	NATE JOHNSON	6-6	215	JR.	12.0
F/C	ALEX SANDERS	6-7	255	SR.	13.7
G	MARQUES MAYBIN	6-3	185	SO.	10.7
G	CAMERON MURRAY	6-0	175	SR.	15.3

Kentucky

POS.	PLAYER	HT.	WT.	CLS.	PT/G
F	SCOTT PADGETT	6-9	240	SR.	11.9
F	HESHIMU EVANS	6-6	215	SR.	14.7
C	MIKE BRADLEY	6-10	235	SO.	11.8
G	WAYNE TURNER	6-2	190	SR.	11.2
G	TAYSHAUN PRINCE	6-8	206	FR.	6.8

"This UofL upset of Wildcats based on solid play, not fluke"
Louisville Courier-Journal

"Cardinals repeat as state champs"
Lexington Herald Leader

There were eleven lead changes in the first half, but the Cards took the lead for good at 30-28 on a Tony Williams lay up with 5:51 before intermission.

With 12:08 to go in the second half, Jamaal Magloire was fouled by UofL's Nate Johnson, followed by the first of their two brief game skirmishes. Each were charged technical fouls and Magloire, hit one of the two free throws he drew from Sander's personal.

UK had cut the deficit to four on that foul shot, 56-52, but that was as close as they could get. Marques Maybin's lay up at the 4:57 mark put the Cards out of reach, 75-60.

Louisville had managed to pull away in the second half, even though at one time they had missed twelve consecutive shots over an almost eight-minute-span, and failed to score a field goal in the final 4:56 of the game. In the closing seconds, Nate Johnson tried to add an exclamation point to the victory with a dunk, when Jamaal Magloire intervened, preventing Johnson from scoring. Johnson immediately protested telling him it was a dirty play. Magloire responded with a shove. The score remained unchanged.

UofL 83-UK 74. Back-to-back is no fluke.

Like last year, the Cards won the battle in three-point territory making 12 of 22 compared to UK's five of 23. Overall UofL shot 52.1 percent to Kentucky's 46.9 percent. They also won the free throw shooting contest, making 27 of 36 for 75 percent, compared to UK's 12 of 20 for 60 percent.

And the point-guard play, Coach Smith's key to the game, favored UofL's Cameron Murray.

When I had my talk show, I used a scoring system I developed after reading an old article about Coach Rupp's tracking system. It is very similar to systems used to gauge the real effectiveness of NBA players. It's quite simple too. Add up the total of points, rebounds, assists, steals and blocks, subtracting missed field-goals, free throws and turnovers. Most fans look at scoring after a game to see how their favorite player performed. In this game Murray scored 14, Turner 11 and that's close. But adjust their stats according to my system and Murray wins 20 to seven. UofL won 83-74.

STATS

Louisville

Player	Min	FG	FG A	3PT FG	3 PT FGA	FT	FT A	Reb	PF	Ast	St	BS	TO	Pts
Tony Williams	36	5	7	3	4	1	3	4	2	4	2	0	5	14
Nate Johnson	23	3	8	0	1	3	5	2	4	0	2	0	0	9
Alex Sanders	30	1	3	0	1	3	4	9	2	2	0	0	4	5
Marques Maybin	26	5	9	2	4	7	9	3	3	2	1	0	4	19
Dion Edwards	8	4	5	0	0	0	0	2	4	0	0	0	0	8
Eric Johnson	17	3	6	1	3	1	2	7	3	0	0	0	1	8
Kevin Smiley	2	0	1	0	1	0	0	0	1	0	0	0	0	0
Tobiah Hopper	17	2	3	0	0	2	2	2	2	0	1	1	3	6

Player	Min	FG	FG A	3PT FG	3 PT FGA	FT	FT A	Reb	PF	Ast	St	BS	TO	Pts
Jeff McKinley	5	0	0	0	0	0	0	0	0	0	0	0	0	0
Cameron Murray	36	2	6	0	3	10	11	3	0	10	1	0	3	14
Team								1						
Totals	200	25	48	6	17	27	36	33	21	18	7	1	20	83

Kentucky

Player	Min	FG	FG A	3PT FG	3 PT FGA	FT	FT A	Reb	PF	Ast	St	BS	TO	Pts
Heshimu Evans	27	3	7	0	3	2	2	4	4	1	2	0	4	8
Scott Padgett	37	6	11	0	3	1	1	5	4	2	4	0	2	13
Michael Bradley	23	6	11	0	0	0	3	7	2	0	0	0	1	12
Wayne Turner	26	5	12	0	1	1	2	4	4	4	2	0	6	11
Tayshaun Prince	18	2	4	1	3	0	0	1	1	1	0	0	1	5
Saul Smith	27	1	3	0	0	3	4	4	4	4	3	1	3	5
Ryan Hogan	19	3	11	1	5	4	5	3	2	1	1	0	1	11
Jamaal Magloire	19	4	5	0	0	1	3	3	3	1	1	1	0	9
Souleymane Camara	2	0	0	0	0	0	0	0	0	1	0	0	0	0
Desmond Allison	2	0	0	0	0	0	0	0	2	0	0	0	0	0
Team								3						
Totals	200	30	64	2	15	12	20	34	26	15	13	2	18	74

POINTS AFTER

"I was glad that I was able to do what I could against the best point guard in the nation. It felt good to go out there and just be on the same floor with him."
CAMERON MURRAY

"It was unnecessary, the game was over. I just told him it was a dirty play."
NATE JOHNSON (on the shove from Magloire)

UK's players did not meet with the press for post-game interviews.

GAME 31

December 18, 1999

	UK	UofL
Record	4-4	5-2
Ranking	unranked	unranked
Series	20	10
Favored	KENTUCKY BY 6	
Location	RUPP ARENA	
TV	CBS	

PRE-GAME REPORT

Borrowing a line from our founding fathers: "We hold these truths to be self-evident," (1) that you can't go into Rupp Arena even though you have three senior starters, in the "Dream Game" with a freshman point-guard and two other first-year guards and expect to win, (2) that UK has never lost more than two consecutive games in the history of the series, and a loss today would be number-three, (3) that sometimes desperation can be the best inspiration, perhaps prompting Coach Tubby Smith to make a change in his starting lineup 10 minutes before the game started, (4) Cat fans were beyond tired, miles and miles beyond fed-up with a current 4-4 record, and two consecutive losses to the Cardinals, and (5) UofL had a better record, 5-2 but they hadn't played anybody in the Top 25 and Jeff Sagarin rated their schedule No. 204 in the nation. However, the Cardinals had forced an average of 24.6 turnovers a game, scoring 35 percent of their points off those miscues.

They're averaging 84.3 points a game which places them ninth in scoring nationally. While UK is averaging only 66 points a game, their worst scoring performance since the 1983-84 season's 65.7.

QUOTES

"Adversity isn't really fun. But it really tests your character."
UK POINT GUARD SAUL SMITH

"They're going to be mad when we're losing because they care so much about it. Basketball means so much to people in this state. I'm like, that's just the nature of Kentucky basketball. That's why they're the greatest fans. Because they care so much.
UK GUARD J.P. BLEVINS

"Any team doesn't want to just keep losing, and they've lost a couple in a row, so they're probably looking at this as the turnaround game. They'll probably come out extra hard at us, especially because it's Louisville-Kentucky."
UofL CENTER DION EDWARD

"We're going to have to get after the shooters, but most important, we're going to have to rebound. I don't worry about the rebounding because I know the guys on my team, we all have big hearts. We see an obstacle like that, somehow it always happens where somebody steps up and does a little bit more than what usually happens. Maybe it will be me, maybe it'll be somebody else, but usually somebody steps up.
UofL FORWARD TONY WILLIAMS

PROBABLE STARTERS

Kentucky

POS.	PLAYER	HT.	WT.	CLS.	PT/G
F	TAYSHAUN PRINCE	6-9	215	SO.	13.2
F	JULES CAMARA	6-11	223	SO.	8.2
C	JAMAAL MAGLOIRE	6-10	260	SR.	10.2
G	SAUL SMITH	6-2	175	JR.	8.1
G/F	DESMOND ALLISON	6-5	214	SO.	6.9

Louisville

POS.	PLAYER	HT.	WT.	CLS.	PT/G
F	NATE JOHNSON	6-6	215	SR.	16.9
F	TONY WILLIAMS	6-7	210	SR.	18.9
C	DION EDWARD	6-9	235	SR.	6.6
G	MARQUES MAYBIN	6-3	185	JR.	15.3
G	REECE GAINES	6-6	185	FR.	6.4

"Ville-ified no more: Cats romp 76-46"
Lexington Herald-Leader

"Cats cut Cards in half"
Louisville Courier-Journal

The Cats 76-46 victory over the Cards, gave them reason to enjoy some r& r and r's; romp, rebirth, restitution, regeneration, renewal, rejuvenation, resuscitation, revitalization, revivification, recovery, recuperation, restoration and renaissance, just to name a few.

Ten minutes before tip-off, Tubby Smith made a change in his starting line-up, giving McDonald's All-American Keith Bogans his first start in nine games as a Wildcat.

With Bogans starting in place of forward Jules Camara, Tayshaun Prince was able to move from small forward to power forward and Desmond Allison from two guard to small forward. Coach Smith explained the reason for the change this way: "We went with a smaller lineup today to get better ball-handling and because I knew it would create some matchup problems for them because of our quickness."

It did energize the Cats, but the full benefits of the move would not be evidenced until the second half. Prince however, played like a king for UK in the first half, scoring 12 of his 20 game-high points. He was averaging just over 13 points a game while playing the small forward position.

Desmond Allison scored seven of his career-high 16 points in the first half, he was averaging just over six points per game at the two guard, but Kentucky led by only one, 35-34 at the intermission.

Then, the Cardinals did the unimaginable. They made only one of their first 22 shots to start the second half. It didn't get a whole lot better, making just two more, they shot only 11.1 percent for the half, and 29.8 percent for the game. They averaged 47.2 percent from the field entering the contest.

Louisville was averaging about two less rebounds per game against their previous seven opponents, prompting Coach Crum to say, "Rebounding concerns me every game, every single game."

The Cats mauled the Cardinals on the glass, 41-24. Magloire led the way with 10, followed by Prince's seven, Saul Smith with six and freshman big-man Marvin Stone's five. Tony William's seven led the Cards.

UK shot a season high 59.6 percent from the field, with Bogans, Allison and Prince beating the Cardinal defenders off the dribble. "That's pretty much my game," said Bogans. "When I could, I turned the corner on them. If I had it, I took it. If they came to me, I passed it out to Tay or Dez for the three."

STATS

Kentucky

Player	Min	FG	FG A	3PT FG	3 PT FGA	FT	FT A	Reb	PF	Ast	St	BS	TO	Pts
Tayshaun Prince	35	8	13	3	5	1	2	7	2	2	1	5	0	20
Desmond Allison	32	6	9	2	3	2	4	3	2	4	2	0	2	16
Jamaal Magloire	30	5	8	0	0	2	2	10	1	1	0	3	3	12
Saul Smith	29	2	5	0	2	0	0	6	3	1	2	0	2	4
Keith Bogans	30	5	6	2	2	0	2	2	2	4	2	0	4	12
J.P. Blevins	8	0	0	0	0	0	0	0	0	0	0	0	0	0
Steve Masiello	3	0	0	0	0	0	0	0	0	0	0	0	1	0
Nate Knight	3	1	3	0	0	0	0	2	0	0	0	0	0	2
Todd Tackett	7	0	1	0	1	0	0	1	0	1	1	0	0	0

Player	Min	FG	FG A	3PT FG	3 PT FGA	FT	FT A	Reb	PF	Ast	St	BS	TO	Pts
Marvin Stone	12	2	4	0	0	0	0	5	3	1	1	1	3	4
Souleymane Camara	11	2	3	0	1	2	2	1	1	0	0	0	1	6
Team								4						
Totals	**200**	**31**	**52**	**7**	**14**	**7**	**12**	**41**	**14**	**14**	**9**	**9**	**16**	**76**

Louisville

Player	Min	FG	FG A	3PT FG	3 PT FGA	FT	FT A	Reb	PF	Ast	St	BS	TO	Pts
Tony Williams	33	4	12	3	7	1	1	7	2	2	0	0	2	12
Nate Johnson	32	4	11	1	2	2	2	5	1	0	0	0	3	11
Dion Edward	26	2	4	0	0	0	0	4	5	0	0	0	1	4
Reece Gaines	31	3	8	0	3	1	1	2	1	0	2	0	4	7
Marques Maybin	31	3	13	1	6	2	2	1	0	2	1	0	2	9
Rashad Brooks	1	0	1	0	1	0	0	0	0	0	0	0	0	0
Hajj Turner	2	0	1	0	0	0	0	1	1	0	0	0	0	0
Quintin Bailey	12	1	3	0	1	0	0	0	2	0	1	0	0	2
Caleb Gervin	11	0	1	0	1	1	2	1	1	0	0	0	1	1
Kevin Smiley	9	0	2	0	1	0	0	0	0	0	0	0	0	0
Tobiah Hopper	12	0	1	0	0	0	0	0	1	0	0	1	1	0
Team								3					1	
Totals	**200**	**17**	**57**	**5**	**22**	**7**	**8**	**24**	**14**	**4**	**4**	**1**	**15**	**46**

POINTS AFTER

"The vision that brought me here was the way we played tonight. It was up-tempo, up and down, just a fast paced game, and that's the way I like to play."
KENTUCKY GUARD KEITH BOGANS

"I know how it is. But the one thing that I heard that I really didn't like is that this team didn't have any Kentucky pride. That they didn't know what it meant to have Kentucky across their shirts. I

told the guys, let's go out there and show them what Kentucky pride's all about, and I think that's what showed on the floor out there today.
KENTUCKY GUARD J.P. BLEVINS

"For some reason, we were in a defensive fog. I'm not sure exactly why our strong side defense was what Abe Lemons used to call the sieve defense. I think that's what it was. We just let them do what they wanted to do."
COACH DENNY CRUM

"When you come down and get easy shots and you're not knocking them down. That's going to take the air out of you on the defensive end."
LOUISVILLE GUARD MARGUES MAYBIN

GAME 32

January 2, 2001

	UofL	UK
Record	4-8	5-5
Ranking	unranked	unranked
Series	10	21
Favored	KENTUCKY BY 8	
Location	FREEDOM HALL	
TV	ESPN 2	

PRE-GAME REPORT

The rivalry was suffering some slippage in superlatives for "Game Day" action. Both teams were unranked, neither had a winning record and CBS had passed national coverage to ESPN 2. But, because it's UK vs. UofL, the game's competitiveness, intensity and entertainment value, remained undiminished, atop college basketball's leader board.

After UK had lost at Michigan State 46-45, Spartan Coach Tom Izzo said, "UK is the best 3-5 team in the history of college basketball." The Cats were trying to build on that compliment, having beaten Indiana 88-74 at Freedom Hall and High Point at home 102-49.

Many of the Wildcats over the years had expressed preference for the "softer" rims in Freedom Hall vs. Rupp Arena. Bogans and Prince had joined the crowd: "Softer" than Rupp." Prince said, "A lot softer. At Rupp, you get a bounce on the rim, it's not going in. The key is to get a shooter's roll. It's hard to get a shooter's roll at Rupp."

Prince and Bogans had made more than 50 percent of their shots in Freedom Hall. Back, just eleven days before, they torched Indiana there. Bogans shot 69.2 percent on nine of 13 from the field, and was three of four from beyond the arc for 75 per cent. Prince was nine of 11 for 81.8 percent, and two of three for 66.7 percent.

Even the rims don't miss rivalry attention. In the early part of the 1992-93 season, I was headed to Lexington for a press conference and practice session that day. I had been asked by my former boss Charlie Jenkins, of WXVW-Radio in Jeffersonville, IN., to have both Denny Crum and Rick Pitino sign a basketball for his Rotary auction. He was retrieving one from Bobby Knight.

As Coach Pitino was signing, I mentioned to him that this basketball was headed to southern Indiana for a Rotary auction against coaches Knight and Crum. Coach Pitino replied, "Like I'm going to beat Bobby Knight at an auction in Indiana!" He did.

As a member of the UK Broadcast Network at that time, co-hosting the post-game talk show with current UK radio play-by-play man Tom Leach, I could go to practices. As I was walking through the back parking lot at Rupp Arena, Coach Pitino drove past me and parked his car. He got out and waited for me to catch up. We walked in to Rupp Arena together discussing different subjects. I mentioned to him that the fans were pretty excited about getting big man, Rodney Dent. I followed that by telling him that the only problem that I saw with Dent, a transfer who had been injured, was that he had been out of action so long that the only people who remember seeing him play are now on Medicare. The coach responded with a chuckle as we went through the door.

I had been asked by the folks at Shively Sporting Goods, who handled the rims that were used at Freedom Hall, to see if I could persuade UK equipment manager Bill Keightley to start using them in Rupp, since the Cats seemed to like them so well when they came to Louisville to play.

Coach Pitino came over and joined our conversation. Bill said that the SEC had some regulation about equipment and would not let him install those rims in Rupp. Coach Pitino said, "Bill! You do whatever you want."

I didn't make a sale that day, but after practice, Coach Pitino came to where I was sitting and asked, "Well, what do you think?" I'm sure what I said helped him make it to the Final Four that year. I was so impressed by how courteous Coach Pitino was to me that day.

Back in Louisville the Cardinals seemed to be tottering on the edge of seasonal oblivion. They had just lost back-to-back games at home by 23 points each to Dayton and Oregon, and were 4-8 overall. Not to mention, in-house bickering between coaches and players. On Sunday, just two days before the UK game, coaches and players met for a seven-hour session that included game film, and plenty of healing conversation; landing the team on the same page for Tuesday night's battle with the Cats.

QUOTES

"If we don't play any better than we have, we don't have much chance at all of beating a team with Kentucky's ability. But sometimes, rival games make kids step up and maybe play harder, play better and concentrate more. You can never predict what will happen."
UofL COACH DENNY CRUM

"If you go according to the way we have played this season, we're going to get dragged by 30. But every game provides us a new opportunity to turn this around. We still really don't doubt our team or our talent. Everybody knows they're talented. They just don't know how to fit-in. If we play like we haven't played all year, we can beat (UK). It's really more about us. It really boils down to just executing and being focused for a whole game, and we haven't done that yet."
UofL FORWARD HAJJ TURNER

"It's a very intense game. It's very competitive. Last year's game was very close in the first half. It's a matter of who can seize the momentum and who can establish the tempo and who can gain the confidence as the game goes along."
UK COACH TUBBY SMITH

"I'm looking forward to it. It's a big game and I like big games. It makes you play harder."
UK FORWARD JASON PARKER

PROBABLE STARTERS

Louisville

POS.	PLAYER	HT.	WT.	CLS.	PT/G
F	ELLIS MYLES	6-8	250	FR.	8.0
G/F	ERIK BROWN	6-5	210	SO.	11.0
C	MUHAMMED LASEGE	6-11	220	FR.	5.0

POS.	PLAYER	HT.	WT.	CLS.	PT/G
G	MARQUES MAYBIN	6-3	185	SR.	20.1
G	REECE GAINES	6-6	195	SO.	14.3

Kentucky

POS.	PLAYER	HT.	WT.	CLS.	PT/G
G/F	GERALD FITCH	6-3	185	FR.	3.5
F	TAYSHAUN PRINCE	6-9	215	JR.	13.7
C	JASON PARKER	6-8	255	FR.	8.7
G	KEITH BOGANS	6-5	205	SO.	17.4
G	SAUL SMITH	6-2	175	SR.	8.2

"UK brings momentum into game vs. UofL"
Lexington Herald-Leader

"Big Blue wins - but not big"
Louisville Courier-Journal

Louisville came out hot, hitting its first six shots, including two three-pointers on the way a 14-4 lead.

Then, the Cats began to claw back. UofL missed seven of its next eight and UK managed to take a 29-27 halftime lead. The Wildcats scored the first eight points of the second half, increasing the margin at one time to a 12-point bulge. But there was no quit in the Cards. They held UK to just four points in the final 4:21 of play.

Cardinal sophomore Reece Gaines who scored a game-high 27 points, connected on consecutive three-pointers late in the game, knotting the score at 62-62 with 58 seconds remaining. UofL smothered the Cats defensively and had the shot clock down to just two seconds, when Luke Whitehead fouled Tayshaun Prince some twenty-five feet from the basket. Prince hit both free throws and the Cats were on top 64-62 with just 26.5 seconds left.

Coach Crum called a timeout with 21 seconds to go. The play called for Gaines to come off a screen set by Joseph N'Sima, which he did, but Erik Brown slipped before he could make the pass, and in the confusion Brown took a three-point shot that bounced hard off the backboard into a crowd of players and rolled out of bounds with 2.1 seconds remaining.

The officials were unable to determine who knocked the ball out of bounds, but the possession arrow was pointing in the Cards favor, giving them one more chance to make something good happen.

Out of timeouts, Ellis Myles floated a pass inbounds intended for Gaines, but it sailed over his head, and the Cats took possession of the ball, giving the Cardinals no chance to tie the game. Final score, UK 64 UofL 62.

STATS

Louisville

Player	Min	FG	FG A	3PT FG	3 PT FGA	FT	FT A	Reb	PF	Ast	St	BS	TO	Pts
Ellis Myles	23	4	5	0	0	0	1	3	3	1	0	0	3	8
Erik Brown	29	3	13	1	6	0	0	3	2	2	4	0	0	7
Muhamed Lasege	8	0	2	0	0	0	0	0	3	0	0	1	0	0
Marques Maybin	38	3	5	1	2	2	2	3	1	2	0	0	2	9
Reece Gaines	32	10	14	5	8	2	2	8	3	4	0	1	1	27
Hajj Turner	7	0	1	0	0	0	0	1	0	0	0	0	1	0
Joseph N'Sima	30	1	3	0	0	0	2	7	2	1	0	3	0	2
Luke Whitehead	21	3	7	0	0	0	0	3	1	2	0	0	1	6
Rashad Brooks	10	1	1	1	1	0	0	2	1	0	0	0	3	3
Simeon Naydenov	1	0	1	0	1	0	0	0	0	0	0	0	0	0
Bryant Northern	1	0	1	0	1	0	0	0	0	0	0	0	0	0
Team								2						
Totals	**200**	**25**	**53**	**8**	**19**	**4**	**7**	**32**	**16**	**12**	**4**	**5**	**11**	**62**

Kentucky

Player	Min	FG	FG A	3PT FG	3 PT FGA	FT	FT A	Reb	PF	Ast	St	BS	TO	Pts
Gerald Fitch	23	2	4	0	1	2	2	2	2	1	1	0	2	6
Tayshaun Prince	40	5	13	1	5	2	2	8	0	6	2	1	1	13
Jason Parker	21	5	7	0	0	1	1	3	3	1	0	0	0	11
Keith Bogans	36	6	15	3	6	1	1	5	2	2	0	0	2	16
Saul Smith	37	2	5	2	5	0	1	1	2	4	1	0	0	6

Player	Min	FG	FG A	3PT FG	3 PT FGA	FT	FT A	Reb	PF	Ast	St	BS	TO	Pts
Marvin Stone	25	5	7	0	0	1	2	6	3	0	0	1	2	11
Erik Daniels	5	0	0	0	0	0	0	0	0	0	0	1	0	0
J.P. Blevins	7	0	1	0	1	0	0	0	0	2	0	0	0	0
Marquis Estill	5	0	0	0	0	1	2	1	1	0	0	1	0	1
Cliff Hawkins	1	0	0	0	0	0	0	0	0	0	0	0	0	0
Team								1						
Totals	**200**	**25**	**52**	**6**	**18**	**8**	**11**	**27**	**13**	**16**	**4**	**4**	**7**	**64**

POINTS AFTER

"I was as proud of this team as any team I've ever coached. To come from where they have been to the level we played today, I've never had a team make that big a turnaround."
UofL COACH DENNY CRUM

"I should have went in harder and then come out. I wanted Ellis to just lob it, but I didn't get close enough for him to make a good pass.
UofL GUARD REECE GAINES

"We played as hard as we could, and I thought they did too. They just kept making big shots, and we didn't do a good job of putting the game away. But a lot of that was Louisville. They kept us off balance, but I thought we did a good job of handling a hostile arena and their gallant comeback."
UK COACH TUBBY SMITH

"This was a step forward for us. We've been on the losing end of enough close games. I think it was important to finally pull one out. We knew this was going to be tough. Louisville is a team with its back to the wall, but we took their shots and came away with the win."
UK GUARD SAUL SMITH

Again, showing what the rivalry brings out of these teams, UofL finished 12-19 after losing the first game in the Conference-USA Tournament.

It would also bring to a close Coach Denny Crum's Hall of Fame thirty-years of work at the University of Louisville. He had taken heat from the press, especially from Billy Reed. Reed was quick to praise him when Crum had beaten UK during Tubby's first season there. But, now after two losses to Coach Smith, Billy was calling for Crum to retire.

In retrospect, it was probably time for Coach Crum to step down, but he was the same coach and man, whether he won a game or lost. What did he remember when he won or forget, when he lost?

One must be careful when responding to environmental stimuli, like Dizzy Dean used to do with Pee Wee Reece when broadcasting the "Game of the Week."

The Yankees had been purchased by CBS and Diz and Pee Wee were broadcasting a Yankees' game. Whitey Ford was a great pitcher. He had been on the DL list due to an injury and now, had returned to the mound for this TV game. Ford looked like his old-self early in the contest. He was mowing down the opposing batters and Dizzy said to Pee Wee something like this, "Pardna, isn't Ford great? He's been out for so long because of injury and it appears like he's never missed a game."

Next inning, Ford can't get the batboy out and Yankees' manager, Ralph Houk removes him from the game. Dizzy's comment, "Well Pardna, you got to realize Whitey's been injured, it's not his fault."

You can't have it both ways.

In talking with Billy Reed about this he said, "I really liked Denny and wanted him to win."

GAME 33

December 29, 2001

	UK	UofL
Record	7-2	9-1
Ranking	#6	unranked
Series	22	10
Favored	KENTUCKY BY 8	
Location	RUPP ARENA	
TV	CBS	

PRE-GAME REPORT

Tickets were hard to come by, and they could cost plenty, but if you got one, you got two games in one. Brian Bennett of the *Courier-Journal* reported that tickets were going for $275 for one upper level seat to $1250 for one lower level seat from one ticket source. A seller on EBAY offered upper level seats for $300 apiece.

Kevin Hacker, president of a ticket company based in Cincinnati said, "This is the hottest ticket I have seen in a long, long, time. It's always one of the biggest games of the year, but with Pitino coming back, it's on a whole other level."

Even the students, staying in line until 3:00 am, took all of their 3500 tickets, leaving none for sale to the public. UK basketball spokesman Brooks Downing confirmed, "That was the most people we have ever had show up for a distribution."

QUOTES

"If they can just remember what this program was like when he came here in '89, then their appreciation for what he did would be magnified 110 percent."
FORMER UK AD C.M. NEWTON

"And I do think people do remember that, and I remember him for that. It's well-documented: Rick is a great coach and a good person."
UK COACH TUBBY SMITH

"This will probably be the biggest regular season event in college basketball, simply because of the unique status of Rick's situation. I don't think anything this season will have quite the same electricity, other than the Final Four. It's a must-see in my mind."
CBS ANALYST CLARK KELLOGG

"The way I look at it, Kentucky was great to me for eight years every time I walked on that floor. As the Louisville coach, it shouldn't matter how you're received because I'm not the Kentucky coach anymore. I'm the Louisville coach. So that's really insignificant and irrelevant personally or professionally in my life.

UofL COACH RICK PITINO

PROBABLE STARTERS

Kentucky

POS.	PLAYER	HT.	WT.	CLS.	PT/G
F	KEITH BOGANS	6-5	205	JR.	13.3
F	TAYSHAUN PRINCE	6-9	215	SR.	18.3
C	JULES CAMARA	6-11	225	JR.	3.8
G	GERALD FITCH	6-3	188	SO.	6.8
G	CLIFF HAWKINS	6-1	190	SO.	8.4

Louisville

POS.	PLAYER	HT.	WT.	CLS.	PT/G
F	ELLIS MYLES	6-8	230	SO.	11.3
F	JOSEPH N'SIMA	6-8	230	SR.	3.5
C	ERIK BROWN	6-5	210	JR.	10.5
G	REECE GAINES	6-6	195	JR.	20.0
G	CARLOS HURT	6-1	180	FR.	7.2

The first game with Rick in red was simple basketball, X's ands O's, three-pointers, slam dunks and etc.

UofL's leading scorer, Reece Gaines picked up two early fouls in the first half, scoring only two points in just 11 minutes of play. However, UK didn't capitalize on the situation, shooting just 37 percent, and were out rebounded 24-20, leading by only four at the half, 36-32.

Gaines picked up his third foul 17 seconds into the second half, but when Cardinal freshman Carlos Hurt nailed a three-pointer, the Cards trailed by one, 38-37. "I hit a three to bring us within one, then it seemed like 30 seconds later it was 47-37, Hurt lamented. That just shows you what kind of a great team they have. They can put a lot of points up on you in a hurry." That's when UK went to work. Prince and Bogans scoring 17 of Kentucky's next 18 points, and with a dozen minutes remaining, the Cats led 54-39.

Louisville never got closer in the game than 13, losing 82-62.

STATS

Kentucky

Player	Min	FG	FG A	3PT FG	3 PT FGA	FT	FT A	Reb	PF	Ast	St	BS	TO	Pts
Tayshaun Prince	31	8	16	1	2	1	3	9	2	3	0	1	1	18
Souleymane Camara	18	1	3	0	0	0	0	2	0	2	1	2	2	2
Cliff Hawkins	30	1	7	0	3	6	8	5	2	5	2	0	6	8
Gerald Fitch	27	3	9	1	6	3	3	5	2	0	0	0	0	10
Keith Bogans	28	7	12	2	6	1	1	7	1	2	1	0	2	17
Rashaad Carruth	13	3	5	2	3	0	0	0	3	0	0	0	0	8
Josh Carrier	2	0	1	0	1	0	0	0	0	0	0	0	0	0
Erik Daniels	14	1	5	0	2	1	2	2	1	1	0	1	0	3
Adam Chiles	8	0	2	0	2	0	0	1	2	4	0	0	2	0
Chuck Hayes	9	2	4	0	0	1	2	3	1	0	1	0	1	5
Marquis Estill	17	5	5	0	0	0	0	5	1	0	0	1	0	10
Matt Heissenbuttel	2	0	1	0	0	1	2	1	0	0	0	0	0	1
Cory Sears	2	0	0	0	0	0	0	0	1	0	0	0	0	0
Team								6						
Totals	**200**	**31**	**70**	**6**	**25**	**14**	**21**	**46**	**16**	**17**	**5**	**5**	**14**	**82**

Louisville

Player	Min	FG	FG A	3PT FG	3 PT FGA	FT	FT A	Reb	PF	Ast	St	BS	TO	Pts
Ellis Myles	23	1	5	0	0	0	2	5	1	0	1	0	3	2
Erik Brown	32	4	10	0	1	1	2	9	3	2	0	0	2	9
Joseph N'Sima	26	4	6	0	0	0	0	7	0	0	0	5	1	8
Carlos Hurt	23	4	11	1	5	1	1	2	4	2	0	0	6	10

Player	Min	FG	FG A	3PT FG	3 PT FGA	FT	FT A	Reb	PF	Ast	St	BS	TO	Pts
Reece Gaines	29	4	10	1	4	1	4	2	5	2	0	1	0	10
Bryant Northern	18	3	10	2	9	2	2	3	2	1	0	0	1	10
Brandon Bender	12	2	3	0	0	0	0	4	0	0	3	1	0	4
Simeon Naydenov	5	1	1	0	0	0	0	0	2	0	1	0	0	2
Luke Whitehead	14	2	9	0	0	0	0	2	4	0	1	0	1	4
Larry O'Bannon	15	0	4	0	0	2	2	3	2	0	0	0	0	2
Otis George	3	0	0	0	0	1	2	1	0	0	0	0	0	1
Team								3						
Totals	**200**	**25**	**69**	**4**	**19**	**8**	**15**	**41**	**23**	**7**	**6**	**7**	**14**	**62**

POINTS AFTER

"He told us we were being out hustled and out rebounded and out worked in all aspects of the game. He didn't lose his composure, but he got on us. He knows what it takes to get us to come out and play hard, and that's what we did."
UK GUARD ADAM CHILES on Coach Smith's Halftime Speech

"The first half was real frustrating because we knew we could do better. The second half we got our groove on and got our spread (offense) working, and after that it was fun."
UK GUARD CLIFF HAWKINS

"We were wide open all night; we just couldn't put the ball in the hole. It was really hard, because our best player was in foul trouble and we were looking for somebody to go to, so everybody tried to step up, and we messed up by trying to do too much."
UofL GUARD CARLOS HURT

"I wouldn't say they shut me down or that I didn't do anything. I created for my teammates and gave them open shots. They just didn't knock them down."
UofL GUARD REECE GAINES

"Now the second game, the game inside the game, requires a refined scrutiny to determine the winners and losers. The return of Rick Pitino has benefited the rivalry immensely. He's one of the best coaches in college basketball. Notice I didn't say the pros." Coach Scott Davenport, current head coach at Bellarmine University, sees things from a unique position, having served as both an assistant to Denny Crum and Rick Pitino.

After one of the first practice sessions with Coach Pitino, as they were walking up the stairs to the basketball office, Coach Davenport asked if he could share something with him and Coach Pitino said, "Feel free to share anything you want with me, anytime." Davenport replied, "Coach. This is where you belong." Scotty didn't mean the University of Louisville in particular, but in college, coaching college basketball.

No matter what you think about Rick Pitino ending up at Louisville, the UK-UofL rivalry is a winner. And the rivalry is No. 1. Had Pitino taken the Michigan job, there would have been a few boos, but Michigan is not Louisville as we saw in the 2013 Final Four. That day in December of 2001, when Pitino returned to Rupp Arena as the coach of the Cardinals, fans had a full-blown chance to vent their mixed emotions.

I love this particular definition of mixed emotions; watching your mother-in-law go over a cliff in your new Cadillac! But the vast majority of fans that day weren't mixed up at all, they knew exactly what they wanted to do—boo Pitino! They had been waiting for some nine months since Rick Pitino was named the UofL coach, to let-off the biggest exhale in "Big Boo" history.

It really started some 18 minutes before tip-off when the crowd started chanting: "Tub-Bee! Tub-Bee! Tub-Bee!" It echoed off and on throughout the game as the Cats built a 28 point second half lead, and reached a crescendo with the final score of UK 82-UofL 62.

Tayshaun Prince responded, "It was overdo, it's never been like that in here before. Coach deserves it." At least for that day Tubby Smith was a winner in more ways than just the score. The ostentatious display by the home crowd, demonstrated they preferred the current coach over the former and Tubby was grateful, "It was great. It makes you feel good to be wanted."

I believe Rick Pitino was a winner and a loser that day. He had to know that this first appearance would be the worst as far as crowd control. He took it and got out. Sure his team lost the game, but they would play it in Louisville next season.

The Cat fans were winners and losers. All the UK fans celebrated the victory. There were those who applauded Coach Pitino, remembering what he done for the University of Kentucky. Kudos!

Booing is something coaches live with. But for those few who made disparaging remarks about Coach Pitino's family—losers. Coach Rupp gave this advice on criticism, "Write or say anything you want about me, but leave my family out of it."

Discussing the lows for sportsmanship in the series, Coach Davenport and I quickly gravitated to the coin thrown from the stands that struck Coach Crum in the head during the March 22, 1984 contest in Rupp Arena. Then, Scotty quickly reversed himself and said, "No, the coin toss was something that occurred in the heat of the game, but those thoughts expressed towards Joanne Pitino, were mean and premediated."

I believe there were only a few fans who allowed their Mr. Hyde persona to take over. Let's say, there were 30 such characters. The Rupp crowd that day was 24,330, so mathematically that represented only 0.001233% of the people in attendance that day who participated in such demeaning behavior.

The Louisville fans were winners and losers that day. Sure they lost the game, but they were anticipating the time when Coach Pitino would return them to their "glory days" of the 1980s.

One more winner that day was the UK Tradition, as the court at Rupp Arena was re-named in honor of the late legendary UK sports broadcaster Cawood Ledford.

GAME 34

December 28, 2002

	UofL	UK
Record	6-1	6-2
Ranking	unranked	#14
Series	10	23
Favored	LOUISVILLE BY 2.5	
Location	FREEDOM HALL	
TV	ESPN	

PRE-GAME REPORT

A little Bob Dylan please, "Don't Think Twice, It's Alright." UK Coach Tubby Smith arrived at Freedom Hall with three consecutive wins over the Cardinals. That translated; UK star senior Keith Bogans was 3-0, and UofL star senior Reece Gaines was 0-3. But, "The Fourth Time Around," "The Times They Are a-Changin."

One reason was "Like A Rolling Stone," Marvin Stone to be exact. Stone had transferred from the University of Kentucky, where he wasn't really happy, just kinda, "Blowin' in the Wind." Some of this could easily be attributed to losing his father and a sister in the previous two years.

Now, in Louisville "Things have Changed" as Marvin's mother Lois pointed out: "I love this city, I love the fans, I love Coach Pitino." Marvin was no longer "Tangled Up in Blue." In his first three games as a Cardinal, Stone scored 56 points, compared to 48 in nine games last year at UK, before he transferred.

"It's All Over Now, Baby Blue" if Coach Pitino's pre-game analysis rings true: "Man to man this game matches up very well. They have a little bit deeper bench in terms of experience, but we have a good bench as well. You won't find two better low post players than Marquis Estill and Marvin Stone, and you won't find two better guards than Reece Gaines and Keith Bogans. You've got guys who work on the glass; Ellis Myles and Chuck Hayes. They're a little more experienced than we are and probably a little bit better at this point in the season than we are. The 'but' part is we're at home."

QUOTES

Bumping into each other in the pre-game warmups.

Bogans: "You ready to play?"

Stone: "Yeah."

Bogans: "Let's go to war, then."

Some two hours later, the identity of the "Masters of War" would be revealed.

Reece Gaines hugging Marvin Stone while Myles looks on

PROBABLE STARTERS

Louisville

POS.	PLAYER	HT.	WT.	CLS.	PT/G
F	ELLIS MYLES	6-8	235	JR.	8.6
F	ERIK BROWN	6-5	210	SR.	4.2
C	MARVIN STONE	6-10	240	SR.	20.0
G	FRANCISCO GARCIA	6-7	175	FR.	10.0
G	REECE GAINES	6-3	205	SR.	19.6

Kentucky

POS.	PLAYER	HT.	WT.	CLS.	PT/G
F	ERIK DANIELS	6-8	214	JR.	9.0
F	CHUCK HAYES	6-6	237	SO.	11.0
C	MARQUIS ESTILL	6-9	236	SR.	6.0
G	GERALD FITCH	6-3	188	JR.	5.0
G	KEITH BOGANS	6-5	213	SR.	14.0

"Card's future is now"
Louisville Courier-Journal

"CARDS STONE UK"
Lexington-Herald Leader

When Marquis Estill, "Lay, Lady, Lay" made a layup that put UK ahead 6-5, it already marked the fourth lead change of the game in a little less than four minutes of play. Kentucky extended its lead to 11, at 20-9 with just under twelve minutes left in the half. But in this day and age if you don't stop the three, "You Ain't Goin' Nowhere". UK had out rebounded UofL in the first half 24-14, and dominated the inside scoring 20-6, but the Cards closed out the final 3:22 of play by making three, three-point shots and trailed, you guessed it, by three, 33-30 at the half.

This boost of confidence would carry the Cardinals through the final twenty minutes of action. Francisco Garcia drilled a three and tied the score at 33-all. Chuck Hayes gave the Wildcats their final lead, 35-33 on a layup. Then Erik Brown made a three-point basket and UofL was off on an 11-0 run.

Jules Camara's dunk, stopped the bleeding, but Taquan Dean answered right back for the Cards by making a three. With 11:43 to go the lead was 55-42, UofL having made seven of its last 10 three-point baskets. UK, travelled a "Narrow Way," getting as close as 60-53, with 9:07 remaining. But Rick Pitino called a thirty-second timeout, and when play resumed, it would be almost five minutes before the Cats would score again.

There is no "Mr. Tambourine Man" that can help when you hit three of 18 three-point shots for 16.7 percent, and the opponent connects on 10 of 21 for 47.6 percent. "Everybody Must Get Stoned" as Marvin scored a game-high 16 points, adding seven rebounds, two blocks and one assist.

"It's All Good," the excitement at Freedom Hall for Cardinal fans, that "All I Really Wanna Do" was running through the mind of UofL signee Brandon Jenkins, who was sitting near the home bench, "Man it was all l could do not to jump in the game. There is some great energy here. The fans were great, the team was great. I can't wait to be a part of it."

The Cats would suffer temporarily from "Subterranean Homesick Blues," but in the greatest rivalry, you're not down long, because maybe the tournament, and for sure, next year's game, offers a chance to redeem those bragging rights.

STATS

Louisville

Player	Min	FG	FG A	3PT FG	3 PT FGA	FT	FT A	Reb	PF	Ast	St	BS	TO	Pts
Ellis Myles	28	3	7	0	0	5	6	14	3	5	0	0	4	11
Francisco Garcia	28	5	11	2	6	0	0	4	4	1	2	1	2	12
Marvin Stone	30	4	7	0	0	8	12	7	3	1	0	2	3	16
Reece Gaines	29	2	5	2	4	4	4	1	4	4	2	1	2	10
Erik Brown	27	2	5	1	2	4	4	0	1	1	1	0	0	9

UK vs. UofL College Basketball's No. 1 Rivalry - Enough Said!

Player	Min	FG	FG A	3PT FG	3 PT FGA	FT	FT A	Reb	PF	Ast	St	BS	TO	Pts
Kendall Dartez	7	0	1	0	0	0	0	2	0	0	0	0	0	0
Bryant Northern	11	3	4	3	3	0	0	3	2	2	0	0	0	9
Taquan Dean	21	4	10	2	6	0	0	3	2	1	0	0	0	10
Luke Whitehead	15	1	2	0	0	2	2	1	3	1	0	0	1	4
Larry O'Bannon	4	0	0	0	0	0	0	0	0	0	0	0	0	0
Team								3					1	
Totals	**200**	**24**	**52**	**10**	**21**	**23**	**28**	**38**	**22**	**16**	**5**	**4**	**13**	**81**

Kentucky

Player	Min	FG	FG A	3PT FG	3 PT FGA	FT	FT A	Reb	PF	Ast	St	BS	TO	Pts
Erik Daniels	24	4	8	0	0	1	1	7	3	2	1	1	1	9
Chuck Hayes	31	3	7	1	2	4	4	5	1	2	0	0	2	11
Marquis Estill	23	2	2	0	0	2	2	6	5	0	1	2	2	6
Gerald Fitch	23	2	10	1	4	0	0	6	3	1	0	0	4	5
Keith Bogans	34	5	15	1	9	3	6	1	2	4	2	0	2	14
Cliff Hawkins	16	0	1	0	0	2	2	1	4	5	0	0	0	2
Brandon Stockton	3	0	1	0	1	0	1	0	0	0	0	0	0	0
Kelenna Azubuike	6	1	3	0	1	1	2	1	0	0	0	0	0	3
Antwain Barbour	21	2	6	0	1	1	1	1	0	0	0	0	1	5
Souleymane Camara	19	4	9	0	0	0	1	4	2	1	0	0	2	8
Team								4						
Totals	**200**	**23**	**62**	**3**	**18**	**14**	**20**	**36**	**20**	**15**	**4**	**3**	**14**	**63**

POINTS AFTER

"We wanted to win this game real bad because of the way they treated Coach (Rick Pitino) last year in Rupp Arena."
UofL FORWARD ELLIS MYLES

"They weren't in shape to keep up with us when we made our run. They weren't used to going up and down like that."
UofL GUARD REECE GAINES

"We could have played that style. We didn't play with energy."
UK GUARD CLIFF HAWKINS

"We were terrible from outside. I thought we got up… in trying to match them."
UK COACH TUBBY SMITH

"It Ain't Me Babe"
BOB DYLAN, song writer

Now for UofL, Freedom Hall holds just fond memories, as they operate out of the YUM Center, making that area of town "Positively 4th Street." And the "Chimes of Freedom" coming from the "Hall", still ring out with the Cats playing there annually.

GAME 35

December 27, 2003

	UK	UofL
Record	7-0	6-1
Ranking	#2	#20
Favored	KENTUCKY BY 7.5	
Series	23	11
Location	RUPP ARENA	
TV	CBS	

PRE-GAME REPORT

There may be 1000 reasons why UK fans suffer discomfort, knowing that Rick Pitino is coaching their arch rival Louisville, but only one has the capability of delivering distress, mingled with fear; that he'll do the same thing to UK that he did to UofL when he was Big Blue-beat them, and often. Two years ago, Pitino came here for the first time as Louisville's head coach, and endured the "Big Boos," and some non-classy ridicule while losing big, 82-62. Last year in Freedom Hall, the Cats won the first half, but were blown out in the second, losing 81-63.

The Cats want to redeem themselves for last year's loss, and certainly need to avoid back-to-back defeats in the rivalry. They have a twenty-seven game regular season and fourteen game home court win streak in process, are undefeated and ranked No. 2 in the AP Poll and No. 1 in the Coaches' Poll.

The Cardinals want to rearrange all the above, and notch that win in Rupp for their coach according to Taquan Dean, "Some of the things the fans here yelled at him when he came here the last time, when I was a senior in high school were cruel. I lost respect for UK fans when they did that. The man gave them eight great years. I understand the rivalry thing, but there's a line you don't cross."

QUOTES

"Francisco Garcia does so many things well, it's hard to figure out who to match up with him."
UK COACH TUBBY SMITH

"They play just like us. The only difference is they have a loss and we don't.
UK FORWARD CHUCK HAYES

"What Kentucky has done is truly extraordinary. It's not necessarily their most talented team, but it's their best team since I've have been at Louisville."
UofL COACH RICK PITINO

"I know their a good defensive team, so I may not be able to go to the hole. I'll just have to pass the ball early, go away from the ball, and try and set some picks."
UofL FORWARD FRANCISCO GARCIA

PROBABLE STARTERS

Kentucky

POS.	PLAYER	HT.	WT.	CLS.	PT/G
F	ERIK DANIELS	6-8	214	SR.	15.7
F	CHUCK HAYES	6-6	247	JR.	13.0
G/F	KELENNA AZUBUIKE	6-5	208	SO.	10.9
G	CLIFF HAWKINS	6-1	187	SR.	11.7
G	GERALD FITCH	6-3	188	SR.	19.1

Louisville

POS.	PLAYER	HT.	WT.	CLS.	PT/G
F	LUKE WHITEHEAD	6-6	220	SR.	14.9
F	FRANCISCO GARCIA	6-7	185	SO.	18.6
C	KENDALL DARTEZ	6-10	225	SR.	4.9
G	TAQUAN DEAN	6-3	185	SO	13.9
G/F	LARRY O'BANNON	6-4	200	JR	7.3

"LOUISVILLE 65, KENTUCKY 56
RICK'S ARENA ONCE AGAIN"
Louisville Courier-Journal

"LOUISVILLE 65, KENTUCKY 56
Rivalry in the red"
Lexington Herald-Leader

Kentucky's energy level was very expendable right from the tip-off. Hawkins and Azubuike each hit a three-pointer, Hayes a put back, followed by an Erik Daniels dunk, and by the first TV timeout, the Cats led 12-2. Almost ten minutes into this affair, UK led 24-10. They hit nine of their first 18 shots and were five out of 13 from three-point land.

UofL's bench played a key role in keeping the Cards close in the first half. Dean and Garcia were held scoreless, but Otis George had 13 points and eight rebounds, and Larry O'Bannon scored 11.

Alhaji Mohammed, Nazr Mohammed's little brother, played big, making two backcourt steals and converting them into five points. Kentucky normally doesn't rely on the three-pointer as much as they did in the first half. You must credit the Cardinal defense for that. Trapping inside, Hayes and Daniels hit only six of 19 shots. The Cats shooting dropped off drastically, only one basket in the final six minutes of the half, and two in the final nine. Despite, the awful shooting, they still led 31-26 at the half.

The Cards' comeback took some time to develop. With 9:43 remaining, Otis George went up for a put back, was fouled, hit the free throw and the game was tied 41-41. Garcia stole the ball and dished to George who slammed it home. On UofL's next possession, Garcia stroked a three and the Cards were on top 46-41.

The Cats responded with and 8-0 run and edged ahead by three. Louisville came right back and a Dartez dunk gave UofL the lead for good. Dean hit his first three for the Cards with 1:42 to go, putting Louisville up 57-51. But Dean fouled Fitch whose three-pointer was good, he made the free-throw and the four-point play made it 57-55 Louisville. Garcia made sure it wouldn't get closer. At the top of the key, he ball faked Keleena Azubuike, then disdaining the pass and the dribble, with Azubuike in his face, he went straight up, drilled the three-point shot and the Cards had breathing room, 60-55.

UofL made just one of its first 10 three-point shots, but connected on three of its last four, in knocking off Kentucky 65-56.

STATS

Kentucky

Player	Min	FG	FG A	3PT FG	3 PT FGA	FT	FT A	Reb	PF	Ast	St	BS	TO	Pts
Erik Daniels	32	4	11	0	1	1	2	8	4	1	1	0	3	9
Kelenna Azubuike	33	4	10	2	5	2	3	1	1	0	3	0	1	12
Chuck Hayes	39	2	8	0	0	0	0	9	2	3	0	4	1	4
Cliff Hawkins	27	4	11	4	6	0	0	2	4	3	3	0	5	12
Gerald Fitch	32	3	12	2	10	1	1	2	1	3	1	0	3	9
Brandon Stockton	19	2	5	1	3	3	3	0	1	1	1	0	1	8
Lukasz Obrzut	8	0	0	0	0	0	0	1	1	0	0	0	0	0
Antwain Barbour	10	1	2	0	0	0	0	3	1	1	0	1	1	2
Team								4					1	
Totals	**200**	**20**	**59**	**9**	**25**	**7**	**9**	**30**	**15**	**12**	**9**	**5**	**16**	**56**

Louisville

Player	Min	FG	FG A	3PT FG	3 PT FGA	FT	FT A	Reb	PF	Ast	St	BS	TO	Pts
Luke Whitehead	33	4	13	0	0	3	4	6	2	2	2	1	3	11
Francisco Garcia	32	4	9	2	5	0	0	7	4	5	1	3	2	10

Player	Min	FG	FG A	3PT FG	3 PT FGA	FT	FT A	Reb	PF	Ast	St	BS	TO	Pts
Kendall Dartez	19	3	4	0	0	0	0	3	1	0	2	0	5	6
Taquan Dean	32	2	11	1	6	0	0	5	3	2	0	0	4	5
Nate Daniels	5	0	1	0	1	0	0	0	0	0	0	0	0	0
Nouha Diakite	2	0	0	0	0	0	0	0	1	0	0	0	0	0
Brandon Jenkins	9	1	1	0	0	0	0	1	1	0	0	0	1	2
Alhaji Mohammed	16	3	4	0	0	1	1	3	2	0	2	0	0	7
Larry O'Bannon	27	1	4	1	1	8	8	3	0	0	0	0	0	11
Otis George	25	5	7	0	1	3	3	8	2	0	0	0	1	13
Team								2						
Totals	**200**	**23**	**54**	**4**	**14**	**15**	**16**	**38**	**16**	**9**	**7**	**4**	**16**	**65**

POINTS AFTER

"I was worried about us getting off to that great start, because we were using a lot of energy…We didn't have our legs after the first ten or fifteen minutes of the first half."
UK COACH TUBBY SMITH

"I'm supposed to make shots, regardless of rhythm or no rhythm. That's why I'm here. I'm supposed to make big shots for my team. I'm not going to make excuses. I'm supposed to make big plays and I didn't, point blank. There's nothing else you can say about that."
UK GUARD GERALD FITCH

"I'm stunned because there were four things I told our players we had to overcome. First, Kentucky is a great basketball team. Second, you're playing the No. 1 ranked team in the country. The third thing is it's on the road in front of the most hostile crowd you'll ever face. And the fourth was that it was a revenge game (for UK). But if you win, it will be one of the greatest wins of your life."
UofL COACH RICK PITINO

"He told us to expect them to come out with that energy. And he told us to keep our poise and hold on. Our game plan was to use their own emotion and aggressiveness against them."
UofL GUARD TAQUAN DEAN

GAME 36

December 18, 2004

	UofL	UK
Record	6-1	6-1
Ranking	#13	#9
Series	12	23
Favored	LOUISVILLE BY 4	
Location	FREEDOM HALL	
TV	ESPN	

PRE-GAME REPORT

The Wildcats had won the preliminary battle returning to the No. 1 status on 84 WHAS Radio, the city of Louisville's 50,000-watt clear channel station. UofL fans and officials weren't happy, they viewed this as betrayal (must be contagious) by the hometown station. Memories wane sometimes when Blue and White, and Red and Black issues converge abruptly.

UK sports had the No. 1 position on WHAS Radio for years until a loophole was discovered in the contract, and UofL left the sister station, WAMZ in the early 80s to take the coveted top spot at WHAS. Neither school has been exiled into broadcasting oblivion by any of these moves, but it's the rivalry, the bragging rights that drives the desire to be mentioned first, or No. 1.

In the early days, there is no doubt that the powerful signal of WHAS Radio helped build a Wildcat following throughout the state, and around the country where the signal could be heard. Cat fans and officials, viewed this as a rightful return to the air wave throne. After last year's loss, sportswriters said that Rick Pitino owned the series. It was his. His record as a coach in the rivalry was 8-3 and Tubby Smith's overall record against Pitino was 2-7.

This game presented a major challenge, not just for Kentucky to break free from this pre-owned state, but no Louisville team had ever won three consecutive games in the series.

Something had to give.

QUOTES

"Now that we've got their coach, it's a little bigger now"
UofL GUARD LARRY O'BANNON on the rivalry.

"The big thing for us is to execute and follow our plays to the end. It's a big challenge for us. If I were them, I'd pound it inside on us because we're a small team and we don't have a lot of depth. But Otis (George) coming back will help us... This game is really big stuff. We had two of our best practices of the season on Thursday, and that's what we need. So I feel good about this game."
UofL FORWARD ELLIS MYLES

"It's depressing (losing two straight games to UofL). It hurts after any loss, but it hurts a lot more when you lose to Louisville."
UK GUARD JOSH CARRIER

"We've got a lot of young guys and it can't get erratic and crazy. But that's the style (Louisville) plays. Their style of play is to make you take bad shots. You have to be patient and play with a lot of poise and not get rattled and rush. That's easier said than done."
UK COACH TUBBY SMITH

PROBABLE STARTERS

Louisville

POS.	PLAYER	HT.	WT.	CLS.	PT/G
F	FRANCISCO GARCIA	6-7	190	JR.	16.1
F	ELLIS MYLES	6-7	245	SR.	11.4
F	JUAN PALACIOS	6-8	245	FR.	8.0
G	LARRY O'BANNON	6-4	200	SR	14.9
G	TAQUAN DEAN	6-3	185	JR	17.0

Kentucky

POS.	PLAYER	HT.	WT.	CLS.	PT/G
F	CHUCK HAYES	6-6	247	SR.	11.9
F/C	KELENNA AZUBUIKE	6-5	220	JR.	14.4
C	RANDOLPH MORRIS	6-10	265	FR.	9.7
G	RAJON RONDO	6-1	171	FR.	6.9
G	PATRICK SPARKS	6-0	180	JR.	12.0

"KENTUCKY 60   LOUISVILLE 58
HAT-TRICK SPARKS UK"
Lexington Herald-Leader

"Sparks burns Cardinals"
Louisville Courier-Journal

The previous two years, UK played its best the first twenty minutes, disappeared the second half and suffered back-to-back losses to UofL. This year, this game, they disappeared in the first half, and appeared lost, trailing 32-16 at the half. But a funny thing happened on the way to the locker room; a dance broke out and the UK players were transformed. When the Cats left the floor, they noticed Cardinal players Francisco Garcia and Taquan Dean dancing to the music played by the Red and Black band.

Wildcat Chuck Hayes, didn't appreciate the action, "That's just disrespect." And that's the first thing they talked about when they entered the locker room.

In that locker room, rebounding and heart were also discussed, and very passionately, "We all kind of lost a little of our religion," said Coach Smith. "I apologize." Adjustments were made. UK led

5-0 with just 1:41 gone in the first half when Louisville called a timeout. With 10:59 left in the half, Kentucky was still stuck on five, UofL had 13 points. The Cards double-teamed UK's big men, Morris and Alleyne, rendering them ineffective offensively.

On offense, the UofL big men did just about what they wanted, freshman Juan Palacios scored 11 first half points, and senior Ellis Myles had eight, and grabbed nine rebounds. UK was only five of 24 from the field for 20.8 percent and were out rebounded 22-13. Coach Smith wanted to feature the smaller Hayes and Azibuike as the big men, to give the Cats more quickness up front, and a pressing defense to wear the Cards down.

This strategy was made a little easier to orchestrate when four minutes into the second half, Cardinal forward Juan Palacios sustained an eye laceration and had to leave the game. Now, the Cardinals would be the team confused on offense. Ellis Myles, even with Palacios out of the game, didn't take a shot in the final twenty minutes.

Still, the comeback wouldn't be easy.

With 12:33 left in the game, Kentucky still trailed by double-digits, 44-30. Substitute Sheray Thomas, who had just returned to the team last week following an undisclosed medical procedure in October, was in the game for only 60 seconds, but his hard drive to the basket, which drew a blocking foul from Ellis Myles, was a turning point in the game according to Coach Smith, "That's Sheray's game. Something we were missing was that aggressiveness, attacking the basket. I was hoping it would do just what it did for us, with guys saying, 'Hey, Sheray's been through a lot, and look what he is doing. I thought that was a big lift for us."

UK scored three of its next four baskets on a dunk and two layups, but when Patrick Sparks hit back-to-back three-pointers in just 33 seconds, UofL called a timeout with 4:58 left, leading by just four, 48-44.

Louisville came right back when Taquan Dean made two threes of his own, pushing the lead back to 10. Sparks would return the fire with another three-pointer, add two points on a ten-foot leaner which drew a foul, followed by the free throw and with 2:50 left, it was UofL 54-50.

Another adjustment Tubby Smith made for the final drive, was switching to a more veteran lineup, with senior Josh Carrier and Junior Ravi Moss replacing the two freshmen, Randolph Morris and Rajon Rondo. This would pay dividends when Moss got a defensive rebound, went down court and drilled a three, cutting the Cardinal lead to one at 54-53. Then Keleena Azuibike would give UK it's first lead of the second half on a pair of free throws 55-54.

The crowd of 20,088 witnessed three lead changes in a 73-second span. Garcia banked in a drive, Louisville's first field goal in some four minutes, 56-55 UofL. Azibuike would score on a layup, 57-56 Kentucky. The Cards' Larry O'Bannon drew a blocking foul and made two free throws, 58-57 UofL.

With 15 seconds left, UK put the ball in play, only to call a timeout five seconds later. Back in play, another timeout, leaving only 4.8 seconds for the final play.

Sparks lobbed the inbounds pass to Azubuike. He is double-teamed, so he gives it right back to Sparks who by now, has moved into three-point position in the left corner. Myles and George go after him. It appears Sparks shuffled his feet, but no call is made and Myles fouled him in the act of shooting, sending an 85-percent free throw shooter to the line with under a second to play.

During the timeout, Coach Smith goes over, puts his arm around Sparks, and starts talking about his guard's plans for Christmas.

Sparks who scored 18 of his game-high 25 points in the second half, makes all three foul shots, and Kentucky wins a thriller, 60-58.

STATS

Louisville

Player	Min	FG	FG A	3PT FG	3 PT FGA	FT	FT A	Reb	PF	Ast	St	BS	TO	Pts
Ellis Myles	30	4	5	0	0	0	0	10	4	2	1	0	3	8
Juan Palacios	20	5	9	0	2	1	1	2	0	0	0	1	0	11
Francisco Garcia	40	3	12	2	7	0	0	6	2	5	0	3	4	8
Taquan Dean	34	3	10	3	8	0	0	7	2	2	1	0	3	9
Larry O'Bannon	38	4	9	2	5	6	6	4	1	1	0	2	1	16
Brandon Jenkins	17	0	0	0	0	0	0	0	1	1	0	0	2	0
Otis George	21	1	1	0	0	4	4	6	3	1	0	1	1	6
Totals	**200**	**20**	**46**	**7**	**22**	**11**	**11**	**35**	**13**	**12**	**2**	**7**	**14**	**58**

Kentucky

Player	Min	FG	FG A	3PT FG	3 PT FGA	FT	FT A	Reb	PF	Ast	St	BS	TO	Pts
Kelenna Azubuike	31	3	12	2	6	4	4	1	2	0	0	1	0	12
Chuck Hayes	36	2	10	0	0	2	2	9	3	4	2	1	0	6
Randolph Morris	17	1	1	0	0	0	2	3	0	2	1	1	1	2
Rajon Rondo	27	2	7	0	2	0	0	4	0	3	1	1	1	4
Ravi Moss	7	1	2	1	2	0	0	3	0	0	0	0	0	3
Ramel Bradley	5	0	0	0	0	0	0	0	1	0	0	0	1	0
Josh Carrier	13	0	1	0	1	0	0	0	2	0	0	0	1	0
Lukasz Obrzut	1	0	0	0	0	0	0	0	0	0	0	0	0	0
Bobby Perry	9	1	2	0	1	0	0	0	0	0	1	0	2	2
Shagari Alleyne	9	0	0	0	0	0	0	2	1	0	0	0	0	0

Player	Min	FG	FG A	3PT FG	3 PT FGA	FT	FT A	Reb	PF	Ast	St	BS	TO	Pts
Sheray Thomas	1	0	1	0	0	1	2	1	0	0	0	0	0	1
Joe Crawford	12	2	6	1	4	0	0	1	0	0	0	0	0	5
Patrick Sparks	32	8	15	5	8	4	4	5	2	3	1	0	2	25
Team								1						
Totals	**200**	**20**	**57**	**9**	**24**	**11**	**14**	**30**	**11**	**12**	**6**	**4**	**8**	**60**

POINTS AFTER

"We had two great wins against them, and they didn't make excuses. And we're not going to make any tonight."
UofL COACH RICK PITINO

"That's my fault. I should have played the walk-ons more. When (Palacios) went down, I thought we'd struggle if we had to go to the walk-ons. But you don't know unless you try. Against a good basketball team that's deep, you can't play six people and win."
UofL COACH RICK PITINO

"It was a tale of two halves. We were getting annihilated on the boards in the first half (22-13), but there was a major difference in the way we played in the second half."
UK COACH TUBBY SMITH

"In the second half, UK won the battle of the boards, 17-13, outscored the Cards 14-4 in the paint and made only two turnovers. Improved their field-goal accuracy from 20.8 percent to 45.5 percent. Keleena Azubuike also scored 10 of his 12 points in the second half. They've probably got a billboard up for Sparks already. (Central City, his hometown)
UK FORWARD CHUCK HAYES

Tom Leach, Voice of the Wildcats said this recently about Patrick Sparks' performance, "It was one of those games where Patrick was in the groove. He couldn't get the ball fast enough."

I'm writing this book in the present tense, while the games are in the past version, which often, can make analysis a little easier. However, I held these opinions at the time the games were played. For fans it is a given, but broadcasters and writers (who have loyalties and feelings too) are prone to jump to conclusions.

Yes, Pitino while he was at UK dominated Denny Crum 6-2, Crum on the downslide of his career. No one expected Coach Pitino to win his first game when he returned to Rupp Arena, but coming into this game he had back-to-back solid wins over Tubby Smith and Kentucky. Hence, the feeling hovering over the Bluegrass State Rivalry, was that Pitino had things well in-hand. He owned the series.

I need to insert a four letter word here—TIME.

Two games is not enough to make such a declaration, especially when previous coaches have warned these "time travelers" that neither team is going to win all the time.

I had this same debate with the late sports talk show host Papa Joe Chevalier. When I was at WTMT-Radio, Papa Joe was one of the national hosts on the Sporting News Network which we carried. He was in town and made a visit to our station on my morning talk show. He was a Pittsburg Pirate fan lamenting the fact that the New York Yankees had won four of the last five World Series titles.

He argued that Pittsburgh was a small market town (just a little bigger than Fern Creek, I guess) and needed revenue sharing from these large TV market area teams to compete. My reply was, "So you believe in socialism for baseball too?" I went on that MLB has produced a greater variety of winners since 1990 than the NBA or NFL. I called in the "facts checkers", and at the time of this show, MLB had six different winners, the NBA five, and I don't believe the 2001 Super Bowl had been played, so the NFL was tied with baseball at six.

These other leagues have tried to level the playing field through various financial means; baseball has not, although the luxury tax may cause some irritation. The richer teams in MLB can still spend all they desire to get the players they want. One must figure too that baseball struck out in 1994, having no post-season because of the players' strike, reducing its number of teams to nine for this comparison, instead of the ten for the other two leagues.

He was afraid the Yankees were going to win every year. I said: "So, what's new? Since, the 20s they have been the dominate team. No one has produced a revised version of the "Damn Yankees" yet, so let's give it some more TIME. If they win the next three, I'll buy in with you.

The Yankees' best World Series winning years before Joe Torre's bunch won four of five titles, was five of six from 1936-1941, and six of seven, from 1947-53.

Looking at the years since the Chevalier-Willman debate, 2001-2014, the Yankees have won only one title. In those thirteen years, the NFL has crowned nine different winners, the NBA six and MLB nine.

His Pittsburgh Pirates won the Series in 1909 and 1925. Thirty-five years expired before they won again in 1960. The Pirates also won in 1971 and 79. If they win in 2013, (and don't hold your breath) - they didn't - it will be thirty-four years since their last title, so what's new?

The Cardinals, after losing to Memphis on February 9th at home, won thirteen consecutive games including the C-USA regular season and tournament titles, and went to the Final Four.

I've talked about avoiding the "What if" syndrome, but in the case of the 2004-5 Cardinals, it may be applicable. What if Rajon Rondo had been a Louisville Cardinal? He was born in Louisville and that's where he wanted to play.

The existing dilemma, UofL had a verbal commitment from Sebastian Telfair, one of the top prospect's in the nation, but that eliminated Rondo. To make matters worse, Telfair wasn't coming. In any business, but especially the radio talk show business, one needs great sources to survive.

When it came to basketball recruiting, I had some of the best. What "Deep Throat" was to Woodward and Bernstein, Bill, from Middlesboro, KY. was to me. (I understand he passed away sometime ago) If you asked what the prospect was going to have for lunch, it seemed that Bill had the answer. He made calls, and calls, and calls. That's how he knew. And when he told me: "This is what will happen!" I was confident I could share it with my listeners.

I said from the very beginning that Telfair would not play for Louisville. I had additional sources who felt the same way.

It happened again with the seven-footer Mark Blount. Jimmy had called my show and said, "Hey, Paul man! You're the best when it comes to recruiting. You had Ron Mercer going to Kentucky before anybody." I said in July of 1994, that Ron Mercer would play for UK. In December of that year, Mercer's Oak Hill team was in town to play, still he had not revealed his college decision, and others like, WAVE-TV Sports, was touting that UK might not be his choice. But, he did announce for UK later. One of my other sources, told me that if Mercer transferred from his high school in Nashville to Oak Hill Academy, he would be a Wildcat. As soon as he announced he was headed to Oak Hill, I made my prediction in July.

Jimmy said Blount was coming to UofL. I informed him that my source (Bill) had him in Pittsburgh and that I was sticking with that. Blount went to Pittsburgh.

So, when somebody wins five consecutive games, which has never been done—then I'll say he owns this series. And will let the wild card "TIME" have it's play, for as Scarlett O'Hara said: "Tomorrow is another day."

In sports that's certainly true.

GAME 37

December 17, 2005

	UK	UofL
Record	6-3	6-0
Ranking	#23	#4
Series	24	12
Favored	KENTUCKY BY 3	
Location	RUPP ARENA	
TV	CBS	

PRE-GAME REPORT

After the dramatic win in Freedom Hall last year 60-58, Smith and Pitino were even with two wins each. I imagine Tubby felt a little more comfortable, knowing that Rick really didn't own the series as advertised.

UofL had gone to the Final Four, losing to Illinois in the semifinals. That trip helped the pollsters cast the Cards in a favorable light for the 2005-06 season, making them the preseason No. 7 team. But upon closer observation, they had lost Francisco Garcia, Otis George, Ellis Myles, Larry O'Bannon and Lorenzo Wade who transferred to Washington. Those players accounted for nearly 60 percent of the Cardinals' scoring and rebounding. Not to mention seven newcomers on this year's roster.

When UofL came to Rupp, ranked No. 4; they were 6-0, had played all their games at home, and none against a top twenty-five team. UK made the Elite 8 the previous year, now, coming into this season they were ranked No. 9. For the Louisville game, they had slipped to No. 23 having beaten No. 13 West Virginia, but lost to No. 18 Iowa, and were blown out on national TV the week before by No. 18 Indiana 79-53. However, forget the wins and losses, Coach Smith and sophomore guard Rajon Rondo were negotiating, hopeful they could work out their differences concerning how Rondo should operate the offense.

QUOTES

"We're looking for a fresh start against Louisville. It's a big game in a big environment, and we've worked on a lot of things to get ready for this."
UK GUARD PATRICK SPARKS

"I'm sure (last season's) loss has been weighing on Louisville's minds for the past year. They're going to come in here ready to play."
UK COACH TUBBY SMITH

"Believe it or not, I don't worry about the freshmen as much as the other guys. I think the freshmen are oblivious. They're not smart enough to be nervous."
UofL COACH RICK PITINO

"It's a lot different. I remember being on the other side (as UK coach), and when we came into Freedom Hall and took the lead, you'd hear 4000 Cat fans come alive. You don't have 40 Card fans in Rupp. It can be very intimidating. It's a strong home-court advantage."
UofL COACH RICK PITINO

PROBABLE STARTERS

Kentucky

POS.	PLAYER	HT.	WT.	CLS.	PT/G
F	SHERAY THOMAS	6-7	230	JR.	4.7
C	LUKASZ ORBZUT	7-0	270	JR.	2.3
G	RAJON RONDO	6-1	171	SO.	15.5
G	PATRICK SPARKS	6-0	180	SR.	10.1
G	JOE CRAWFORD	6-4	210	SO.	6.8

Louisville

POS.	PLAYER	HT.	WT.	CLS.	PT/G
F	JUAN PALACIOS	6-8	255	SO.	11.5
F	TERRENCE WILLIAMS	6-6	220	FR.	9.2
F/C	DAVID PADGETT	6-11	250	SO.	10.2
G	TAQUAN DEAN	6-3	185	SR	20.5
G	BRANDON JENKINS	6-3	185	JR.	11.5

"RONDO RINGS IN NEW GEAR
Kentucky 73, Louisville 61"
LEXINGTON HERALD-LEADER

"Rondo earns his stripes"
Louisville Courier-Journal

Coach Smith and Rondo were on the same page for this game. UK scored the first eight points and went on to lead 39-24 at the half. On two of UK's first four possessions, Rondo drove to the basket and scored, then on the fifth, dished off to Orbzut for a dunk.

The Cards scored on just one of its first 11 possessions and fell quickly behind 13-3. Adding to the trouble was David Padgett going to the bench with two personal fouls in the first 1:26 of play. Palacios later joined Padgett on the bench for the same reason. Despite shooting just three for 19, UofL was only behind 15-11 when Rondo scored all of UK's points in an 8-2 run that made the score 23-13.

Coach Pitino didn't blame foul trouble for Louisville's dilemma, the key factor was UK shot 50 percent in the first half compared to UofL's 26.5 percent.

In the second half UofL cut a twenty-three point deficit to thirteen, 66-53, but Rondo made six free throws down the stretch to help preserve the victory for Kentucky, 73-61. Rondo scored a career and game-high 25 points, dished out seven assists, had three rebounds and two steals. His teammates benefited from his leadership with Sheray Thomas scoring a career-high 11 points and grabbing six rebounds. Rondo also played some fine defense on his Cardinal counterpart, senior guard Taquan Dean, who was five of fourteen from the field, including two of ten three-point attempts. He missed all five of his shots in the final 10.5 minutes while his teammates made nine of their 12. Padgett and Palacios combined for 27 points during that span of play.

Remember, the newcomers, the freshmen, in what Pitino called "a circus environment," made just three of their 21 shots under Rupp's Big Top.

STATS

Kentucky

Player	Min	FG	FG A	3PT FG	3 PT FGA	FT	FT A	Reb	PF	Ast	St	BS	TO	Pts
Sheray Thomas	29	3	6	1	1	4	4	6	3	1	0	1	0	11
Lukasz Obrzut	30	2	3	0	0	0	1	9	3	0	0	2	0	4
Rajon Rondo	35	7	12	1	3	10	15	3	2	7	2	0	3	25
Patrick Sparks	20	2	3	0	0	2	2	2	3	0	0	0	2	6
Joe Crawford	31	3	8	0	0	3	4	7	2	0	1	1	1	9
Ravi Moss	18	1	4	1	3	2	2	3	2	0	0	0	0	5
Ramel Bradley	17	3	6	1	4	1	2	0	3	2	0	0	2	8
Bobby Perry	8	0	1	0	1	0	0	1	1	1	0	0	1	0
Shagari Alleyne	4	2	3	0	0	0	0	1	0	0	0	2	1	4
Rekalin Sims	8	0	2	0	1	1	4	3	0	1	0	0	1	1
Team								1					1	
Totals	**200**	**23**	**48**	**4**	**13**	**23**	**34**	**36**	**19**	**12**	**3**	**6**	**12**	**73**

Louisville

Player	Min	FG	FG A	3PT FG	3 PT FGA	FT	FT A	Reb	PF	Ast	St	BS	TO	Pts
Terrance Williams	22	1	7	0	3	3	3	1	1	1	0	0	0	5

Player	Min	FG	FG A	3PT FG	3 PT FGA	FT	FT A	Reb	PF	Ast	St	BS	TO	Pts
Juan Palacios	26	6	9	2	5	1	2	7	4	0	0	2	1	15
David Padgett	20	5	8	0	0	2	4	3	3	1	0	0	1	12
Taquan Dean	34	5	16	2	10	2	2	5	4	6	0	0	4	14
Brandon Jenkins	34	2	6	2	2	0	0	4	4	2	0	0	0	6
Brad Gianiny	10	0	0	0	0	2	2	1	2	1	1	0	0	2
Chad Millard	14	0	0	0	0	0	0	2	1	1	0	1	1	0
Jonathan Huffman	4	0	2	0	0	0	0	1	2	0	0	0	1	0
Andre McGee	19	1	5	1	4	2	5	1	3	2	1	0	4	5
Terrance Farley	1	0	0	0	0	0	0	1	0	0	0	0	0	0
Brian Johnson	16	1	7	0	1	0	0	5	2	0	0	1	0	2
Team								4						
Totals	**200**	**21**	**60**	**7**	**25**	**12**	**18**	**35**	**26**	**14**	**2**	**4**	**12**	**61**

POINTS AFTER

"He was like a captain out there, like a general. We're comfortable when he's running the show, and he made great decisions all day."

UK GUARD RAVI MOSS (regarding Rondo)

"This was our best effort, best all-around effort in all phases of the game."

UK COACH TUBBY SMITH

"All the things they did, we saw then do on tape. Everything we didn't want to let them do, they did."

UofL FORWARD TERRENCE WILLIAMS

"We were getting great effort, but that was the only silver lining. We still took poor shots...You don't catch up doing that. Every time we got the ball inside to Padgett something good happened. So we're playing like an inexperienced team, but we are one."

UofL COACH RICK PITINO

Louisville finished 21-13 that year, losing the first game in the Big East Tournament. The Cards won all three of their NIT games in Freedom Hall, but lost in the semifinals to South Carolina at Madison Square Garden.

Kentucky was 22-13, lost to South Carolina in the SEC Tournament semifinals, and to Connecticut in the NCAA East Region second round. Kentucky had beaten South Carolina twice during the SEC regular season, but not in the tournament with the NCAA automatic bid on the line. Connecticut beat the Cardinals twice during regular season play. Team chemistry is such an important element in winning.

Nothing against Brandon Stockton, but when Tubby was playing him over Rondo, it was painful. But a coach has to be in control. Even if Rondo had come to Louisville, would his relationship with Pitino have been any better?

Remember these lines from the poet John Greenleaf Whittier: "Of all sad words of tongue or pen, the saddest are these, it might have been." Maud Miller pamphlet.

GAME 38

December 16, 2006

	UofL	UK
Record	6-3	5-3
Ranking	unranked	unranked
Series	12	25
Favored	LOUISVILLE BY 2	
Location	FREEDOM HALL	
TV	CBS	

PRE-GAME REPORT

Slippage, dreamless, some of the non-endearing terms attached to this rivalry game. It was only the third time since the series was renewed that both teams came into the game unranked in the national polls. But it is still: *UK vs. UofL - College Basketball's No. 1 Rivalry - Enough Said!* Even in the thin times, it matters who wins.

I interviewed a Nebraska football fan before the 2013 Louisville-Florida International game. I mentioned that his team was struggling. His reply was, "We're No. 1 no matter what!" Likewise in this series, even if the teams are down in the rankings they'll still No. 1 with their fans and that makes the difference in the long run on the national scene.

In reviewing these games, it has been interesting at times, to find how quickly those covering the games revert to describing the rivalry as "waning" in interest. One team has too many wins, neither team has a chance to "go all the way," not ranked, not winning enough games, not enough players from the state, the game was "brutal" and etc.

But then we have read this quote so often attributed to the fans: "If you only win one game this year—let it be UK/UofL!"

Now, doing all those other things will certainly bring more national attention, but this rivalry is the best because the fans in this state are the most passionate whether their team is up or down at the tip-off. And there were writers at this time, like the C-J's Brain Bennett that covered this last point as well. "But in reality, as important as this game is to the fans, go 1-26, and this brand of 'get out of jail free card' won't be validated for very long."

Sure, the December the 28th, 2013 game in Rupp Arena was the most anticipated game in the series. Each school has won a national championship in the previous two years. This rivalry has pushed ahead once again of Duke/North Carolina in NCAA titles, 11-9. You don't dismiss the Blue Devils and Tar Heels, but the Cards and Cats are receiving the most attention heading into the 2013-14 season locally and nationally. There have been some thin times for Duke and North Carolina, but they didn't cancel their series.

From 1939, first year of the NCAA tournament through the 1958 season, Kentucky won four NCAA championships and one NIT in 1946. Louisville won the NAIB in 1948 and the 1956 NIT championship, North Carolina won one NCAA title in 1957. At the end of the 1986 season, UK/UofL had won seven NCAA titles, North Carolina/Duke two (Blue Devils none).

For 48 years, UK and UofL were way out in front. The next 25 years, it was Duke and UNC that dominated. That is one reason the Tobacco Road rivalry is viewed as the best. Current events obscure history, dominating the scene.

We've heard for the last few years that the Big East Conference was the best in basketball. Examining the major conferences before the Cardinals won the NCAA in 2013, here is the record since the Big East Conference was formed in 1979:

	NCAA Titles	Teams in Final Four
BIG EAST	6	18
SEC	6	18
ACC	10	28
BIG 10	5	22
BIG 12	2	13
PAC 12	2	9

Brainwashing not only occurs in the "Manchurian Candidate," we've been told over and over that the SEC is weak in basketball, but it was dead even with the Big East in the comparison that really counts, until Louisville won in 2013. Louisville's win gives the Big East seven titles, and with Syracuse also making the 2013 Final Four, totals 20 teams making it to the "big dance."

Let's not mention that the ACC was the best by this comparison standard. Now, with the addition of UofL to the ACC Conference, beginning with the 2014-15 season, one can see why the already best basketball conference since 1979, has even gotten better. Re-emphasizing the point, that just because we're told something is so, that doesn't make it true.

In football it's not even close since our comparison year of 1979:

NATIONAL CHAMPIONSHIPS

Football

	Titles
SEC	13
BIG 12	6
ACC	4
BIG East	2
BIG 10	2
PAC 12	0*

*USC had to vacate title

By tabulating total number of champions in college sports' two major categories, here are the following results:

	Basketball	**Football**	**Total**
SEC	6	13	19
ACC	10	4	14
BIG EAST	7	2	9
BIG 12	2	6	8
BIG 10	5	2	7
PAC 12	2	0	2

It's easy to understand why this book is centered on basketball, none of the four I am talking about have won a football national championship, but at the time of writing, and I don't care about the strength of schedule argument, that's always been by used by both schools trying to diminish the accomplishments of the other, Louisville is closer than the other three of cashing in on that possibility in football. And now with the Big East Conference as we knew it, laid to rest; the added element that enriches this rivalry is that UK and UofL are in the best conferences. State, conference and national championship bragging rights are now at stake.

I can hear Dick Vitale: "Hey baby! It's the ACC vs. The SEC! It doesn't get any better than this baby!"

On game day here in Louisville on December 16, 2006, both teams were desperately in need of a win. Each team was starting one senior and one freshman. UK had six other freshmen on the bench, and UofL four.

Kentucky was using a three-guard attack with freshman, Derrick Jasper at the point and Louisville would counter with three on the frontline against Randolph Morris and Bobby Perry.

QUOTES

"Neither Kentucky or Louisville is struggling. Neither one of us are great right now. We both aspire to be great at the right time, and both teams are working extremely hard and both have very good potential. And which one is going to be very good, I don't know."
UofL COACH RICK PITINO

"One of the big keys for us is to get B.J. (Flynn) and David Padgett playing up to their level."
UofL COACH RICK PITINO

"They're expecting us to be shaky with the ball. That's one of the things teams are doing. We have to understand that and handle that."
UK COACH TUBBY SMITH

"Our fans around (Lexington) are saying, 'Just beat up on those Cards.' They're still hyped about it, regardless of how we're playing, how they're playing. It's still Kentucky-Louisville. It's still, who's going to be king of the Bluegrass this year."
UK FORWARD BOBBY PERRY

PROBABLE STARTERS

Louisville

POS.	PLAYER	HT.	WT.	CLS.	PT/G
F	TERRENCE WILLIAMS	6-6	210	SO.	12.3
F	JUAN PALACIOS	6-8	250	JR.	12.1
C	DAVID PADGETT	6-11	245	JR.	7.3
G	EDGAR SOSA	6-1	175	FR.	12.3
G	BRANDON JENKINS	6-3	185	SR.	5.9

Kentucky

POS.	PLAYER	HT.	WT.	CLS.	PT/G
F	BOBBY PERRY	6-8	215	SR.	8.4
C	RANDOLPH MORRIS	6-11	259	JR.	16.9
C	DERRICK JASPER	6-6	213	FR.	3.1
G	RAMEL BRADLEY	6-2	176	JR.	12.4
G	JOE CRAWFORD	6-5	211	JR.	14.0

"Kentucky 61   Louisville 49
UK FINDS PLENTY IN RESERVES"
Lexington Herald-Leader

"Other guys' key Cats"
Louisville Courier-Journal

This game rated ho-hum status, but for the Cats it was exciting as they won by double-digits, 61-49. UK's leading scorer and rebounder Randolph Morris picked up two fouls in the first four minutes of play and went to the bench for the rest of the half. But the Cats didn't need to expend any of it's "nine lives" with the relief administered by the bench.

Jody Meeks, who had scored just eight points in the previous three games, scored nine of his career-high 18 points in the first half to help keep the Cats in contention. Lukasz Orbzut who had made just four baskets all season, tallied three in the first half.

UofL's freshmen center, Derrick Caracter had troubles of his own, fouling out in just eight minutes and missing all three of his shots. And the team had major problems, shooting just 27 percent from the floor, the lowest percentage for a Cardinal coached Pitino team since a 71-46 loss to TCU in February of 2004.

UK wasn't red-hot either, shooting 41 percent, but the Cats were six of 18 from three-point range for 33 percent, while UofL was just three of 24 for a miserable 12.5 percent. There should be something in the Bible about "living and dying by the three!"

Randolph Morris picked-up just where he left off in the first half, committing another foul in only 34 seconds. Ramel Bradley, however got hot scoring seven points to give UK it's biggest lead up until that time, 36-29. With the exception of Jodie Meeks' nine points, non-scoring stuck to the rest of the players from the 10:43 to 4:00 mark of the second half. Meeks was the only player in the game on either side to score during this blackout period.

Kentucky went on to defeat Louisville 61-49.

STATS

Louisville

Player	Min	FG	FG A	3PT FG	3 PT FGA	FT	FT A	Reb	PF	Ast	St	BS	TO	Pts
Terrance Williams	28	3	11	1	5	0	1	6	3	2	2	0	2	7
Juan Palacios	36	4	12	0	4	2	4	6	2	0	2	0	1	10
David Padgett	32	4	4	0	0	8	10	10	4	2	0	3	1	16
Brandon Jenkins	26	1	5	0	3	1	1	4	1	2	2	0	1	3
Andre McGee	20	1	8	0	4	0	1	4	2	1	1	0	2	2
Earl Clark	3	0	2	0	0	0	0	2	0	0	0	0	0	0
Edgar Sosa	14	2	7	0	1	1	1	1	2	0	1	0	1	5
Brad Gianiny	7	1	3	1	2	0	0	1	1	0	0	0	0	3
Will Scott	8	0	1	0	1	0	0	0	0	1	0	0	0	0

Paul Willman

Player	Min	FG	FG A	3PT FG	3 PT FGA	FT	FT A	Reb	PF	Ast	St	BS	TO	Pts
Derrick Caracter	8	0	3	0	0	0	0	2	5	0	0	0	3	0
Jerry Smith	18	1	7	1	4	0	0	7	1	0	0	0	1	3
Terrance Farley	0	0	0	0	0	0	0	0	0	0	0	0	0	0
Team								1						
Totals	200	17	63	3	24	12	18	44	21	8	8	3	12	49

Kentucky

Player	Min	FG	FG A	3PT FG	3 PT FGA	FT	FT A	Reb	PF	Ast	St	BS	TO	Pts
Bobby Perry	12	0	6	0	2	0	0	2	3	1	1	0	2	0
Randolph Morris	16	0	1	0	0	2	2	3	4	0	1	0	0	2
Ramel Bradley	31	4	10	1	4	6	7	6	1	2	0	1	3	15
Derrick Jasper	20	3	3	0	0	0	0	3	2	0	1	0	2	6
Joe Crawford	31	2	9	0	3	1	4	4	0	5	2	1	1	5
Michael Porter	15	1	2	1	2	1	2	5	1	1	0	0	2	4
Lukasz Obrzut	26	3	5	0	0	0	0	5	4	0	0	1	0	6
Jodie Meeks	21	5	10	4	7	4	5	3	2	2	1	0	1	18
Perry Stevenson	10	1	1	0	0	0	0	0	1	1	0	0	1	2
Sheray Thomas	18	1	1	0	0	1	2	5	3	1	0	1	1	3
Team								4						
Totals	200	20	48	6	18	15	22	40	21	13	6	4	13	61

POINTS AFTER

"That's the most open shots we've had. That's the best we have reversed the ball, the best we've gone inside-out. Our guys did a good job of spacing and move. But we've got to make easy put backs and two-point shots. We're not going to change the outside shooting; it is what it is. But those little bank shots, you've got to make those."

UofL COACH RICK PITINO

"Me personally, I haven't lost any confidence, but I think as a team we're starting to get a little down. We've been losing a lot of early games, and we feel like we're letting Coach "P" down. He predicted us to be a good team and we've got four losses."
   UofL GUARD EDGAR SOSA

"I believe guys are on the team for a reason. Because they can help us win basketball games. And they stepped up and produced."
   UK COACH TUBBY SMITH

"What happens sooner or later the game turns to substance. A lot of times it is emotion early. In the long run, as long as you don't get beat by emotion, victory can be achieved."
   UK ASSISTANT HEAD COACH DAVID HOBBS

This was Coach Smith's third consecutive victory over Pitino, but no one was writing or talking about Tubby owning the series, as they did when Pitino had won back-to-back games against the Wildcats. It's one thing to criticize fans that are riding the coach about his substitution patterns, recruiting or one of a thousand other things, but didn't Tubby deserve the same comments in the press that he "owned" the series, as was done for Pitino, when he had won just two in a row? No racism here. That's not to say you won't find some folks in either camp who still abide by these miserable feelings, but it was not the case with Tubby Smith, neither Joker Phillips or Ron Cooper.

Tubby Smith wasn't fired, he left.

His overall record in the rivalry was six and four, with a 4-2 advantage against Pitino, that was huge. And he was four and three against North Carolina, but only one and three when matched up with Roy Williams. Add five double-digit loss seasons, and no Final Fours since his first year, the program was on a downward trend; that's pressure that is so very difficult to withstand.

Then, mediocrity exploded under Billy Gillispie. One of the worst decisions in UK sport's history. Now, the only time big name recruits were mentioning Kentucky was at KFC. In 75 years of NCAA history, with 15 Final Fours and eight National Championships, UK averages a trip to the Final Four every five years and a title every 9.4 years.

Tubby was close to the title average, but it was on the back-end of his tenure, and he was behind in Final Fours.

If Coach Rupp was on the scene today, he would be feeling pressure. He described the feelings of a professor whom he met on campus one day, and asked him how the team was going to fare that season? Coach Rupp said, "We're not going to be very good." The professor stomped his foot, turned around and walked away mad. Rupp continued: "They just don't want to know the truth!" This is the truth. Coach Rupp's first 20 years of NCAA play, (tournament started in 1939) he set the standard; a Final Four every four years, a title every five.

However, during his last 14 years, he made only one Final Four reducing his numbers to 5.7 and 8.5 years. Add Rupp's three NIT finals and one championship (since there are some who still think the NIT was the No. 1 post-season tournament even back in 1956 when UofL won this championship) his numbers are every 3.9 years for Final Fours and every 7.0 years for a title.

Coach Hall made a Final Four every 4.3 years, a title every 13.

Coach Pitino, 2.7 years for a Final Four, a title in eight. Don't count the first two years because UK was on a two-year probation period, and Pitino is every two years for a Final Four and a title every six.

At UK, John Calipari is a Final Four every two years and a title in four.

From the UofL end of the bench. Coach Crum, a Final Four every five years, a title every 15. Coach Pitino, a Final Four every four years, one title in 12.

It's the numbers that drives the fans. If the winning numbers are down too long, and/or the fans don't buy as many tickets, you'll see the moving vans circling the coach's home.

In football, UK changed a street name to Hal Mumme Pass. A mistake; did not allow for TIME to reveal the true situation. I believe it was a mistake to crown Joker Phillips the new coach before Rich Brooks left. Racism had nothing to do with the dismissal of Ron Cooper. I have a Louisville friend who believes it did, but it didn't. The hiring of Charley Strong, who did an excellent job proves that. Same for Steve Kragthorpe, numbers too low.

Coach Pitino at this time was also talking about living in a "microwave world," according to *Lexington-Herald Leader* writer Chip Cosby. "Criticism does not bother me at all because I'm not part of the microwave society. I just eat my food out of the microwave. I love the microwave, because of my wife and the talent she has in the kitchen. That is my best friend. Every evening I go home, and I pop something in the microwave. If I eat at home it's never a cooked meal, it's always a microwave. I just want to eat food out of it."

UofL junior forward Terrence Williams was thinking along those same lines concerning fan criticism, "Once you're out of the microwave and hot, everybody wants you. But when you're cool, nobody likes you. Nobody likes to eat cold food."

Pitino then analyzed the criticism in the NFL, "I thought everybody was going to jump out of the stadium and kill themselves about five weeks ago in Cincinnati with the Bengals. Then I saw the Dallas Cowboys and thought everybody would do the same thing as well. Then they change quarterbacks and everything's unbelievable in Dallas, and everything's unbelievable in Cincinnati. It's not even by seasons anymore; it's by a couple of games. It's that microwave I keep telling you about." Coach Pitino continued, "When you look at coaches and how unhappy they are, sometimes you say, why stay in it? That's not going to happen to me. It did happen to me in Boston. So there's nothing you can write, there's nothing you can say, there's nothing you can piss me off with at all to get me not to love coaching. I love coaching; I love teaching my guys. I love perfection. I want to see them become a great basketball team. You cannot get under my skin. So rest assured, you're still going to be my friends long after I am gone."

Right now I believe Rick Pitino is the most dangerous man in this rivalry. Throw out age, he is now displaying the same passion at UofL that he did in his younger days at Kentucky. In his earlier years at UofL something was just a little different in my opinion.

Many of my Kentucky friends thought he should have been fired over the Karen Sypher affair. I did myself at first. But, try looking at things this way. It just may have been tougher punishment to let him keep his job. He certainly waded through minutes, hours, days, weeks, months and yes, even years of embarrassment and shame. Their were fans that wanted him gone for not winning, but the Final Four trip in 2012, when it appeared Florida was going to win—turned it all around.

Sure he lost to Kentucky twice that year, but in 2013, the Cardinals beat the Cats in the regular season and won the NCAA Championship. In Coach Pitino's Hall of Fame induction interviews, he admitted to character flaws, but his countenance has changed. He is refreshed, happy and ready to win again.

Rick Pitino is the most dangerous man in the rivalry because he will finish his career at UofL. His contract has been extended, and recruits know he's not going anywhere else. If Pitino beats Calipari's Cats at Rupp Arena on December 28, 2013, he won't own the series, but he will have the upper hand.

Fred Cowgill, WLKY-TV Sports Director was in school at Boston University when Coach Pitino was there. He has covered the legendary coach for many years and has from that standpoint, a unique perspective, "Pitino has suffered three major falls in his life, (1) the death of his son Daniel Pitino, (2) the death of his brother-in-law and closest friend Billy Minardi in the 9-11 attacks and (3) the Karen Sypher extortion case. He was down, but got up each time and is happy at home and is at the top of his game."

One thing about the fans that ought never be forgotten. They are the paying customers. They pay huge sums of money to follow their teams. They expect more, and they expect it now. I remember when Cincinnati was the "Big Red Machine" in the 70s, and my Atlanta Braves were struggling.

The schedule masters always had the Braves and Reds playing something like six of the first nine games. Atlanta was already 2-7 and their was some forlorn Braves' fan holding up a sign that read, "Wait Until Next Year!"

What a tribute to the fans who pay the money to follow their teams, knowing so often they have little chance of winning a championship. Without the fans, John Calipari, and Lebron James might be operating a plumbing business together.

GAME 39

January 5, 2008

	UK	UofL
Record	6-6	9-3
Ranking	unranked	unranked
Series	26	12
Favored	KENTUCKY BY 1.5	
Location	RUPP ARENA	
TV	CBS	

PRE-GAME REPORT

Coach Rick Pitino was back at Rupp Arena for the fifth time since he took the UofL job in 2001, and for the second time in less than a year. The opposing coach was Billy Gillispie.

In that span, Pitino was 1-2 against UK and 0-1 versus Texas A&M. Last March 17, at Rupp in an NCAA South Region game, Billy Gillispie's No. 9 A&M squad beat Louisville 72-69.

At UK it's a different story. Not just anyone can coach there. The expectations, demands and pressure make finding a compatible match difficult at best. The Wildcats were 6-6, with a loss at home to Gardner-Webb by 18. Attendance was already down some three thousand per game. Cat fans were on the prowl.

Pitino had been very understanding towards Gillispie in the press, urging the fans to be patient. But fans, seldom find patience a virtue in regards to winning. Maybe patience in this case, is an example of Coach Pitino's oft referenced phrase, "fool's gold."

"Fool's gold" being, that which is perceived as of extraordinary value, but discovered later to be something of no worth, causing another helpless victim to fall prey to its glittering deception.

Questions concerning injuries nagged each team as Juan Palacios and David Padgett for UofL and Jodie Meeks and Derrick Jasper for the Cats were ailing. In addition for the Cards, Earl Clark was serving a one game suspension, reasons for were unexplained. With both teams unranked and sporting a combined ten losses, national attention may have suffered some slippage, but none of that was apparent here in the Bluegrass.

As always shooting the three would be vital to victory. In Louisville's nine wins they have shot 38.2 percent from three-point land, in the four losses, just 24.2 percent. On the defensive side of the three, the Cards in victory, have held their opponents to shooting just 29.5 percent, and in defeat, the opponents have improved to 40.2 percent.

QUOTES

"The key for us in the game we've won is we've done a good job guarding the three. In the games we've lost we haven't."
UofL CENTER DAVID PADGETT

"Sometimes we get very technical in our explanation of why you win and lose. Then you watch the tape and you realize it is very simple: You had open shots and then the ball didn't go in."
UofL COACH RICK PITINO

"It's a very important game to us all. The one thing you have to do is, no matter what the result is, you have to move on after the game. But leading up to the game, you need to understand that it is a very, very, very important game, and you have to hold it in the highest esteem."
UK COACH BILLY GILLISPIE

"We got some confidence (from beating Florida International) but we're not a very good team right now."
UK GUARD DERRICK JASPER

PROBABLE STARTERS

Kentucky

POS.	PLAYER	HT.	WT.	CLS.	PT/G
F	PATRICK PATTERSON	6-8	232	FR.	17.7
C	MARK COURY	6-8	238	SO.	3.1
C	RAMON HARRIS	6-6	213	SO.	4.0
G	RAMEL BRADLEY	6-2	191	SR.	13.8
G	JOE CRAWFORD	6-5	207	SR.	15.8

Louisville

POS.	PLAYER	HT.	WT.	CLS.	PT/G
F	JUAN PALACIOS	6-8	250	SR.	8.9
F	TERRENCE WILLIAMS	6-6	215	JR.	12.4
C	DERRICK CARACTER	6-9	265	SO.	12.0
G	ANDRE McGEE	5-10	180	JR.	7.1
G	JERRY SMITH	6-1	200	SO.	10.3

"LOUISVILLE 89 KENTUCKY 75
    Call 'em Flash Cards"
    Louisville Courier-Journal

"LOUISVILLE 89 KENTUCKY 75
    RED ALL ABOUT IT"
    Lexington Herald-Leader

In the rivalry, when Rick Pitino was at Kentucky, among others, he threshed some "Wheat" and now at Louisville, among others, he has contained Marquis Estill and you can add Patrick Patterson's name to that list.

They wanted to take Patterson out of the game said Rick Pitino, "We didn't want (Patterson) to catch the basketball. They run everything through him, and he's very fundamentally sound for a freshman. I haven't seen a freshman as good as that for a longtime from a fundamental standpoint." The plan worked, as Patterson went just three of 14 from the field, scoring only six points while committing an equal number of turnovers.

UK guard Derrick Jasper analyzed the trapping defense on Patterson, "Padgett and Palacios did a great job of collapsing on him and denying him the ball. They're really big bodies, so I think Patrick had a really tough time." And except for Ramel Bradley, who had a career-high 27 points, hitting eight of 12 from the field, including his only three-point attempt, and cashing in on eight of nine from the foul line, and Ramon Harris who was three for three, the rest of the team struggled against a new-look matchup zone.

UK was shooting 48.8 percent from the field in its previous 12 games, against the Cards it dropped to 41.1 percent. They were seven of 22 from three-point range, 31.8 percent and committed 22 turnovers.

Juan Palacios played a surprising 34 minutes, scoring 17 points and grabbing six rebounds while helping to contain UK's Patterson on defense. Williams, McGee, Smith and Sosa also scored in double figures.

Louisville trailed 31-30 at the half, but shot 56 percent in the second half. UK made just two field goals in the first 13-plus minutes of the second half, committing ten turnovers while taking only eight shots. With 8:13 left in the game, UofL center David Padgett was fouled hard by Ramel Bradley as he went up for a layup, coming down awkwardly under the basket. Padgett had missed ten games this season with a fractured kneecap.

Terrence Williams, coming to the defense of his teammate, took exception to the play and confronted Bradley which ended up in a brief skirmish between the two players. They were quickly separated, with Padgett who was not injured, pulling Williams away. And intentional foul was called on Bradley and a technical was charged to Williams.

Terrence Williams recalled the play, "I thought it was a hard foul; I really didn't see the play. That's my center, just coming back from injury. So I'm going to protect him from injury and be like his shield. I got in the middle of it to see if my center was alright, I got pushed by somebody, I pushed somebody back. I'm the one who got the technical, but I'll take the technical and the win."

Bradley's version was a little different, "The big guy had a wide-open layup, and I was just trying to make a good, hard foul and not let him get the basket. I tried to help him up even, after the play was over. The guy, No. 1 (Williams) he just came in and acted like a clown, and Joe (Crawford) had my back. I just tried to get us to walk away from it. We couldn't afford anything bad to go wrong."

Bradley made both of the technical free throws, and Padgett missed both of his foul shots.

Louisville registered its first double-digit win over the Cats in Rupp Arena 89-75.

STATS

Kentucky

Player	Min	FG	FG A	3PT FG	3 PT FGA	FT	FT A	Reb	PF	Ast	St	BS	TO	Pts
Ramel Bradley	40	8	12	3	6	8	9	2	4	5	1	0	4	27
Jodie Meeks	31	1	8	1	5	4	4	1	2	2	3	0	1	7
Ramon Harris	14	3	3	1	1	1	2	4	3	0	0	0	0	8
Mark Coury	6	0	1	0	0	0	0	0	4	1	0	0	0	0
Patrick Patterson	32	3	14	0	2	0	0	7	5	0	1	2	6	6
Derrick Jasper	31	2	4	2	3	0	0	7	3	0	0	0	2	6
A.J. Stewart	3	0	0	0	0	0	0	2	3	0	0	0	0	0
Perry Stevenson	8	1	1	0	0	0	0	1	4	0	1	0	1	2
Joe Crawford	35	5	13	0	5	9	12	8	3	3	0	0	7	19
Team								2					1	
Totals	**200**	**23**	**56**	**7**	**22**	**22**	**27**	**34**	**31**	**11**	**6**	**2**	**22**	**75**

Louisville

Player	Min	FG	FG A	3PT FG	3 PT FGA	FT	FT A	Reb	PF	Ast	St	BS	TO	Pts
Terrance Williams	40	4	11	1	4	6	7	6	1	3	0	3	5	15
Juan Palacios	34	5	9	1	4	6	7	6	5	4	1	0	1	17
Derrick Caracter	19	2	5	0	0	2	4	5	5	0	3	1	2	6
Andre McGee	21	3	6	1	3	4	6	1	2	4	1	0	1	11
Jerry Smith	23	4	7	1	4	8	9	4	4	2	1	1	2	17
Preston Knowles	17	1	4	0	2	0	0	2	1	0	2	0	0	2
David Padgett	15	2	3	0	0	5	11	5	4	1	0	2	2	9
Edgar Sosa	23	3	6	2	3	2	2	3	0	1	0	0	1	10

Player	Min	FG	FG A	3PT FG	3 PT FGA	FT	FT A	Reb	PF	Ast	St	BS	TO	Pts
Josh Chichester	4	1	1	0	0	0	0	0	1	0	0	0	0	2
Terrance Farley	4	0	0	0	0	0	0	0	2	0	0	0	0	0
Team								3						
Totals	**200**	**25**	**52**	**6**	**20**	**33**	**46**	**35**	**25**	**15**	**8**	**7**	**14**	**89**

POINTS AFTER

"When something isn't given to us, we have to take it. We haven't done that yet. Until we do, we're going to continue down this path."
UK COACH BILLY GILLISPIE

"We saw on film that they turned up the aggressiveness in the second half. They just did a good job of getting their hands out and stealing the ball."
UK GUARD DERRICK JASPER

"He (Juan Palacios) gave us a spark to start the game. He looked athletic and back to his old self."
UofL DAVID PADGETT

"In the first half we were just driving and looking for our shots individually. In the second half we drove to get people open, and that really helped us."
UofL FORWARD JUAN PALACIOS

GAME 40

January 4, 2009

	UofL	UK
Record	8-3	11-3
Ranking	#18	unranked
Favored	LOUISVILLE BY 8	
Series	13	26
Location	FREEDOM HALL	
TV	CBS	

PRE-GAME REPORT

This time around, the Cats' record was much improved, 11-3, compared to last year's 6-6 mark, when they lost to the Cards in Rupp Arena 89-75. But they're still seeking a signature win over a top team, and what better time to secure it, than in the rivalry game. The degree of difficulty would be greater with the Cards at home in Freedom Hall. If history means anything, since the regular season rivalry games were resumed in November of 1983, Kentucky was 7-5 in Louisville with coaches Sutton and Pitino winning there first game there, while coaches Smith and Hall did not. (Joe Hall only played one game there)

However, the Cards, who were the preseason No. 3 favorite, had slipped to No. 18, losing two of their last three games to unranked UNLV at home, and to Tubby Smith's Minnesota Golden Gophers at the Stadium Shootout in Phoenix, Arizona. They had also lost to Western Kentucky earlier in the season in Nashville.

Kentucky needs to take care of the ball, they are averaging 18.3 turnovers a game, but are 7-0 when they commit fewer turnovers than the opponent. The Cats are shooting better from the field and the free throw line than the Cards, and have an advantage with Patterson inside.

Louisville has improved its free throw shooting of late, averaging about 76 percent compared to its season average of 64.5 percent. The Cards are dishing out assists at the rate 17.5 per game, but in their losses, they averaged only nine per game.

A key point to watch will be the play of Edgar Sosa. Coach Pitino suggested that he would be happier if he transferred. Coming into the rivalry game, Sosa had been averaging just five points a game on 30 percent shooting from the field and 20 percent from beyond the three-point arc.

QUOTES

"They can always put five guys out there that you have to guard. That sounds simple. But not too many teams do that. They do a really good job of spreading the floor and getting the ball where they want it."

UK COACH BILLY GILLISPIE

"If I was playing us, I'd definitely try to take Pat (Patterson) and Jodie (Meeks) away. I think that's what everyone will do. We'll have to be good in other spots."
UK COACH BILLY GILLISPIE

"Our defense never really gets a chance to do the things they'll capable of doing unless we take good shots. It all starts with our offense, not our defense because if we take high percentage shots we can get our pressure on and maybe cause some damage to people."
UofL COACH RICK PITINO

"But this is where I want to be. I committed to Louisville before I had even seen the campus."
UofL GUARD EDGAR SOSA

PROBABLE STARTERS

Louisville

POS.	PLAYER	HT.	WT.	CLS.	PT/G
F	TERRENCE WILLIAMS	6-6	215	SR.	11.6
F	EARL CLARK	6-9	220	JR.	13.1
F/C	SAMARDO SAMUELS	6-8	240	FR.	14.7
G	EDGAR SOSA	6-1	175	JR.	5.0
G	JERRY SMITH	6-1	200	JR.	7.7

Kentucky

POS.	PLAYER	HT.	WT.	CLS.	PT/G
F	PERRY STEVENSON	6-9	207	JR.	6.9
C	PATRICK PATTERSON	6-9	235	SO.	19.3
G	DeANDRE LIGGINS	6-6	202	FR.	6.8
G	MICHAEL PORTER	6-3	198	JR.	3.1
G	JODIE MEEKS	6-4	208	JR.	24.1

"No. 18 Louisville 74, Kentucky 71
Three and out"
Louisville Courier-Journal

"Louisville 74, Kentucky 71
SAY IT AIN'T SOSA"
Lexington Herald-Leader

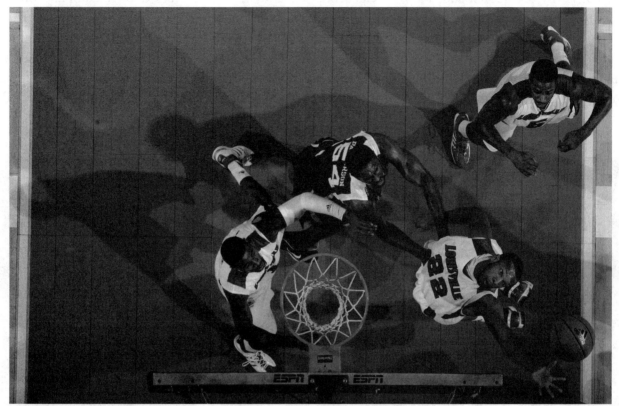

Terrence Williams - #1 - UofL, Patrick Paterson - #54 UK, George Goode - #22 - UofL
Earl Clark - #5 UofL

Maybe, it was because this would be the last game of the series played in storied Freedom Hall, with the Cards scheduled to move downtown to their new state-of-the art-facility, but most observers, including UofL Coach Rick Pitino felt this was a great game, "This is a great rivalry, but most of them have not been great basketball games. Tonight, was a great basketball game."

UK's start however, was not tending in that direction. The Cats made two turnovers in the first minute, seven in the first six minutes and a total of 14 in the first half. Surprisingly, UofL would only score two more points (24) than UK off turnovers for the entire game.

The Cardinal defense had Patterson and Meeks covered, neither player scored a basket in the first six minutes. UofL led by nine early. Meeks was the first to recover, hitting back-to-back-threes that started a 10-0 run for the Cats' junior guard. Meeks and Patterson combined for 18 straight points, to keep UK in the game, which trailed at the half, 38-35.

Starting the second half, the duo continued its torrid streak, scoring UK's first 15 points and 21 of its first 24. With 17:17 left in the game, back-to-back put backs by Patterson, actually gave Kentucky a one-point lead, 43-42. This was their first lead of the game. But the momentum shifted right back to UofL, after Coach Gillispie was called for a technical foul as Louisville scored the next 12 points to build its first double-digit lead, 57-45 with 13:07 to go.

Led by Meeks and Patterson, UK got within five points twice before the final television timeout. Then a foul line jumper with 4:32 left gave the Cards a 66-61 lead. Porter's three-pointer cut the deficit to 66-64 with just 2:53 remaining.

What's amazing, counting Sosa's game winner, the Cardinals managed only two baskets in the final 9:04 of play, but never relinquished their lead to Kentucky. At the 50.7 seconds mark, Sosa's two free throws put the Cards into a seemingly safe zone, leading 71-64. Enter Jerry Smith, fouling Jodie Meeks who was shooting a three. Meeks makes all three free throws, 71-67. Earl Clark throws the ball away on the inbounds pass, Meeks scores via a layup 71-69. Clark does it again and Meeks goes to the free throw line making two: UofL 71, UK 71.

Meeks was about to inherit the earth. With 22 seconds remaining, Edgar Sosa entered for the Cards and went right to work. Sosa was out near mid-court waving off Will Scott, who was ready to set the pick. UK's Porter is the defender, but Sosa watches him continue to backpedal. He makes his move and goes up from 25 feet and buries the three. Cardinal fans go into celebration mode as UofL prevails 74 to 71.

Patrick Patterson - #54 - UK, Jared Swopshire - #21 - UofL

STATS

Louisville

Player	Min	FG	FG A	3PT FG	3 PT FGA	FT	FT A	Reb	PF	Ast	St	BS	TO	Pts
Terrance Williams	36	7	12	3	5	2	2	8	2	1	5	0	3	19
Earl Clark	36	2	11	0	4	6	8	8	5	3	1	3	7	10
Samardo Samuels	11	2	3	0	0	0	0	1	4	1	0	0	1	4

Player	Min	FG	FG A	3PT FG	3 PT FGA	FT	FT A	Reb	PF	Ast	St	BS	TO	Pts
Edgar Sosa	26	4	7	2	4	8	9	1	1	2	2	0	2	18
Jerry Smith	29	3	3	3	3	2	2	0	1	2	0	2	1	11
Preston Knowles	10	1	2	1	1	0	0	1	2	0	1	0	0	3
Kyle Kuric	4	1	1	1	1	0	0	0	0	0	1	0	0	3
Will Scott	2	1	1	1	1	1	2	0	0	0	0	0	0	4
Jared Swopshire	4	0	1	0	0	0	0	0	0	0	0	0	0	0
George Goode	22	0	2	0	0	0	0	1	4	2	1	2	0	0
Terrence Jennings	6	0	2	0	0	0	0	1	1	0	0	1	1	0
Andre McGee	14	1	2	0	1	0	0	1	1	3	0	0	0	2
Team								0						
Totals	**200**	**22**	**47**	**11**	**20**	**19**	**23**	**22**	**21**	**14**	**11**	**8**	**15**	**74**

Kentucky

Player	Min	FG	FG A	3PT FG	3 PT FGA	FT	FT A	Reb	PF	Ast	St	BS	TO	Pts
Perry Stevenson	31	3	5	1	1	0	1	6	4	2	0	3	4	7
Patrick Patterson	40	8	13	0	0	6	7	15	1	4	1	0	3	22
Kevin Galloway	4	1	1	0	0	0	0	0	0	0	1	0	1	2
Michael Porter	33	2	5	2	4	2	2	0	4	1	1	0	0	8
Jodie Meeks	40	8	19	3	9	9	9	3	3	0	2	0	6	28
Darius Miller	13	0	1	0	0	0	0	0	0	1	0	0	0	0
A.J. Stewart	3	0	0	0	0	2	2	1	1	0	0	0	0	2
Ramon Harris	23	0	3	0	1	0	0	3	3	1	0	0	1	0
DeAndre Liggins	8	1	1	0	0	0	1	0	1	2	1	1	3	2
Josh Harrellson	5	0	1	0	1	0	0	1	0	0	0	0	3	0

Player	Min	FG	FG A	3PT FG	3 PT FGA	FT	FT A	Reb	PF	Ast	St	BS	TO	Pts
Team								3	1					
Totals	200	23	49	6	16	19	22	32	18	11	6	4	21	71

POINTS AFTER

"Man he pulled up from deep. I didn't think there was a chance in heck he'd made it."
UK GUARD MICHAEL PORTER

"We didn't make the statement. The score is up there. We lost."
UK FORWARD PATRICK PATTERSON

"(Porter) was backing up, and I really didn't know where I was on the floor. It's probably not going to hit me until later tonight when I see it on ESPN. Twenty years from now I can tell my kids I played for Louisville and hit the shot that beat Kentucky."
UofL GUARD EDGAR SOSA

"It would have been difficult if we had lost. We played great, basically outplayed them for 38 minutes. To lose that game would have been emotionally and physically devastating. I wouldn't have wanted to be in the locker room trying to motivate those guys if we had lost that game."
UofL COACH RICK PITINO

Like his Kentucky team had done so often before, Rick Pitino's Louisville team won the game by shooting the three-pointer in the rivalry game at an unbelievable clip. Against UK the Cards shot 55 percent, hitting 11 of 20.

On the season, they were hitting 34.7 percent. It was also their best game of the year from the foul line. Averaging 64.5 percent coming into the contest, the Cards hit 19 of 23 for 82.6 percent.

UK had the big advantage off the boards, 32-22. Patterson collected six offensive rebounds, Louisville had seven. The Cats outscored the Cards 23-5 on second chance points.

Edgar Sosa had made only seven of 35 three-point shots all season, but today he was two for four and scored 18 points, and he was eight of nine from the foul line.

Coach Gillispie's team would finish 22-14, losing in the quarterfinals of both, the SEC and NIT tournaments. Problems continued to plague Gillispie off the court, making a coaching change necessary.

I liked DeAndre Liggins from the first time I saw him play. In my opinion, he should have been playing more under Gillispie. The point Gillispie made about Pitino having five players that could score, was echoed by Oklahoma State Coach Hank Iba to me about Coach Rupp, "When you played other teams you worried about two or three players being able to score, but against a Rupp coached team, you had to worry about all five."

Edgar Sosa - #10 - UL, Jerry Smith - #34 - UL

GAME 41

January 2, 2010

	UK	UofL
Record	14-0	10-3
Ranking	#3	unranked
Series	26	14
Favored	KENTUCKY BY 7.5	
Location	RUPP ARENA	
TV	CBS	

PRE-GAME REPORT

When two top gunfighters meet in a classic western, we hear such things as, "This town's not big enough for the both of us," or "Prove it," and "we have to find out which one of us is the best." In this shootout, excuse me, rivalry, it is big enough for both of these top coaches, John Calipari and Rick Pitino. And we are the beneficiaries of watching them prove it.

Pitino turned around UK when he arrived. "Others may have been able to do what he did, but not in the manner or time that he did," said Coach Scott Davenport.

Pitino has come to Louisville and has done the same thing for the Cardinals, although it took a little more time, turning their program around after Coach Crum's retirement.

Paul Rogers, the "Voice of the Cardinals," told me that, "it was unrealistic to have expected Rick Pitino to accomplish what he did at Kentucky in the same period of time here at Louisville. It's a different time, a different place. He's been able to get his pieces in place and they are in good shape."

Paul also agreed with this Paul, that some fans were complaining about Pitino as coach before he won the NCAA Regional against Florida and went on to meet UK in the Final Four. Fans complaining about Pitino's coaching, Rogers couldn't agree with.

Now at Kentucky, they weren't on probation when Coach Calipari arrived, but they were going absolutely nowhere, stuck in the NIT. The new order of things, "One and Done," would make an instant reversible of post-season tournament play. This is why this rivalry is back on top, college's basketball's best, because of the ability and visibility of these two coaches. They look like champions, they coach like champions and each has won an NCAA championship in the previous two seasons.

Some Louisville fans said Calipari couldn't win a title, using "One and Dones." Now, the word is he can't win another.

Some Kentucky fans were in the process of scanning Pitino's picture in that conglomeration of faces on the cover of the Sgt. Pepper's Lonely Hearts Club album, when back-to-back Final Fours, a national championship and induction into the Basketball Hall of Fame rejuvenated this coach for years to come.

Sure you need players. Coach Crum told me, "I'll tell you one thing. I was a better coach when I had better players." And these two coaches can recruit them.

This rivalry was about to enter a new dimension.

Darius Miller - #1 - UK; Jared Swopshire - #21 - UofL; DeMarcus Cousins - #15 - UK

QUOTES

'We need to be better than that. We don't need it. It's about the players on the court. Let's keep it about the players."
UK COACH JOHN CALIPARI.

"Referring to his exhortation urging UK fans not to bring signs or direct any chanting towards Coach Pitino regarding the Karen Sypher case. Coach Pitino admitted to an affair with Sypher earlier that summer. It'll get you off track; it'll will get you off focus. I just tell my teammates to concentrate. You can listen to what the fans are saying; you can read the signs. Just make sure that you concentrate on the game.
    UK FORWARD PATRICK PATTERSON

"They're an extraordinary team statistically, first of all. They have great speed. They can erase their mistakes with their hand speed and their foot speed."
    UofL COACH RICK PITINO

"It will be, like walking into hell (Rupp Arena)."
    UofL GUARD EDGAR SOSA

PROBABLE STARTERS

Kentucky

POS.	PLAYER	HT.	WT.	CLS.	PT/G
F	PATRICK PATTERSON	6-9	235	JR.	16.6
F	DeMARCUS COUSINS	6-11	260	FR.	15.2
G	DARIUS MILLER	6-7	223	SO.	8.2
G	JOHN WALL	6-4	195	FR.	17.2
G	ERIC BLEDSOE	6-1	190	FR.	10.1

Louisville

POS.	PLAYER	HT.	WT.	CLS.	PT/G
F	SAMARDO SAMUELS	6-9	260	SO.	16.4
F	JARED SWOPSHIRE	6-8	220	SO.	8.0
G	EDGAR SOSA	6-2	175	SR.	13.3
G	REGINALD DELK	6-5	200	SR.	6.7
G	JERRY SMITH	6-2	190	SR.	8.7

"CATS FIGHT 'EM OFF"
Lexington Herald-Leader

"NO. 3 KENTUCKY 71, LOUISVILLE 62

CATS push to the top at Rough Arena"
Louisville Courier-Journal

Game preliminaries.

"Have Intimidation Will Trash Talk!" Text all players Lexington, KY.

Players bumping other players after the National Anthem.

No opposing cheerleaders allowed. No handshakes before the tip-off. Was Pat Riley in the building?

That was the friendly stuff, because 45 seconds into the game, DeMarcus Cousins was going for a loose ball and instead, got Jared Swopshire's head. But the officials called technicals on Swopshire and Reginald Delk. Following further review, Cousins also received a technical, but was not ejected from the game for applying his elbow to Swopshire's head.

Swopshire would miss his first six shots, including a three-point airball. He could use the Cousin's encounter to plead for mercy, but what about the rest of the team. The Cardinals made only one of their first 19 shots, finishing the first half five for 29. UK was up 15-3 early, but didn't put the Cardinals away. UofL hit five free throws down the first half stretch and trailed by eight at the intermission, 27-19.

Louisville started the second half with a 7-2 run. Swopshire, Sosa and Jerry Smith scored 27 of their 32 points in the second half helping to keep the Cards in contention, and with 9:51 left in the game, Terrence Jenning's free throw turned, staying in contention, to a 42-41 Louisville lead. Suddenly, Rupp Arena's record crowd of 24,479 became the largest mausoleum in the U.S.

The silence was brief, for the Cards slammed into a Wall. John Wall's driving basket 20 seconds later, leaning back to get the shot over Terrence Jennings, put the Cats back on top for good, 43-42. The Cards committed a turnover on their next possession, and while waiting for the inbounds pass, Wall and Jerry Smith received a warning for trash talking, followed by technical fouls.

Wall claimed that Smith tried to bump him out of his spot; whatever, it was inspirational therapy for Wall. He followed the exchange with a 15-foot jumper and two free throws and UK led 47-42. Louisville would never get closer than four, losing 71-62.

Darius Miller - #1 - UK, Chris Smith - #5 - UofL

STATS

Kentucky

Player	Min	FG	FG A	3PT FG	3 PT FGA	FT	FT A	Reb	PF	Ast	St	BS	TO	Pts
DeMarcus Cousins	26	7	14	0	0	4	8	18	3	3	1	2	2	18
Patrick Patterson	38	7	10	1	1	2	5	4	1	1	1	0	1	17
Darius Miller	8	0	1	0	0	0	0	2	3	0	0	0	1	0
John Wall	36	5	10	0	3	7	12	1	3	4	2	0	5	17
Eric Bledsoe	30	3	8	0	3	6	6	2	2	4	2	0	4	12
Darnell Dodson	13	0	5	0	4	2	2	4	1	1	1	0	1	2
Ramon Harris	23	1	3	1	3	0	0	2	4	1	0	0	3	3
Perry Stevenson	10	1	1	0	0	0	0	2	0	0	0	1	0	2
Daniel Orton	8	0	0	0	0	0	1	0	4	0	1	2	1	0
DeAndre Liggins	8	0	0	0	0	0	0	1	0	1	1	0	0	0
Team								2						
Totals	**200**	**24**	**52**	**2**	**14**	**21**	**34**	**38**	**21**	**15**	**9**	**5**	**18**	**71**

Louisville

Player	Min	FG	FG A	3PT FG	3 PT FGA	FT	FT A	Reb	PF	Ast	St	BS	TO	Pts
Samardo Samuels	25	3	9	0	0	3	5	9	4	2	1	1	3	9
Jared Swopshire	30	4	13	2	4	0	2	4	4	0	0	1	3	10
Jerry Smith	25	4	7	2	4	1	2	6	3	0	4	0	2	11
Edgar Sosa	34	3	11	0	4	5	6	2	2	2	0	0	6	11
Reginald Delk	28	2	3	1	2	4	4	4	4	1	1	0	0	9
Preston Knowles	17	1	8	0	2	5	5	1	3	0	2	0	0	7

Player	Min	FG	FG A	3PT FG	3 PT FGA	FT	FT A	Reb	PF	Ast	St	BS	TO	Pts
Peyton Siva	6	0	1	0	1	0	0	0	1	0	1	0	1	0
Rakeem Buckles	10	0	2	0	0	0	0	3	4	0	0	0	2	0
Kyle Kuric	10	0	2	0	0	0	0	3	2	0	0	0	0	0
Terrence Jennings	15	2	3	0	0	1	2	4	3	0	0	3	1	5
Stepham Van Treese	0	0	0	0	0	0	0	0	0	0	0	0	0	0
Team								3						
Totals	**200**	**19**	**59**	**5**	**17**	**19**	**26**	**39**	**30**	**5**	**9**	**5**	**19**	**62**

POINTS AFTER

"They're a Big East team. They love being physical, they love pushing, they love smacking, they love hacking. That's what they do a lot of, trying to get us out of our game or trying to get in our heads. I thought my teammates did a good job of handling it.
UK FORWARD PATRICK PATTERSON

"As heated, and emotional and physical, grabbing, pushing a game as I have coached in."
UK COACH JOHN CALIPARI

"We thought we could win the game. But they made big plays and deserved to win."
UofL COACH RICK PITINO

"This was going to be a dogfight. They came out—I guess they tried to come out—with the tough-boy acts. Like they were going to scare us and we (didn't) back down. We were ready for whatever."
UofL GUARD EDGAR SOSA

GAME 42

December 31, 2010

	UofL	UK
Record	10-2	11-1
Ranking	#11	#22
Series	14	27
Favored	LOUISVILLE BY 2	
Location	THE YUM CENTER	
TV	CBS	

PRE-GAME REPORT

Xs and Os, match-ups, stats and etc.; forget, it. This is the Josh Harrellson Report. How about some possible headlines: "Rudy Transfers to UK," "Mr. Harrellson Goes to the YUM CENTER," "When You Wish Upon a Wildcat," and "One Shinning Moment for Josh." He was poised to break loose in the North Carolina game, but didn't shoot from the wing several times when he had the opportunity, or drive to the basket. He was saving his coming out party for the Cats' first game in the Yum Center, which turned out to be Josh's best.

Josh Harrellson - #55 - UK, Preston Knowles- #2 - UofL
Terrence Jones - #3 - UK

PROBABLE STARTERS

Louisville

POS.	PLAYER	HT.	WT.	CLS.	PT/G
G	PRESTON KNOWLES	6-1	195	SR.	15.2
G	PEYTON SIVA	5-11	175	SO.	11.5
C	GORGUI DIENG	6-10	225	FR.	5.8
G	CHRIS SMITH	6-2	200	JR.	8.7
G	KYLE KURIC	6-4	185	JR.	7.9

Kentucky

POS.	PLAYER	HT.	WT.	CLS.	PT/G
F	JOSH HARRELLSON	6-10	275	SR.	5.4
F	TERRENCE JONES	6-8	244	FR.	18.2
G	DARIUS MILLER	6-7	228	JR.	9.4
G	BRANDON KNIGHT	6-3	185	FR.	17.4
G	DeANDRE LIGGINS	6-6	210	JR.	10.3

Career Game, Powers
CATS PAST CARDS
Lexington Herald-Leader

"It's Josh, by gosh!"
Louisville Courier-Journal

Rick Bozich of the Courier-Journal pointed out that 15 NBA scouts had requested credentials for the game, Josh Harrellson countered, "They probably weren't here to see me." But what they saw was a player who had put himself in condition to be used. When watching film of Harrellson's earlier days, close observation was required to reveal the existence of potential, not Dan Issel potential, but the ability to contribute nonetheless. No meticulous observation was necessary however, to know that he was not in shape.

Earlier in the season in a Blue-White scrimmage, Harrellson had 26 rebounds, but was sulking because he drew no praise from Coach Calipari and vented his feelings on Twitter. Coach Cal wasn't amused, and suspended the big man's tweeting privileges and placed him on a 30-day conditioning program.

Harrellson didn't let the punishment get in his way, expanding on the program, he got into the best shape of his college career and became a team leader. They saw Terrence Jones and Harrellson working together as a team, complimenting each other on that frontline.

They saw a bigger, slower player take on all comers: the quick, the tall and the small. They saw a center, who didn't play in last year's UK-UofL game, play 37 minutes, make dunks, hit a three-pointer, score 23 points, grab a game-high 14 rebounds, hand out two assists, block a shot, make a steal and only commit one turnover in those most productive 37 minutes of play.

They saw DeAndre Liggins use his size and quickness against UofL's point-guard, Peyton Siva to keep the Cards stranded on the perimeter in the first half, as the Cats built a comfortable 35-24 halftime advantage.

They saw Brandon Knight score 25-points and hand out four assists leading the Cats' attack. Even though Louisville made nine straight shots in the second half, trimming the deficit to 10, at 59-49, UK had the answers and rolled on to a surprising 78-63 win.

QUOTES

"I think Siva is really, really good and that's why we put DeAndre on him."
UK COACH JOHN CALIPARI

"Anybody sit next to our bench last year? We had some back and forth. There's no back and forth."
UK COACH JOHN CALIPARI

"We felt that if they were going to take away the perimeter shot on us, then we had to go inside. We only went inside four times, and that was our Achilles' heel in the first half."
UofL COACH RICK PITINO

"They were better on the glass, (36-25) they were better at executing and they played a terrific game."
UofL COACH RICK PITINO

STATS

Louisville

Player	Min	FG	FG A	3PT FG	3 PT FGA	FT	FT A	Reb	PF	Ast	St	BS	TO	Pts
Chris Smith	33	6	8	1	1	2	5	6	3	4	0	0	3	15
Kyle Kuric	37	3	7	1	4	0	0	3	4	2	2	0	2	7
Gorgui Dieng	12	2	4	0	0	0	0	4	1	0	0	0	1	4
Preston Knowles	37	8	16	6	10	0	0	2	2	3	4	0	3	22
Peyton Siva	33	2	9	0	3	2	3	2	4	4	2	0	3	6
Tim Henderson	0	0	0	0	0	0	0	0	1	0	0	0	0	0
Elisha Justice	3	0	0	0	0	0	0	1	0	0	0	0	0	0
Terrence Jennings	28	4	6	0	0	1	3	4	1	1	1	2	1	9
Russ Smith	5	0	1	0	0	0	0	0	1	0	1	0	0	0

UK vs. UofL College Basketball's No. 1 Rivalry - Enough Said!

Player	Min	FG	FG A	3PT FG	3 PT FGA	FT	FT A	Reb	PF	Ast	St	BS	TO	Pts
Mike Marra	11	0	3	0	2	0	0	1	1	0	0	1	0	0
Stepham Van Treese	1	0	0	0	0	0	0	0	0	0	0	0	0	0
Team								2						
Totals	200	25	54	8	20	5	11	25	18	14	9	3	13	63

Kentucky

Player	Min	FG	FG A	3PT FG	3 PT FGA	FT	FT A	Reb	PF	Ast	St	BS	TO	Pts
Terrence Jone	33	5	11	0	2	2	2	8	2	5	1	3	1	12
Josh Harrellson	37	10	12	1	1	2	3	14	3	2	1	1	1	23
Darius Miller	29	3	6	0	1	1	1	3	4	0	0	1	2	7
Brandon Knight	36	7	13	4	6	7	8	3	2	4	0	0	5	25
DeAndre Liggins	39	1	7	0	4	0	0	4	2	2	4	2	4	2
Jon Hood	1	0	0	0	0	0	0	0	0	0	0	0	0	0
Doron Lamb	23	3	6	1	2	2	2	3	2	1	0	0	0	9
Eloy Vargus	2	0	2	0	0	0	0	0	0	0	0	0	0	0
Team								1						
Totals	200	29	57	6	16	14	16	36	15	14	6	7	13	78

POINTS AFTER

It was mentioned that DeAndre Liggins had played an uneventful eight minutes in the game at Rupp the previous year, which UK won 71-62. Examining the box score from that contest, Liggins had one rebound and one assist. By using the scoring system that I developed for myself, based on the Coach Rupp system that appeared in the CJ, Liggins scored a +2 in that game, making one point every four minutes. (Note: The system works like this; add points, rebounds, assists, steals and blocks, then minus the turnovers, and missed field goals and free throws for your final number.) This game, he played 37 minutes and was a +4, a point every 9.3 minutes.

By this comparison the uneventful eight minutes was better per/minute played. But Liggins defense was also a key factor in this UK win, which this system is not specifically designed to quantify. However, Liggins' job was to control UofL's point-guard Peyton Siva. Siva played 33 minutes and was a +3. That correlates to a point every 11 minutes.

217

The combined 19 mintues played for Elisha Justice, Russ Smith and Mike Marra at guard, was a minus-one, now the value of Liggins performance on defense is easier noted.

Preston Knowles had a fine game from the two guard position. He scored 22 points and rated a 20 in 37 minutes of play. He was six of 10 from three-point range, leading the Cardinals in scoring.

One more shot with the numbers to illustrate the invaluable contribution from Harrellson. He played 37 minutes like Liggins and Knowles, but his Willman rating was a superb +37. A point a minute, truly a remarkable game.

Fans are going to talk, but one must be careful when he or she is a fan, and a manager inside business premises on duty. I was inside a Walgreens, where I could easily hear a snide remark, made by a manager to a Wildcat fan before the East Region NCAA game in 2011 against No. 1 Ohio State. He said something like this, "Boy! You're sure going to get your butts kicked tonight."

As a customer, I was surprised that he would risk making such a statement surrounded by other customers. Remember! The fans wield the mightiest weapon, sponsor the recall proof referendum, cast the veto that cannot be overturned and hold within their very pockets, the ultimate right of nullification—their hard earned money—that goes for tickets to games, pay-per-view telecasts and purchases in stores.

GAME 43

December 31, 2011

	UK	UofL
Record	12-1	11-1
Ranking	#3	#4
Series	28	14
Favored	KENTUCKY BY 13.5	
Location	RUPP ARENA	
TV	CBS	

PRE-GAME REPORT

The "Dream Game" was reaching new heights among it's fans, and greater notoriety around the nation. Never before had both teams clashed when ranked among the top-five. Their combined record of 23-2 was the best since the 20-1 mark back in the 1996-97 season.

Kentucky had the No. 1 recruiting class again led by Anthony Davis, Michael Gilchrist, Marquis Teague and Kyle Wiltjer. But they also had some experience in the "house." Senior Darius Miller, along with sophomores Terrence Jones and Doron Lamb.

Louisville wasn't empty-handed. It's recruiting was getting better and they also had a combination of experience and talented newcomers with seniors Chris Smith and Kyle Kuric, along with junior Peyton Siva, sophomore Russ Smith and freshman Kevin Ware at guard. On the frontline 6-10 Sophomore Gorgui Dieng would be joined by Chane Behanan and Wayne Blackshear, who could also play guard.

The two main returning players were UK Coach John Calipari and UofL Coach Rick Pitino.

CBS Sports reporter Jeff Goodman interviewed Pitino concerning these comments made by Calipari, "It's a unique thing. There's no other state, none, that's as connected to their basketball program as this one. Because those other states (do) have other programs. Michigan has Michigan State, California has has UCLA, North Carolina has Duke. It's Kentucky throughout this whole state, and that's what makes us unique."

Pitino responded, "Four things I've learned in my 59 years about people. I ignore the jealous, I ignore the malicious, I ignore the ignorant and I ignore the paranoid." Is he talking about Coach Calipari? Surely not.

Maybe Coach Calipari was trying to point out that UK has more fans throughout the state. Take IU and Purdue for example. Indiana is a basketball crazy state too, but you hear things like: if you go so far up I-65 you'll hit Boilermaker country. That doesn't mean IU fans don't reside up north but Purdue will have a bigger base there, and vice a versa further south.

Whereas Kentucky would have large fan bases throughout the state—border to border. On the other hand, Louisville, since winning its first NCAA national championship in 1980, has made inroads in different areas outside of Jefferson County.

Then, Coach Calipari may just be looking to keep his team's name in the press, like UK All-American Lee Huber from Louisville St. Xavier told me about his coach, Adolph Rupp, "The rules makers took the center jump out of college basketball in 1937. Before that change, you had a jump ball after every basket made. We're in New York and the headline the next day in the paper read, 'Coach Rupp Wants the Center Jump Brought Back." Before 1937, a jump ball was required after every basket scored. Huber saw Coach Rupp later that day and said, "Coach do you really believe that?" Rupp's reply, "Hell, no! But there were a lot of writers in the room and I thought it would be good press for the university."

Otherwise, it provides unnecessary bulletin board material for the other team. The "feuding" between the coaches makes the rivalry better on the floor and the debates more interesting among the fans.

QUOTES

"Neither one gives ground to the other, ever."
TIM WELSH ESPN BASKETBALL ANALYST

"It's all part of the psychological warfare that comes about when you have two great programs with two great coaches and rabid fan bases. It's like Rommel and Montgomery, Ali and Frasier, Bobby Fischer and Boris Spassky.
There was a time not long ago when Kentucky-Louisville wasn't a game you really cared about watching if you were a casual fan. Now because of the importance of the game and hostility between the coaches, it's a game you have to watch. I really want to stay neutral on this, but it's all great theater."
FRAN FRASCHILLA ESPN BASKETBALL ANALYST

"Who are the happiest people in our town right now? The ticket scalpers. They're ecstatic."
UK COACH JOHN CALIPARI

"We can't buy into any of that. We know they're just as athletic. We know they're a really good team, too. We can't come in thinking we're more athletic or a better team. We have to come in and play, because we know they will do the same."
UK GUARD DARIUS MILLER responding to Coach Pitino's comments that UK is a better team.

PROBABLE STARTERS

Kentucky

POS.	PLAYER	HT.	WT.	CLS.	PT/G
F	DARIUS MILLER	6-8	225	SR.	10.5
F	DORON LAMB	6-4	210	SO.	15.8
G	ANTHONY DAVIS	6-10	220	FR.	11.6
F	M. KIDD-GILCHRIST	6-7	232	FR.	13.5
G	MARQUIS TEAGUE	6-2	195	FR.	9.9

Louisville

POS.	PLAYER	HT.	WT.	CLS.	PT/G
F	KYLE KURIC	6-4	195	SR.	13.5
F	CHANE BEHANAN	6-6	250	FR.	8.7
C	GORGUI DIENG	6-11	235	SO.	10.5
G	PEYTON SIVA	6-0	180	JR.	9.5
G	CHRIS SMITH	6-2	195	SR.	9.9

"KENTUCKY 69, LOUISVILLE 62
GRITTY, UGLY, BEAUTIFUL"
Lexington Herald-Leader

"BLOCK AND TACKLE"
Louisville Courier-Journal

Doron Lamb - #20 - UK, Russ Smith - #2 - UofL
Michael Kidd-Gilchrist - #14 - UK

Make it three consecutive wins for Calipari vs. Pitino in the UK-UofL rivalry as the Cats won 69-62. Calipari is 3-0 against Pitino in this series, but overall, the two are tied with eight wins a piece.

Michael Kidd-Gilchrist loves contact. Michael Kidd-Gilchrist loves this game; 52 total fouls called, 29 against UofL as Gilchrist notched career-highs in both points and rebounds with 24 and 19 respectfully. Two other Wildcats scored in double figures, Davis with 18 and Lamb had 10.

Russ Smith came off the bench for Louisville to score a career-high 30 points, in just 27 minutes of play. He was the only Cardinal to score in double figures. The Cards had only one lead in this entire game, that's when Chris Smith hit a jumper just 17 seconds into the first half to give UofL a 2-0 lead.

Marquis Teague hit a jumper and a layup in the next 62 seconds, putting UK on top 4-2. Six minutes later UK was out in front 12-8.

The two teams combined for only seven field goals in the first nine minutes of play. Shooting came at a premium in this game. The Cards shot 40.7 percent in the first half and trailed 36-33 at the intermission. UK shot only 27.8 percent.

Foul trouble limited UofL's Chane Behanan to less than four minutes of play in the first half, and UK's Anthony Davis saw just seven minutes of action. Davis' first half box score stats would have been great, had he been playing golf. No points scored, no shots attempted, one block and four rebounds. It was a very low round. However, he finished with 18 points, 10 rebounds and six blocked shots. And, he worked magic from the charity stripe, connecting on 12 of 13 free throws.

UofL tied the game at 40-40 when Russ Smith turned a four-point play. Old math; new math, add a three-pointer and a free throw and you total four. But Kentucky scored the next seven points and went on to win by the same margin, 69-62.

Louisville shot 32.3 percent to Kentucky's 29.8 percent. But you must remember that coming into this game, UK was ranked No. 1 in field-goal defense, and UofL was No. 6.

Rebounding and free throw shooting were the major differences in the game. UK out rebounded the Cards 57-31, and hit 32 of 43 free throws for 74.4 percent. The Cardinals were 18 of 27 from the foul line for 66.7 percent.

STATS

Kentucky

	Min	FG	FG A	3PT FG	3 PT FGA	FT	FT A	Reb	PF	Ast	St	BS	TO	Pts
M. Kidd-Gilchrist	39	7	16	2	4	8	13	19	3	1	0	0	0	24
Anthony Davis	27	3	4	0	0	12	13	10	3	0	3	6	2	18
Darius Miller	32	2	8	1	3	2	2	4	4	1	0	0	8	7
Doron Lamb	24	1	7	0	3	8	9	0	4	2	0	0	4	10
Marquis Teague	29	1	8	0	3	2	2	3	5	5	0	1	4	4
Terrence Jones	30	1	9	0	1	0	4	11	1	0	3	0	1	2
Twany Beckham	2	0	0	0	0	0	0	0	0	1	0	0	0	0
Eloy Vargus	2	0	0	0	0	0	0	0	0	0	0	0	0	0
Kyle Wiltjer	15	2	5	0	2	0	0	2	2	0	0	0	1	4
Team								8	1				1	
Totals	**200**	**17**	**57**	**3**	**16**	**32**	**43**	**57**	**23**	**10**	**6**	**7**	**21**	**69**

Louisville

Player	Min	FG	FG A	3PT FG	3 PT FGA	FT	FT A	Reb	PF	Ast	St	BS	TO	Pts
Kyle Kuric	38	1	4	0	2	0	0	2	4	1	1	0	1	2
Chane Behanan	15	1	3	0	0	2	2	5	5	1	0	0	1	4
Gorgui Dieng	33	2	5	0	0	1	2	5	4	0	1	6	3	5
Peyton Siva	29	2	13	0	4	4	6	2	4	4	1	1	3	8
Chris Smith	21	2	10	1	3	2	2	3	3	0	3	0	0	7
Russ Smith	27	10	20	3	8	7	10	5	3	0	3	0	3	30
Rakeem Buckles	15	1	4	0	0	0	0	3	4	0	0	0	2	2
Jared Swopshire	17	1	2	0	1	2	3	2	2	0	3	1	0	4
Elisha Justice	1	0	0	0	0	0	0	1	0	0	0	0	0	0
Kevin Ware	4	0	1	0	0	0	2	0	0	0	0	0	1	0
Team								3						
Totals	**200**	**20**	**62**	**4**	**18**	**18**	**27**	**31**	**29**	**6**	**12**	**8**	**14**	**62**

POINTS AFTER

Articles, written before the game, had symbolized Calipari with the present and Pitino the past. It wasn't mentioned that Calipari owned the series, but his real success was now filling that category.

In his two previous years at UK, he was 7-2 in the NCAA, with a Final Four and an Elite-Eight appearance, while Pitino was 0-2, which included a loss to another in-state rival, Morehead in the second round of the NCAA tournament.

Pitino was filling that "past" category. There were Louisville fans that were murmuring. They were also thinking past, in terms of Pitino, not being at Louisville anymore. But those glorious days at Kentucky also included a surprise, disappointing loss to Marquette, in the second round of the NCAA Southeast Regional. That was followed by an Elite-Eight, back-to-back Final Fours and a national championship.

Aren't rivalries and comparisons fun? Of course, they are lot more fun when your team is hot and the other team is not.

GAME 44

March 31, 2012

	UK	UofL
Record	37-2	30-9
Ranking	#1	#17
Favored	KENTUCKY BY 8.5	
Series	29	14
Location	SUPERDOME NEW ORLEANS, LA	
TV	CBS	

PRE-GAME REPORT

The last time two teams from the same state played in the Final Four against each other was back in 1962, when Ohio State and Cincinnati met for the second consecutive year in the national title game. The Bearcats beat the Buckeyes both times. Still, these two in state rivals do not play each other during the regular season, and there appears to be no driving force to change that current policy as occurred in this rivalry.

UK and UofL have made two Final Fours together. In 1975 Kentucky advanced to the title game beating Syracuse 95-79, but the Cardinals lost a game they could have won to UCLA, 75-74 in overtime and UCLA went on to beat the Cats 92-85 in the championship game, John Wooden's last stand.

Comparing UK-UofL to North Carolina and Duke, the Tar Heels and Blue Devils have only been to the same Final Four once, in 1991, but failed to play each other for that championship. Some point out that Duke and North Carolina have not had the same number of opportunities to play in the Final Four, because the NCAA did not allow more than one team from the same conference to participate in the tournament until 1975.

That is true, but the difference is not as great as some have surmised. The NCAA tournament started in 1939 and through the 1950 season, only eight teams were invited to participate. Of those 48 spots, nine were independents.

In 1950 the NCAA decided that Kentucky and North Carolina State should have a playoff to determine which of the two teams would be invited to play in the tournament.

Coach Rupp felt that since his team had won back-to-back NCAA Championships, and was ranked No. 4 with a 22-4 record, and NC State was 21-5 and ranked No. 8, that his team should be the invitee. He was not willing to be part of a play-in game.

Three men cast ballots to determine the participant, two were from the Southern Conference where NC State played and one from the SEC, UK's conference. In a big surprise, NC State won 2-1. One of those voting from the Southern Conference was Duke's Eddie Cameron, for whom their basketball facility is named. This is the original Duke irritant for the Cats. The silver thread in this dark tapestry of intrigue, is that Coach Rupp threw such a fit, that the tournament was expanded to 16 teams the following year.

The 1951 East Regional marked the first time that UK and UofL met in the NCAA tournament. They would meet again in the 1959 Mideast Regional. Although they could meet in regional NCAA play, it was not until 1964, when Louisville became a Missouri Valley Conference member, whose champion played in the NCAA Midwest Regional, that the Cards and Cats had the opportunity to meet in the Final Four.

It's always advisable to check things out before declaring how things really stand. I have always thought that the NCAA Selection Committee favored Duke and NorthCarolina for possible tournament match-ups over Kentucky and Louisville. It has, but the disparity is not as great as I had imagined. Still, it would take a good leap to get across the disproportionate chasm that does exist.

Starting with the 1975 Final Four, more than one team from a conference could be invited to the NCAA tournament. From that point to today, 39 opportunities to meet in a Final Four have been possible, if the brackets were so designed.

In this 39-year time frame, the Selection Committee's bracket configurations netted Duke-North Carolina 18 opportunities to meet for the national championship, while UK-UofL were limited to 13. Obviously, none have occurred. Final Four semifinal match-up possibilities are even at eight for each pair of schools. With 26 opportunities to meet in the Final Four, Duke and North Carolina have only done it once, in 1991, and did not play each other in the championship game, although Duke did win its first of four championships, beating Kansas 72-65.

During this same time period, the Cards and Cats twice arrived together for the Final Four. In the aforementioned 1975 Final Four, UCLA played the villain's part beating UofL in the semifinals and UK in the championship game.

Now, in 2012 it happened. Here, today they would play. This was no April Fool, there would be plenty of time for that tomorrow. This was only the fourth time in NCAA history that two teams from the same state would play each other in the Final Four.

The first was in 1954, when La Salle from Philadelphia beat Penn State in the semifinals 69-54 (Kentucky had beaten La Salle 73-60 in Lexington that year, but because Hagan, Ramsey and

Tsioropoulos were graduate students, they were not permitted to participate in the NCAA tourney, so UK declined the bid.).

The Cats were the AP Poll National Champion for 1954, and the Helms Foundation Champion as well. Only four times since 1939, when the NCAA tournament began, has the Helms organization given it's national championship to a team other than the NCAA winner.

Cincinnati beat Ohio State 70-65 in the 1961 title game and 71-59 the following year. What would we see different today, that we didn't see on New Year's Eve in Rupp Arena, when UK celebrated the New Year with a 69-62 victory? Two times in a season they would play, but this time, the bragging rights were expanded to include the right to play for the national championship.

Calipari and Pitino were 8-8 all-time, something had to give.

QUOTES

"I put it like this: Anthony Davis, he should be worried about Gorgui Dieng really. For us as a team, we're going to try to stop (Davis) cold, really, not feed into his shot-blocking. We've got to get him in foul trouble, and that will pretty much give us the game."
UofL GUARD CHRIS SMITH

"I think you never know, when the ball is thrown up in the Final Four, who is going to handle and overcome the nervousness of playing in a Final Four and who's going to be totally focused in and not bothered by it. There are some players I've coached in the past I thought would be really cool and calm, and they weren't. And others I thought wouldn't be (who) were. You really can't tell by their demeanor before the game or how they act."
UofL COACH RICK PITINO

"They pressed us (in Rupp Arena) and it rattled some cages. I mean, we were not ready for that."
UK COACH JOHN CALIPARI

"We worked on playing through the hits and being extra physical with each other."
UK GUARD SAM MALONE

PROBABLE STARTERS

Kentucky

POS.	PLAYER	HT.	WT.	CLS.	PT/G
F	DARIUS MILLER	6-8	225	SR.	10.5
F	DORON LAMB	6-4	210	SO.	15.8
G	ANTHONY DAVIS	6-10	220	FR.	11.6
F	M. KIDD-GILCHRIST	6-7	232	FR.	13.5
G	MARQUIS TEAGUE	6-2	195	FR.	9.9

Louisville

POS.	PLAYER	HT.	WT.	CLS.	PT/G
F	CHANE BEHANAN	6-6	250	FR.	9.5
F	KYLE KURIC	6-4	195	SR.	12.6
C	GORGUI DIENG	6-11	235	SO.	9.1
G	CHRIS SMITH	6-2	195	SR.	9.7
G	PEYTON SIVA	6-0	180	JR.	9.1

"BIG BLUE SUNDAY
HEADS OF STATE"
Lexington Herald-Leader

Blue State
Wildcats Win One Dream Game, Earn Another Monday
Louisville Courier-Journal

On New Year's Eve UK scored 69 points. Today UK scored 69 points. UofL dropped one-point, from 62 to 61. The Cards trailed by double-digits in the first half of both games, but also tied the score in the second half both times, only to have Kentucky make runs in both games that led to victory.

With 13:18 left in the first half, Terrence Jones' dunk gave UK it's first double-digit lead 16-6.

Wayne Blackshear made two free throws and a dunk to cut the deficit to six, but it was Miller "time" as Darius added a layup and two free throws of his own to put the Cats ahead by 10 again, 20-10. Louisville would continue to battle and with 1:30 remaining. Gorgui Dieng's dunk and free throw reduced the Kentucky lead to just three at 31-28.

Kyle Wiltjer would only play seven minutes and score just five points, but they were B-I-G. A tip-in at the 8:18 mark put the Cats up by 10 again, and 14 seconds after Dieng's old fashioned three-point play, Wiltjer hit a three-pointer. UK led at the half 35-28.

UK controlled the start of the second half, and with 15:37 left in the game, was on top 46-34. But there was no quit in the Cardinals.

Peyton Siva made a jumper and a three-point bucket within a 24-second span and it was a new game at 49-49. Now it was time for Kentucky to make another run. Anthony Davis missed a layup but got the rebound, and made a pass to Kidd-Gilchrist who scored on a layup. Russ Smith turned it over on UofL's next possession, and Kidd-Gilchrist followed with a dunk.

Siva made two free throws with 7:34 left, to pull the Cards within two, 53-51. But they couldn't get any closer. Over the next four minutes and 40 seconds of play, UK scored seven unanswered points; a jumper by Jones and a three-pointer and two more free throws by Miller. The Cards missed nine consecutive shots before Chris Behanan dunked the ball with only 2:54 left in the game. It was over as Kentucky prevailed 69-61. UK shot 57.1 percent in this game compared to the 29.8 percent on New Year's Eve.

Louisville shot about the same as they did in the first meeting, but stayed in this game on rebounding. Earlier in the season, UK won the battle of the boards 57-31, but this time it was Louisville with 16 offensive rebounds in their total of 40 compared to UK's 33. The Cards had 15 second-chance field goal attempts, but only made five out of that 15 for 33.3 percent.

Paul Willman

Anthony Davis was the most consistent player, averaging 18 points, 12 rebounds, 5.5 blocks, two steals and one assist per/game.

STATS

Kentucky

	Min	FG	FG A	3PT FG	3 PT FGA	FT	FT A	Reb	PF	Ast	St	BS	TO	Pts
Terrence Jones	33	3	8	0	0	0	3	7	2	0	2	2	0	6
M. Kidd-Gilchrist	23	4	6	0	0	1	4	4	3	1	0	0	4	9
Anthony Davis	39	7	8	0	0	4	6	14	2	2	1	5	3	18
Doron Lamb	35	4	9	0	2	2	3	1	1	1	0	0	4	10
Marquis Teague	33	4	8	0	0	0	0	2	4	5	1	0	2	8
Darius Miller	29	4	7	1	4	4	4	3	2	0	2	0	1	13
Eloy Vargus	0	0	0	0	0	0	0	0	0	0	0	0	0	0
Kyle Wiltjer	8	2	3	1	1	0	0	1	0	0	1	0	0	5
Team								1						
Totals	**200**	**28**	**49**	**2**	**7**	**11**	**20**	**33**	**14**	**9**	**7**	**7**	**14**	**69**

Louisville

Player	Min	FG	FG A	3PT FG	3 PT FGA	FT	FT A	Reb	PF	Ast	St	BS	TO	Pts
Kyle Kuric	28	3	8	1	2	0	1	5	3	0	1	0	0	7
Chane Behanan	34	4	9	0	2	2	2	9	1	0	0	0	2	10
Gorgui Dieng	40	3	10	0	0	1	1	12	2	2	2	4	3	7
Peyton Siva	31	4	11	1	2	2	2	3	2	3	0	0	3	11
Chris Smith	23	3	11	1	2	1	2	1	1	1	0	0	1	8
Russ Smith	26	4	15	0	1	1	2	3	2	1	2	0	3	9
Jared Swopshire	4	0	0	0	0	0	0	0	1	0	0	0	0	0

Player	Min	FG	FG A	3PT FG	3 PT FGA	FT	FT A	Reb	PF	Ast	St	BS	TO	Pts
Elisha Justice	1	0	0	0	0	0	0	0	0	0	0	0	0	0
Wayne Blackshear	14	3	5	1	2	2	3	4	4	0	0	0	0	9
Team								3						
Totals	**200**	**24**	**69**	**4**	**11**	**9**	**13**	**40**	**16**	**7**	**5**	**4**	**12**	**61**

POINTS AFTER

"I think that's neat. When I was at UMASS, I can remember hugging him and telling him,, 'I'm happy for you and I really want you to win the national title.' He did the same thing to me tonight, so I think it's kind of neat."
UK COACH JOHN CALIPARI talking about Coach Pitino's post game congratulations.

"It's our fans; our fans are great to us. Our fans travel a long way. We want to go out here and give them a show and give them what they want, which is a national championship."
UK CENTER ANTHONY DAVIS

"Anthony Davis is just the No. 1 player in the draft. When you're playing against Bill Russell on the pro level, you realize why the Celtics won 11 world championships."
UofL COACH RICK PITINO

"They were the better team today."
UofL GUARD PEYTON SIVA

"Kentucky has won the state championship, now it's on to Monday night and the national championship."
JIM NANCE, CBS SPORTS

As stated before, I believe that the 2012 meeting in the Final Four exceeds the original 1983 "Dream Game" in excitement and meaning. And that game, was at the top of the fan meter and interest across the nation. But WLKY-TV's Sports Director Fred Cowgill, seized a unique perception of this game's importance from an empty seat in the arena: "Just before the tip-off, a person from the San Antonio News vacated his seat close to the floor, and I slipped into it. It was the only open seat available. It was a festive time. I saw pictures being taken of the players and the teams, but then the moment went beyond all of that, when I was able to grasp the fabric; the real meaning of this trip to New Orleans---and that was just how much the fans really care for the game. It was a special moment." Fred was able to remain in that magical seat for about 15 minutes of the first half, but it left upon him and indelible impression, that places this game at the top of the rivalry countdown. Duke and North Carolina fans, no matter how many great games their teams have played, still lack the exhilarating experience of competing against each other in college basketball's showcase, and this is just one of the many reasons why UK vs. UofL is No. 1.

GAME 45

December 29, 2012

	UofL	UK
Record	11-1	8-3
Ranking	#4	unranked
Series	14	30
Favored	LOUISVILLE BY 7.5	
Location	KFC YUM CENTER	
TV	CBS	

PRE-GAME REPORT

There has never been a coach in this series to win five consecutive games. Rick Pitino won four straight from December 29, 1990 through November 27, 1993. Pitino's bid for five consecutive wins ended in Freedom Hall on New Year's Day 1995, when Samaki Walker registered the rivalry's only triple-double and UofL won 88-86.

Now, it's John Calipari's turn. His first game was January 2, 2010 and the Cats prevailed 71-62 with Wall and company. Later that year on New Year's Eve, Josh Harrellson and company surprised the Cards 78-63. Then last year, it was two fine teams playing twice, but UK was just better, winning at home and in the NCAA tournament. That was Davis and Company, INC.

Now, Rick Pitino according to Steve Jones of the Courier-Journal, was dismissing any advantages that his team might have and was building up the Cats; that they were formidable at every position and come February would be a difficult ballclub to play against. But this was late December.

Rick Pitino is a master of disguise. He had three returning starters that played two times against UK last season, plus two top reserves, in Russ Smith and Wayne Blackshear. Not to mention returning guard Kevin Ware (who had to take a medical redshirt season), and two promising newcomers in Luke Hancock and Montrezl Harrell.

UK had one returning player, Kyle Wiltjer, who played 15 minutes in the first UofL game last year and eight minutes in the Final Four contest. Nerlens Noel, Alex Poythress and Archie Goodwin were the heralded new freshmen along with Willie Cauley-Stein.

Some may say that's their fault, they are going for the "one and dones." As Calipari assistant coach, and former UofL star Kenny Payne told me, "We have to be on our toes every minute. We are working in "unchartered waters." Although Coach Pitino has chosen the more conventional way of building for the long haul, don't forget he's had some of those players too. And, he has missed out on some of those players, like Marquis Teague, who was UK's point-guard last year. And let's be honest, nobody would turn down Anthony Davis if he called up and said he wanted to play for you "for one year only" (Sounds like a James Bond movie theme.).

Gorgui Dieng was returning after sitting out with a broken wrist, and it was at the YUM Center. UofL was No. 4 and after losing to Baylor at home on December 1. Kentucky's ranking set another record; quickest drop from the Top 25 in recorded history.

As Tom Leach, the "Voice" of the Wildcats" said in an interview, "Except for the matchup in Louisville when Harrellson had such a great game, everything in the series has gone about as expected."

Gorgui Dieng - #10- UofL, Willie Cauley-Stein - #15 UK

QUOTES

"They are a well-oiled machine. We are a work in progress."
UK COACH JOHN CALIPARI

"We're definitely looking forward to proving people wrong. We're going to come in there and play hard and show the progress we've made."
UK CENTER NERLENS NOEL

"I forgot Gorgui was on the team (joking). It gave us confidence to know that we could play without Gorgui, even though he'll give us a great presence in the middle."
UofL FORWARD WAYNE BLACKSHEAR

"One of the toughest things to figure out is rivalry games. One thing that you'd like to see is both teams play great and give their best performances."
UofL COACH RICK PITINO

PROBABLE STARTERS

Louisville

POS.	PLAYER	HT.	WT.	CLS.	PT/G
G/F	WAYNE BLACKSHEAR	6-5	230	SO.	10.0
F	CHANE BEHANAN	6-6	250	SO.	10.8
C	ZACK PRICE	6-10	250	SO	1.6
G	PEYTON SIVA	6-0	185	SR.	11.4
G	RUSS SMITH	6-0	165	JR.	19.7

Kentucky

POS.	PLAYER	HT.	WT.	CLS.	PT/G
F	NERLENS NOEL	6-10	228	FR.	10.7
F	CAULEY-STEIN	7-0	244	FR.	7.6
G	ARCHIE GOODWIN	6-4	198	FR.	16.0
G	RYAN HARROW	6-2	170	SO.	7.0
G	JULIUS MAYS	6-2	192	SR.	9.3

Louisville 80   Kentucky 77
THRILLING FINISH EARNS CARDS' WIN
Louisville Courier-Journal

Red Rival
Lexington Herald-Leader

Russ Smith, 21 points and seven rebounds, Chane Behanan, 20 points, seven rebounds and three steals and Peyton Siva with 19 points led the way for Louisville as the Cardinals snapped their four-game losing streak to Kentucky 80-77.

Coach Pitino had placed a media ban on Behanan in October for reasons that weren't enumerated. So, he became the silent assassin in this contest as he used his strength to help force Noel and Cauley-Stein off the block.

UofL called a timeout with 13:58 remaining in the first half, after Kyle Wiltjer made a three-pointer that tied the game at 10-all. Gorgui Deng who did not start, scored on a dunk ten-seconds later to nudge the Cards in front 12-10, but the Cats got a little wild and ripped-off an 8-0 run to grab back the lead at 18-12. After Chane Behanan's dunk produced another tie at 18-18 with a little over eight minutes left in the first half, UofL led by Siva's two three-pointers, outscored the Cats 18-10 to take a 36-28 lead at intermission.

The first two minutes of the second half belonged to UofL as the Cards scored five unanswered points via three free throws and a layup by Russ Smith, expanding their lead to double-digits, 41-28. When Smith made another layup with 14:56 left, the Cardinals were on the verge of running away with the game, when Wiltjer made two threes for the Cats in a matter of 35 seconds. Goodwin added a jumper and Harrow a layup in the next 40 seconds and UK, just like that had trimmed the deficit to seven, at 51-44.

Russ Smith stopped the Wildcat run with a layup of his own and at the next TV timeout, UofL led 53-44. But the Cards hampered by foul trouble, were outscored by Kentucky 15-10 and with 6:16 remaining and the Cards' clinging to a 63-59 lead, the outcome was very much in doubt.

That was still the situation with UofL leading 77-74, when Russ Smith made his first free throw, but missed the second and Nerlens Noel grabbed the rebound. Then Goodwin took control of the ball for the Cats, Behanan made a steal and his dunk put Louisville on top 80-74 with just 17 seconds remaining in the game.

Archie Goodwin scored 13 of UK's last 18 points, but his final three-point bucket with five seconds to go was not enough as Louisville snapped Kentucky's four-game rivalry winning streak, 80-77.

STATS

Louisville

Player	Min	FG	FG A	3PT FG	3 PT FGA	FT	FT A	Reb	PF	Ast	St	BS	TO	Pts
Wayne Blackshear	31	2	7	1	2	0	2	7	1	0	0	0	0	5
Chane Behanan	35	8	13	0	0	4	6	7	3	3	3	1	1	20
Zach Price	2	0	0	0	0	0	0	0	1	0	0	0	0	0
Russ Smith	30	9	20	0	1	3	6	7	4	3	3	0	3	21
Peyton Siva	31	6	11	2	4	5	5	2	5	1	1	0	3	19
Kevin Ware	14	1	4	0	0	0	0	0	2	1	2	0	0	2
Gorgui Dieng	20	3	4	0	0	0	0	7	4	1	0	2	1	6
Luke Hancock	14	0	0	0	0	0	0	1	0	2	0	0	1	0

Paul Willman

Player	Min	FG	FG A	3PT FG	3 PT FGA	FT	FT A	Reb	PF	Ast	St	BS	TO	Pts
Montrezl Harrell	23	1	3	0	0	5	6	4	1	0	0	1	0	7
Team							1							
Totals	200	30	62	3	7	17	25	36	21	11	9	4	9	80

Kentucky

	Min	FG	FG A	3PT FG	3 PT FGA	FT	FT A	Reb	PF	Ast	St	BS	TO	Pts
Nerlens Noel	31	4	5	0	0	0	1	8	4	0	2	2	2	8
Willie Cauley-Stein	23	3	4	0	0	0	4	8	4	2	0	3	0	6
Archie Goodwin	36	8	15	3	5	3	4	5	3	2	1	0	5	22
Ryan Harrow	39	6	15	1	1	4	6	5	4	3	2	0	0	17
Julius Mays	35	1	8	1	6	0	0	3	3	2	0	0	2	3
Jarod Polson	2	0	0	0	0	0	0	1	0	0	0	0	0	0
Alex Poythress	15	2	4	1	2	2	6	5	2	0	0	0	2	7
Kyle Wiltjer	19	4	7	4	7	2	2	3	1	1	0	0	3	14
Team								1	1				1	
Totals	200	28	58	10	21	11	23	39	22	10	5	5	15	77

POINTS AFTER

Pitino would go on that season to win his second national championship - his first with the Cardinals - giving UofL its third NCAA title beating Michigan in Atlanta 82-76. UK is the preseason No. 1 team and UofL is No. 3.

When the Cards come to Rupp Arena on December 28, 2013, Calipari will have beaten Pitino nine times in his career and Pitino will have beaten Calipari nine times in his career. Calipari leads 4-1 in the rivalry games. Calipari has one national championship and two Final Fours in the last three years and Pitino has one national championship and two Final Fours in the last three years. Pitino is working on three consecutive Final Fours which if UofL achieves in the 2013-14 campaign; he said at a news conference "would constitute a mini-dynasty for the Cardinals."

The WWE was in Lexington in September of 2013, but the main bout was delayed over to December 28th when the Cards and Cats clashed once more in college basketball's No. 1 rivalry.

Chane Behanan - #24 - UofL, Nerlens Noels- #3 - UK, Julius Mays - #34 - UK, Kyle Wiltjer - #33 - UK
Payton Siva - #3 - UofL, Ryan Harrow - #12 - UK

Chapter Seven
Football and Other Things

Although the people of Kentucky consider basketball a religion, they love their football too. No matter how much money basketball produces, football delivers more of it. A successful football operation is an absolute requirement for an overall successful athletic program.

UK's greatest success in football was under the leadership of Paul "Bear" Bryant with victories in the Sugar Bowl, Cotton Bowl and Great Lakes Bowl and a loss in the Orange Bowl. There was also an SEC Championship. I mentioned to former UK All-American and UofL head coach Howard Schnellenberger that the UK fight song is about football. His reply: "That's right. You've never heard of a fight song with basketball wording, have you?"

I'm still working on that.

I had walked into Coach Schnellenberger's office one day wearing a Louisville Shooter's basketball shirt. He saw the basketball on my shirt and yelled out: "Paul! I can't believe you came in here wearing a basketball shirt!"

The Shooters were a member of the GBA, Global Basketball Association and I did the play-by-play. It lasted one year and I believe two games. Johnny Neuman was the first-year coach and former Louisville great, Derek Smith was the coach for that following year, which was highlighted by brevity. (The book written about the ABA, The American Basketball Association was entitled: Loose Balls. I said if a book was written about the GBA, it would be entitled: No Balls). I was led into his private closet, he preceded to select a UofL football shirt to his liking, had me put it on and tossed the basketball shirt into the waste basket.

Regarding basketball however, the coach likes to point out that when he played for Louisville Flaget High School, he had an opportunity to guard future UK All-American, Cliff Hagan of Owensboro High School in a game. Schnellenberger made this comment about the encounter: "I held Cliff Hagan to six points. He took three shots."

The University of Louisville football team has come a long way as well. In 1923 and '24, Fred Enke coached both the football and basketball teams as many coaches around the country did. He was the last coach to play UK in the regular season in football until the series was resumed in 1994. The Cards lost under Enke to the Cats, 29-0. In two years Enke was 8-8 with one tie. His basketball record in that same period of time was 14-20.

I found a source that had Enke also coaching the Calumet Club of the Falls City League. It was like a semi-pro organization, fellows past their college age. On February 22, 1924 when UofL played Calumet on the road (in New Albany, IN.), Enke lost to himself 43-25, but the following year he beat himself January 19, 1925 on the road at Calumet 24-15.

Fred Enke left the Cardinals and took the job at Arizona where he compiled a basketball coaching record of 509-324. Lute Olsen succeeded him as the winningest coach in Arizona history.

Former C-J sports editor Earl Ruby was working part-time for the Courier-Journal when he was playing football at Louisville DuPont Manual High School. After graduation, he went to the University of Louisville where he played football for a brief period of time.

Speaking of the equipment in 1924 he told me: "We used wood to fill the openings on the trousers where normally pads are inserted. You get hit there pretty hard, and you'd have splinters as well as the tacklers to contend with on the following play." It was a long and winding road to Papa John's Cardinal Stadium.

I have seen the drawing of a hoped for football stadium that would have been on the UofL campus in the 30s. In the 40s, there was a plan proposed for a new stadium around Eastern Parkway. But it was Parkway Field, Manual Stadium, Cardinal Stadium and the expanded Cardinal Stadium that were the main housing areas for the Cardinals until Papa John's.

Louisville football under Frank Camp, who integrated the program in the 50s, was a pioneer for integration in the South. Among his players was the great Lenny Lyles. In UofL's first Bowl game, the 1958 Sun Bowl, Lyles, the nation's leading rusher, was injured in the first quarter, but Ken Porco carried the ball for 119 yards on 20 carries and the Cardinals beat Drake 34-20. Ken said to me: "All we wanted back then was a chance to play and show that we could kick some ass."
I remember the days when you go to a UofL football game for a dollar.

I was there in the primitive "Crunch Zone" before Nestles' sponsored that popular section of the old Cardinal Stadium. I was with my sons, Rhett and Adam. They had their pictures taken with my then, future brother-in-law Jeff Griffin (My sister Melanie and Jeff have five children today), who was a backup quarterback on that UofL team.

It was September the 1st, 1984. Louisville had just scored to take a lead over Murray with about 34 seconds left in the game. Pandemonium had broken out on the Cardinal sideline as they started a premature celebration. I pointed to the clock and told my sons: "Don't ever do what they're doing. You never celebrate until there are all zeros in that time section on the scoreboard and you're ahead."

Two plays later a Murray player is running our way toward the end zone. He scores a touchdown and the Racers win and a valuable piece of advice is immortalized on the spot.

I mentioned to former UofL A.D. Bill Olsen that had to be the final nail in Coach Bob Weber's coffin to lose to Murray. He agreed.

Bill talked about the challenge to make UofL football profitable: "When I took over one could buy a season ticket package of six home games for $18.00. We sold three thousand season tickets. Syracuse comes to play and wants a guarantee of $100,000. Let's say the crowd is 30,000:

Season Ticket Holders: 3,000 x $3.00 = $9,000

General Admission: 27,000 x $1.00 = $27,000

Total Gate Receipts: $36,000.

Old math, new math; it wasn't going to be easy. Oh, and you needed a new football stadium and the campus configuration needed changing because it was land-locked-no chance for real growth.

Bill Olsen said the following three things were critical in establishing football as a profitable program at Louisville. First, was getting top billing on 84 WHAS-Radio. For some 50 years Kentucky football and basketball had the prime spot on WHAS. UofL was heard on other stations in town including WAVE and then WHAS broadcasted the Cardinal games on its sister station, WAMZ.

Most public comments made said that UofL found a loophole in the contract and was able to take Kentucky's spot. Bill Olsen sees it this way: "Jim Host of Host Communications was hoping to make a proposal to UofL officials about setting up a state-wide network for the Cardinals, similar to the one he had with UK.

I was a neighbor of Bob Scherer, who was the General Manager at WHAS. The contract with UK was expiring. WHAS was interested and so was I in forming a broadcasting relationship. WHAS was going to save a lot of money going with us instead of paying the broadcast fees to carry Kentucky Sports, and it would be very helpful for us."

The deal was made and UofL won the media rivalry this time around. Louisville got top billing in the fall of 1985. New sponsorship money benefited both parties involved and UofL would continue to gain marketing strength and expertise.

Second, was the hiring of Howard Schnellenberger. The Orlando-Sentinel recently rated Schnellenberger the eighth-greatest college football coach of all-time. He came here and sold football to the city just as he had done in Miami. Schnellenberger said: "To be really successful you have to have community leadership. You need an inner circle of four people that are aware of what is going on in the program at all times." This he put in place.

Third, Bill Olsen said "winning the Fiesta Bowl was a major turning point." Alabama really didn't care about the game. One gets so sick and tired of hearing that excuse. As great a coach as Bear Bryant was; from 1968-75 he lost seven bowl games and tied one. And non-major bowl games like the Gator and Bluebonnet were included in that stretch. Maybe that part of the tradition carried over here too. Since that time UofL has won two BCS Bowl games, but there are still mountains to climb to achieve a national championship.

Remember the "Battle Cry" Coach Schnellenberger penned when he was here: "UofL is on a collision course with the national championship, the only variable is time." Of course, many believe that time variable is eternity, but that's just another factor that makes this rivalry No. 1.

The Fiesta Bowl victory was instrumental in helping Olsen and Schnellenberger make UofL's negotiation position stronger back in 1994 with UK Athletics Director, C.M. Newton, and Wildcat football Coach Bill Curry in resurrecting the football annual rivalry game that had been stuck in the locker room since 1924.

C.M. Newton in a recent interview said: "We weren't going to help Louisville build their new stadium. They were going to do that anyway." Coach Rupp felt the same way in the 60s when he told UK Sports Information Director, Russell Rice, "It doesn't make any sense for us to play them (football) and help build their new stadium."

Coach Jerry Claiborne felt that way too. But Bill Curry thought, like Schnellenberger, that it would help high school football in Kentucky. I mentioned to C. M. Newton that it had to help Kentucky expand Commonwealth Stadium and he replied, "It did."

The first game was played on September 3, 1994 before 59,162 fans in Lexington. UK won 20-14 and it was the first time that UofL had scored in a game with the Cats. In the previous six games from 1912-1924, the Cards had been outscored 210-0.

After the first four games were held in Lexington, the series moved to Louisville's new Papa John's Cardinal Stadium in 1998 drawing 42,643 fans, and has been on a home-and-home basis ever since.

Starting in 1999 through 2009, the two teams played before six crowds of over 70,000 at Commonwealth Stadium, the largest was 70,998 in 2009. In 2010 under Coach Charlie Strong, the game was played in Louisville's expanded stadium drawing 55,327 fans, followed by 55,386 in 2012.

Tom Jurich has pointed out: "I could have 70,000 seats here if we had not gone with all chair backseats, but I didn't want to do that."

The stadium has 55,000 chairback seats and 70 luxury suites. It's a beautiful venue to play football.

This series had helped both teams. And as Coach Schnellenberger says: "It has helped to increase the number of Division-1 college prospects in the Bluegrass state by a substantial margin.

C.M. felt the game should be the first one on the schedule, giving fans the opportunity to talk about something all summer long rather than basketball. But then the game could be forgotten as you moved on to the conference schedule. He thought: "if you couldn't beat Louisville and Indiana, you really didn't have any business playing in the SEC."

It's amazing how things come full circle. Bill Olsen said, "Coach "Peck" Hickman always felt that it would be the best for the Cardinals to be a member of the ACC. That's why he tried to play so many teams from that part of the country"

In 2014 the Cardinals will be nesting where the builder of the Louisville basketball tradition envisioned, and the Wildcats are trying not only to beat Louisville on a regular basis, but to be competitive in the SEC and do what only Paul "Bear" Bryant and Fran Curci have done—win an SEC championship.

The football aspect of this rivalry has added a new dimension that actually intensifies the basketball rivalry and carries over that competitive spirit to all other teams, both men's and women's who are an integral part of this wonderful rivalry. UofL has played in two BCS bowls and who would have imagined that some 30 years ago, when Coach Schnellenberger was working his team out at Manual Stadium (a wonderful old high school stadium in Louisville)?

Now with UK's Mark Stoops and UofL's Bobby Petrino fighting each other for recruits in Florida, as well as victories on the gridiron, coupled with John Calipari and Rick Pitino on the hardwood, this rivalry is going to keep the fans in a "frenzied" state of mind.

Chapter Eight
The Defectors

The Berlin Wall was erected on August 13, 1961. The first phase consisted of fence, mingled with barbed wire. Two days later, concrete was added for the first time. The Wall, which was designed to keep East Germans under the rule of the Soviet Union, was built to keep East Germans from joining the free West German society, and to keep the West German ideas about freedom and such from coming to the East.

The Wall passed through three more generations of modifications before it was torn down on the ninth and tenth days of November 1989. During that time period from 1961-1989, it is estimated that 100,000 East Germans attempted to escape their awful life under the Soviets by going over, around or under that wall of repression and slavery. Between 5000 and 10,000 were successful defectors, while two hundred lost their lives trying.

I remember a story about one man, the poor "devil," and the only one, who went from the West to the East. The Online Merriam-Webster Dictionary defines defector this way: (1) one who forsakes one cause, party, or nation for another often because of a change in ideology, (2) one who leaves one situation (as a job) often to go over to a rival.

On the other hand, a traitor seems to be vastly different: (1) one who betrays another's trust or is false to an obligation or duty, (2) one who commits treason.

And finally, the dictionary definition of the dastardly turncoat: (1) a person who stops being a member of a group in order to join another group who opposes it.

The synonyms and related words for a turncoat, certainly reveal this despicable culprit; accommodationist, apostate, backstabber, betrayer, blabbermouth collaborator, defector, deserter, double-crosser, double-dealer, gossipmonger, informer, intriguer, Judas, rat, recreant, rumormonger, serpent, snake, snitch, squealer, stool pigeon, talebearer, telltale and traitor.

Hopefully, these definitions will help remove the bitterness and the "gruesome" mind games that are conjured-up when anyone speaks of the No. 1 defector in this rivalry, one Richard Pitino.

We may be able to classify him as a defector, but surely not a traitor or turncoat.

I knew a girl in Austria whose parents were divorced. Her mother re-married. Every Sunday at church she would sit with her mom and step-father, but every Sunday she would also give her father a hug and a kiss. Now, if her father and step-father were basketball coaches, I wonder which one she would have pulled for? Would it have been like Governor John Y. Brown at the "Dream Game" in Knoxville when he sat on the UK side the first half and the UofL side the second half?

This comparison works and it doesn't work. Hopefully, it will help both UK and UofL fans appreciate more what they do have and get over what they don't have.

Howard Schnellenberger asked me if I felt any animosity towards him, having played for Kentucky and then becoming the head coach of the Louisville football team? I said, "No."

Looking at our timeline of defectors, one source stated that Russell "Duke" Ellington was the first to transfer from Louisville to the University of Kentucky in 1924. But this is incorrect. Ellington was a member of the UK freshmen team for the 1933-34 season. The UofL 1924 Yearbook lists an unnamed player that left for an unnamed institution, but I find no transfer appearing on the UK rosters in the following years.

In 1988, I interviewed Dave Lawrence, a UK All-American in 1935. He was a real gentleman. He told me he was unhappy with Coach Rupp because he didn't think the coach did enough to help him find a job after his graduation. But the job he secured on his own was where he met his future wife.

#25 Co - Captain Lawrence

In 1934, Kentucky finished 16-0 in the regular season and met a "weak" Florida squad in the first round of the SEC Tournament. The Cats suffered a 38-32 upset at the hands of the Gators. Dave told me the game was played in an old theater in Atlanta, and when one went in for a layup, the floor was on a downward slope and then abruptly, went back up again.

The slope upwards, reminds me of the outfield at old Crosley Field, home of the Cincinnati Reds from 1912 to June 24, 1970. He said, "I missed several layups, uncomfortable with the floor configuration under the baskets that contributed greatly to our defeat." And Coach Rupp was uncomfortable with Dave after the game.

He became an assistant coach at UofL and was on the bench with Coach Hickman when the Cards lost to the Cats in the Olympic Trials game in 1948 and the 1951 NCAA East Region game in Raleigh, North Carolina.

He was the Dean of Men from 1952-1963, and the Dean of Students from 1963 until 1978, and a well respected man in his profession. His granddaughter, Jennifer Lawrence is a young super-star Hollywood actress. He passed away in 2000.

Chet Wynne, the head football coach at Kentucky from 1934-37 had fired one of his assistant coaches, Bernie Shively.

I once saw a picture of Shivley shaking hands with Dr. Raymond Kent, the president of the University of Louisville at that time. Shively was in town to interview for the UofL Athletics Director job. He didn't get it, but Adolph Rupp got Shively the job as the UK Athletics Director. One must make allowances for those who are seeking a job for their family's livelihood.

These other Wildcats from the 1940s all transferred to Louisville. Clyde Parker wanted to be a dentist so he transferred to Louisville after his freshman year at UK.

Clyde "Ace Parker"   UK   1942-43

Games/Starter	FG	FTM/FTA	PTS	AVG
20 5	17	24/42	68	3.4

Clyde "Ace" Parker   UofL

1944-45	Fourth Leading Scorer	6.8
1945-46	Fourth Leading Scorer	7.5
1946-47	Fourth Leading scorer	7.0

Glenn Parker (Clyde's brother) UK   1943-44

Games	FG	FTM/FTA	PTS	AVG
8	6	0/1	12	1.5

Glenn transferred but did not play basketball for the Cardinals.

Another freshman, Truitt DeMoisey, the brother of Adolph Rupp's first recruit "Frenchy," who became an All-American, transferred after his freshman year. He spent some time at Ohio State and in the military, which prevented him from wearing the UofL uniform until the 1948-49 season.

"Frenchy"

Paul Willman

Truitt DeMoisey   UK   1943-44

Games	FG	FTM/FTA	PTS	AVG
18	21	18/29	60	3.3

Truitt DeMoisey   UofL   1948-49

Games	FGM/FGA	FTM/FTA	PTS	AVG
26	44/107	45/67	133	5.1

Deward Compton played two years at Kentucky.

Deward Compton   UK   1944-45   Freshman

Games	FG	FTM/FTA	PTS	AVG
4	8	0/0	16	4.0

Deward Compton   UK   1945-46   Sophomore

Games	FG	FTM	PTS	AVG
6	4	2	10	1.7

Deward Compton's defector story is my favorite. I interviewed former UofL Coach "Peck" Hickman in 1992. After he got the UofL job in 1943, he went to the University of Kentucky to get a master's degree. He was living in one of the dorms on campus and met an unhappy Wildcat by the name of Deward Compton. Compton tells the coach: "I'm not getting much playing time here." (As the previous stats confirm) Coach Hickman invited Compton to start wearing a new uniform to help him with the building process at UofL.

In 1947, Deward Compton was tied for fifth as the team's leading scorer with a 6.6 points per game average.

Deward Compton UofL   1947-48

Games	FG	FT	PTS	AVG
34	135	87	357	10.5

Louisville won the small college N.A.I.B. National Championship that year over John Wooden's Indiana State team 82-70. Former UofL AD Bill Olsen said: "Deward Compton was a life-long, true supporter of the University of Louisville."

UK vs. UofL College Basketball's No. 1 Rivalry - Enough Said!

Ralph Beard of the Fabulous Five thought about transferring from UK to UofL his freshman year, after he injured his shoulder playing for the football Cats. Upon telling Coach Rupp of his thoughts, the Baron replied: "I don't know why you want to go to that 'Normal' school, but I'll tell you one damn thing Beard, we won't cancel our schedule if you leave."

Gene Rhodes, Ralph's longtime friend who played with Beard on Louisville Male High's first State Champion basketball team in 1945, told me "that Coach Harry "Pap" Glenn counseled Ralph that he would be better off remaining at UK."

There was another prospective defector lurking in the shadows that might truly surprise some people—the Baron himself, Adolph Rupp.
His son Herky told me that his father was set to take the Duke job after his retirement from UK and that Herky was going to be his top assistant, but the manager of their farm died of a heart attack and the Rupp's stayed at home in Lexington.

December 28, 2002, as soon as the jump ball started the game, Marvin Stone became the first defector to have played for both teams in the rivalry game. He had a big game that night, scoring 16 points and grabbing seven rebounds as the Cards beat the Cats 81-63.

Marvin Stone UK 1999-2002 vs. UofL

12/18/99 RUPP ARENA   UK 76   UofL 46

MIN	FGM/A	FTM/A	R	TO	B	S	A	PF	PTS
12	2/4	0/0	5	3	1	0	0	3	4

1/2/2001   FREEDOM HALL UK 64 UofL 62

MIN	FGM/A	FTM/A	R	TO	B	S	A	PF	PTS
25	5/7	1/2	6	2	1	0	0	3	11

Marvin's last game with UK was one week before the December 29, 2001 Louisville game.

Marvin Stone   UofL 2002-03 vs. UK

12/28/2002 FREEDOM HALL UofL 81   UK 63

MIN	FGM/A	FTM/A	R	TO	B	S	A	PF	PTS
30	4/7	8/12	7	3	2	0	1	3	16

Marvin died of a heart attack playing a basketball game in the Saudi Arabian Federation Play-offs in 2008.

Of course, the main defector in the series that frustrated the Blue and energized the Red was the hiring by Tom Jurich of Rick Pitino to coach the Louisville Cardinals on March 21, 2001. I was tempted to say something like: "A 2001 Coaching Odyssey," but I resisted the temptation as you can see.

It's been almost 13 years, and surely for most, the animosity is now history or under control. However, that's why I began this chapter with definitions, synonyms and other juicy related words to those that still need help in understanding the situation.

Obviously, Pitino was not a traitor. He was free contractually from the University of Kentucky and looking for a job.

Many of those tender feelings by Kentucky fans would have been aptly justified had the coach gone directly to Louisville—but he got a get-out-of-jail free card when he went to Boston and back to the NBA. His position has always been that he gave the best eight years he could to UK and brought them back from the brink of basketball oblivion. He's right.

However, I believe Wildcat fans have been dealt an injustice when the other side celebrates Pitino's arrival while allowing no margin of error for the Big Blue to vent.

I was there March 21, 2001 for the coronation with my friend Scott Trager of Republic Bank. He leaned over at one point in the meeting and said: "Paul, for eight years I hated his guts, but now— he's the best."

There's that word hate again that was discussed in chapter one. Scott must not have hated Pitino while he was in Boston because he confined his statement to eight years; the exact time the coach was at Kentucky. But Wildcat fans are quickly chastised if they want to say: "for eight years we adored him, but now we hate his guts."

When he was the Big Blue coach, I had an idea that I let die on the drawing board. The women were such big fans that I wanted to manufacture the "Rick Pitino Doll." Pull the string on the back and it says things in that New York brogue: "Shoot or transfer, that's fool's gold, or Kentucky is the Roman Empire of college basketball."

Those Louisville fans that now cheer him on used to say things like: "You can't believe what he says. They get away with hacking. Call all the fouls and they'd all foul out. Corrupt Rupp. And my personal favorite—they don't play anybody."

If Cat fans chime in with some of the same trash talk such as UofL gets away with hacking, call the fouls and they can't win. The reply is: "You're just sore losers because he's not at UK anymore."

"It would never happen in North Carolina," said Vince Taylor, who went to high school in Lexington, played for Duke, was an assistant coach at UofL and is now an assistant coach with Tubby Smith at Texas Tech. That is, the Duke coach going to North Carolina or a Tar Heel head coach going to Duke. In fact, he continued, "The Duke fans couldn't stand it if I was even an assistant coach at North Carolina."

Kenny Payne, a former UofL player, is well liked at Kentucky as a Calipari assistant coach. And Walter McCarty, Tony Delk and now Wayne Turner, all former Pitino players at UK, have been treated with the same respect at UofL. But when a job and your livelihood is concerned, shouldn't allowance be made by the fans? Maybe in the movies you say.

With Pitino at Louisville, it has made the rivalry even more competitive. Former Wildcat guard Sean Woods, now the coach at Morehead State agrees: "The rivalry will always be big in the state, but with the present two coaches, Pitino and Calipari; it will be bigger."

I think national broadcaster Tom Hammond goes directly to the center of the issue for many Big Blue fans in speaking of Pitino now at UofL: "As a Kentuckian, I think its great he came back to the state. But as a UK fan, I wish he would have never left."

He started his thirteenth year at UofL in 2013. He spent eight years at UK. The best way for a Kentucky fan to get over it is to see Calipari's Cats beat him.

Chapter Nine
Near Misses

Near misses are the opportunities to play each other in the NCAA tournament, that never materialized, because one, or both, of the teams lost. The most famous, or most talked about is March 11, 1982 in the NCAA Mideast Regional played in Nashville. All Kentucky had to do was beat the Blue Raiders of Middle Tennessee State and the Cards and Cats would have battled for the first time in 23 years. Middle Tennessee won 50-44.

A close second has to be the 1975 NCAA Final Four in San Diego. UK beat Syracuse 95-79 in the first semifinal game and all the Cardinals had to do was beat UCLA. They did, but they didn't, losing 75-74 in overtime.

The first near miss has to be March of 1916. The two teams split the regular season contests. The Cats challenged the Cards to play on any floor, anywhere, to determine the state champion. The Cards gladly accepted the invitation. However, this third game between the schools was only played out on paper. The 1916 state championship remains undecided, but then maybe not.

In the 2012 Final Four semifinal game in New Orleans, after UK beat UofL 69-61, CBS's Jim Nance said: "Kentucky has won the state championship, now it's on to Monday night and the national championship."

The rivalry went into hiding after the last two games were played in 1922, creating our near misses stat sheet. It is interesting to note the comments found in the 1922 UK Yearbook read: "January 17 the Wildcats defeated the University of Louisville, at Louisville, 38 to 14. That was satisfactory to the Wildcats and the fans, but it didn't mean anything.

Louisville came down on January 21 for another beating, and got it, 29 to 22. The Cardinals were disciples of the hypothesis or whatever it is that distance lends enchantment, and they made goal after goal from distances that were almost preposterous, but they finished to the rear despite their remarkable efforts. Basil Hayden (UK's first All-American) was back in the game on this occasion."

In 1948, 26 years later, the Cards and the Cats met for the first time in postseason play in New York City for the Olympic Trials. Both schools were in the college division of the tournament. A college winner would meet a semi-pro team from the other division for the title game and the right to have their coach, the head coach for the Olympic Team that would play in London. The coach of the runner-up team would be the assistant coach and his starting five, along with the starting five from the head coach's team would form the U.S. team roster.

Alternates were also chosen in case one of the ten players was unable to participate. Kentucky beat Louisville 91 to 57, then, Baylor 77-59 which had defeated local favorite New York University in its first game. Kentucky lost the title game to the Phillips Oilers 53-49.

Three years later the two schools met again in the 1951 NCAA East Regional in Raleigh, NC. UK won again, but this game was much closer: 79-68. Then for seven years their paths would not cross each other in postseason competition. UK lost in the second game in the 1952, '55 and '56 NCAA East Regional.

Kentucky's 1952-53 schedule was canceled as a result of the point-shaving scandal and in 1954, the 25-0 Wildcats declined the NCAA bid because their three best players on that team, Frank Ramsey, Cliff Hagan and Lou Tsioropoulos were disqualified from tournament play because they were in graduate school.

In 1957 the Cats were beaten by Michigan State 80-68 on their home floor in the NCAA Midwest Regional. In 1958, the Wildcats were back at home for the Mideast Regional, winning both games and advancing to Louisville for the Final Four where Rupp won his fourth national championship 82-70 over Elgin Baylor's Seattle team.

From 1952-56, UofL went to the NIT. They lost to Western Kentucky in the first game in 1952 62-59. In 1953, the Cards beat the Georgetown Hoyas but lost to Manhattan in the second game. In 1954, they lost to St. Francis of New York in the first game. In 1955, the Cardinals beat Manhattan, this time by a 91-86 score, but lost to No. 6 Duquesne 74-66.

Then, in the game that "Peck" Hickman would say three years later was more important than beating UK in the 1959 NCAA, because it was a game that won a national tournament, the Cards beat No. 3 Dayton for the third time that year 93-80 to win the NIT. The next two years Louisville was on probation for recruiting violations and were prohibited from participating in postseason play.

In 1959 the Cardinals were back, and I'd say they were back, winning the NCAA Mideast Regional, beating UK along the way 76-61 to qualify for its first ever Final Four which was held on its home floor in Freedom Hall. When they met in 1959, it had been eight years since the two teams had played and Coach Rupp would finish 2-1 against the Cards and "Peck" Hickman finished 1-2 against the Cats for time would keep on delaying a rematch for 24 years until the teams would meet again in Knoxville for the 1983 "Dream Game."

Neither team qualified for postseason play in 1960, but in 1961 the collision course was set up to play out on UofL's home court in the 1961 NCAA Mideast Regional at Freedom Hall. The six teams on hand included three entries from the Bluegrass State; UK, UofL and Morehead. The other three were from Ohio; the defending national champion Ohio State, Ohio University and Xavier. Seeding had UofL against Ohio in a first round game and Morehead was to play Xavier.

The Cards won 76-70 setting up a semifinal matchup against Ohio State. Morehead stopped Xavier 71-66, making its next opponent the Wildcats. After Morehead beat Xavier making the game official with in-state rival Kentucky, who they had never played, the Eagles started this chant: "UK. . . Then all the way." For most of the game that chant seemed to be working its magic.

UK had a nine-point advantage in the first half, and led by eight points several times in the second. Overall the score was tied nine times and the lead changed hands on six different occasions. But with 2:52 left in the game, Morehead was on top 64 to 63 until Roger Newman made one for the Cats giving them the lead 65 to 64, which they did not relinquish.

Carol Burchett followed with two free throws, and a Newman tip-in with just 43 seconds left in the game. UK led 69-64 and won by a final margin of 71-64. The March 18, 1961 *Courier-Journal* article sums up the in-state rivalry battle this way: "When it was over, a howling mob, in which noise, it appeared was evenly divided for both state teams had gotten its money worth."

This first collision ever between two-state-supported schools was played briskly but without incident between players or, as far as could be determined, between their rooters." However, this is not the case. Kentucky played Eastern Kentucky in 1928.

Ken Porco, former UofL football player remarked: "Some UK creep threw a beer bottle at us during the regionals."

A friend of mine, John Gibson was the second-leading scorer for Morehead in that game with 14 points. I asked him when he was growing up in Paintsville, Ky. if there were any Louisville fans in his Eastern Kentucky home area. He said: "Louisville who? What is Louisville?"

Today, he says, "There are a few Cardinal fans there, but they're mostly graduates of UofL who are doctors and dentists." I'll tell you he continued, "We did play Louisville in track when I was in college but they weren't much." He talked about picking up messages in that charged atmosphere in Freedom Hall, "A lot of talk was coming from the Louisville players about playing Kentucky."

When I mentioned that with the former UofL players, who have breakfast every Thursday at Wagner's Pharmacy near Churchill Downs, Howard Stacey said, "He didn't remember that." But Bud Olsen exclaimed, "I sure do. I wanted to beat Kentucky badly because they still looked down on us."

Former UofL football and basketball players who meet every Thursday morning to
talk sports and enjoy a good breakfast at Wagner's Pharmacy next to Churchill Downs:
1) Mario Cheppo, 2) Dale Orem, 3) Ken Porco, 4) Chuck Nabor, 5) John Hunt, 6) Elmer Collina,
7) Ray Farmer, 8) Don Rossoll, 9) Rich Keeling, 10) Phil Rollins, 11) Don Hockensmith,
12) Dave Hall, 13) Lou Bryon, 14) John Reuther, 15) Howard Stacey, 16) Bud Olsen,
17) Lou Sutherland, 18) Larry Broaden, 19) Ken Kortas, 20) Dennis Clifford, 21) Bill Windchy,
22) Larry Najjar, 23) Bill Pence, 24) Tom Montgomery, and 25) Gil Sturtzel

I brought up the fact to Gibson that he scored 14 points against UK, but only two in the consolation game with UofL losing 83-61. John replied: "I didn't care about the consolation game. Anyway, after you play Kentucky it doesn't matter who you play in the next game."

We had moved back to the city from Fern Creek in March of 1961 to Murray Avenue and I was with my dad the night of the Louisville-Ohio State game steaming wallpaper. The Cardinals and the Buckeyes were engaged in a fierce battle. Ohio State was the defending national champion and was favored over UofL by 11.

With just under three minutes to play, the Cardinals were leading by five points. Former Cardinal player and Assistant Coach Howard Stacey remembers: "We had a five-point lead and I told Coach Hickman that my legs were gone. He elected to take Jadie Frazier out and replace him with Ron Rubenstein. Jadie was young, a sophomore, but he could handle the pressure. Ron was a good ball handler but I felt going with Frazier was best."

The Cards led 54-49 with 2:46 left in the game. John Havlicek hit a 15-foot jump shot for the Buckeyes to make it 54-51, and then another turnover hurt the Cards as Larry Siegfried stole a pass from Ron Ruebenstein and went in for a layup, 54-53. The turnover was compounded by a foul and Siegfried made the free throw to tie the game at 54-all. When Ohio State got the ball again, their intent was to go for one shot but Halicek was called for traveling. But the Cards turned it over again as John Turner lost the ball off his foot.

State's Mel Nowell missed a shot with 29 seconds left but Bob Knight got the rebound. The Buckeyes called a timeout with 18 seconds remaining and 12 seconds later Havlicek hit a miracle 20-footer to put Ohio State on top 56-54. In a 1992 interview Bob Knight, then the head coach at IU said, "Coach Taylor told us not to foul."

According to the account in the *Courier-Journal*, Siegfried fell down in front of Turner and John tripped over him, drawing the foul. Turner hit the first free throw making it 56-55. With that shot Turner had made seven consecutive free throws. He missed the second, the ball was tipped back to Turner who tried a follow shot but it was no good. The Cardinals had played a great game. John Turner had 23 points and 13 rebounds, but they just couldn't close the deal.

Jadie Frazier had been a surprise starter, but Howard Stacey says, "The substitution late in the game, when Stacey said his legs were gone, and Rubenstein came in to replace Frazier, was a decision that Coach Hickman regretted."

Of all the games I've watched or heard, that one ranks in the top-three on my all-time disappointing games list, as a ten-year-old listening and helping his father steam wallpaper back on March 17. 1961. The Buckeyes beat UK 87-74 to make their second consecutive Final Four.

Kentucky went back to the Mideast Regional in 1962, but lost to Ohio State once again in the regional championship by a score of 74-64 which sent Ohio State to its third consecutive Final Four. The Cats missed the tournament in 1963 but returned to the Mideast Regional in 1964 in Minneapolis, MN.

Louisville missed the tournament in 1962 and 63 but was back in the Mideast Regional in 1964. The Cards had to play Ohio University in the first round of the regional in Evanston, IL. UofL was playing Ohio for the third time that season. They beat the Bobcats at home on December 30, 1963 69-61, but had lost just 10 days ago at Ohio 88-79.

Louisville wasn't playing its best basketball down the stretch losing four of its last five games before the tournament. A win over Ohio meant the Cards would travel to Minneapolis for a second round game with the Wildcats.

Ten minutes into the first half Ohio led 23-14. With 4:21 left in the half and Louisville a little closer at 29-23, Coach Hickman sent the faster Dennis Clifford into the lineup for Judd Rothman who had picked up his third foul. Hickman called for a pressing defense and the Bobcats committed three turnovers. The Cards were able to score 12 consecutive points and ended up in front at the half 37-32.

The first ten minutes of the second half hinged on the foul calls. Judd Rothman picked up his fourth foul after 3:27 and Ron Hawley followed with his fourth personal two minutes and thirty seconds later. The Bobcats were in the bonus with 11:12 left and went 9:27 without being whistled for a foul of their own.

Ohio finally took the lead at 51-50, but UofL would outscore the Bobcats 10-4 that included three consecutive buckets by John Reuther to put the Cards on top once again at 60-55.

Ohio fought back and tied the score at 65-all. They took the last shot, Reuther grabbed the rebound and the teams were headed to overtime. Ohio scored first in the overtime and built a 69-65 lead. UofL was able to tie the score at 69-69, with 1:54 remaining.

The Bobcat's Jackson hit the front end of a one-and-one to give Ohio a 70-69 lead, but he missed the second free throw. However the ball was batted outside where Ohio regained possession and Storey was fouled sending the Bobcats to the free throw line once again for the one-and-one. Storey made the first but missed the second. Ohio led 71-69.

Louisville worked the ball down court with 12 seconds left in the game. Ron Hawley tried to get the ball to Reuther, but with three seconds to go, Hilt for Ohio stole the ball and the Bobcats were moving on to Minneapolis to play the Wildcats.

In the last 25 minutes of the game (second half and overtime) the Cards shot just three free throws making two while Ohio connected on 15 of 24 from the charity stripe.

Ohio had no problem with Kentucky beating the Wildcats 85-69. Cotton Nash was going in for a meaningless layup late in the game and I remember as a disgruntled fans yelling out, "You bum! Why didn't you do more of that earlier in the game?"

Neither team played in the postseason in 1965. In 1966, UK went to the NCAA Championship game losing to Texas Western 72-65, while Boston College beat Louisville 96-90 in the first round of the NIT.

Louisville was now playing in the Missouri Valley Conference, so more than likely; the Cards would be placed in the Midwest Region instead of the Mideast with Kentucky.

The Cats missed the tournament in 1967 as Rupp experienced his only non-losing season, finishing 13-13. From 1968-72 UK won five consecutive SEC Championships and went to the Mideast Regional five consecutive years, but never made it to another Final Four under Rupp.

The Cardinals went to the NCAA Midwest Regional in 1967 and 68, losing in the first round each time. Coach Hickman retired after the 1967 campaign and John Dromo took over for the 1967-68 season. For the next three years, UofL was an NIT participant winning only one first round game in 1969.

Coach Denny Crum took over for the 1971-72 year and made the Final Four his first season as a head coach on the Division-1 level. He said, "After being with Coach Wooden, I thought going to the Final Four is what you did at that time of year."

In 1973 the Cards went to the NIT winning just one game and were beaten in the first game of the 1974 NCAA Midwest Regional by Oral Roberts 96-93. Denny also lost his first game to Eddie Sutton, as Creighton won the consolation game 80-71.

Coach Joe B. Hall replaced Adolph Rupp for the 1972-73 season and lost to Indiana in the second game of the Mideast Regional 72-65. The Cats stayed home in 1974 finishing with a non-losing record of 13 and 13.

The 1975 NCAA tournament was the first that allowed more than one team from a conference to go to the "Big Dance." Kentucky was the SEC co-champion with Alabama and Louisville won the Missouri Valley Conference. The Cards and the Cats both made it to San Diego for the Final Four, both would lose to UCLA.

UK beat Syracuse in the first semifinal game 95-79. Then it was UofL's turn, David Meyers scored first for UCLA but the Cards came right back with two baskets, the last by Phil Bond and UofL was on top 4-2. The score was tied 8-8 when the hot shooting Cardinals, who hit seven of their first nine shots, used that shooting accuracy to score nine unanswered points and took a 17-8 lead.

UCLA got it down to 19-14, but with about 12:30 in the half, UofL added four points of their own and led by nine once again, 23-14. With 10:31 remaining in the half the Cards were on top 25-18. UofL was shooting 67 percent, UCLA 60 percent. The Cards were out rebounding the Bruins 10-2, led by Wesley Cox with five.

The Cards scored to make it 27-18, marking the fourth time in the game they had led by nine. Substitutions were made by both teams, freshman Ricky Gallon was in at center, Danny Brown at guard and Ike Whitfield on the frontline for the Cards.

Wooden made a switch at center sending the 7-1 Ralph Drollinger into the contest. It would be difficult for the Cards to continue that torrid shooting percentage of almost 70 percent, but now, their shooting was on a downward spiral headed for 50 percent, and they committed too many turnovers.

With 5:06 remaining, it was now UofL 29, UCLA 27. The Cardinals were 14 of 28 from the field and UCLA 13 of 23. The Cards still lead the rebounding battle 15-9, but the Bruins had the advantage 7-5 during this crucial five-minute span.

Washington tied the game 29-29. Cox moved Louisville ahead 31-29. UCLA took its first lead 33-32 with 2:45 left to play.

Allen Murphy and Bill Bunton retaliated for UofL, making it 36-33 and the Cards added another free throw to their total for a 37-33 halftime advantage.

Speaking of that Bruin first half comeback Ralph Drollinger said: "We've had teams all season get the jump on us. We're not really the aggressive steamed-up kind of team UCLA has been before. But Coach Wooden just tells us to go slowly and patiently and gradually come back." CJ March 30, 1975.

David Myers added, "They were making us keep the ball on the wings and we weren't running our offense. We really didn't get around to running it the whole game, not even on Washington's winning shot. We just started making it harder for them to do what they wanted." CJ March 30, 1975

Junior Bridgeman thought: "They did start playing harder." Bridgeman scored four baskets in the early part of the game, but only made free throws the rest of the way. He explained why: "They started getting help from the weak side of me when I would go low. But we have another option if that happens. We didn't take advantage."

In the second half Wooden used an extremely tall frontline to counter the Cardinals quickness and leaping ability. He had 7-1 Drollinger, 6-10 Washington and 6-8 Meyers in the game at the same time. For a few minutes in the second half he used his other starter, 6-7 forward Marques Johnson in place of his 6-4 starting guard Pete Trgovich.

Still, the Cards could have just as easily won the game in regulation and overtime. Louisville's largest second half lead was six, UCLA's three. The teams slugged it out starting the second half. The score was 47-all, then, 49-all.

When the Cards edged ahead 51-49 with 10:32 left in the game, they were shooting 48 percent from the field, on five for 12, while the Bruins were seven of 15, for 47 percent. Richard Washington stole the ball, raced down the court and laid it in, making 51-all the 13th tie of the game.

Allen Murphy who had a game-high 33 points, buried a 20-ft jumper off the right wing giving the Cards a 53-51 advantage. Trgovich missed for UCLA and Murphy missed at the other end for Louisville, but Gallon and Drollinger tied it up on the rebound and a jump ball was called.

The tipped-ball on the jump goes out of bounds and the officials called it Cardinal basketball. With 8:08 left in the game, the Cards put it back in play. Murphy gets under the basket and makes a smooth one-handed back over the head shot. UofL 55-51.

Just 12 seconds later McCarter hits a jumper. Still, Louisville led 55-53. The Cards are called for walking, but Drollinger's shot at the other end is disallowed as he committed a foul on the attempt. On UofL's next possession, Cox rebounded Bridgeman's missed shot and was fouled, but missed at the free-throw line.

UCLA's Meyers walked at the other end and the Cards were right back on offense clinging to that 55-53 lead. Junior Bridgeman missed a shot, but Wesley Cox was fouled on the put back attempt by Drollinger who fouled out, committing his fifth personal foul.

This time Cox cashed in on both freebies and the Cards led 57-53. Louisville gets it back, but Bridgeman and Cox both missed shots as Meyers grabs the rebound for UCLA, but in the process travelled with the ball. Murphy gets open for an eight-footer, drilled it and Louisville led 59-53.

It's UCLA's turn to put together an 8-0 run of its own. Trgovich hits a jumper and it's 59-55. Bond missed for UofL. The Bruins head the other way and it's Meyers for two, 59-57. Bridgeman walks. The Cards commit their seventh turnover of the half. Cawood Ledford calling the game for The University of Kentucky Basketball Network said: "This is a barn burner." Earlier in the game he remarked: "This is not for the timid."

He was right.

Washington scored next for the Bruins and we're tied 59-59. It's the 14th tie of the game. Cawood cautions: "Hang on! Hang on!"

Louisville turned it over, as Murphy can't control the ball and it went out of bounds along the UofL left baseline. Washington's good for two more and UCLA took the lead, 61-59, completing that 8-0 run. Washington now had 20 points with 3:48 remaining in the game.

Murphy missed but Cox got the rebound and put it in, 61-61 for the 15th tie of the game. Meyers missed two free throws and back on offense, Bill Bunton found Murphy inside for two points. Louisville 63-61 with 2:06 on the clock.

Dave Meyers tried a long shot from the right side that was no good, and Bond grabbed the rebound and quickly headed the other way for Louisville. McCarter knocked the ball out of bounds. But UofL retained possession. With less than two minutes remaining, Terry Howard checked in for the Cards.

With Bond and now Howard, both excellent ball handlers, the Cards went to the four corner delay game. Bond is fouled, he calmly made the two free throws and with 1:03 left, Louisville had a four-point lead, 65-61.

That might make one think that the Cards were in great shape, but don't forget, the man on the other bench had won nine national championships in the past 11 years. Nothing was certain until that buzzer sounded "Game Over."

Washington cut it to just a two-point lead with 48 seconds left, 65-63. Then, quick as lightning, the Bruins stole the ball, Spillane missed the jumper off the left side but Marques Johnson tied the game 65-65 with the follow shot.

Instant replay! UCLA stole the ball again and now they had 34 seconds to close the deal. At this point, Louisville had committed 11 turnovers in the second half, two on the last two possessions and 21 for the game.

UCLA had committed 14 turnovers, but now they're back on offense. Wooden's team was now running the delay, but the Cardinal defense deflected UCLA's shot and Louisville had the ball first, and 94 feet to go, with just seven seconds remaining.

Bond takes the ball up the floor and finds Junior Bridgeman in the left corner. He shoots from about 25-feet and misses. Score 65-65. Standby for overtime.

In a personal interview, Bridgeman described what happened on that fateful last shot: "The Sports Arena in San Diego had a bank of lights that encircled the entire floor. When I went up for the shot, all I could see was that bank of lights on the other side. I never saw the basket. I was just hoping it would go in."

Louisville only shot 36 percent in the second half, hitting 10 of 26 field goal attempts. UCLA was a little better, making 14 of 35 for 40 percent. UofL controlled the tap and Murphy's eight-footer gave them a 67-65 lead.

Jim Spillane, filling in for Pete Trgovich who had fouled out, made his jumper from the left side, 67-67. Murphy's "Law" rules as he scores again, was fouled, added the free throw and it was the Cards by three, 70-67. Washington scored for UCLA, 70-69.

Murphy shot the ball, but was fouled by Washington. Allen was three for three from the line, missed the first, and made the second, 71-69 with 3:30 left in overtime. Washington missed, Louisville got the rebound but Bridgeman missed his shot on the offensive end. Andre McCarter turned the ball over on a traveling violation for UCLA.

Allen Murphy is fouled by Washington again, and like before, Allen missed the first, made the second and UofL led 72-69. Marques Johnson took a missed shot, went back up and put it in, 72-71. Phil Bond missed, but the Bruins' McCarter can't control the ball as it went out of bounds; Cardinal ball. Murphy missed, Bridgeman missed, but Cox got it to go, 74-71.

On the other end, Cox fouled Dave Meyers. Meyers had missed two a little earlier, but redeemed himself with these two free throws. UofL 74-73.

Terry Howard was back in the game with 50 seconds left. The Cardinals are content to run time off the clock with their two sure ball handlers, Bond and Howard in the game together.

Terry Howard was fouled with 20 seconds left in overtime. He was 28 for 28 from the line on the year. I interviewed Terry several years ago. During the season sportswriters kept reminding him that he hadn't missed a free throw all year. Terry's response: "Stop! You keep bringing it up and I might miss." He told me, "When it left my hand, I felt it was in." It wasn't.

It didn't go through the net but came out and UCLA had the rebound. The Bruins called a timeout. They now had 13 seconds to win the game. The ball came to Washington about ten feet away on the right side. He turned, shot the ball without using the backboard. He didn't need it—it swished.

The Cardinals took a timeout, but there were only two precious seconds on the clock. The in bounds pass was thrown to Murphy who was on the right side, not far from the mid-court line, but he was unable to grab the pass initially. When he did get his hands on the ball, he heaved it toward the rim, but it wasn't even close.

The final score was: UCLA 75 UofL 74

Watching the game on television, I was like most Louisville fans—stunned. I must have stayed in my chair for about 15 minutes. I couldn't get up. I felt as though I was under the power of same strange paralysis. Now, granted some of that feeling was due to wanting Wooden to get beat.

One observer quoted in the paper said: "God must be a UCLA Bruin."

The Cardinals were a good shooting free throw team averaging around 76 percent. But against UCLA, they slipped to 59.3 percent making only 16 of 27 shots. However, the problem was infectious because UCLA wasn't a whole lot better from the line, nine of 14 for 64.3 percent.

But the Bruins had eight more field goal attempts than UofL, 73-65. They made four more than the Cards, 33 to 29. The field goal shooting percentages were close. UCLA 45.2 percent to UofL's 44.6 percent. The Cards had 13 more attempts at the foul line, which meant that in reality, UCLA only had 1.5 more attempts from the field.

In the second half, the Cards shot just 38.5 percent, making 10 of 26 attempts. UCLA wasn't much better; they shot 40 percent but took nine more shots (35) and made four of those for a total of 14 made field goals in the second half.

Now, Louisville's poor free throw shooting resulted in a compound fracture. Couple that with committing 22 turnovers compared to UCLA's 14, with the majority of those turnovers made after the first 20 minutes of play, and we have a better understanding of how the Cardinals won in regulation, but lost and won in overtime, but lost.

In an interview with Phil Bond he said, "I received a copy of the game and have watched some of it, but I just couldn't watch the end."

I like what Dave Meyers said after the game, "Usually we have to play against a lot of other factors besides basketball talent. Players talk at you, cuss at you. Here were two teams not saying a word, doing everything they could to win a basketball game, playing hard, playing clean. That's what it's all about. It was a great game. I haven't been in a game like that in a long time. I thought there were two UCLA teams on the court."

Memories are stirred for what might have been—the Cards and the Cats battling for the national championship. Coach Crum and Coach Hall still debate the outcome of that never-to-be rivalry matchup for all the marbles. Coach Crum says, "Look Joe, we only allowed them to score 75 points in 45 minutes, you allowed them to score 92 in just 40 minutes of play."

Looking at that defensive interpretation by Coach Crum is interesting. Like the Louisville game, UCLA shot 64 percent from the line, making 16 of 25. UK was 19 of 25 for 76 percent. That was the same percentage UofL shot during the season, except against UCLA.

Now from the field, the Bruins were better vs. the Cats than against the Cards. UCLA hit 38 of 78 for 48.7 percent, compared to its 33 of 73 vs. the Cardinals for 45.2 percent. Kentucky was only 38.4 percent from the field connecting on just 33 of 86 attempts. Defense was a key as UofL shot 44.6 percent in their game with UCLA.

Louisville out rebounded UCLA 47-37. UCLA out rebounded Kentucky 55-49. The Bruins' Ralph Drollinger played a key role here by grabbing 13 rebounds in only 16 minutes of action.

UK committed only 12 turnovers against UCLA, UofL made 22.

We see some of the major differences between the Cards and Cats when they played the "Wizard of Westwood," but the result was the same, UCLA won the game. From 1964 thru that last Final Four against the Bluegrass state in 1975, John Wooden won 44 of 45 tournament games and 10 national championships. Don't look for anyone to beat that anytime soon.

The following year the collision course reappeared, but was found in a vastly different location. Instead of the NCAA Final Four, this road to the "Dream Game" ran through New York City to Madison Square Garden for the NIT. UK beat Niagara 67-61 in the first round while Providence defeated North Carolina A&T 84-68.

The Kentucky Wildcats then beat the Kansas State Wildcats 81-78 advancing to play the winner of the Louisville-Providence game. The Cardinals had lost to Providence on the road, January 10, 1976 by three, 63-60. Louisville then proceeded to win its next 11 games before losing to No. 2 Marquette at home 72-62.

They didn't recover, losing two of their next four games, one to Memphis in the first game of the Metro 6 Tournament 87-76.

Phil Bond told me, "Just like the game against UCLA in the Final Four, I wasn't looking past Providence either, thinking about playing Kentucky. You take them one game at a time."

He continued, "For some reason we just weren't playing our best basketball at this particular time."

Providence wrecked the collision course beating UofL 73-67. Kentucky beat Providence 79-78 and UNC-Charlotte 71-67 to win its second NIT, 30 years after its first in 1946 when freshman Ralph Beard sank a free throw giving Kentucky a 46-45 victory over Rhode Island. From 1976 to 1981 the collision course was under repair. UofL went to the West Region in 1977, the Midwest Region in 1978, '79 '80 and 1981. They lost to UCLA in the first game in 1977, lost to DePaul in the first game in '78, lost to Arkansas in the second game in '79 and in 1980 won it all over UCLA in Indianapolis 59-54.

In 1981 U.S. Reed hit his miracle shot from around mid-court to eliminate the defending national champion Cardinals 74-73 in the Midwest Regional first round. During that same time period, UK lost in the NCAA East Regional championship game to North Carolina 79-72. In 1978 they were in the Mideast Regional and went all the way beating Duke 94-88 in the Checker Dome in St. Louis.

In 1979 the Cats lost to Clemson at home in the first game of the NIT 68-67. In 1980, UK lost to Duke on its own floor in the second game of the Mideast Regional 55-54 and dropped a 69-62 decision to UAB in the first round of the Mideast Regional in 1981 Tuscaloosa, AL. So maybe, just maybe after losing like they did the previous three years, and minus Sam Bowie due to injury, the loss to Middle Tennessee wasn't as surprising as everyone surmised.

Headline: *Lexington-Herald Leader*: UK-UofL match fires up state.

Mark Bradley wrote, "In a state where the advent of March turns the citizenry into madmen and madwomen, however, Joe Hall was likely the only one thinking about Middle. Everyone else zoomed in on the name of the team the Wildcats would play in the second round of the NCAA tournament. The magic name, Louisville. What the media and the legislature and a million fans could not bring to pass, the NCAA Selection Committee probably will. If Kentucky defeats Middle Tennessee Thursday in Nashville, Saturday will feature the match made only once every third decade. Kentucky and Louisville, so rich in tradition, so near in miles, so far apart in philosophy. And now, one game from confrontation."

The late Derek Smith responded to the news of the possible matchup this way: "When I came to Louisville, I wanted to win a national championship. (He did in 1980) When I did that, I always felt that I wanted to play against Kentucky."

Stan Simpson, the coach of Middle Tennessee was quoted as saying: "I feel like the ugliest boy in the class. At the last minute, he was invited to the senior prom by the most beautiful girl in the class. He's glad to have the opportunity, but not sure he can dance with her." But dance he did, as the Blue Raiders waltzed past UK 50-44 and got another date, this time with Louisville.

Looking back recently, Coach Joe B. Hall said: "We died. We jumped out to a big lead, and then, just absolutely we're looking ahead. I don't think there's any question about it. All the conversation, all the questions were about playing Louisville in the second game and I think our players just switched from Middle Tennessee to thinking about the Louisville game. And after we had gotten a comfortable lead we, just fell apart."

The Cardinals were pretty fine dancers themselves beating Middle, then Minnesota and UAB to advance to another Final Four where they lost to Georgetown in New Orleans in a semifinal game, 50-46.

The real "Dream Game" finally became reality the following year, 1983 in Knoxville where the Cards won a thriller 80-68 in overtime and went to their third Final Four in four years losing to Houston in a semifinal game 94-81.

In 1984 UK beat UofL in the Mideast Regional in Lexington 72-67, then beat Illinois, advancing to the Final Four to lose to Georgetown in the semifinals 53-40. In 1985 UK won two games in the West Regional before losing to St. John's 86-70 in Coach Hall's final year.

Louisville was back in the NIT in 1985 winning two at home before being beaten by UCLA in the semifinals 75-66. In 1986, the Cards lost to the Cats in the regular season 69-64 at Rupp, but now they were really rolling, winning 11 straight games, including the Metro Conference Tournament over Florida State 87-80.

The Wildcats were rolling too, having won 14 straight as they prepared to meet LSU for the fourth time that season in the championship game of the Southeast Regional in Atlanta. In the previous game the Cats beat Alabama for the fourth time that year, 68-63. But the fourth time against LSU wasn't a charm as the Tigers won 59-57. LSU, instead of Kentucky went to the Final Four in Dallas to play the Cards in a semifinal game, losing to UofL 88-77.

The Cards went on to beat Duke 72-69 for UofL's second national championship in seven years with Denny Crum. Denny shared his conservation with Coach Bobby Knight the following day, "Coach Knight told me that the best team didn't win the national championship this year." Coach Crum responded: "I'll tell you one thing, the best team won that game last night."

In 1988 another opportunity was up for grabs. Both teams were in Birmingham, AL. for the NCAA Southeast Region semifinals. A win for UK over Villanova and a win for UofL over Oklahoma, and they meet in the region championship game for the right to go to the Final Four. UK lost to Villanova 80-74 and Oklahoma beat Louisville 108-98. Even had they played, it would not have been official, since part of UK's NCAA sanctions included the removal of their two victories and one defeat in the tournament that year.

In 1996, Rick Pitino was at his zenith at Kentucky. After beating Utah in the Midwest Regional semifinal 101-70, the Cats had outscored their three opponents in the tournament by 89 points, were 31-3 and on a roll. UofL was 22-10 and a victory over Wake Forest in the Midwest Regional semifinal would secure the Cards a matchup with the Wildcats for the right to go to the Final Four.

From a shooting standpoint, the Cardinals had played a poor game connecting on 23 of 69 shots for only 33.3 percent. Their star player, DeJaun Wheat was just three of 15 from the field. The previous week in the region's first two rounds, he was 15 of 28 which included nine of 19 from three-point range. He scored a total of 52 points in the victories over Tulsa and Villanova and led the team with six assists. UofL won the rebound battle versus Tim Duncan's Wake Forest squad 40-32. The Cards turned it over only six times while Wake committed 17 miscues. Samaki Walker had a solid performance against Duncan with 18 points and 10 rebounds. B.J. Flynn was a huge contributor off the bench with 11 points, four rebounds, three assists and two steals. Tick Rogers also added 13 points. It was real battle between these two, trying to advance to the next round.

Wake Forest led at the half 30-27. The Demon Deacons sprinted out to a 38-29 advantage with 16:50 to play. The Cardinals cut it to six, at 38-32 on Flynn's three-point play, but Tim Duncan answered with a 22-footer as the shot clock expired, 41-32 Wake Forest.

Samaki Walker countered with back-to-back three-point plays as Louisville continued to scrap, and it paid-off when Tick Rogers made a three-pointer to finish a 16-6 run giving the Cards a 48-47 lead with 10:26 on the clock.

The score was tied 51-all but UofL found itself on top once again, this time 59-54 with 4:52 left.

Louisville didn't score again.

The Cardinals experienced a similar drought in the first half going 4:42 before Tick Roger's scored on a dunk with four seconds left in that half. LaRue hit a three for Wake Forest trimming the Cardinal lead to two, 59-57 with a whole lot of time left, 4:31. Wake Forest was the third best three-point shooting team in the nation. They made 10 of 18 in this game. Coach Crum was quoted by the C-J: "We did not want to give up (so) many threes, but when you double-team Duncan, it leaves you vulnerable."

With the score still 59-57 in favor of UofL, Tim Duncan scored on a controversial three-point play to give Wake the 60-59 lead. Down inside, Duncan made a move, hit the basket and was fouled by Damion Dantzler. Duncan added the free throw. A replay on the overhead screens showed that Duncan traveled at least once and perhaps twice before scoring the inside basket. No replay screen is necessary. Assistant Jerry Jones simply stated: "He walked." Still, Louisville had 1:16 to provide a makeup call

After a series of six passes, Wheat tried a difficult three-point shot off the left-side and missed. Wheat back on defense drew a charge from Wake Forest guard Jerry Braswell near the time-line. Wheat got in position to shoot, by making a cross-over dribble to the left, then he flashed back to his right. He had an opening, but then Tim Duncan (still playing for the San Antonio Spurs) came at

Wheat forcing him to pull-up for a jump shot. LaRue had shifted back alongside Wheat's left shoulder, DeJaun dipped his body to the right and took a shot from his side and missed.

Kentucky beat Wake Forest 83-63, advancing to the Final Four beating Calipari's UMASS team 81-74 and Syracuse 76-67 for the 1996 NCAA National Championship.

It's been 17 years since the last near miss, but the Cards and Cats played a sure round in the 2012 NCAA Final Four, UK winning that game 69-61 and its eighth national championship beating Kansas in the title game 67-59.

Chapter Ten
We're Number One

The main purpose of this book is to prove that UK vs. UofL truly is college basketball's No. 1 rivalry.

When freshmen were ineligible to play for the varsity team at the colleges and universities, it was always a treat to arrive to the main event early, to see the freshmen play. It was a preview of coming attractions for the following season. That changed in the fall of 1972, when freshmen became eligible to compete on the varsity level.

Like those freshmen games of a bygone era, the first nine chapters in this book play the preliminary role, to the unveiling of what really is the number one rivalry in all of college basketball. Former Louisville Cardinal Coach Denny Crum said: "I don't know how you would measure which rivalry is the best?

Coach Crum is not the only one that feels that way. However, I have selected a closing technique used by salesmen for ages, which I feel provides a sure quantifiable measuring stick, by which we with certainty can declare the UK-UofL rivalry No. 1 in all of college basketball.

It's called the Ben Franklin "T" close. It goes like this, "Mr. and Mrs. Prospect, Ben Franklin is considered one of the wisest men in American history. Whenever he had a decision to make, he simply took a piece of paper and on it, drew a big T. On one side of the T he would list all the reasons why he should do a certain thing, on the opposite side, he listed all the reasons why he should not. Whichever side had the most reasons, wise old Ben would follow.

Then the salesman proceeds to list all the reasons why Mr. and Mrs. Prospect should buy his product and then lays the pen down, and asks the prospects to list all the reasons why they should not. On paper, the prospects are in deep trouble if they chose to follow this closing technique.

As wise as the publisher of Poor Richard's Almanac was, I have always felt there was a flaw to Franklin's system. What if there was one reason and just one reason only, that was so compelling, it could overpower the other side's reason, logic, emotion and number of reasons listed to finalize the person's decision?

In life insurance selling for example, there are basically two "real reasons" why people don't buy: (1) They can't qualify for the policy because they are uninsurable, and (2) They can't afford it.

There are life insurance policies today that cover any health risk. That takes care of number one (maybe not the amount they wish, but adequate, affordable coverage is available). If money is the problem and no way can be found to overcome that hurdle, the fact remains they still would like to have the policy.

Franklin's system is not a true pros and cons list. The con's side would address negative reasons being listed why one should not pursue a certain course. The "T" close is so designed that positive reasons can be listed on both sides of this decision-making equation.

When Dwayne Casey was still an assistant coach for the UK basketball team, I explained the Ben Franklin "T" close to him at a game, so he could try it with Derrick Miller who was debating either to go to Auburn or UK. I said, "Dwayne you list all the reasons why Derrick should attend UK, then lay your pen down and let him list all the reasons why he should go to Auburn." Now if it was football, one would not use the T method, but because it was basketball, and Auburn didn't have a chance.

When I saw Casey later at another event, Miller had already committed to Kentucky. Dwayne was in a hurry to leave, but I yelled out to him, he turned around and I said did you use the "T" close with Miller? He replied, "Yes!"

Derrick Miller ranks No. 1 in the rivalry's single-game scoring category with 34 points.

Now, let's see how the T method helps us answer our rivalry question. First, I will use the media guides from each school because therein, the media person for basketball, highlights their school's particular achievements and second, the 2013-14 NCAA Record Book.

I will also utilize other information sources that definitely have bearing on the outcome of the issue at stake. But I feel the reasons listed should mainly reflect something won; games, conference championships, conference tournament titles and NCAA National Championships.

Supplementary indicators of winning such as the AP Poll results, number of titles, number of championships, victories and winning percentage are all vital in making the final determination. Awards per/se are not. No coach begins the season thinking of the number of players he can get on the all-conference team. However, certain awards such as player of the year and NBA drafted players I will include.

It is also imperative to include categories in which fans make the difference, like attendance, travel and etc. Another important category to consider is what a university or coach has done to make the game, or life a little better for all concerned.

I will use personal subjectivity in this case, or in other words, intangible evidence may be applicable at certain times.

In studying the media guides of UK, UofL, Duke, UNC and UCLA I have found some contradictions in facts that have been used to highlight accomplishments and construed to establish a certain intent. For example, UCLA still claims 18 Final Fours, which makes them tied with North Carolina for the record in that category. But the NCAA vacated their spot in the 1980 Final Four when they lost to Louisville in the title game 59-54 which reduces UCLA to 17, good for second-place.

UNC has UCLA with 17 in its media guide making the Tar Heels a stand-alone No. 1 in Final Four appearances with 18. No surprise there, that's how it should be. But North Carolina counts the vacated Final Four for former player and Assistant Coach Larry Brown on page 49 of the 2013-14 media guide. It reads: "Roy Williams is one of four coaches (with Frank McGuire, Larry Brown and Rick Pitino) to lead two schools to the national championship game."

Brown led UCLA in 1980 and Kansas in 1988 to the finals, but the NCAA vacated UCLA's 1980 appearance. You can't have it both ways. UNC uses the same Final Four to reduce UCLA's number from 18 to 17, but counts it when crediting their own Larry Brown. It's also interesting that they don't mention John Calipari with these other four coaches, because he did the same thing with Memphis in 2008 and UK in 2012. Here again, the NCAA vacated Memphis's 2008 runner-up spot and North Carolina agrees with the NCAA in Calipari's situation, but not with their own Larry Brown.

I will simply follow the declarations of the NCAA.

When the media guide states a record is based since a particular time period, or is a record among active coaches, it will not be counted unless it is actually the record including all-time results. Then, there are simply some mistakes included in these guides. For example, UCLA's guide states that John Wooden's 81.5 percent winning percentage is the best of all-time.

We have a two-way problem with the stated percentage. (1) Clair Bee of Long Island University is the all-time winning percentage leader at 82.6 percent and Adolph Rupp is second with 82.2 percent. (2) Coach Wooden's actual winning percentage at UCLA was 80.8 percent winning 620 and losing 147 games. At Indiana State he was 44-15 making his overall winning percentage 80.4 percent with 664 wins and 162 losses.

In analyzing All-American teams, so many different organizations were cited before the AP Poll started naming its All-Americans in 1948 that it resembles professional wrestling.
I remember as a young man in the 60s, there were so many different wrestling championship belts up for grabs it was confusing. It got to the point were you would hear something along these lines: "Ladies and gentleman! Tonight's bout is for the Inter-Continental Midwest Heavyweight Championship of the World, within a 40-miles radius of the North Platte River."

Keeping this in mind, I will credit the AP All-American teams that were selected beginning with the 1947-48 basketball season.

On the right side of the T, I will list all the reasons why UK-UofL is No. 1 and on the left, Duke-UNC. Any points elaborated on below the T's will be designated as the corresponding number and R for Kentucky and Louisvlle or the corresponding number and L for Duke and UNC.

Since we have determined that basketball is a religion in Kentucky and Duke claims they are the Blue Devils; the biblical symbolism of on the right hand and the left, and the sheep and the goats is a perfect fit for our comparison study.

Duke and UNC No. 1	Kentucky and Louisville No. 1
1. Duke Coach Mike Krzyzewski is the winningest Division 1 coach of all-time in number of victories entering the 2013-14 season: 957	1. 11-9-UK-UofL have more NCAA National Championships than Duke-UNC.

1R. I could lay the pen down now and walk away and feel completely justified in making the case that the Cards and the Cats are the No. 1 all-time college basketball rivalry. All other records appear a shade or shades paler in comparable significance.

There are some who don't agree that the number of national championships is the reason I referred to earlier that can overpower all other logic, reasoning and number of items listed for pursuing a particular decision. But that is easily countered. When I mention that no team in Major League Baseball will break my Atlanta Braves' record of 14 consecutive division titles, the instant reply remains: "You only won one World Series, who cares?" I care, because your team hasn't and won't break that record. As a Braves' fan purely speaking, we should have won the World Series in 1991 and 1996 as well.

Lelo Prado, former UofL head baseball coach remembered this about the 1996 World Series. The Braves had taken the first two games in New York and lost the next four, making the Yankees World Champions again. Prado said, "My brother-in-law, Yankees' first baseman Tino Martinez told me that when the team was leaving the stadium down 0-2, teammate Wade Boggs exclaimed: 'We're in good shape, we're going to win this thing." Faith, ill-advised base running and questionable pitching changes precede the miracle.

Coach Rupp said in his speech at BYU in 1958, "If a man is found on top of a mountain; he didn't fall to get there, he had to climb."

If the climbing doesn't ascend to the top; the majority of the time, the fans disregard the distance achieved in the attempt. Championships matter.

Remember the dictionary definition of rival that was used in Chapter One: "One of two or more striving to reach or obtain something that only one can possess." We're not talking about MVP's, All-Tournament Team etc.. No one goes into the championship game striving to win those awards. Now don't get me wrong, it certainly is a bonus for the schools to have their participants so honored. However, the above definition reduces the argument to only one conclusion: "The National Championship."

UK can't win the ACC Conference and the other three can't win the SEC.

It's great to make it to the Final Four, but that's not the championship. UK and UofL have the advantage in the most important category. That's why I mentioned one might find a weakness in the Franklin System, but the system still serves the purpose here; one reason or the most, the Cards and the Cats are the winners.

Duke and UNC No. 1	Kentucky and Louisville No. 1

2. Duke-UNC have the top three coaches in NCAA tournament wins: 3
 	
    (1) Mike Krzyzewski-82
    (2) Dean Smith-65
    (3) Roy Williams-62
	2. No other school, let me repeat myself, no other school has accomplished, what UofL did in the 2012-2013 season.

2R. (1) The men's basketball team won the national championship, (2) the women's basketball team was the runner-up for the national championship, (3) the football team won a BCS bowl defeating Florida in the Sugar Bowl and (4) the baseball team went to the College World Series. This is unchartered territory. No other school has ever accomplished this feat.

Granted, this includes more than just basketball, but I think Reagan's "trickle down" theory really works well in sports.

UK vs. UofL College Basketball's No. 1 Rivalry - Enough Said!

The stronger the rivalries in basketball and football here, the better the other sports do. UK-UofL draws more fans for basketball and football than Duke and UNC. You have to sneak into the UK-UofL baseball game now. Volleyball, softball all do better from the trickle down effect. Rick Pitino said recently: "If Cal and I were to pitch horseshoes, five-thousand would show-up."

Duke and UNC No. 1	Kentucky and Louisville No. 1
3. Coach K has the most 30-win seasons as a coach, Duke and UK are tied with 13-30 win seasons.: 13	3. Louisville is the only school to have won the N.A.I.B., NIT and NCAA tournaments.

3R. NAIB stood for the National Association for Intercollegiate Basketball. It was the first national tournament started in 1937 specifically for smaller colleges. Louisville beat John Wooden and his Indiana State team in 1948, 82 to 70 for that title. The NAIB is the NAIA today.

Duke and UNC No. 1	Kentucky and Louisville No. 1
4. North Carolina ranks first in the number of Final Four appearances: 18	4. UofL was a pioneer for having racially integrated teams in the South.

4R. Frank Camp's Cardinal football team did it in the 50s and UofL's basketball team signed Wade Houston, Eddie Whitehead and Sam Smith for the 1962-63 season. This not only was a key factor in Louisville becoming a basketball powerhouse, but it was good for the community as well.

Duke and UNC No. 1	Kentucky and Louisville No. 1
5. North Carolina ranks first in number of players to have participated in a Final Four: 154	5. UK is the all-time winningest team in college basketball. (Total wins entering the 2013-14 season: 2,111
6. North Carolina is tied with Houston and LSU for the most players selected on the NBA's 50 All-Time Greatest Players Team: 3	6. UK leads college basketball in all-time winning percentage: 76.1%
7. North Carolina is the only school in the country with 12 wins over the No. 1-ranked team in the AP Poll: 12	7. UK is the all-time leader in NCAA appearances: 52
8. Carolina has been a No. 1 seed in the NCAA Tournament more than any other school in NCAA history: 14	8. UK is the all-time leader in NCAA games played: 157
9. Michael Jordan is the ESPN Athlete of the Century	9. UK is the all-time leader in NCAA tournament victories: 111

Duke and UNC No. 1	Kentucky and Louisville No. 1
10. Carolina has appeared in the AP Poll more times than any other school in history: 808	10. UK leads in all-time NCAA Elite Eight appearances: 34

10L. The AP Poll started for college basketball during the 1948-49 season and college football in 1936. Two different numbers are used in the UNC media guide and a different number is cited in the NCAA Record Book. I'll use this one; they win regardless of number used.

Duke and UNC No. 1	Kentucky and Louisville No. 1
11. Michael Jordan is considered the greatest NBA player of all-time.	11. UK leads in all-time NCAA Sweet 16 appearances: 39

11R. I used the numbers for the pre-1975 era. Most of the college media guides do too. It would really only change the Sweet 16 appearances in UNC's favor. UNC used the pre-1975 figures as well.

Duke and UNC No. 1	Kentucky and Louisville No. 1
12. 45-UNC has the greatest number of first-round players drafted by the NBA.	12. UK has the most combined post season tournament appearances. (NCAA and NIT): 61
13. National Media favors Duke/North Carolina as the best college rivalry	13. UK is the only school to win multiple championships in both the NCAA (8) and the NIT (2).
14. National audience favors Duke/North Carolina as the best college rivalry.	14. UK has the most 20-win seasons: 57
15. (1) geography, the two schools are so close together it makes for a really intense atmosphere.	15. 13-UK is tied with Duke for the most 30 win seasons: Coach K has all the 30 win seasons for the Blue Devils.
16. (2) The two schools have been playing longer. That is on a consecutive basis. Actually UK and UofL started first on 2-15-1912 with Kentucky winning 34 to 10	16. UK has the most number of 35 win seasons: 5

15-16L. Matt Plizga, Duke Associate Director of Sports information for men's basketball and men's golf, named the two reasons (above in bullet point 15 and 16) why they believe Duke/North Carolina is the best college basketball rivalry.

16L. Duke-UNC began 1-24-1920 with the Tar Heels taking the game, 36 to 25. Playing longer doesn't necessarily guarantee a better product, although Duke and North Carolina are awfully good teams, especially since 1986. Check Army-Navy. They reek with tradition, but the glory has faded.

Duke and UNC No. 1	Kentucky and Louisville No. 1
17. Public versus private. Most fans of this rivalry always list this as one of the reasons.	17. UK has the most number of coaches who have won an NCAA national championship: 5. Adolph Rupp has four and Joe B. Hall, Rick Pitino, Tubby Smith and John Calipari have one each
18. Dean Smith holds the record for most consecutive 20-win seasons: 27	18. UK is #1 all-time for most weeks ranked in the AP Poll Top-Ten: 634
19. Dean Smith holds the record for most consecutive trips to the NCAA tournament: 23	19. UK is #1 all-time for the most weeks ranked in the AP Poll Top-Five: 422
20. Roy Williams is the only coach with a win in 20 consecutive NCAA tournament appearances: 20	20. UK is #1 all-time in the Final AP Poll for Top 25-finishes: 48
21. The edge for athletic academic achievement goes to Duke-UNC. UK-UofL are getting better and better with AD's Barnhart and Jurich, and coaches Calipari and Pitino.	21. UK is #1 all-time in the Final AP Poll for Top-20 finishes: 48
22. Mike Krzyzewski has four Gold Medals and Dean Smith was the coach of the 1976 Olympic team.	22. UK is #1 all-time in the Final AP Poll for Top-15 finishes: 43

22R. UK has ten players that have Olympic Gold Medals, but when you combine the number of players with the successful coaches, Duke-UNC wins here.

I think John Wooden was disappointed that his country didn't call on him to coach the Olympic Team. We talked about that when I was in his home in December of 1991. He wasn't angry, but I believe he was disappointed. With his record, he should have been the coach.

Duke and UNC No. 1	Kentucky and Louisville No. 1
23. Duke is the only team to finish No.1 in the final regular season AP Poll for four consecutive years. (1999-2002).	23. UK is #1 all-time in the Final AP Poll for Top-Ten finishes: 40
24. Roy Williams is one of only three coaches to lead two schools to the national championship game. (The others are Rick Pitino and Frank McGuire)	24. UK is #1 all-time in the regular season Final AP Poll for number-one finishes: 9
25. Roy Williams is the only coach to lead two schools to two appearances in the finals. (Kansas in 1991 and 2003); and North Carolina in 2005 and 2009)	25. UK is #1 in all-time winning percentage against AP-ranked opponents: 60.9%
26. Roy Williams reached 700 wins faster than any other coach in history. Only Adolph Rupp (82.5%) had a better winning percentage than Roy Williams (79.5%) of all the coaches who have reached the 700-win plateau	26. UK is #1 all-time in the UPI/Coaches' Poll for Top 25 finishes: 46
27. Roy Williams is the only Carolina coach to have three consecutive 30-win seasons. (2007-09)	27. UK is #1 all-time in the UPI/Coaches' Poll for Top-20 finishes: 45
28. UNC leads all other schools in the number of players who have scored at least 1,000 points in their careers: 68	28. UK is #1 all-time in the UPI/Coaches' Poll for Top-15 finishes: 42
29. Dean Smith retired as the winningest coach in Division 1 history: 879	29. UK is #1 all-time in the UPI/Coaches' Poll for Top-Ten finishes: 38
30. A 2012 report by the Wall Street Journal found that since 1985, NBA-bound players from Carolina have earned over $853 million, more than basketball alumni from any other university.	30. UK is #1 all-time in the UPI/Coaches' Poll for Top-Five finishes: 29

30L. "It's absolutely fair to say, that the Tar Heels are the first college team-possibly in any sport-whose former athletes have earned more than one billion in salary playing that sport professionally. If you factor in endorsement income, (Michael) Jordan alone might make the Tar Heels lead insurmountable."

Duke and UNC No. 1	Kentucky and Louisville No. 1
31. John Gabriel, New York Knicks Scouting Director has said: "UNC is a plus-four school, meaning that if I rate a player as the 10th-best player in the NBA Draft, being a Tar Heel automatically jumps him to number six. The plus-four rating is based upon the success of former Tar Heels in the NBA."	31. The YUM Center is the "jewel" of the rivalry facilities.

31L. I don't know if I would be using anything or anyone that is associated with the New York Knicks at this time. This includes the Statue of Liberty.

Duke and UNC No. 1	Kentucky and Louisville No. 1
32. 7-0 -UNC is undefeated in games when No. 1 verses No. 2. 4-0 as No. 1 and 3-0 as No. 2.	32. UK is #1 in average number of losses per season played: 6.0090909
33. Upper Deck produced a set of Carolina basketball trading cards, making UNC the first basketball program to receive a school-exclusive set from the company.	33. UK is #1 all-time for most head coaches with a NCAA Championship game appearance: 5
34. Entering the 2013-14 season, Duke has been ranked in the AP Poll an NCAA-best 116 straight weeks.	34. UK is #1 all-time for most head coaches with multiple NCAA Championship game appearances: 3
35. Coach K is the all-time leader for most times ranked No. 1 in the AP Poll in different seasons: 16. He has done it 11 times in the last 16 years. John Wooden is second, (12) Roy Williams third (10) and Dean Smith fourth (10).	35. UK is #1 all-time in total decades with a NCAA Championship: 5
36. Coach K was voted the best coach by Time Magazine and CNN in 2001.	36. UK is #1 all-time in total decades with multiple NCAA Championships: 3
37. Coach K was the first college basketball coach to be elected Sportsman of the Year by the Sporting News in 1992.	37. UK is #1 all-time in total decades with multiple NCAA Championship game appearances: 4

Duke and UNC No. 1	Kentucky and Louisville No. 1
38. Coach K is the all-time leader in number of games coached in the NCAA tournament: 107	38. UK is #1 all-time in total decades with a Final Four appearance: 7
39. Duke has won NCAA-best 101 consecutive non-conference home games. I did not see this listed in the NCAA record book, but it will be counted here.	39. UK is #1 all-time in total decades with multiple Final Four appearances: 5
40. Coach K has been named the National Coach of the Year by 12 various organizations. Using the AP Poll as the "determiner," Coach Wooden leads as a five-time award winner.	40. UK is #1 all-time in Top Five total wins in total decades since 1930: 4
41. Duke's 1991-92 team is one of only 12 schools in college basketball history to be ranked No. 1 for the entire season.	41. UK is #1 all-time in Top Ten total wins in total decades since 1930: 7
42. Seth Curry and his older brother Stephen Curry became the highest scoring brother tandem in NCAA history during the 2012-13 season. The two combined for 4,736 points during their college careers.	42. UK is #1 winning percentage leader in total decades since 1930: 2

42L. Seth scored 2,101 career points, including 1,394 as a Blue Devil. Stephen, a current member of the Golden State Warriors, finished his career at Davidson with 2,635.

Duke and UNC No. 1	Kentucky and Louisville No. 1
43. ESPN, Sports Illustrated, Sporting News and Fox Sports named Roy Williams the Coach of the Decade for 2000-2009. He led Kansas and North Carolina to 33 NCAA tournament wins in that span, eight more than any other coach and won Championships at North Carolina in 2005 and 2009.	43. UK is #1 all-time in Top Five winning percentage in total decades since 1930: 6

Duke and UNC No. 1	Kentucky and Louisville No. 1
44. The Sporting News surveyed a panel of 50 former ACC standout players in 2010 asking them which current ACC coach they would want to play for other than their alma mater's-Roy Williams received 19 votes. No other coach received more than 8.5 votes.	44. UK is #1 all-time in top Ten winning percentage in total decades since 1930: 7
45. In February of 2009, Forbes named Roy Williams the best basketball coach in the country, choosing him by analyzing win-loss percentages, NCAA Tournament appearances, Final Fours, national championships and recruiting.	45. UK has won more regular season conference championships (47) than UNC (36), UofL (23) and Duke (22).

45R. The Cat's 47 includes two, UNC's includes seven and Duke's includes three Southern Conference titles. The Cardinals won titles in the KIAC, Missouri Valley, Metro, Conference-USA and Big East conferences.

Duke and UNC No. 1	Kentucky and Louisville No. 1
46. UNC became the first national champion to win all six games by a dozen or more points.	46. UK is #1 all-time winning conference tournament championships: 28. This total includes the 1921 SIAA Conference Tournament title.
47. Roy Williams holds the record for most wins in a season by a Tar Heel coach: 36	47. UK is #1 all-time in national attendance titles: 25
48. During the 2013-14 season when UNC plays at Duke, it will be a GameDay record for UNC for most appearances on the show: 11	48. UK has won eight consecutive attendance titles and 17 of the last 18.

48R. That may be, but Kentucky set the record for GameDay attendance. Winning is what matters. Just because you are sitting in a garage, that doesn't make you a car. Just because some guy tells you Duke-UNC is the best, that doesn't necessarily make it so.

These points listed on the Franklin "T" System, show that titles, number of wins, great players and especially the fans doing their part, really comprise the composite winner.

Duke and UNC No. 1	Kentucky and Louisville No. 1
49. Dean Smith was named the second-best coach behind John Wooden by the NABC. (National Association of basketball Coaches).	49. UK has the most passionate fan base. Dick Vitale agrees.
50. In 2006, Dean Smith was named to the inaugural class of the National Collegiate Basketball Hall of Fame along with James Naismith, John Wooden, Oscar Robertson and Bill Russell.	50. UK fans travel better than any another fan group. UofL does a great job as well.
51. Frank McGuire was the first coach in history to win 100 games at three different schools. (St. John's, North Carolina and South Carolina).	51. UNC's media guide states that the Tar Heels are annually among the leaders in selling officially licensed merchandise. They are, but UK wins among our Big Four finishing #5 this past season. (2012-13).
52. Frank McGuire and John Calipari are the only coaches to lead three different schools to a No. 1 ranking.	52. The UK-UofL rivalry is considered by most nationally as the best non-conference rivalry. This alone could give the edge to the Cards and the Cats.

52L and R. Before 1975 only one team from a conference could participate in the NCAA tournament. Now that multiple teams from a conference are allowed to play, if you lose in the conference qualifier, so what? One still has a chance too go all the way in the NCAA.

This diminishes the importance of the conference tournament. They exist primarily now, just to make money. If pre-1975 NCAA rules were still in vogue, and only the one team that won the conference qualifier went to the tournament, UK would not have won their 1996 and 2012 national championships. Mike Krzyzewski would have three championships and six Final Fours instead of four and 11, and North Carolina would not have been the ACC representative in 1993, 2005 and 2009 when they won the title in those years. Louisville has been the conference qualifier each time they have won the championship.

This brings me to my next point. Let's don't say; in the beginning of the NCAA tournament, you only had to win three games to take the title, so that was easy. But, on the other hand you got right to the meat of the tournament in those three games. Eras are different. There are advantages and disadvantages in both and we will applaud and validate those conquering heroes in days of old, in the present tense and in years to come.

Duke and UNC No. 1	Kentucky and Louisville No. 1
53. Frank McGuire is the only coach to win ACC titles at two schools. (North Carolina and South Carolina).	53. UK-UofL can also count geography, historical and social differences to make this rivalry No. 1.

53R. The Cards and the Cats win the mileage battle. Hostility builds as you drive the 70 miles or so to reach the other team's home base.The two cities have been competitive almost since Daniel Boone came through the Cumberland Gap. Lexington was actually the largest city in the state when the first U.S. Census laid out the game stats in 1790. Lexington was the population tournament leader until 1830.

Back then, there were more millionaires in Lexington's central part of the state. In fact, wealthy gentry and other landowners may be the genesis according to some why a undetermined percentage of Wildcat fans still turn-up their noses and cast their eyes downward at what are considered unworthy Cardinal fans and their meager accomplishments in the world of collegiate athletics.

The history of the River City with areas such as Shippingport, tend one to think more of the average "Joe." Louisville didn't become a part of the state college system until 1970, but UK remains the flagship university in the state.

In politics, its always the "city slickers" in the big town; Louisville, against the rest of the state. UofL has more fans out in the state now than ever before thanks to Cardinal Coach Denny Crum, A.D.s Bill Olsen and Tom Jurich and current Coach Rick Pitino, but UK also has it's largest alumni base in Louisville.

I think we should add a rivalry referendum to the 2016 U.S Presidential Ballot here in Kentucky. Which team is your favorite? Then we will know the number across the Bluegrass and finally be able to determine which team has the largest fan base right here in Louisville. You must be 18 to vote, so we'll have to hold elections in the schools to include the youth's preferences.

One might ask: "If you know which team has the most fans in Louisville, wouldn't that diminish the frenzied debates about which team prevails in number in Jefferson County?" Absolutely not! The loser will claim foul. Election machines either malfunctioned or were tampered with, and the war of words will be entrapped forever in a dangling "chad" conversation.

Duke and UNC No. 1	Kentucky and Louisville No. 1
54. Bill Guthridge has played or coached in more Final Fours than any other person in NCAA history: 14 (Two as a head coach at North Carolina, 10 as a Tar Heel assistant coach, and one each as a player and assistant coach at his alma mater, Kansas State).	54. Adolph Rupp

54R. Adolph Rupp dominated college basketball until 1969 when John Wooden became the winningest NCAA Championship coach.

Next to Wooden's run of 12 Final Fours and 10 NCAA titles from 1962-1975, I believe Rupp's run from 1942-58 is the greatest.

In that period of time, he went to eight Final Fours, five in the NCAA tournament, winning four, and three in the NIT, winning one.

He won 407 games while losing only 58 for a 87.5 percent winning percentage. He finished first in the 1949, 1951, 1952 and 1954 Final Regular Season AP Poll. One must remember that the AP Poll didn't start for college basketball until the 1948-49 season. Rupp would have won in 1948 and probably 1947 as well.

He won a Helms Foundation National Championship in 1933 but won again in 1954. There are only four times the Helms Foundation has not awarded the NCAA Champion its title, and one of those years was 1954, when UK finished 25-0 but declined the NCAA bid because its top three scorers were ruled ineligible for being graduate students.

He was also the 1948 assistant Olympic coach as the U.S. Won the Gold Medal with UK's Fabulous Five comprising half of the ten member team.

He won 13 SEC regular season conference championships in 16 years (UK's 1952-53 season was cancelled) and nine SEC tournament titles in 11 years. The tournament was disbanded after 1952 and resumed in 1979. Rupp won 22 of the 27 SEC titles for an amazing championship winning percentage of 81.5 percent.

UK-UofL dominated the rivalry, the Bluegrass was far ahead of those guys down on Tobacco Road. After the NCAA championship in 1958, the UK-UofL tandem had four titles, UNC-Duke had one. The Cards and the Cats had been to six Final Fours, the Tar Heels and Blue Devils just two.

Analyzing the first 38 years of play after the 1977 season, it was still four to one in titles, but Duke-UNC led 10-9 in number of Final Fours.

UK beat Duke in 1964 which was the same year that the Blue Devils made the Final Four losing to UCLA in the championship game. The Wildcats ranked No. 1 beat No. 2 Duke in the 1966 semifinals, 83-79. I'll never forget that game for several reasons.

Naturally, it placed UK in the championship game to face Texas Western. But I had to watch the game from behind the Chevron Station that sat on the triangle where Bardstown Road, Taylorsville Road and Trevillian Way intersected. I was at a church dance.

The leader, a fellow we called "Uncle Donnie," asked me to attend so the other guys would too. I told him: "Your nuts! Kentucky plays in the Final Four that night." He continued to beg: "Paul! Don't you have a portable TV?" I said: "Yes."

He said: "That's it. You bring the TV and when the game begins you can go into a separate room and watch the game. When it's over, you can return to the dance." That sounded plausible so I agreed to attend. Doesn't hurt to dance with a pretty young lady either.

After a while, Uncle Donnie left for some reason. I told another adult that I had known since I was young, that I was going to take my TV and watch the UK game. He said he knew nothing about the arrangement and I wasn't allowed to use a separate room to watch the game. This dance was being held in the Uncle's office building which had a huge room that could be converted into a dance floor.

I was trying to be reasonable, holding on for dear life, hoping to remain calm in this ridiculous situation that never should have entered my young life. I responded with what I thought was the logical approach to solving the problem. I could remain out in the open in an adjacent area to the dance floor, so everyone could see me and if they so desired, watch the game as well.

He flatly said: "No." I calmly left the building. He called me a "punk" and I said something to this effect: "So it had come down to this." He was wrong and he knew it, because all he had to comeback with was I was a punk. I grabbed my portable TV and headed out the door. The Bambi Bar was across the street but that was no solution for a 15-year-old or anyone else I might add, plus I was at a church dance. I didn't live terribly far from the office, but I didn't want to miss any of the game.

I went to the Chevron Station and asked this guy if I could plug my TV into the outlet behind the gas station and watch the Kentucky-Duke game. He gave an enthusiastic "yes" answer and I was in business. He wasn't the manager but he said he would comeback there during intervals to watch the game with me. Hey! I thought I was behaving like a mature adult, because I asked for permission, I just didn't assume it would be okay.

The station worker was so exited that he could see the game in stretches, for he had no hope of watching the game at all before my arrival. Then, the manager pulled onto the lot. Immediately he came to where I was standing and asked what I was doing. I gave him a brief description of the evening's activities and he allowed me to stay, but his kindness died inside his office when he told my friend, the station worker, that he could no longer run back there to watch the game.

Periodically, the worker would look around the corner of the building and yell to me: "What's happening?" I would give the score and break NCAA broadcast rules by using my own description of the telecast. It was exciting watching the Cats beat the Blue Devils 83-79 under those circumstances.

Adolph Rupp finished his career in 1972 with an overall 7-1 record against Duke, and a 5-6 ledger versus North Carolina. The rivalry for the best rivalry started its second half with a big bang in 1978 when Joe Hall's Cats beat Bill Foster's Blue Devils 94-88 for UK's fifth national championship. Nobody stomped on anyone's chest, there was no last second miracle shot, but Jack Givens gave an MVP performance scoring 41 points, hitting 18 of 27 field-goals.

Duke and UNC No. 1	Kentucky and Louisville No. 1
55. Bill Guthridge and Fred Taylor of Ohio State are the only two coaches to lead their teams to two Final Fours in their first three seasons.	55. Denny Crum

55R. Denny Crum left John Wooden's side and became UofL's coach before the start of the 1971-72 season. He went to the Final Four his first year, losing to Wooden's Bruins in the semifinals. He was back in 1975, but would lose to UCLA again, which postponed the "Dream Game" between UK and UofL until March of 1983. Kentucky was also in this Final Four. The Cats had beaten Syracuse to advance to the title game, but lost to Wooden 92-85.

Crum's third Final Four was in 1980, he played UCLA again, but this time in the title game, he beat the Bruins coached by former Tar Heel Larry Brown 59-54. Denny Crum was the "Coach of the 80s." He went to three more Final Fours in 1982, '83 and 1986, beating Duke that year in the championship game 72-69.

After the 1986 NCAA title game the rivalry looked like this since the tournament began in 1939:

UK-UofL had seven national championships and 16 Final Fours to their credit. Duke-UNC had two national championships and 14 Final Fours to their credit. And both Kentucky and Louisville had beaten Duke for the ultimate bragging rights—the national championship.
Clearly, the first 48 years belonged to the state of Kentucky, but we don't hear much about this from today's commentators. We should. It matters.

Duke and UNC No. 1	Kentucky and Louisville No. 1
56. Bill Guthridge won more games in his first two seasons than any other coach: 58	56. Final Four Efficiency (FFE)

56L. I certainly don't want to discredit a team for making it to the Final Four, but the UCLA media guide highlights titles and the North Carolina media guide highlights Final Four appearances. In the Tar Heel media guide, one page reads: This is Carolina basketball. The three categories mentioned are (1) Academic Excellence, (2) NBA Success and (3) 18 Final Fours. The next page begins with national championships.

One thing I must mention here about the Tar Heels, they hang their Helms National Championship banner next to their five NCAA title banners, but the word Helms is nowhere to be found on that 1924 banner. The Tar Heels lead in this category (Final Four appearances) so this is understandable in a way. But the ultimate goal as I have stated previously is not just to make it to the Final Four, but to win the national championship.

To determine Final Four Efficiency, simply divide the number of Final Fours by the number of titles won. The following table shows the average number of Final Fours necessary for each rival team to produce a national championship:

UK	UofL	UNC	Duke
(15)	(10)	(18)	(15)
1.88	3.3	3.6	3.8

Calculating FFE on a percentage basis of titles won, compared to the number of Final Four appearances, the table shows the percentage rate of success for national championships:

UK	UofL	UNC	Duke
53.3%	30%	27.8%	26.7%

UK-UofL are the FFE Champions.

Duke and UNC No. 1	Kentucky and Louisville No. 1
57. Bill Guthridge has more wins in his first season than any other coach: 34	57. Post-Season Competition

57R. UK-UofL have played each other in the NCAA tournament, that's where the passion, the tension, the expectations, the exhilaration, and the misery index are at their zenith. Duke-UNC have not. They could not until 1975 when the NCAA made a change and allowed more than one team from a conference to participate in the tournament.

UK and UofL played in the 1951 East Region with Kentucky winning 79-68. They met again in the 1959 Mideast Regional, this time the Cards won 76-61. When UofL joined the Missouri Valley Conference in 1964, their invitation to the NCAA tournament would normally begin in the Midwest Regional, making a matchup with Kentucky possible only in the Final Four.

Both Kentucky and Louisville advanced to the same Final Four in 1975 and 2012. They didn't play each other in 1975, but UK took the 2012 semifinal matchup over the Cardinals 69-61, advancing to the title game beating Kansas for the Wildcat's eighth national championship.

They played the "Dream Game" in the 1983 Mideast Regional in Knoxville. Louisville won 80-68 in overtime advancing to the Final Four in Albuquerque, N.M. losing to Houston in the semifinals 94 to 81.

The following year, Kentucky beat Louisville 72 to 67 on its home floor in Lexington in a 1984 Mideast Regional game. Then UK beat Illinois for the regional crown, advancing to the Final Four in Seattle where they lost in the semifinals to Georgetown 53-40.

Duke and North Carolina were in the same Final Four in 1991 but did not play each other.

They have had ample opportunities to play each other in the NCAA tournament, but have failed to do so.

Definite advantage, UK-UofL.

Duke and UNC No. 1	Kentucky and Louisville No. 1
58. UNC has been ranked in the top-ten of the AP Poll for the most weeks in ACC history: 621	58. Rick Pitino

58R. Rick Pitino taking the Louisville job makes this rivalry distinctly unique, the importance of winning this game only greater and the animosity between fans more like a cage match.

Vince Taylor, a former assistant at UofL to Rick Pitino and Denny Crum played his high school basketball at Tates Creek in Lexington, and his college hoops at Duke told me: "This would never happen at Duke or North Carolina. It would not even be advisable for me to serve as a Carolina assistant coach having played for the Blue Devils." Checking the history of the rivalry on Tobacco Road there were some defectors in the early days of their feud.

Frank McGuire who won North Carolina's first national championship in 1957, later became the coach at South Carolina in 1964. Now, the Gamecocks are not the rival that the Blue Devils are, but they can be found on the UNC hate list.

Vic Bubas, who took Duke to its first three Final Fours, played for a fine coach, Everett Case, at hated North Carolina State. But playing N.C. State is still not the same as North Carolina and Duke playing each other. Mike Krzyzewski fumigated any N.C. State influence on Duke with his four national championships and 11 Final Fours.

Big Time Advantage-UK-UofL.

Duke and UNC No. 1	Kentucky and Louisville No. 1
59. UNC became the first-ever unanimous preseason No. 1 in the 2008-09 AP Poll.	59. John Calipari and Frank McGuire are the only two coaches in history to coach three different teams to a No. 1 ranking. (Calipari-UK, Memphis and UMASS) (McGuire-South Carolina, North Carolina and St. John's).
60. UNC was ranked No. 1 in the 2007-08 season joining UNLV as the only school to be ranked as the preseason favorite in back-to-back years.	60. John Calipari and Rick Pitino; enough said. These two have put UK-UofL back on top in the rivalry battle.

60R. Pitino has been at it for 13 seasons at Louisville while Calipari is in his fifth year at UK. The intensity of both has lowered the boiling point in the rivalry. Both fan bases accuse the other coach of double-speak, while hanging their mental stability on every word uttered by their own roundball gladiators.

Duke and UNC No. 1	Kentucky and Louisville No. 1
61. Carolina has been ranked the preseason favorite more times than any other school: 7	61. Vince Taylor, former Duke player and current assistant coach at Texas Tech told me he believes UK-UofL is the hottest rivalry right now. It took a little time for him to say that, because he is a Duke man and proud of it.
62. Duke has three No. 1 overall NBA Draft picks. John Calipari is the only coach with three (Memphis 1 UK 2)	62. UK-UofL play fewer games. In the rivalry competition; less is more. One reason Duke and Carolina claim their rivalry is the best- they play more often

62L. The Tar Heels and the Blue Devils play at least twice a year during the regular season and may face-off a third time in the ACC tournament. Whichever team loses the first game, only has to wait a few weeks for the opportunity to annex revenge.

The Cards and Cats play one regular season contest. Bragging rights are reserved for a year, unless you meet again in the NCAA.

Win both of those games like Kentucky did in 1983-84 and 2012, and that's one definition of heaven you won't hear about in church. On the other hand, I wouldn't bet against it.

But that's not all folks. The team that lost twice in this rivalry during a single-season, is oozing from every pore with motivation to make amends the following year.

Louisville did it in the 2012-13 campaign, beating UK during the regular season and winning its own national championship.

Now, which team will win the rivalry and national championship rubber match in 2013-14?

Advantage: UK-UofL

Duke and UNC No. 1	Kentucky and Louisville No. 1
63. Duke has six NABC (National Association of Basketball Coaches) Defensive Players of the Year, named nine times, more than any other school	63. Rick Pitino

63R. At UK, Rick Pitino accomplished the best, and quickest rebuilding job in the history of college basketball. Without his eight-year stay in Lexington, the UK-UofL rivalry would have slipped behind Duke-UNC.

Duke and UNC No. 1	Kentucky and Louisville No. 1
64. Duke has more Associated Press College Players of the Year than any other school. Seven players honored nine times.	64. Rick Pitino is one of only three coaches (Frank McGuire and Roy Williams) to lead two different schools to the national championship game.
65. North Carolina has more Associated Press 2nd Team All-Americans than any other school. 20 players named 22 times.	65. Rick Pitino is the only coach to win a national championship at two different schools. (Kentucky and Louisville)
66. UNC has 11 First-Team players named 14 times, 20 Second-Team players named 22 times and 9 Third-Team players named 10 times for a total of 40 players named 46 times, the most of any school when combining all three AP All-American teams from 1947-48 through 2012-13.	66. Rick Pitino is the only coach to take three different schools to the Final Four.
67. 457-Duke's J.J. Redick is the career leader in three-point field goals made: 457 (1,126 attempts)	67. UK holds the single-season record for recruiting the most McDonald All-Americans: 6

Duke and UNC No. 1	Kentucky and Louisville No. 1
68. UNC's Tyler Hansbrough is career leader for free throws made during a four-year period: 982 (1,241 attempts)	68. UK is the only school in history to have both the No. 1 and No. 2 picks in the same NBA Draft. (2012) Anthony Davis and Michael Kidd-Gilchrist.
69. 91.2%-Duke's J.J. Redick is the career free throw percentage leader, minimum made-600.	69. UK holds the record for most players selected in the first-round of the NBA Draft: 5 (2010)
70. Duke's Bobby Hurley is the career assists leader: 1,076 (140 games from 1990-1993).	70. UK holds the record for the most number of players selected in the first two-rounds of the NBA Draft: 6 (2012). Four chosen in the first-round and two in the second-round.
71. UNC's Billy Cunningham is the career leader for most consecutive games making a double-double: 40	71. The NCAA record book has Duke with the most victories in a four-year period, 133. That beats UK's mark of 132 which was accomplished twice, from 1992-1995 and 1996-1999

71R. Duke provided a loophole in its media guide by mentioning a Krzyzewski-led Duke team setting that record.

Therefore, I will combine John Calipari's last season at Memphis, 2008-09 (these games were not vacated by the NCAA) and his first three years at UK:

2008-2009 Memphis	33-4
2009-10 UK	35-3
2010-11 UK	29-9
2011-12 UK	38-2
Total Wins	135

Duke and UNC No. 1	Kentucky and Louisville No. 1
72. 32-Duke holds the record for overcoming the greatest deficit to win a game. Duke (74) vs. Tulane (72), Dec. 30, 1950 (trailed 22-54 with 2:00 left in the first half).	72. UK is the leader for most victories over a three-year period: 104 (1996-1998). The Cats are also tied for second place with Montana State winning 102 games from 1947-49 and 2010-2012.
73. Duke holds the record for overcoming the greatest halftime deficit to win a game: 29. Duke (74) vs. Tulane (72), Dec. 30, 1950 (trailed 27-56 at halftime).	73. UK holds the record for most consecutive games won on its home court: 129. The streak began on 1/4/1943 with a win over Ft. Knox 64-30, and was ended by a loss to Georgia Tech 59 to 58 on 1/8/1955.
74. Duke is tied with Kentucky for overcoming the greatest second half deficit to win a game: 31. Duke (74) vs. Tulane (72), Dec. 30, 1950 (trailed 27-58 with 19:00 left in the second half); Kentucky (99) vs. LSU (95), Feb. 15, 1994(trailed 37-68 with 15:34 left in the second half).	74. John Calipari holds the single-season record for most wins by a coach: 38
75. 94.1%-UNC holds the record for best field-goal percentage in a half, North Carolina vs. Virginia, Jan. 7, 1978 (16 of 17).	75. Calipari has had 17 players drafted by the NBA in his first-four years at UK, the most by any coach in a four-year span.
76. Duke holds the record for fewest points allowed in a half since 1938, Duke (7) vs. North Carolina (0), Feb. 24, 1979 (first).	76. Calipari has had three No. 1 overall NBA Draft picks in his career, the most by any coach: 3
77. Blue Devils and the Tar Heels hold the record for fewest points scored by both teams in a half since 1938, Duke (7) vs. North Carolina (0), Feb. 24, 1979 (first).	77. Adolph Rupp was voted the Coach of the Century in 1967 by the Columbus Touch-down Club.
78. 20:48 .Duke holds the record for the longest time holding the opponent scoreless, Duke vs. North Carolina, Feb. 24, 1979. (UNC scored its first points of the game at 19:12 of the second half)	78. Adolph Rupp retired as the winningest coach in Division-1 history: 876

Duke and UNC No. 1	Kentucky and Louisville No. 1
79. Duke holds the record for most free throws made in a season, 1990: 888 (1,165 attempts).	79. LSU head coach Dale Brown honored coaches John Wooden and Adolph Rupp back in the 70s at a banquet as the two greatest basketball coaches of all-time. The film of this event was available in 1991 at the Naismith Memorial Basketball Hall of Fame.
80. UNC holds the record with Indiana for most number of wins in a perfect season, 1957: 32	80. When former Oklahoma State Coach Hank Iba died in 1993, Bobby Knight said: "Hank Iba had cast the greatest shadow across college basketball."

80R. Former UNC Coach Frank McGuire gave a rebuttal to Knight's statement saying he was incorrect. It was Adolph Rupp who cast the biggest shadow across college basketball.

Duke and UNC No. 1	Kentucky and Louisville No. 1
81. North Carolina leads all-time in number of 25-win seasons: 34	81. In October of 1991, Lee Williams, then, executive director of the Basketball Hall of Fame said to me: "Without Adolph Rupp, there would be no Basketball Hall of Fame. He was the driving force behind it. He went out and raised the money so it could be built."

81R. Just one of the many examples of how the Baron cast his shadow across the college basketball world.

Duke and UNC No. 1	Kentucky and Louisville No. 1
82. 95.3%-Duke's J.J. Redick is the sophomore season all-time free throw percentage leader.	82. UofL sat the record for most steals in a NCAA tournament game in 2013 against North Carolina A&T: 20
83. UNC's Kendall Marshall is the sophomore season all-time assist average leader: 9.75.	83. UofL is the No. 1 school for producing basketball revenue.

Duke and UNC No. 1	Kentucky and Louisville No. 1
84. Duke's Bobby Hurley is the all-time assists leader for a single-season, 1990, 38 games: 288	84. The Metro Louisville area has been the No. 1 viewing site for college basketball over the last ten years, even when its own teams don't make the finals. This is another example of how Cards' and Cats' fans make a huge difference
85. 513 players have scored at least 2,000 points over their careers, Duke leads all-time with 12.	85. There are no professional teams in Kentucky, giving the Bluegrass state a better opportunity to make college basketball a real rivalry. I would like to count this in the total, but I don't know if it's a real advantage since the last time I checked, I'm not sure the Charlotte Bobcats can be considered a professional team.
	86. It's the only game in the state.
86. 64.8%-UNC's Brad Daugherty was the 1986 annual individual field-goal percentage champion.	

86R. No disrespect to Western, Eastern, Murray State, Morehead State or Northern Kentucky, but UK vs. UofL is really the only game in the state. I asked a fellow who used to live in North Carolina, but has now been in Lexington for around 12 years which rivalry he thought was the best?

He voted for UK-UofL. His reasoning: "They are the only game here, but in Carolina, N.C. State and Wake Forest are always chipping in, 'don't forget about us."

On Tobacco Road there is some opposition to the Tar Heels and Blue Devils being the only show in town. In the Bluegrass, UK-UofL is the show.

Duke and UNC No. 1	Kentucky and Louisville No. 1
87. 69.7%-UNC's Brendan Haywood was the 2000 annual individual field-goal percentage champion	87. The other side claims their games are more exciting, but I believe the "Dream Game" in 1983 and the Final Four battle in 2012 top any game they have played. Remember, the other side has never played each other on the NCAA tournament stage.

Duke and UNC No. 1	Kentucky and Louisville No. 1
88. UNC's Kendall Marshall was the 2012 annual individual assist-to-turnover ratio champion: 3.48	88. The other side claims their better because of the number of close games they have played.

88R. In number they are better; they play more often, but percentage-wise, that's another story. The Cards and Cats have also provided some great close encounters, and some are of the three-point kind. Cedric Jenkin's last second tap gave UK a 76-75 victory in game #14. Samaki Walker's triple-double and DeJuan Wheat's big shots put UofL over the top 88-86 in game #26.

Patrick Sparks was fouled as time was about to expire. He made all three free throws and the Cats escaped 60-58 on the Cards' home floor in game #36. Edgar Sosa drilled a three-pointer as time expired, giving Louisville a thrilling 74-71 victory in game #40.

When there was a question about a stat or team record etc., the great New York Yankees manager Casey Stengel gave this sound advice: "Look it up!"

Taking Casey's advice, I checked the games played by UK and UofL since their regular season competition resumed on November 26, 1983, and examined the games Duke and North Carolina played during that same time period.

Before I examined the games, I chose a one to five-point victory margin as the standard for close games, and over 25 points for a blowout. In the time frame from November 26, 1983 until the beginning of the 2013-14 season; UK-UofL played 32 games and Duke-UNC 71.

The Cards and the Cats played nine close games for a 28.1 percentage of all 32 games played.

The Tar Heels and Blue Devils played 21 close games, for a 29.6 percentage of all 71 games played.

The Cards and Cats produced two blowout games (34 and 30) for a 6.3 percentage of all games played and Duke-UNC four blowouts, (32, 29, 26 and 25) for a 5.6 percentage of all games played. The totals are virtually the same percentage-wise. Casey didn't strike out in this situation.

Duke and UNC No. 1	Kentucky and Louisville No. 1
89. 3.19-UNC's Dexter Strickland was the 2013 annual individual assist-to-turnover ratio champion	89. The North Carolina media guide states that Dean Smith and Bobby Knight are the only two persons to have played on a national championship team and coached a national championship team.
	Now, UK's Joe B. Hall didn't play in the title game, but he was a member of the '49 squad (you can see his picture in the media guide) and coached UK to the 1978 NCAA championship. But Coach Hall did something the other two did not, playing and coaching at the same school.

Duke and UNC No. 1	Kentucky and Louisville No. 1
90. 24.6-Duke was the scoring margin leader for 1999. UK also had this number as the scoring margin leader in 1948.	90. The Tar Heel guide also states that Dean Smith, Bobby Knight and Pete Newell are the only coaches to have won the NCAA championship, a NIT title and a Gold Medal as the coach of the U.S. Olympic team.

90R. Again, Joe Hall won a NCAA championship, a NIT title, but did not coach the Olympic team. But Joe Hall did something the other three did not. He was also the top assistant coach in a Final Four in 1966.

Duke and UNC No. 1	Kentucky and Louisville No. 1
91. 21.5-Duke was the scoring margin leader for 1998.	91. Former Wildcat All-American Pat Riley is the only person to have won an NBA title as a player, assistant coach, five championships as a head coach of two different teams, two NBA rings as a team president and has a former assistant coach, Erik Spoelstra, who has won two NBA titles himself. If you can find another person with this resume, I'll use Riley's time as a Lakers' broadcaster for the tie-breaker.
92. UNC was the field-goal percentage leader in 1986: 55.9%	92. UK has the largest collegiate basketball radio-network.
93. Duke was the leader in three-point field goals made in 2001: 407	93. Gary Gupton's Red and Blue Review is very popular, sells out its advertising inventory at a brisk rate and is the only show of its kind featuring UK versus UofL exclusively.

93R. Gary says he hasn't heard of another show like it anywhere and Bellarmine University Coach Scott Davenport agrees.

Now another show in another state may have begun right before or since the printing of this book. If it has-they're in second-place.

Duke and UNC No. 1	Kentucky and Louisville No. 1
94. 10.44-Duke was the leader in three-point field goals made per game in 2001.	94. 22,144-In 2010 UK fans sat the ESPN GameDay attendance record. GameDay hosts proclaim Cat fans the most passionate.
95. Duke was the leader in free throw percentage in 1978: 79.1%	95. 2010-11 UK media guide states that Kentucky is the most watched college team.
96. UNC was the rebound leader in 2012: 1,711	96. UK under Joe B. Hall popularized "Midnight Madness." The best fans deserve the best.
97. UNC was the rebound leader in 2008: 1,695	97. Among attendance leaders, fans traveling with their team and those buying officially-licensed merchandise, UofL is doing its part, making this duo No. 1 against Duke-UNC.
98. UNC was the assist leader in 1986: 800	98. Adolph Rupp is the only coach to have played on two Helms Foundation National Championship teams, won two Helms Foundation National Championships as a coach, four NCAA National Championships, one NIT title and was an assistant coach of a Gold Medal U.S. Olympic team champion.
99. UNC was the assist leader in 1989: 788	99. Largest losing margin by a No. 1 ranked team, Kentucky (81) vs. St. John's (40) 12-17-51: 41
100. UNC was the assist leader in 1987: 782	100. UK is the only school that finished in the Top 20 in wins in every decade since 1930.
101. UNC was the assist leader in 2005: 706	101. UK has the highest overall ranking in wins in all decades since 1930.
102. UNC was the assist leader in 1991: 699	102. UK has the highest number of players drafted in NBA history. This total includes Enes Kantor, but UK is the winner even without him: 108

102R. Kantor was enrolled at Kentucky, but was ruled ineligible by the NCAA to play. Shawn Kemp is not included in this total since he was at Trinity Valley Community College in Texas when he was drafted.

North Carolina counts two players that had transferred to other schools and therefore should not be included in the Tar Heels' total.
Clifford Rozier transferred to Louisville and was drafted the 16th pick overall by the Golden State Warriors in the 1994 draft. Fritz Nagy transferred to Akron and was drafted in the BAA Draft in 1947.

I use the NBA Draft Index/Basketball Reference.com for my information. Here are the numbers for the schools researched:

(1) UK-107. Adding Kantor makes 108.
(2) UCLA-106
(3) UNC-104.
(4) Duke-81
(5) UofL-65

Duke and UNC No. 1	Kentucky and Louisville No. 1
103. UNC was the assist leader in 1998: 699	103. Lou Tsioropoulos who played on UK's 1951 national championship team made this remark about his playing time with the Boston Celtics: "There were those in the organization who commented that the University of Kentucky players came into the NBA better prepared fundamentally to play basketball than the players from any other school."
104. Duke was the assist leader in 2001: 701	104. 15/17-UK has the most number of players selected as AP First Team All-Americans.

104R. These 15 players were selected a total of 17 times. UCLA has 12 players selected a total of 18 times, edging the Cats in number of times so honored. The balloting for All-American honors by the Associated Press began during the 1947-48 college basketball season.

Duke and UNC No. 1	Kentucky and Louisville No. 1
105. 23.5 per/game-UNC was the assists per game leader in 1986.	105. Coaches To Fastest Milestone Wins Adolph Rupp (400, 500, 600, 700, and 800.).

Duke and UNC No. 1	Kentucky and Louisville No. 1
106. 21.7 per/game-UNC was the assists per game leader in 1987.	106. First to Milestone Wins. 800-Adolph Rupp 2-8-69 vs. Ole Miss 104-68.
107. 21.3 per/game-UNC was the assists per game leader in 1989.	107. In the top ten best career starts by percentage category, Adolph Rupp is the percentage leader for 23 seasons, more than any other coach
	Final Four Records:
108. Duke was the blocked shots leader in 1999: 245	108. UK is tied with Duke for overcoming the largest second half deficit to win a game: 31

108R. Kentucky (99) vs. LSU (95), Feb. 15 1994 (trailed 37-68 with 15:34 left in the second half); Duke (74) vs. Tulane (72) Dec. 30, 1950 (trailed 27-58 with 19:00 left in the second half) UK did it with less time left, should the Cats be No. 1 in this category? I'll answer my own question—yes!

Duke and UNC No. 1	Kentucky and Louisville No. 1
109. Duke was the steals leader in 2001: 411	109. 9-fewest field goals Oklahoma State vs. Kentucky 3-26-1949 championship game.
110. UNC was the rebounding margin leader for 2008: 11.0	110. Most assists by Louisville vs. LSU semi-finals 3-29-1986: 26
111. Duke was the turnover margin leader in 1998: 7.44	111. Most blocks Kentucky vs. Kansas 4-2-2012 championship game: 11
112. UNC led in fewest personal fours per game in 1995: 14.00	112. 111-Most points in a half by two teams, Louisville (57) vs. North Carolina (54) third-place game 3-5-1972. (second half)
113. UNC led in fewest personal fouls per game in 1998: 14.03	113. Most free throws made by two teams, North Carolina (33) vs. Louisville (27), third-place game 3-25-1972: 60

Duke and UNC No. 1	Kentucky and Louisville No. 1
114. UNC was the won-lost percentage champion for 1957. (32-0)	114. Most blocked shots by two teams, Kentucky (11) vs. Kansas (5) championship game 4-2-2012: 16
115. UNC was the won-lost percentage champion for 1982: 94.1%	115. Most personal fouls by two teams, Kentucky (31) vs. Syracuse (30), semifinals 3-29-1975: 61
116. UNC was the won-lost percentage champion for 1993: 89.5%	**Championship Game Individual Records** 116. 100%/5-5 three-point field goal percentage, minimum five attempts, Luke Hancock Louisville vs. Michigan 4-8-2013.
117. UNC was the won-lost champion for 2009: 89.5%	**Championship Game Team Records** 117. Three-point field goals made, Kentucky vs. Syracuse 4-1-1996: 12
118. Duke was the won-lost percentage champion for 1986: 92.5%	118. Largest halftime deficit overcome, Kentucky vs. Utah, Half; 31-41 3-30-1998: 10
119. Duke was the won-lost percentage champion for 1992: 94.4%	119. Most field goals by two teams, UCLA (38) vs. Kentucky (33), 3-31-1975: 71
120. Duke was the won-lost percentage champion for 1999: 94.9%	120. Most points by two teams, Kentucky (94), vs. Duke (88), 3-27-1988: 182
121. 91.8 Avg.-Duke led the nation in scoring offense for 1999.	121. Most players disqualified by fouls, Kentucky (4), vs. Arizona (1), 3-31-1997 (ot): 5
122. 88.0 Avg.-Duke led the nation in scoring offense for 2000	**Semifinal Game Records - Individuals** 122. 90.9%, 10-11 best field-goal percentage, minimum 10 attempts, Billy Thompson Louisville vs. LSU, 3-29-1986, tied with Jerry Lucas, Ohio State vs. St. Joseph's, 3-24-1961.
123. 88.0 Avg.-UNC led the nation in scoring offense for 2005	**Team Records** 123. Most steals Kentucky vs. Minnesota 3-29-1997: 14

Duke and UNC No. 1	Kentucky and Louisville No. 1
124. 51.1% Duke was the field-goal percentage champion for 1963.	Final Four Two-Game Records 124. 84.2%, 16-19-best field-goal percentage, minimum 15 attempts, Billy Thompson, Louisville, 1986.
125. 53.6%-Duke was the field-goal percentage champion for 1992.	125. Most blocks, Anthony Davis, Kentucky, tied with Jeff Whitney, Kansas: 11
126. 51.7%-UNC was the field-goal percentage champion for 1966.	126. Most blocks, Kentucky, 2012: 18
127. 52.8%-UNC was the field-goal percentage champion for 1972.	Final Four Two-Game Records 127. 100% 15-15, best field-goal percentage, minimum 15 attempts, Clifford Rozier, Louisville vs. Eastern Kentucky , 12-11-1993.
128. 52.7%-UNC was the field-goal percentage champion for 1973.	Team Records 128. Most rebounds in a single-game, Kentucky vs. Mississippi 2-8-1964: 108
129. 51.8%-UNC was the field-goal percentage champion for 1998.	129. Fewest points allowed, Kentucky (75) vs. Arkansas State, (6) tied with Temple (6) vs. Tennessee (11), Dec. 15, 1974.
130. 78.5%-Duke was the free throw percentage for 1973.	130. Fewest field-goals since 1938, Kentucky versus Arkansas State 1-8-45, tied with Duke vs. North Carolina State: 2
131. 79.1%-Duke was the free throw percentage champion for 1978.	Season Records 131. Most rebounds, Kentucky, 1951. (34 games): 2,109
132. UNC was the rebound margin leader for 2012: 10.5	132. Most blocks, Kentucky, 2012. (40 games): 344
133. UNC is one of seven teams that set the record of most consecutive weeks with a different No. 1 Jan. 3 to Feb. 14, 1994.	133. Most consecutive overtime wins all-time: 11. Louisville 2-10-1968 to 3-29-1975. Tied with Massachusetts (John Calipari coach) and Virginia.

Duke and UNC No. 1	Kentucky and Louisville No. 1
134. UNC is one of seven teams that sat the record for most teams ranked No. 1 in a season. 1983.	134. Number of unbeaten teams since 1938: 12. Kentucky tied with 11 others.

Final Four Records

All-Time Individual Leaders

135. 100% (12-12), Jim Spanarkel holds the record for free throw percentage, minimum 10 made, Duke vs. Notre Dame 3-25-1978 in the national semifinals.

135. 100%, 15-15, field-goal percentage leaders, minimum 12 field-goals made. Clifford Rozier vs. Eastern Kentucky 12-11-1993.

136. 100% (12-12), Christian Laettner, Duke vs. Kansas, 4-1-1991, championship game free throws.

Top Season Performances by a Freshman

136. Most blocks in a season by a freshman, Anthony Davis, Kentucky, 2012: 186 (40 games).

137. UNC's Ty Lawson holds the record for most steals in a championship game: 8. North Carolina vs. Michigan State, 4-6-2009.

137. The UNC media guides states that only one coach reached 700 wins with a winning percentage better than Roy Williams-Adolph Rupp with 82.2 percent compared to Williams' 79.5 percent.

138. Duke holds the record for largest deficit overcome to win: 22. Duke vs. Maryland, 17-39 with 6:37 left in the first half, final 94-84, national semifinals, 3-31-2011

138. The University of Kentucky Cheerleading squad has won the Universal Cheerleaders Association National College Cheerleading Championship an unprecedented 19 times

139. 14-North Carolina, and Kansas are tied for having the largest lead before the other team scored, North Carolina vs. Houston with 14:57 left in the first half, Final: 68-63, national semifinals, 3-27-1982; Kansas vs. Duke with 13:14 left in the first half, Final: 66-59, national semifinals, 4-2-1998.

139. The UK cheerleading squad has won the National Championships 16 times and four times has placed second.

140. Michael Jordan is a member of the All-Time Final FOUR Team along with Wilt Chamberlain, Lew Alcindor, Earvin "Magic" Johnson and Larry Bird. All selections made prior to the 1988 tournament.

140. UofL's large co-ed cheerleading squad has won 15 National Cheerleading Association championships.

140R. The all-girl's squad has won nine National Cheerleading Association championships and the small co-ed cheerleading squad has won seven National Cheerleading Association championships.

Duke and UNC No. 1	Kentucky and Louisville No. 1
141. Mike Krzyzewski reached 900 wins faster than any other coach. (1,183 games).	141. 78,129-is the single-game attendance record, Kentucky (79) vs. Michigan State (74), 12-13-2003 at Ford Field Detroit (regular-season game).
142. Roy Williams leads all coaches in top 10 best career starts by wins: 17 (from season nine through 25).	142. 885,953-full-season total attendance record, all games, home, road, neutral, tournaments, Kentucky, 2012. (40 games).
143. North Carolina vs. Loyola Marymount, second-round, NCAA, 3-19-1988, UNC is the assist leader: 36	143. 74,326-record crowd for a Final Four and national championship game, Louisville (82) vs. Michigan (76) 4-8-2013.
144. Iowa (10), Duke (8) NCAA second-round, 3-21-1992, most blocks by two teams.	144. Dick Vital said on the Terry Meiners Show in December of 2013: "I would work the UK-UofL game for nothing". He was lamenting the fact that his network is not covering the game.
145. 100% (10-10), Christian Laettner, Duke vs. Kentucky, NCAA Regional Final, 3-28-1992 (ot) is tied with Marvin Barnes of Providence for best field-goal percentage, minimum ten field-goals made.	145. In the 2009 ESPN Encyclopedia Kentucky was ranked the No. 1 program of all-time.
146. 100% (5-5) Hubert Davis is tied with Jamaal Mashburn and William Scott of Kansas State for best three-point field-goal percentage in a NCAA Regional Final, minimum five, three-point field-goals made	146. Kentucky holds the record for consecutive non-losing seasons: 60 (includes 500 Record), 1928-1952, 54-88# (two 500 seasons) Kentucky did not play basketball during the 1953 season.
147. UNC is the leader for most consecutive appearances in the Sweet 16: 13	147. UK was the scoring margin leader for 1954: 27.2

Duke and UNC No. 1	Kentucky and Louisville No. 1
148. 100% (6-6) UNC's Ranzino Smith is the leader for three-point field-goal percentage in four games in 1987, minimum 1.5 three-point field-goals per game, 2.0 per game since 2002. (NCAA tournament games)	148. UK was the scoring margin leader for 1952: 26.9
149. Duke's Christian Laettner, 1989-92 (23 games) is the tournament's all-time points leader: 407 (Two year minimum for averages and percentages.	149. UK was the scoring margin leader for 1948: 24.6. Duke had the same number as scoring margin leader for 1999
150. Duke's Christian Laettner, 1989-92 (23 games) is the tournament's all time free throws made leader: 142	150. UK was the scoring margin leader for 1949: 24.3
151. Duke's Bobby Hurley, 1990-93 (20 games) is the tournament's all-time leader in assists: 145	151. UK was the scoring margin leader for 1951: 22.2
152. Duke's Grant Hill, 1991-1994 (20 games) is the tournament's all-time leader in steals: 39	152. UK was the scoring margin leader for 1996: 22.1
153. Duke's Christian Laettner, 1989-1992 is the tournament leader in number of games played: 23	153. 55.6%-UK was the field-goal percentage leader for 1983
154. Most points scored in one overtime period, Texas A&M vs. North Carolina, 2nd round NCAA tournament 3-9-1980: 25	154. Louisville was the leader in three-point field goals made in 2005: 361. Arkansas had the same number in 1995.
155. UNC holds the record for most overtime periods in one tournament: 6. 1957 (two games).	155. UK was the leader in three-point field goals made in 1993: 340
156. 60.4% (113-187), North Carolina holds the record for best field-goal percentage, 1975 (three games) (Three-game minimum for averages and percentages).	156. UK was the leader in three-point field goals made per game in 1990: 10.04

Duke and UNC No. 1	Kentucky and Louisville No. 1
157. Duke has beaten the most No. 1 seeds in the NCAA tournament: 8	157. UK was the season rebound leader in 1952: 1,817
158. North Carolina is the only team to beat the first four teams in a AP Preseason Poll (2013-14).	158. UK was the assist leader in 1996: 783
159. The Nov. 2009 ESPN the Magazine, polled 100 Division-1 men's basketball players. North Carolina was the overwhelming favorite as the "Best Program in the Country," winning 62 percent of the vote.	159. UK was the assist leader in 1997: 776
160. Frank McGuire is one of three coaches to have won at least 100 games at three different Division 1 school. (St. John's, North Carolina and South Carolina).	160. 21.8 per/game-UK was the assist per game leader in 1996.
161. Roy Williams is one of 10 coaches with 200 or more wins at two different Division 1 schools.	161. UK was the blocked shots season leader in 2010: 273
162. 75%-(99-33) Duke has the best winning percentage in NCAA tournament games.	162. UK was the blocked shots per game leader for 2012: 8.60
163. Rick Pitino said that Mike Krzyzewski is the modern John Wooden.	163. UK was the steals leader in 1997: 480
164. Most points scored in a Final Four half by two teams, North Carolina vs. Louisville, third place game, 3-25-1972: 111	164. UK was the steals leader in 1996: 435
165. North Carolina has the edge over the other three teams in head-to-head games. UNC 23-13 over UK, 9-3 over UofL and 133-105 over Duke (Totals through the 2013-14 regular season).	165. UofL was the steals leader in 2013: 430
166. North Carolina has the edge over UK and UofL in NCAA tournament games played. UNC-2-1 vs. UK and 3-1 vs. UofL.	166. UK was the turnover margin leader in 1997: 7.95

Duke and UNC No. 1	Kentucky and Louisville No. 1
167. Most points scored by two teams in a Final Four game in one half, Uof L (57) vs. North Carolina, (54) third-place game, 3-25-1972. (Second half): 111	167. UK was the won-lost percentage champion for 1949: 94.1
168. Most points scored by two teams in a championship game, Kentucky (94) vs. Duke, (88), 3-27-1978: 182	168. UK was the won-lost percentage champion for 1954: 100%
169. Most free throws made by two teams in a Final Four game, North Carolina (33) vs. Louisville (27), third-place, 3-25-1972: 60	169. UK was the won-lost percentage champion for 1978: 93.8%
170. Dean Smith, Bob Knight and Pete Newell are the only three coaches to have won an NCAA Championship, a NIT title and a Gold Medal as the coach of the U.S. Olympic Team.	170. UK was the won-lost percentage leader for 2003: 88.9%
171. Roy Williams and Rick Pitino are the only two coaches to have taken two different schools to at least three Final Fours each.	171. UK was the won-lost percentage leader for 2010: 92.1%
	172. UK was the won-lost percentage champion for 2012.: 95.0%
	173. Avg.-UK led the nation in scoring offense for 1952: 82.3
	174. UK was the scoring margin champion for 1957: 14.8
	175. UK was the scoring margin champion for 1995: 18.4
	176. UK was the scoring margin champion for 1997.: 20.3
	177. UK was the scoring margin champion for 2012.: 16.8

Kentucky and Louisville No. 1

178. UK and UCLA are the only teams to win the scoring margin championship three consecutive seasons.

179. UK is the all-time leader for scoring margin seasonal champions from 1947-48 through 2012-13: 10

180. UK was the field-goal percentage defense champion for 2012: 36.1%

181. UK was the turnover margin leader for 1996: 6.81

182. 6/7 of the four schools, UK has the greatest number of Most Outstanding Players in the Final Four. Six different players named seven times.

183. Austin Carr (52), Dan Issel (44) most points scored by two opposing players in a regional semifinal, 3-12-1970: 96

184. 100% (11-11), Kenny Walker, Kentucky vs. Western Kentucky, 2nd round, 3-16-1986 is the leader for field-goal percentage, minimum 10 field-goals made.

185. 100% (18-18), Kentucky vs. Utah, 2nd round, 3-23-2003, UK is the leader for free throw percentage, minimum 15 free throws made.

Kentucky and Louisville No. 1

186. 100% (5-5) Jamaal Mashburn is tied with UNC's Hubert Davis and Kansas State's William Scott for best three-point field-goal percentage in a NCAA Regional Final, minimum five three-point field-goals made.

187. UK is the leader in most blocked shots in a NCAA Regional Final, Kentucky vs. UCLA, 3-20-1998.: 14

188. West Virginia (18) vs. Louisville (11), most three-point field-goals two teams in NCAA Regional Final, 3-26-2005. (ot): 29

189. UK holds the single tournament record for most assists, 1996 (six games): 143

190. UK holds the single tournament record for blocked shots, 1998 (six games): 48

191. Rick Pitino is one of only four coaches (also Mike Krzyzewski, Dean Smith and Jim Boeheim) ever to guide a school to the Final Four in four separate decades: 4

192. Rick Pitino and Roy Williams are the only coaches to have led two different schools to at least three Final Fours each: 3

193. UK is tied with Duke for most No. 1 finishes in the Coaches' Poll: 8

Paul Willman

Kentucky and Louisville No. 1

194. John Calipari is one of 13 coaches with 100 or more wins at three different schools. (UMASS, Memphis and Kentucky)

195. Rick Pitino is one of 10 coaches with 200 or more wins at Two Division 1 schools.

196. Eddie Sutton is one of 10 coaches with 200 or more wins at two Division 1 schools.

197. Tubby Smith is one of three coaches to have won the NCAA championship their first year at a school. Kentucky, 1998.

198. Denny Crum is one of nine coaches who took their team to the Final Four their first season as coach.

199. Rick Pitino is one of eight coaches who have taken four different teams to the NCAA tournament. (Boston University, Providence, Kentucky and Louisville)

200. Tubby Smith is one of eight coaches who has taken four different teams to the NCAA tournament. (Tulsa, Georgia, Kentucky and Minnesota)

201. Eddie Sutton is one of eight coaches who has taken four different teams to the NCAA tournament. (Creighton, Arkansas, Kentucky and Oklahoma State)

Kentucky and Louisville No. 1

202. UofL's DeJuan Wheat is the only player in NCAA Division 1 history to have career totals of at least 2,000 points, (2,183) 450 assists, (498) 300 three-point goals, (323) and 200 steals. (204)

203. Russ Smith tied an NCAA record for most steals in a tournament game vs. North Carolina A&T in 2013: 8

204. The ranking for Louisville 10 weeks prior to reaching No. 1 in the final 2008-09 Associated Press poll, the largest jump to the top spot by any school in the 22-year history of the 25-team AP rankings.: 23

205. UofL's dance team, The Ladybirds have won 10 national championships: 10

206. Kentucky leads Duke head-to-head games 11-9.

207. UK has a 3-2 advantage over Duke in NCAA games.

208. UK beat Duke 94-88 in 1978 for the NCAA title.

209. Louisville has a 2-0 lead over Duke in NCAA games played.

210. UofL beat Duke 72-69 in 1986 for the NCAA title.

211. The bottom line, the game means more to the people of Kentucky. They truly live it 24/7.

212. UofL overcame the state's No. 1 opinion maker. On the editoral page of the Courier-Journal's May 23, 1952 edition it reads: The Future of the UofL Does Not Lie in Sports.

212R. The Arts and Sciences faculty of the University of Louisville has laid before the board of trustees a statement of unanimous sentiment as to the university's athletic program. Bluntly put, it is that university funds now budgeted for intercollegiate athletics could be better spent on teachers.

There is much to justify the faculties position. Louisville is not an enthusiastic football city, and football is not only the most spectacular college sport; it is also the most costly. It would take years and many hundreds of thousands of dollars to establish UofL as a great football school. And it did, but overcoming the editorial board is another reason why UofL is known at the "Fighting Cardinals."

When I talked with Steve Kirschner, who is in charge of communications and media relations for UNC Men's basketball, about Rupp's strength of schedule, he broke-in and said: "You don't need to talk about that, Kentucky would be Kentucky wherever they played."

It is interesting however, that Duke is 5-6 against the SEC in tournament play. The Blue Devils are 2-3 vs. UK, so that makes them 3-3 against the rest of the league.

Duke has a 65% winning percentage versus the ACC, and its just a little better against the SEC, 67.4% (118-57). It goes to show as Coach Scott Davenport said: "It's just so hard to win a national championship."

I feel that I have tried to be fair to all four schools. In most cases, I did not use active coaching records unless they were the all-time best. Records like most shots attempted stayed in the file cabinet. Both sides of the T are very impressive.

But using the Ben Franklin "T" Close (my wife says the "T" stands for titles, she's not only beautiful, she's sharp too) UK vs. UofL is truly college basketball's No. 1 rivalry.

Chapter Eleven
Stats and Such

THE GAMES

UK LEADS 31-15

#46 in Lex.	12/28/2013	#18 UK 73 #6 UofL 66
#45 in Lou.	12/29/2012	#4 U of L 80 UK 77
#44 Final Four	3/31/2012	#1 UK 69 #17 UofL 61
#43 in Lex. #3	12/31/2011	UK 69 #4 UofL 62
#42 in Lou.	12/31/2010	#11 UK 78 #22 UofL 63
#41 in Lex.	1/2/2010	#3 UK 71 UofL 62
#40 in Lou.	1/4/2009	#18 UofL 74 UK 71
#39 in Lex.	1/5/2008	UofL 89 UK 75
#38 in Lou.	12/16/2006	UK 61 UofL 49
#37 in Lex.	12/17/2005	#23 UK 73 #4 UofL 61
#36 in Lou.	12/18/2004	#9 UK 60 #13 UofL 58
#35 in Lex.	12/27/2003	#20 UofL 65 #2 UK 56
#34 in Lou.	12/28/2002	UofL 81 #14 UK 63
#33 in Lex.	12/29/2001	#6 UK 82 UofL 62
#32 in Lou.	1/2/2001	UK 64 UofL 62
#31 in Lex.	12/18/1999	UK 76 UofL 46
#30 in Lou.	12/26/1998	UofL 83 #3 UK 74
#29 in Lex.	12/27/1997	UofL 79 #4 UK 76
#28 in Lou.	12/31/1996	#3 UK 74 #16 UofL 54
#27 in Lex.	12/23/95	#4 UK 89 #25 UofL 66

#26 in Lou.	1/1/1995	UofL 88 #5 UK 86
#25 in Lex.	11/27/93	#2 UK 78 #7 UofL 70
#24 in Lou.	12/12/1992	#3 UK 88 #9 UofL 68
#23 in Lex.	12/28/1991	#17 UK 103 #21 UofL 89
#22 in Lou.	12/29/1990	#18 UK 93 UofL 85
#21 in Lex.	12/30/1989	#8 UofL 86 UK 79
#20 in Lou.	12/31/1988	#14 UofL 97 UK 75
#18 in Lou.	12/27/1986	#18 UK 85 UofL 51
#17 in Lex.	12/28/1985	#13 69 #15 UofL 64
#16 in Lou.	12/15/1984	#14 UofL 71 UK 64
#15 in Lex.	3/22/1984	# 3 UK 72 UofL 67 NCAA Mideast Regional Semifinals
#14 in Lex.	11/26/1984	#2 UK 65 #6 UofL 44
#13 in Knoxville	3/26/1983	#2 UofL 80 #12 UK 68 (ot) NCAA Mideast Regional Final
#12 in Evanston, IL.	3/13/1959	UofL 76 #2 UK 61 NCAA Mideast Regional Semifinals
#11 in Raleigh, NC.	3/20/1951	#1 UK 79 UofL 68 NCAA East Regional First Round
#10 in New York, NY.	3/27/1948	UK 91 UofL 57 Olympic Trials
#9 in Lex.	1/21/1922	UK 29 UofL 22
#8 in Lou	1/17 1922	UK 38 UofL 14
#7 in Lou.	2/22	UK 32 UofL 24
#6 in Lex.	2/12/1916	UofL 28 UK 22
#5 in Lou.	2/27/1915	UofL 26 UK 15
#4 in Lex.	1/23/1915	UK 18 UofL 14
#3 in Lou.	3/3/1914	UK 26 UofL 13
#2 in Lex.	2/7/1914	UK 22 UofL 17
#1 in Lex.	2/15/1913	UK 34 UofL 10

Here is a look at the rivalry by some of the numbers. Games 13-46.

MOST POINTS-SINGLE GAME

DERRICK MILLER UK	GAME 20	34
KENNY WALKER UK	GAME 16	32
TONY DELK UK	GAME 27	30
RUSS SMITH U of L	GAME 30	30
CLIFF ROZIER U of L	GAME 25	29
JODIE MEEKS UK	GAME 40	28
RAMEL BRADLEY UK	GAME 39	27
REECE GAINES U of L	GAME 32	27
JAMAAL MASHBURN UK	GAME 24	27
REX CHAPMAN UK	GAME 18	26
JOHN PELPHREY UK	GAME 23	26
LaBRADFORD SMITH U of L	GAME 22	26
LANCASTER GORDON U of L	GAME 15	25
BRANDON KNIGHT UK	GAME 42	25
JAMAAL MASHBURN UK	GAME 23	25
RAJON RONDO UK	GAME 37	25
PATRICK SPARKS UK	GAME 36	25

MOST REBOUNDS-SINGLE GAME

DEMARCUS COUSINS UK	GAME 41	18
DERON FELDHAUS UK	GAME 21	16
KENNY WALKER UK	GAME 16	15
ANTHONY DAVIS UK	GAME 44	14
JOSH HARRELLSON UK	GAME 42	14
ELLIS MYLES U of L	GAME 34	14
PATRICK PATTERSON UK	GAME 15	14

CLIFFORD ROZIER U of L	GAME 24	14
KENNY WALKER UK	GAME 17	14
MICHAEL KIDD-GILCHRIST UK	GAME 44	13
CLIFFORD ROZIER U of L	GAME 25	13
LaBRADFORD SMITH U of L	GAME 15	12
GORGUI DIENG U of L	GAME 44	12
BILLY THOMPSON U of L	GAME 16	12
ANTOINE WALKER UK	GAME 27	12

MOST FREE THROWS SINGLE-GAME

ANTHONY DAVIS UK	GAME 43	12/13
CAMERON MURRAY U of L	GAME 30	10/11
RAJON RONDO UK	GAME 37	10/15
JIM MASTER UK	GAME 14	9/9
JODIE MEEKS UK	GAME 40	9/9
MARK McSWAIN U of L	GAME 16	9/10
KIP STONE U of L	GAME 22	9/10
JOE CRAWFORD UK	GAME 39	9/12
LARRY O'BANNON U of L	GAME 35	8/8
SCOTT PADGETT UK	GAME 28	8/8
LaBRADFORD SMITH U of L	GAME 20	8/8
RAMEL BRADLEY UK	GAME 39	8/9
DORON LAMB UK	GAME 43	8/9
JERRY SMITH U of L	GAME 39	8/9
EDGAR SOSA U of L	GAME 40	8/9
DAVID PADGETT U of L	GAME 38	8/10
JOHN PELPHREY UK	GAME 23	8/10
LaBRADFORD SMITH U of L	GAME 21	8/11
MARVIN STONE U of L	GAME 34	8/12

MOST 3-POINTERS SINGLE-GAME

RUSS SMITH U of L	GAME 43	7/10
PRESTON KNOWLES U of L	GAME 42	6/10
JEFF BRASSOW UK	GAME 22	6/11
JAMAAL MASHBURN UK	GAME 24	5/7
REX CHAPMAN UK	GAME 18	5/8
REECE GAINES U of L	GAME 32	5/8
PATRICK SPARKS UK	GAME 36	5/8
TONY DELK UK	GAME 25	5/11

MOST BLOCKS SINGLE-GAME

SAMAKI WALKER U of L	GAME 26	11
ANTHONY DAVIS UK	GAME 43	6
GORGUI DIENG U of L	GAME 43	6
SAM BOWIE UK	GAME 16	5
ANTHONY DAVIS UK	GAME 44	5
TAYSHAUN PRINCE UK	GAME 31	5
JOSEPH N'SIMA U of L	GAME 33	5
GORGUI DIENG-U of L	GAME 44	4
PERVIS ELLISION U of L	GAME 17	4
CHUCK HAYES UK	GAME 35	4
MANGOK MATHIANG U of L	GAME 46	4
FELTON SPENCER U of L	GAME 21	4
BILLY THOMPSON U of L	GAME 16	4
SAMAKI WALKER U of L	GAME 27	4

Paul Willman

MOST ASSISTS SINGLE-GAME

CAMERON MURRAY U of L	GAME 30	10
LaBRADFORD SMITH U of L	GAME 20	8
TRAVIS FORD UK	GAME 24	7
RAJON RONDO UK	GAME 37	7
SEAN WOODS UK	GAME 21	7
TAQUAN DEAN U of L	GAME 37	6
CAMERON MURRAY U of L	GAME 29	6
TAYSHAUN PRINCE UK	GAME 32	6
LaBRADFORD SMITH U of L	GAME 19	6
BILLY THOMPSON U of L	GAME 16	6

MOST STEALS SINGLE-GAME

DICKY BEAL UK	GAME 15	6
TERRENCE WILLIAMS U of L	GAME 40	5
JEFF BRASSOW UK	GAME 22	4
ERIC BROWN U of L	GAME 32	4
ALLEN EDWARDS UK	GAME 29	4
PERVIS ELLISON U of L	GAME 19	4
ANTHONY EPPS UK	GAME 27	4
TRAVIS FORD UK	GAME 24	4
PRESTON KNOWLES U of L	GAME 42	4

MOST POINTS-TWO GAMES

REX CHAPMAN UK	GAMES 18, 19	47
JIM MASTER UK	GAMES 13, 14	37
CLIFFORD ROZIER U of L	GAMES 24, 25	37
ANTHONY DAVIS UK	GAMES 43, 44	36

REGGIE HANSON UK	GAMES 20, 21	35
MELVIN TURPIN UK	GAMES 13, 14	34
MICHAEL KIDD-GILCHRIST UK	GAMES 43, 44	33
LANCASTER GORDON U of L	GAMES 13, 14	32
GREG MINOR U of L	GAMES 23, 24	32
JAMAAL MASHBURN UK	GAMES 22, 23	31
PATRICK SPARKS UK	GAMES 36, 37	31
EVERICK SULLIVAN U of L	GAMES 20, 21	31
SAMAKI WALKER U of L	GAMES 26, 27	31

MOST POINTS-THREE GAMES

JAMAAL MASHBURN UK	GAMES-22, 23, 24	58
LANCASTER GORDON U of L	GAMES-13,14,15	57
JODIE MEEKS UK	GAMES-38,39,40	53
REGGIE HANSON UK	GAMES-20,21,22	52
JIM MASTER UK	GAMES-13,14,15	52
MELVIN TURPIN UK	GAMES-13,14,15	48
LaBRADFORD SMITH U of L	GAMES-19,20,21	46
DeJUAN WHEAT U of L	GAMES-25,26,27	46
KEITH BOGANS UK	GAMES-31,32,33	45
GREG MINOR U of L	GAMES-23,24,25	45
PATRICK PATTERSON UK	GAMES-39,40,41	45
HERBERT CROOK U of L	GAMES-17,18,19	44
TONY DELK UK	GAMES-24,25,26	44
DERRICK MILLER UK	GAMES-18,19,20	44
JOHN PELPHREY UK	GAMES-21,22,23	44
MILT WAGNER U of L	GAMES-13,14,15	44

MOST POINTS-FOUR GAMES

TONY DELK UK	GAMES-24,25,26,27	74
LaBRADFORD SMITH U of L	GAMES-19,20,21,22	72
MILT WAGNER U of L	GAMES-13,14,15,17	63
RUSS SMITH U of L	GAMES-42,43,44,45	60
KEITH BOGANS UK	GAMES-31,32,33,34	59
PERVIS ELLISON U of L	GAMES-17,18,19,20	57
DERRICK MILLER UK	GAMES-18,19,20,21	57
TAYSHAUN PRINCE UK	GAMES-30,31,32,33	56
KENNY WALKER UK	GAMES-13,14,15,16	55
DeJUAN WHEAT U of L	GAMES-25,26,27,28	54
JUAN PALACIOS U of L	GAMES-36,37,38,39	53
EVERICK SULLIVAN U of L	GAMES-20,21,22,23	52
RAMEL BRADLEY UK	GAMES-36,37,38,39	50
DERRICK MILLER UK	GAMES-18,19,20	44
JOHN PELPHREY UK	GAMES-21,22,23	44
MILT WAGNER U of L	GAMES-13,14,15	44

STATS FOR SIX PLAYERS WHO HAVE PLAYED IN FIVE RIVALRY GAMES
(Extra players added in Addendum I at the back of book)

RUSS SMITH LOUISVILLE

	FG/A	3/A	FT/A	R	PF	A	S	B	TO	PTS
GAME #42	0/1	0/0	0/0	0	1	0	0	0	0	0
GAME #43	10/20	3/8	7/10	5	3	0	3	0	3	30
GAME #44	4/15	0/1	1/2	3	2	1	2	0	3	9
GAME #45	9/20	0/1	3/6	7	4	3	3	0	3	21
GAME #46	7/20	0/5	5/10	2	4	4	1	0	4	19
TOTALS	30/76	3/15	16/28	17	14	8	9	0	13	79

KENNY WALKER KENTUCKY

	FG/A	FT/A	R	PF	A	S	B	TO	PTS
GAME #13	1/3	0/0	1	1	0	0	0	1	2
GAME #14	6/9	1/4	3	0	0	3	0	0	13
GAME #15	2/7	4/4	6	3	3	2	1	0	8
GAME #16	14/25	4/5	15	2	2	1	0	1	3
GAME #17	5/13	1/5	14	3	0	0	0	0	11
TOTALS	28/57	10/18	39	9	5	6	1	2	66

WINSTON BENNETT   KENTUCKY

	FG/A	FT/A	R	PF	A	S	B	TO	PTS
GAME #14	0/6	2/4	7	4	1	1	1	3	2
GAME #15	4/9	2/4	5	3	0	0	0	1	10
GAME #16	6/14	2/4	9	5	0	0	0	4	14
GAME #17	8/13	7/8	7	3	2	3	1	1	23
GAME#19	6/11	2/4	6	5	2	0	0	2	15
TOTALS	28/57	10/18	39	9	5	6	1	2	66

PEYTON SIVA LOUISVILLE

	FG/A	3/A	FT/A	R	PF	A	S	B	TO	PTS
GAME #41	0/1	0/1	0	0	1	0	1	0	1	0
GAME #42	2/9	0/3	2/3	2	4	4	2	0	3	6
GAME #43	2/13	0/4	4/6	2	4	4	1	1	3	8
GAME #44	4/11	1/2	2/2	3	2	3	0	0	3	11
GAME #45	6/11	2/4	5/5	2	5	1	1	0	3	19
TOTALS	14/45	3/14	13/16	9	16	12	5	1	13	44

BILLY THOMPSON LOUISVILLE

	FG/A	FT/A	R	PF	A	S	B	TO	PTS
GAME #13	2/4	0/1	2	1	1	0	0	1	4
GAME #14	2/6	0/0	6	4	2	1	1	5	4
GAME #15	6/14	2/4	9	5	0	0	0	4	14
GAME #16	7/13	3/7	12	1	6	1	4	3	17
GAME #17	3/6	2/2	8	4	3	0	2	4	8
TOTALS	16/37	5/13	33	14	13	2	7	17	37

JEFF HALL LOUISVILLE

	FG/A	FT/A	R	PF	A	S	B	TO	PTS
GAME #13	0/0	0/0	0	1	0	1	0	0	0
GAME #14	3/9	0/0	1	2	1	1	1	2	6
GAME #15	1/4	0/0	0	3	0	1	0	0	2
GAME #16	3/8	4/4	2	2	1	1	0	5	10
GAME #17	3/5	0/0	3	3	3	0	0	2	6
TOTALS	10/26	4/4	6	11	5	4	0	9	24

MOST FIELD-GOALS MADE
(minimum 20 made, 35 attempted)

FGA/FGM	PLAYER	#GAMES	%
28/49	MILT WAGNER UOFL	4	57.2
26/52	TONY DELK-UK	4	50.0
25/51	LANCASTER GORDON-UOFL	3	49
23/48	KEITH BOGANS-UK	4	47.9
23/46	TAYSHAUN PRINCE-UK	4	50
22/51	PERVIS ELLISON-UOFL	4	43.1
22/49	DERRICK MILLER-UK	4	44.9
22/46	LaBRADFORD SMITH-UOFL	4	47.8

FGA/FGM	PLAYER	#GAMES	%
20/36	JIM MASTER-UK	3	55.6

MOST free throwS MADE
(minimum 13 made, 15 attempted)

FT/FTA	PLAYER	#GAMES	%
16/16	LARRY O'BANNON-UOFL	4	100
25/28	LaBRADFORD SMITH-UOFL	4	89.3
17/18	JODIE MEEKS-UKL	3	94.4
16/18	EDGAR SOSA-UOFL	4	88.9
16/19	ANTHONY DAVIS-UK	2	84.2
16/28	RUSS SMITH-UOFL	5	57.1
15/18	RAMEL BRADLEY-UK	4	83.3
15/17	CAMERON MURRAY-UOFL	2	88.2
15/25	DAVID PADGETT-UOFL	3	60.0
13/18	JOE CRAWFORD	4	72.2
13/15	ED DAVENDER-UK	4	86.7
13/15	PERVIS ELLISON-UOFL	4	86.7
13/16	PEYTON SIVA-U of L	5	81.3

MOST 3-POINT FIELD-GOALS
(minimum seven made)

NO.	PLAYER	#GAMES	TOTAL	AVG SHOTS PER GAME	%
12	TONY DELK-UK	4	12/28	3	42.9
9	DERRICK MILLER-UK	4	9/28	2.24	32.1
8	KEITH BOGANS-UK	4	8/23	2	34.8
8	TAQUAN DEAN-UOFL	4	8/30	2	26.7
8	REECE GAINES-UOFL	4	8/19	2	42.1

NO.	PLAYER	#GAMES	TOTAL	AVG SHOTS PER GAME	%
8	DeJUAN WHEAT-UOFL	4	8/22	2	36.4
8	JODIE MEEKS-UK	3	8/21	2.7	38.1
7	REX CHAPMAN-UK	2	7/17	3.5	46.7
7	JERRY SMITH-UOFL	4	7/15	1.8	46.7
7	EVERICK SULLIVAN-UOFL	4	7/23	1.8	30.4

MOST REBOUNDS
(minimum 25)

NO.	PLAYER	#GAMES	AVG
39	KENNY WALKER-UK	5	7.8
34	WINSTON BENNETT-UK	5	6.8
33	BILLY THOMPSON-UOFL		6.6
32	ELLIS MYLES-UOFL	4	8.0
31	PERVIS ELLISON-UOFL	4	7.8
28	GORGUI DIENG-UOFL	4	7.0
27	CORNELIUS HOLDEN-UOFL	4	6.8
27	CLIFFORD ROZIER-UOFL	2	13.5
26	TERRENCE JONES-UK	3	8.7
25	RICHARD MADISON-UK	4	6.3

MOST ASSISTS
(minimum 12)

NO.	PLAYER	#GAMES	AVG
21	LaBRADFORD SMITH-UOFL	4	5.3
16	CAMERON MURRAY-UOFL	2	8.0
16	MILT WAGNER-UOFL	4	4.0
16	SEAN WOODS-UK	4	4.0

NO.	PLAYER	#GAMES	AVG
14	KEITH WILLIAMS-UOFL	4	3.5
13	DICKY BEAL-UK	3	4.3
13	CLIFF HAWKINS-UK	4	3.3
12	TRAVIS FORD-UK	3	4.0
12	TAYSHAUN PRINCE-UK	4	3.0
12	PEYTON SIVA-UOFL	5	2.4

MOST STEALS
(minimum six)

NO.	PLAYER	#GAMES	AVG
9	SCOTT PADGETT-UK	3	3.0
9	PRESTON KNOWLES-UOFL	4	2.3
9	RUSS SMITH-UOFL	5	1.8
7	TERRENCE WILLIAMS-UOFL	3	2.3
6	ALLEN EDWARDS-UK	4	1.5
6	TERRENCE JONES-UK	3	2.0
6	JODIE MEEKS-UK	3	2.0
6	SAUL SMITH-UK	3	2.0

MOST BLOCKED SHOTS
(minimum six)

NO.	PLAYER	#GAMES	AVG
15	SAMAKI WALKER-UOFL	2	7.5
12	GORGUI DIENG-UOFL	4	3.0
12	PERVIS ELLISON-UOFL	4	3.0
11	ANTHONY DAVIS-UK	2	5.5
8	SAM BOWIE-UK	2	4.0
8	JOSEPH N'SIMA-UOFL	2	4.0

NO.	PLAYER	#GAMES	AVG
7	FRANCISCO GARCIA-UOFL	3	2.3
7	TAYSHAUN PRINCE-UK	4	1.8
7	CLIFFORD ROZIER-UOFL	2	3.5
6	TERRENCE JENNINGS-UOFL	3	2.0

TOTAL TEAM NUMBERS FOR GAMES 14-46

	UK	Uofl
FG/FGA	878/1970 44.6%	808/1907 42.4%
3FG/3FGA	191/552 34.6%	153/489 31.3%
FT/FTA	517/740 69.9%	509/721 70.6%
TOT. POINTS	2464	2278
AVG	74.7	69.0
REBOUNDS	1241	1158
AVG	37.6	35.1
ASSISTS	463	413
AVG	14.0	12.5
STEALS	246	214
AVG	7.5	6.5
BLOCKS	137	163
AVG	4.2	4.9
PERSONAL FOULS	666	668
AVG	20.2	20.3
TURNOVERS	485	511
AVG	14.7	15.5

FIRST REGULAR SEASON GAME SERIES 1913-1922: UK 7   U of L 2

UK's Karl Zerfoss is the winningest player in the total history of the series with a record of 5-2.

Leading scorers for Kentucky:

PLAYER	POINTS	GAMES
DERRILL HART	30	2
RALPH MORGAN	29	4
R.C. PRESTON	25	2
PAUL ADKINS	24	2
JIM SERVER	22	4

Leading scorers for Louisville:

PLAYER	POINTS	GAMES
HARDING McCALEB	33	4
CLARENCE RODGERS	32	4

RUPP vs. Hickman

Adolph Rupp and Bernard "Peck" Hickman met three times in post-season play. (1) The Olympic Trials in New York City, (2) NCAA East Region in Raleigh, N.C. and (3) NCAA Mideast Regional Semifinals in Evanston, I.L.

UK won two of the three contests. U of L's win in 1959 solidified its position in the national spotlight.

THE RIVALRY RECORD ALL SPORTS
(Compiled before the 2014 season)

MEN'S SPORTS

BASKETBALL	UK-31	UofL-15
FOOTBALL	UK-14	UofL-12

The Cards lead the series 12-8 since it resumed in September of 1994. The Cats were 6-0 in the early years and Louisville never scored in those first six games. The Wildcats outscored the Cardinals 230-0.

Since Tom Jurich arrived, the Cards lead the series 10-6.

BASEBALL	UK-59	UofL-35	1 TIE

Since Tom Jurich arrived in October of 1997, The Cats lead 16-11.

SOCCER	UK-13	UofL-11	4 TIES

The Cats lead the series 7-5-1 since Tom Jurich's arrival.

SWIMMING & DIVING	UK-14	UofL-5

The UK men won 14 consecutive matches but the Cards have won five straight starting in 2009.

TENNIS	UK-26	UofL-0

WOMEN'S SPORTS

BASKETBALL	UK-32	UofL-17

The series is 9-9 since Tom's Jurich's arrival.

VOLLEYBALL	UK-27	UofL-24
FAST PITCH SOFTBALL	UK-18	UofL-14

This series began March 29, 2000.

SOCCER	UK-11	UofL-5	1 TIE
TENNIS	UK-15	UofL-0	
SWIMMING & DIVING	UK-16	UofL-4	

Like the UK men, the women's team won the first 16 matches but the Louisville women are on a four-game winning streak.

The sports information tells me that track and field, cross-country and golf don't break down into individual matchups.

UK currently doesn't have a women's field hockey team, but the two did play eight matches from 1976 through 1980 with the Lady Cards going undefeated.

I think Mitch Barnhart and Tom Jurich are another reason why the rivalry is so good. They have improved recruiting, academics, facilities and made the atmosphere much stronger to help the rivalry continue its excellence in so many areas of competition.

Congratulations to UK's Gimel Martinez, the only player in rivalry history to go 4-0.

The late Marvin Stone, the only player to have played for both teams in the rivalry, finished 3-0. Winning two at UK and one at U of L.

There are several players who were 2-0 and 1-0.

Chapter Twelve
Looking Ahead and Final Thoughts

GAME 46

December 28, 2013

	UK	UofL
Record	9-3	11-1
Ranking	#18	#6
Series	30	15
Favored	PICK	
Location	RUPP ARENA	
TV	CBS	

THE PRE-GAME REPORT

Earlier in the book I mentioned that this would be the most anticipated game in the history of the rivalry. UK was No. 1 and U of L was No. 3 in the Associated Press Preseason Poll, which quickly ignited a hotly contested debate about the poll's positioning.

Calipari was 4-1 vs. Pitino while at UK, and the two coaches were 9-9 in overall competition when you include Pitino's time at both UK and UofL and Calipari's tenure at UK, UMASS and Memphis. And the last two NCAAs belonged to Calipari in 2012 and Pitino won it all in 2013. This game would give one man the advantage in games won in head-to-head match-ups, with the possibility of a rematch in this year's national championship which is just around the corner?

The Cats didn't stay No. 1 very long, losing to Michigan State three games into the season, 78-74. Then after dropping close games to Baylor 67 to 62 and North Carolina 82-77, UK had to work its way back into the top 20. This young Wildcat team is very much a work in progress, but disregarding all their mistakes, and a little better free throw shooting, they could have been undefeated and No. 1 going into the Louisville game. There I go again with the 'IF' game.

The Cardinals on the other hand, are the defending national champions, losing only two players from that championship team, but oh-those two players. Gorgui Dieng, the 6-11 big man inside, and Peyton Siva, their point-guard, whose improvement throughout his four-year career, culminated with that national title.

Chris Jones, the junior college transfer, is an outstanding scorer, but like Russ Smith is not really a point-guard. That's one of the challenges to be overcome, if the Cardinals want to make their third consecutive Final Four and win back-to-back championships.

Injuries have slowed Luke Hancock and Kevin Ware's progress (later, Ware will decide to take a medical redshirt year). Another big question for the Cardinals is the availability of Chane Behanan, who was very much a key factor in winning their national championship. He had been suspended from the team on October 17, 2013 and we were told that his return was predicated on his following instructions to get his life turned around. He struggled early, violating his new guidelines in the first week, but was reinstated after the season opener against Charleston (For further rules violations, Behanan was dismissed from school 12-30-13).

UofL will rely heavily on sophomore Montrezl Harrell on the frontline and they need freshman big man Mangok Mathiang to fill Gorgui Dieng's shoes as quickly as possible.

QUOTES

"This is a team game. It's not a collection, it's a team game. We're only now beginning, to be that kind of team. We'll see where we are against a top opponent. We'll see, and we'll figure out from there, where we gotta go."
UK COACH JOHN CALIPARI

"It means a lot to me. As a kid growing up in Kentucky, you want to be able to play for Kentucky, play against Louisville and hopefully beat them. That's a rivalry team that usually Kentucky fans don't like at all."
UK GUARD DOMINIQUE HAWKINS

"It's an overpowering place (Rupp Arena), but I think our guys have responded well there in the past, and I expect them to do that again."
UofL COACH RICK PITINO

"He can block (a shot) two players away. He's a dangerous weapon. He keeps the ball alive. A lot of shot blockers throw the ball out of bounds…He keeps it alive and it leads to fast breaks."
UofL COACH RICK PITINO talking about Willie Cauley-Stein.

PROBABLE STARTERS
Kentucky

POS.	PLAYER	HT.	WT.	CLS.	PT.
F/G	JAMES YOUNG	6-6	215	FR.	13.4
F	CAULEY-STEIN	7-0	244	SO.	9.3
F	JULIUS RANDLE	6-9	250	FR.	18.2
G	AARON HARRISON	6-6	218	FR.	15.1
G	ANDREW HARRISON	6-6	215	FR.	10.6

Louisville

POS.	PLAYER	HT.	WT.	CLS.	PT.
F	WAYNE BLACKSHEAR	6-5	220	JR.	10.3
F	MONTREZL HARRELL	6-8	235	SO.	12.5
C	MANGOK MATHIANG	6-10	210	FR.	5.0
G	RUSS SMITH	6-0	175	SR.	16.8
G	CHRIS JONES	5-10	170	JR.	13.5

Harrison Twins Deliver When Cats Need Them the Most
Lexington Herald-Leader

With Randle Out, Others Step-up Against Cards
Louisville Courier-Journal

The first 2:22 it was all Louisville. UK missed five shots while Montrelz Harrell sandwiched a steal and a layup between two Chris Jones' three-point baskets. U of L took the advantage 8-0. The next 1:25 belonged to UK's Julius Randle. He scored five of his first half 17 points on a free throw, a dunk and a layup. Russ Smith made a layup for the Cards, then Alex Poythress, had a layup for UK, followed by Andrew Harrison's jumper, layup and free throw and Kentucky had its first lead at 12-10 with 14:23 left in the first half. This was the first of five lead changes in the half.

Mangok Mathiang added a layup for UofL about a minute later, registering the first of three ties in the half at 12-12. The second tie was 14 to 14 and Louisville's Chris Jones hit another three-pointer at the 9:49 mark for the third tie at 19-19. Chris Jones hit a jumper to move U of L ahead 21-19, then the Cats followed with a 7-0 run that put them on top 26-21. Cauley-Stein's layup with 4:06 left, gave the Wildcats their biggest lead of the half, nine-points at 34-25.

The Cardinals shot right back with five unanswered points on a jumper by Russ Smith, and a three-point basket by Terry Rozier making it 34-30. Finishing the half, James Young had a jumper and two free throws, while Julius Randle added a jumper and a free throw of his own giving the Cats 41 first half points.

Luke Hancock broke loose for a layup, Russ Smith added a layup and a highlight dunk, making the half time score UK 41; Uof L 36 - it's anybody's game.

U of L was guarding Julius Randle one-on-one much of the time, and he took advantage of it scoring 17 first half points. James Young and Andrew Harrison added valuable support to Randle's effort. Young had two three-pointers in his 12 first half points, and Andrew Harrison added seven to UK's 41 point total. Chris Jones was trying to keep up with the Randles in the first half, leading the Cards in scoring with 15 points. Russ Smith added 10 and Terry Rozier five.

The Cardinal's 36 points were guard dominated while the Wildcats had a more balanced scoring attack. Down in the paint, the Cats outscored the Cards 24-12 and were ahead in second chance scoring 12-0. But then again this series has often been dominated by the three-point shot.

Louisville was four for five from the foul line while Kentucky continued to struggle from that "so called charity stripe," connecting on just nine of 16 for a puny 56.3 percent.

Aaron Harrison struck first in the second half, his jumper moving UK ahead 43-36, but U of L went on a two-minute drill with Russ Smith scoring five of their seven unanswered points, tying the game at 43-43. The real bad news for the Cats however, was the fact that Julius Randle was plagued with muscle cramps, limiting his total playing time to 21 minutes and no points in the second half.

With 11:01 remaining in the game, a Chris Jones free throw gave Louisville the lead at 52-51 and the game hung by a delicate balance. Would the young Cats succumb to the more experienced Louisville team, or could they, without their scoring leader, make great strides and pull this one out at home in the precious final 11 minutes that remained?

In the next 3:18, Andrew Harrison and James Young began to provide some answers to those looming questions. Harrison had two layups and Young one, while UofL was limited to just one Russ Smith free throw, giving Kentucky a 57-53 lead. And the Cats would never trail again.

Aaron Harrison had two layups, his brother Andrew one and James Young a three-pointer leading a nine to three run and stretching UK's lead to ten, 66-56, with 5:21 left in the game. Within that run, Louisville had cut the lead to four, at 60-56, but Young's clutch three-point basket sealed the deal, for the now hustling and confident Wildcats.

The final score of 73-66, gives Calipari a 5-1 games lead against Pitino in the series, a 10-9 overall matchup lead over Pitino and his Cards. This was UK's first win over a ranked team for the season and bragging rights for another year. Even without Randle in the second half, UK still won the scoring battle in the paint 42-24 and outscored the Cardinals 17 to six on second chance points.

Both teams have the potential to produce a rematch in the tournament, but only time and the tournament pairings will tell.

STATS

Kentucky

	Min	FG	FG A	3PT FG	3 PT FGA	FT	FT A	Reb	PF	Ast	St	BS	TO	Pts
Willie Cauley-Stein	35	1	3	0	0	0	0	10	4	0	1	3	0	2
Julius Randle	21	7	8	0	1	3	6	3	1	0	0	0	2	17
James Young	36	5	17	3	8	5	9	10	2	4	1	1	2	18
Aaron Harrison	30	5	12	0	3	0	0	4	2	1	0	0	4	10
Andrew Harrison	34	6	16	0	1	6	12	4	3	2	1	0	3	18
Alex Poythress	21	3	4	0	0	1	2	5	3	0	0	0	0	7
Dominique Hawkins	15	0	1	0	1	1	1	3	4	0	0	0	0	1
Dakari Johnson	8	0	1	1	0	0	0	1	0	1	0	0	0	0
Team								4						
Totals	**200**	**27**	**62**	**3**	**14**	**16**	**30**	**44**	**19**	**8**	**3**	**4**	**11**	**73**

Louisville

Player	Min	FG	FG A	3PT FG	3 PT FGA	FT	FT A	Reb	PF	Ast	St	BS	TO	Pts
Mangok Mathiang	22	2	2	0	0	0	0	3	1	0	0	4	1	4
Wayne Blackshear	12	1	4	0	2	3	4	3	5	0	1	0	0	5
Montrezl Harrell	21	2	2	0	0	2	2	4	3	0	1	1	0	6
Russ Smith	30	7	20	0	5	5	10	2	4	4	1	0	4	19
Chris Jones	31	7	13	3	9	1	1	3	3	2	1	0	2	18
Terry Rozier	13	1	3	1	2	2	2	1	2	0	1	0	1	5
Luke Hancock	28	3	11	2	8	0	1	3	2	2	1	0	0	8
Tim Henderson	3	0	0	0	0	0	0	0	0	0	0	0	0	0
Chane Behanan	20	0	3	0	0	0	0	7	2	0	0	0	3	0
Akoy Agau	2	0	0	0	0	0	0	2	2	0	0	0	0	0
Stephan Van Treese	18	0	0	0	0	1	2	5	1	0	0	0	1	1
Team								3					1	
Totals	**200**	**23**	**58**	**6**	**26**	**14**	**22**	**36**	**25**	**8**	**6**	**5**	**13**	**66**

POINTS AFTER

"This team is becoming a good team. We haven't been all year. Now, we're starting. You know why? Because they knew if they didn't play together, they had no shot in this game."
UK COACH JOHN CALIPARI

"They had a lot of small guards, so I knew I could get a lot more rebounds. I saw a lot of loose balls, so I tried to go for every loose ball."
UK FORWARD JAMES YOUNG

"We had a shot in the second half, and missed free throws, made a big defensive mistake in giving up the three. But give them credit; they did a good job against our pressure."
UofL COACH RICK PITINO

"They out hustled us to every loose ball. And as far as what we were going to do, rebounding as a team, we didn't do that. We got annihilated on the backboard. We didn't come in ready to play, and we got beat for that."

UofL CENTER MONTREZL HARRELL

I have only played church ball. I got cut at Atherton High School in Louisville twice, but never came to a game expecting to lose. But guess what? Teams I played on are not undefeated. There are some nights when you just don't have your "A" game. It's just the way sports' performances are. There are even theories about what causes these lapses of performance.

Like Coach Rupp said in a 1958 speech, "I don't go into a ballgame, hoping we play a good game, I go into the ballgame to try and win. They still keep score don't they?" In another setting he talked about that old adage that it doesn't make any difference if you win or lose, it's how you play the game. In reviewing a loss at home to Purdue, 89-83 on December 19, 1970 he said, "Not one of the 11,500 fans in attendance came down and said, 'Well, Adolph you played a good game."

All athletes take their whippings at times. When I was younger, I remember getting beat in a game by an older bunch of guys from Johnson City, TN 53 to four. We were playing at a junior high school in Lexington. The score was there on the wall for all to see. However, I am proud to say that I did score 50 percent of our total points. Then when my fellow players and I were high school seniors, we had our day and beat a Lexington church team 127-17 in a 32 minute game with a running clock (We'd probably be excommunicated for that today).

The one excuse that any player, in any sport should never use is, "I didn't come ready to play." But being ready sometimes has a mind of its own. It may be the biggest game of the year for the fans with no justification for not being ready to play, save for physical injury, but the players emotions may not come ready and that is unpredictable and catches coaches scratching their collective heads. If he doesn't come ready to play, let someone else take his place who is ready to play. You owe that much to your teammates and the coaching staff. Maybe you'll get ready while sitting on the bench.

The one thing I am proud about my meager playing days is my nickname "Z." One day while we were playing in our beloved church gym on Eastern Parkway, all 5-9 of me was playing center. I was making hook shots, blocking shots and grabbing rebounds. My childhood friend Steve White said, "This man is playing like Zelmo Beatty!" Its been shortened to "Z" over the last 48 years, but I still deem it an honor, to have for some 30 minutes in my life, played a stretch, that caused someone to consider me, in the very least, to play like my namesake—Zelmo Beatty.

This has truly been a delightful research project. The subject matter is so compelling-Kentucky vs. Louisville and Duke vs. North Carolina are in my estimation truly the two best rivalries in all of college basketball. When we look at the facts of the case the evidence is overwhelming; 20 NCAA National Championships and 58 Final Fours for these four schools.

Chapter ten satisfies the major premise of this book, and that is UK vs. U of L is the No. 1 college basketball rivalry. In that process, I have also pointed out the merits of our "Tobacco Road" competitors, Duke and UNC.

I also wanted to persuade more people in the Commonwealth of Kentucky to pull for their arch nemesis, if they advance on to win the national championship. The polling data will never reflect 100 percent agreement, but I feel secure in my conversations with many fans that a solid 45 percent will pull for the other state school to be successful. There will always be those who will never pull for the other team (Cards/Cats). But if they win the national championship, I say give them the credit due such an achievement. It's better for both programs if one of them wins a National Championship. Twice we have had an NCAA winner who lost the season match-up with their in-state rival.

Going into this past game on December 28, 2013, U of L fans were harping on those few Cat fans, who said UK was going to go 40-0. Some were making money on this idea selling tee-shirts I do believe. But a wise man (Heber J. Grant) once said, "You must judge by the average and not the exception." Too many exceptions led to frustration in trying to savor the ups and downs of our rivalry teams.

After UK's win 73 to 66, I heard these kind of comments, "We never lose a game, we just don't win 'em all," and, "You can't win when it's seven against five." Was the other official for your team, they have been using three officials now for a long-time if you'll recall.

The opposition says things like this, because they want to divert the sting of losing. Bragging rights are established on the scoreboard, no matter what else is claimed or debated (although that can be a lot of fun), the Wildcat contingent have those rights for another year, unless they meet in the NCAA tournament and the outcome is different. And that is the way the rivalry grows.

Down the road, as long as the two schools have Mitch Barnhart and Tom Jurich in the administrative offices, and Calipari and Pitino pacing the sidelines, it will continue to be the hottest game in town.

One aspect the Wildcat fans have to deal with is how long will Coach Calipari stay? Pitino is in Louisville for sure, but Calipari, more than likely, will not make UK his last stop. One giant back-step with the one-and-dones, could be disastrous. I think it is appropriate that a trophy be created to award the school that has the most wins in all of the rivalry sports for the season. Basketball and football should be weighted a little heavier in the points.

Football with Mark Stoops trying to establish his program at UK, and Bobby Petrino returning to the sidelines for the Cards should be very interesting over the next fews years. As we've already pointed out, the other sports are doing very well when it comes to competition and attendance between these two rivals.

There is one challenge for the rivalry today. Many in media circles feel that objectivity has taken a major blow on some of the talk shows, in the articles written and whether or not one can wrangle an interview with certain personalities.

When I had a sports talk show, if a hair on my arm happened to be turned in a certain school's direction, fans would be uneasy. Today, there are some pretty powerful body punches thrown at the schools and their representatives, with no regards to accuracy or decency. It's a shame. Both schools have great programs.

In the final analysis I think it is wise to follow the counsel of Coach Schnellenberger. I told him that some of the writers and commentators were expressing their opinions that Teddy Bridgewater is the best quarterback to ever come out of the University of Louisville, including Johnny Unitas. Schnellenberger responded as only he can, "Who gives a damn! What did Unitas win at Louisville?" I replied, "Nothing. But some of his teammates say he is the best." Coach Schnellenberger replied, "So, What? They played with him, what else are they going to say? Now, let me tell you how we are going to judge this thing. Comeback in 15 years after that young man has played in the NFL, then we'll know the answer."

We'll know about the rivalry as time goes on. UK and U of L dominated from 1939-1986. Duke and UNC were fantastic from 86 up to the present time, but the Bluegrass fellows have been more consistent over the entire time—especially these last two championship seasons. UK and U of L are at the top of college basketball rivalries right now! We'll let time reveal further details down the road.

Speaking of the rivalry's future Coach Joe B. Hall sees it this way since his retirement from coaching in 1985, "I think the rivalry is good for both teams. It's sharpened up their demands from the fans, to maintain the program at a high level. Louisville has reached that pinnacle with two national championships, now three. The rivalry grows with every success that either team has. Calipari as added a championship, as did Rick and Tubby Smith, and that just makes the rivalry that much hotter. And the more success the individual teams have, the more attention it brings each year to that game. And that's good. It's good for national recruiting. It makes local in-state recruiting a real battle. That rivalry keeps everybody on their toes."

There have certainly been some hateful interchanges over the years in the UK-U of L rivalry, but the fact that players from both schools now or have coached at both schools, and of course, with Rick Pitino coaching at both schools (even though some still don't like it), shows that deep-down, this rivalry is not based on hate, but on a massive, highly competitive desire to beat the other team.

My Mount Rushmore of the greatest college basketball coaches looks like this, (1) John Wooden, (2) Adolph Rupp, (3) Mike Krzyzewski and (4)_____.

I am going to assign you readers some parting homework. If you see me or get to talk to me, who would you put in that fourth spot? I could go with Bobby Knight, Dean Smith, Jim Calhoun, Rick Pitino or Denny Crum. If Coach Pitino wins another championship, I would feel confident of placing him in that fourth position. You might not agree with my first three choices, but I feel those are solid choices. I'm giving the test question, so please fill in the number four spot.

My buddies Steve White, Rick Bolus and I went to the 1998 Final Four in San Antonio. Kentucky edged Standford in a tight battle, and I was worried about Monday night's game for the championship. That night I had a dream of Coach Rupp, There I told him of my concerns about the championship game and he said, "I'm worried about it too. I worry about all the games." He was about winning basketball games!

And Coach Rupp shared this philosophy at BYU after winning his fourth NCAA Championship in 1958 with the Fiddlin' Five:

…"I do believe that in competitive sports, you get something out of being in sports that you do not get if you fail to participate. You learn to give the best that's in you. You learn to pull out a little extra whenever you have to have it. If you can force your nerve, and heart, and sinew to serve their term long after they are gone, and so hold on when there is nothing in you, except the will which says to them hold on.

That's one lesson that I have learned in sports. I've learned that the boys that have got it, that'll stay in there, that'll stick to their task till it sticks to you---beginners are many, but finishers are few. Honor, power, place and praise, will come in the time to the one who stays. Stick to your task till it sticks to you, bend at it, sweat at it, smile at it too. For out of the bend and the sweat and the smile, will come life's victories after awhile.

And I am convinced that there's no finer philosophy in life than that. You've got to stick to these tasks and it's the boys that will stay in there, in these games when it just seems that they just can't hold on. When they think that it's hopeless, but there's just that will that tells them they must hold on—sometimes the victory will be there. . .

There isn't a greater satisfaction in life than taking a bunch of boys, especially when they are underdogs, the way we have been this year in almost every game and takin' them in there and seeing those kids walk of afterward successful.

Well, sometimes you can't win. You can't always win. I realize that. You're beaten! Well, well what's that? Come up with a smiling face! It's nothing against you to fall down flat—but to lie there—that's the disgrace. And so if you're beaten, you must bounce back and comeback. You're not always successful. You don't sell everybody that walks into your store or into your automobile place. You don't sell everybody---everything that they look at, but you don't give up. You stay in there. You're defeated in business at times, but you're going to get up there and go to work again."

Coach Rupp has given us a blueprint for success, but in the final analysis, he and Coach John Wooden were in total agreement on what constitutes success:

. . . "I think that everybody ought to do the best that they can. . . Now in sports they're certain things you have to do. There's no shortcut to success. There's no shortcut to make a touchdown. There's no shortcut to win a basketball game. There's no shortcut to run a mile or to win a 100-yard dash, or to throw the javelin or put the shot. There are no shortcuts in sports. It takes hard work to do that."

"There isn't any shortcut to success in this world. When you come in at night, if you can go to the mirror and look at that mirror and say: 'Today has been a good day, I have given this old world everything that I could give it. I couldn't do any better---this is the best that I can do.' If you can do that, then the world in return will give the best back to you."

If you watch sports, enjoy yourself, but use those principles you see displayed in the realm of competition to improve your own life. It's in the best interest of both programs to turn this rivalry into a much friendlier competition by pulling for each other when they are not playing each other.

These two programs are No. 1 with their fans and foes. Nobody likes winning more than these programs... And nobody likes beating these two teams more than their foes. It is widely recognized that a team can have a losing season but if they beat either of these two teams in the regular season, to them, and their fans, it is a winning season.

To all the thousands of great Cardinal and Wildcat fans, enjoy being a part of the rivalry, have fun, and no matter what happens in the great debate concerning who's best, there is always one-point where agreement can be found----UK vs. U of L is College Basketball's No. 1 rivalry. Enough said!

Go Cards!
Go Cats!

However, when they are playing each other:
GO CATS!!!!
GO CARDS!!!!

INDEX

(Names in this index were supplied by the author. Because of the multitude of people presented in this book, not every name will be accounted for in the index.)

The Royal Pedigree
of College Basketball Coaches

In the early days of basketball, there were many outstanding coaches and a few who are the foundation of the game. Forrest "Phog" Allen, who played for James Naismith, the game's inventor, was the driving force behind the organization of the National Association of Basketball Coaches (NABC) and is known today as the "father" of basketball coaching. He also won two Helms Foundations titles in his early days and the 1952 NCAA Championship.

Doc Meanwell, who coached Wisconsin and Missouri, won three Helms Foundation National Championships, and among his many contributions to the game, was removing the football-like laces from the basketball, making it one continuous seam.

Ward "Piggy" Lambert (He was known for hogging the ball during a game, they began to call him "Piggy") won a Helms Foundation title and coached John Wooden at Purdue. Hank Iba at Oklahoma A&M (Now known as Oklahoma State) was the first coach to win-back-to-back NCAA titles (1945-46).

Nat Holman was a member of the "Original Celtics" (No connection with the Boston Celtics) who was the only coach to win both the NCAA and the NIT in the same year, 1950 with CCNY. Joe Lapchick, a teammate of Nat Holman, coached St. John's to a record four NIT championships. Clair Bee of Long Island University is the all-time percentage winningest coach at 82.6 percent and is known for developing the one-three-one zone defense. Howard Cann was also a fixture in the East at NYU and Sam Barry out West at USC.

In order to truly appreciate the profound effects these great early coaches had on the game, we need only to search the coaching pedigrees of the four universities found in this book. Looking at the records, I will include NCAA Championships won, Final Four appearances, NBA Titles and NBA Finals.

This will resemble a search for one's family history pedigree on any number of websites designed for that purpose. I will start with Dr. James Naismith the inventor of the game, in what I will call his coaching downline (Those coming after him through his pedigree). To qualify as a member of our rivalry coaching tree, an individual must have played for, or coached with, the person indicated.

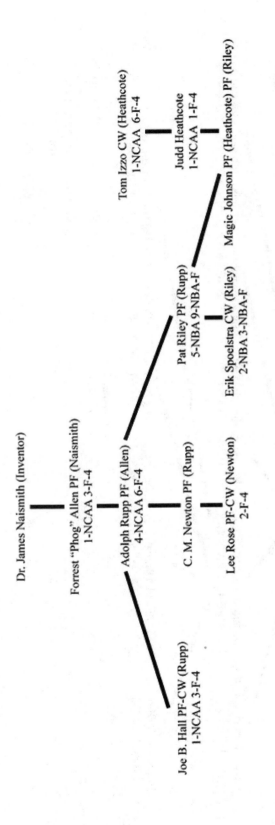

Dr. James Naismith (Inventor)

Forrest "Phog" Allen PF (Naismith)
1-NCAA 3-F-4

Adolph Rupp PF (Allen)
4-NCAA 6-F-4

C. M. Newton PF (Rupp)

Lee Rose PF-CW (Newton)
2-F-4

Joe B. Hall PF-CW (Rupp)
1-NCAA 3-F-4

Pat Riley PF (Rupp)
5-NBA 9-NBA-F

Erik Spoelstra CW (Riley)
2-NBA 3-NBA-F

Magic Johnson PF (Heathcote) PF (Riley)

Tom Izzo CW (Heathcote)
1-NCAA 6-F-4

Judd Heathcote
1-NCAA 1-F-4

NCAA=TITLE F-4= FINAL FOUR

NBA=NBA TITLE NBA-F=NBA
FINALS

PF=PLAYED FOR

CW=COACHED WITH

Coaches Pedigree Chart page 1

The Forrest "Phog" Allen coaching lines give us:
18 NCAA Championships
56 Final Fours
13 NBA Championships
24 NBA Finals

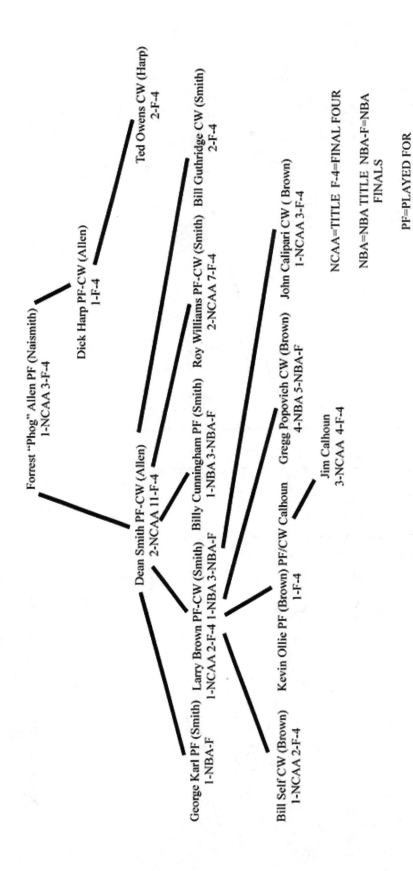

Ted Owens CW (Harp)
2-F-4

Bill Guthridge CW (Smith)
2-F-4

Dick Harp PF-CW (Allen)
1-F-4

Forrest "Phog" Allen PF (Naismith)
1-NCAA 3-F-4

Roy Williams PF-CW (Smith)
2-NCAA 7-F-4

John Calipari CW (Brown)
1-NCAA 3-F-4

Gregg Popovich CW (Brown)
4-NBA 5-NBA-F

Billy Cunningham PF (Smith)
1-NBA 3-NBA-F

Jim Calhoun
3-NCAA 4-F-4

Dean Smith PF-CW (Allen)
2-NCAA 11-F-4

Larry Brown PF-CW (Smith)
1-NCAA 2-F-4 1-NBA 3-NBA-F

Kevin Ollie PF (Brown) PF/CW Calhoun
1-F-4

George Karl PF (Smith)
1-NBA-F

Bill Self CW (Brown)
1-NCAA 2-F-4

NCAA=TITLE F-4=FINAL FOUR

NBA=NBA TITLE NBA-F=NBA
FINALS

PF=PLAYED FOR

CW=COACHED WITH

Coaches Pedigree Chart page 2

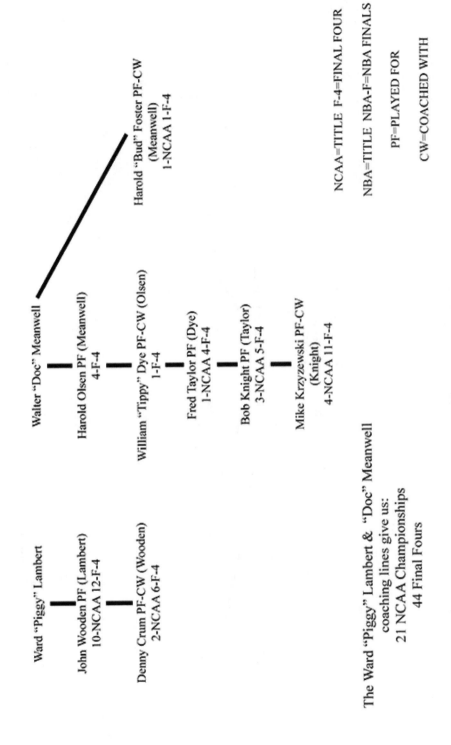

Ward "Piggy" Lambert

John Wooden PF (Lambert)
10-NCAA 12-F-4

Denny Crum PF-CW (Wooden)
2-NCAA 6-F-4

Walter "Doc" Meanwell

Harold Olsen PF (Meanwell)
4-F-4

William "Tippy" Dye PF-CW (Olsen)
1-F-4

Fred Taylor PF (Dye)
1-NCAA 4-F-4

Bob Knight PF (Taylor)
3-NCAA 5-F-4

Mike Krzyzewski PF-CW
(Knight)
4-NCAA 11-F-4

Harold "Bud" Foster PF-CW
(Meanwell)
1-NCAA 1-F-4

NCAA=TITLE F-4=FINAL FOUR

NBA=TITLE NBA-F=NBA FINALS

PF=PLAYED FOR

CW=COACHED WITH

The Ward "Piggy" Lambert & "Doc" Meanwell
coaching lines give us:
21 NCAA Championships
44 Final Fours

Coaches Pedigree Chart page 3

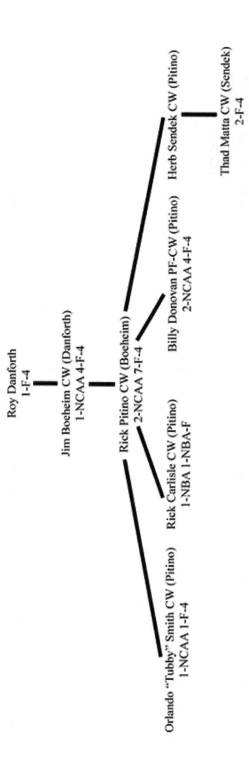

Roy Danforth
1-F-4

Jim Boeheim CW (Danforth)
1-NCAA 4-F-4

Rick Pitino CW (Boeheim)
2-NCAA 7-F-4

Orlando "Tubby" Smith CW (Pitino)
1-NCAA 1-F-4

Rick Carlisle CW (Pitino)
1-NBA 1-NBA-F

Billy Donovan PF-CW (Pitino)
2-NCAA 4-F-4

Herb Sendek CW (Pitino)

Thad Matta CW (Sendek)
2-F-4

The Roy Danforth coaching lines give us:
6 NCAA Championships
19 Final Fours
1 NBA Championship
1 NBA Final

NCAA=TITLE F-4= FINAL FOUR

NBA=TITLE NBA-F=NBA FINALS

PF=PLAYED FOR

CW=COACHED WITH

Coaches Pedigree Chart page 4

From Page 1 Coaches Pedigree Chart

Adolph Rupp

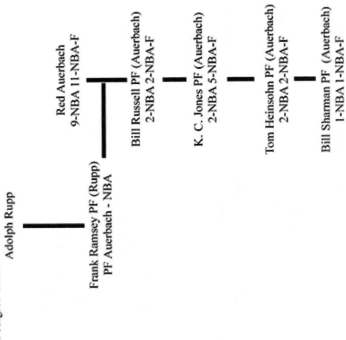

Frank Ramsey PF (Rupp)
PF Auerbach - NBA

Red Auerbach
9-NBA 11-NBA-F

Bill Russell PF (Auerbach)
2-NBA 2-NBA-F

K. C. Jones PF (Auerbach)
2-NBA 5-NBA-F

Tom Heinsohn PF (Auerbach)
2-NBA 2-NBA-F

Bill Sharman PF (Auerbach)
1-NBA 1-NBA-F

NCAA=TITLE F-4= FINAL FOUR

NBA=TITLE NBA-F=NBA FINALS

PF=PLAYED FOR

CW=COACHED WITH

The Red Auerbach downline lineage is
a product of the Adolph Rupp
Coaching Pedigree which give us the
following:
16 NBA Championships
21 NBA Finals

Coaches Pedigree Chart page 5

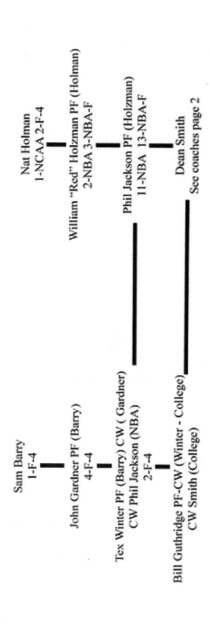

Sam Barry
1-F-4

John Gardner PF (Barry)
4-F-4

Tex Winter PF (Barry) CW (Gardner)
CW Phil Jackson (NBA)
2-F-4

Bill Guthridge PF-CW (Winter - College)
CW Smith (College)

Nat Holman
1-NCAA 2-F-4

William "Red" Holzman PF (Holman)
2-NBA 3-NBA-F

Phil Jackson PF (Holzman)
11-NBA 13-NBA-F

Dean Smith
See coaches page 2

The Sam Barry and Nat Holman downline
lineages are a product of the Dean Smith
Coaching Pedigree which gives us the
following:
13 NBA Championships
16 NBA-Finals
1 NCAA Championship
9 Final Fours

NCAA=TITLE F-4= FINAL FOUR

NBA=TITLE NBA-F=NBA FINALS

PF=PLAYED FOR

CW=COACHED WITH

Coaches Pedigree Chart page 6

The results shown by the coaching pedigree charts reveal additional evidence why UK-UofL and Duke-North Carolina are the No. 1 and No. 2 rivalries in all of college basketball--------their success is rooted in the richest "Blue Ribbon" coaching pedigrees of all-time.

The Forrest "Phog" Allen line is the group leader with 18-NCAA Championships, 56-Final Fours, 13-NBA titles and 24-NBA Finals. The grand total including the Lambert, Danforth and Meanwell pedigree lines is 45-NCAA Championships, 119-Final Fours, 14-NBA Championships and 25-NBA Finals.

The 45 NCAA titles represent 60 percent of the 75 championship games played, and the 14 NBA titles, equal 20.9 percent of the 67 professional championships. But the numbers continue to multiply when the four pedigrees are connected by mutual links, found in other coaching pedigree lines.

For example, Frank Ramsey played for Coach Adolph Rupp at UK, but he also played for the Boston Celtics under Coach Red Auerback. Now, by this mutual association, we can add Red Auerback's 9-NBA championships and 11-NBA Finals. However, we don't stop there. Bill Russell also played for Auerback and he won 2-NBA titles and went to 2-NBA Finals. Extend the relationship another step; Russell played for Coach Phil Woolpert in college at San Francisco making it possible to include Woolpert's 2-NCAA Championships and 3-Final Fours.

K.C. Jones, (2-NBA titles, 5-NBA Finals) Tom Heinsohn (2-NBA titles, 2-NBA Finals) and Bill Sharman (1-NBA title, 1-NBA Final) were teammates of Russell in Boston who also played for Red Auerback. Bob Cousy was another teammate of Russell's, who won an NCAA Championship in 1947 playing for "Doggie" Julian at Holy Cross. Coach Julian has 1-NCAA and 2-Final Fours.

Interlinking different coaching pedigrees is fun, easy and profitable, adding to our accomplishments' list. One more example. Sam Barry at USC coached Jack Gardner and Tex Winter. Gardner has 4-Final Fours to his credit and Tex Winter, who also coached with Gardner has two. But Winter, also coached with Phil Jackson who is the winningest championship coach in the NBA with 11-titles and 13-NBA Finals. Jackson played for Red Holzman who had 2-NBA Championships and 3-NBA Finals with the New York Knicks. Holzman played at The City College of New York (CCNY) for Nat Holman (who I interviewed in 1991). Holman won 1-NCAA Championship in 1950 and went to 2-Final Fours. He also won the NIT in 1950, making him the only coach to win both titles in the same year.

Our not-so missing link, is Bill Guthridge, who coached with Dean Smith at North Carolina but also played for and coached with Tex Winter at Kansas State. Guthridge makes the assist in adding these additional coaching lines to our already "Blue Ribbon" Pedigree. By the way, Jack Gardner was the head coach, and Tex Winter was one of his assistants when Kentucky beat Kansas State for the National Championship in 1951, 68-58. Frank Ramsey was a member of that UK championship team. This mutual linkage is made possible when an individual has either played for, coached with or done both with coaches from multiple pedigrees.

By combining lines, our four "Blue Ribbon" Coaching Pedigrees now have won 73 of the 75 NCAA Championships for an amazing 97.3 percent of those games played. And, by this method we can also count 67 of the 67 NBA Championships, for a perfect score of 100 percent.

Remarkable.

Remarkable is not finished for the 2013-14 season. Kevin Ollie played for Coach Larry Brown on the 2001-02 Philadelphia 76ers, allowing us to add Connecticut coach Jim Calhoun's three NCAA titles, four Final Fours and Ollie's one Final Four to our total. That makes all of the 2014 Final Four contestants eligible to improve our remarkable total to 74 of 76, for a 97.4 winning percentage of all NCAA Championship games played (I am counting Bo Ryan because he is at the same school, Wisconsin, as the head of the pedigree----Doc Meanwell). If Kentucky wins its ninth national championship; UK-UofL will lead Duke-UNC in that category 12 to 9.

ADDENDUM I
These players were added after the book was made ready for press.

FIVE OF THE ELEVEN PLAYERS WHO HAVE PLAYED IN FIVE RIVALRY GAMES

JAMES BLACKMON-UK

	FG/A	3/A	FT/A	R	PF	A	S	B	TO	PTS
GAME #14	3/5	0/0	0/1	2	3	4	3	0	2	6
GAME #15	1/1	0/0	0/0	1	0	0	0	0	1	2
GAME #16	0/1	0/0	0/0	0	2	1	1	0	1	0
GAME #17	3/12	0/0	3/4	4	1	1	0	0	1	9
GAME #18	4/7	3/3	0/2	1	2	2	2	0	1	11
TOTALS	11/26	3/3	3/7	8	8	8	6	0	6	28

ROGER HARDEN-UK

	FG/A	3/A	FT/A	R	PF	A	S	B	TO	PTS
GAME #13	0/0	0/0	0/0	0	0	0	0	0	1	0
GAME #14	0/0	0/0	0/0	1	2	2	0	0	1	0
GAME #15	0/0	0/0	0/0	0	1	0	0	0	0	0
GAME #16	6/9	0/0	0/0	2	1	2	1	0	2	12
GAME #17	3/6	0/0	4/4	2	2	4	2	0	3	10
TOTALS	9/15	0/0	4/4	5	6	8	3	0	7	22

MARK McSWAIN-UofL

	FG/A	3/A	FT/A	R	PF	A	S	B	TO	PTS
GAME #14	5/5	0/0	0/0	2	4	0	0	0	2	10
GAME #15	0/1	0/0	0/0	0	1	1	0	0	0	0
GAME #16	2/5	0/0	9/10	4	3	0	1	0	0	13
GAME #17	0/0	0/0	3/4	0	2	0	0	1	0	0
GAME #18	1/2	0/0	0/1	4	0	1	0	0	0	2
TOTALS	8/13	0/0	9/11	10	10	2	1	1	2	25

DARIUS MILLER-UK

	FG/A	3/A	FT/A	R	PF	A	S	B	TO	PTS
GAME #40	0/1	0/0	0/0	0	0	1	0	0	0	0
GAME #41	0/1	0/0	0/0	2	3	0	0	0	1	0
GAME #42	3/6	0/1	1/1	3	4	0	0	1	2	7
GAME #43	2/8	1/1	2/2	4	4	1	0	0	8	7
GAME #44	4/7	1/4	4/4	3	2	0	2	0	1	13
TOTALS	9/23	2/6	7/7	12	13	2	2	1	12	27

KYLE KURIC-UofL

	FG/A	3/A	FT/A	R	PF	A	S	B	TO	PTS
GAME #40	1/1	1/1	0/0	0	0	0	1	0	0	3
GAME #41	0/2	0/0	0/0	3	2	0	0	0	0	0
GAME #42	3/7	1/4	0/0	3	4	2	2	0	2	7
GAME #43	1/4	0/2	0/0	2	4	1	1	0	1	2
GAME #44	3/8	1/2	0/1	5	3	0	1	0	0	7
TOTALS	8/22	3/9	0/1	13	13	3	5	0	3	19

GAME 47
March 28, 2014

	UK	UofL
Record	26-10	31-5
Ranking	unranked	#5
Series	31	15
Favored	LOUISVILLE BY 4.5	
Location	LUCAS OIL STADIUM INDIANAPOLIS, IN	
TV	CBS	

THE PRE-GAME REPORT

It's hard to separate this rivalry into time segments because of its eternal nature-----constantly in play. The all-consuming passion displayed by these Card and Cat fans' may at any moment ignite the bottomless pit into a raging Mt. Vesuvius. And the ultimate trigger mechanism is----the NCAA tournament, where the rivalry looms even larger because the national championship is at stake.

This marks the fourth time the Cards and Cats have tangled in NCAA competition since 1975 when more than one team from each conference is allowed to participate in the same tournament. Duke and North Carolina, the runner-up rivalry have never battled each other in NCAA tournament play. Complaints have been made about the seeding and placement of both UK and UofL in the same Midwest Region. The seeding could have been a little better for both teams; UofL is a No. 4 seed and UK is a No. 8, but the real irritant is the fact that both teams have landed in the Midwest Region.

This is the sixth time that the Cards and Cats have been linked in the same region since 1975 while Duke and UNC have suffered the same fate only twice. But the SEC has absorbed the brunt of this "shabby" affront by the Selection Committee as two of its only three tournament teams; Kentucky and Tennessee are crammed together in this same Midwest Region. Some have contended that the committee dealt this hand because of Kentucky's low-seeding, but this proposition lacks credence since the last time I checked there is still a No. 8 seed in all four of the regions.

The paralysis by analysis has been amongst us since the 2014 AP Preseason Poll was released on October 31, 2013. The "One and Dones" of Kentucky were ranked No. 1, followed by No. 2 Michigan State and No. 3 Louisville. Halloween must have conjured this spell that five freshmen starters were the best in the land. This preseason poll had 11 of its' 25 members in this 2014 NCAA Sweet 16 including six of the Top Ten; Kentucky, Michigan State, Louisville, Arizona, Michigan and Florida.

It seems that we hear incessantly from various sources the same hopes and longings: Harrell is better now than when they played in Rupp, Dakari Johnson is better now than when they played in Rupp, Luke Hancock is better now than when they played in Rupp, Randle missed most of the second-half when they played in Rupp, UofL has the advantage on the perimeter, UK has the advantage inside, Vegas has the Cardinals winning, so UofL fans don't have anything to worry about, Kentucky has turned things around so UK fans don't have anything to worry about, and so forth and so on.

UofL Coach Rick Pitino says: "It's not defense that wins championships, you win by scoring." UK Coach John Calipari says: "You don't have to make all your shots, but you can't miss all your shots." Louisville has won seven consecutive games and 18 of its last 20. Kentucky has overcome lackluster effort, a negative patience rating and selfish play to win six of its seven games in the post-season. But can this continue?

An analogy comes to mind. Remember when you bought your first car? Unless you were related to someone like Bill Gates, your first was pretty close to a "clunker." Let's assume it was an old Dodge Dart. Now, your oil pan and radiator were both leaking, your timing belt was out of time and all four tires resembled your favorite bald person. And you tell me you're going on a trip all the way from Louisville to Los Angeles. My response has me come immediately to attention; I salute and say: "Good luck Captain!" Later that night I receive a collect call from the captain who is stuck in a Memphis barbecue joint pleading his case: "Hey Man! Do you belong to AAA!"

In 1980, "The Ville" went to Poncho Wright's stomping grounds----Indianapolis and beat a UCLA team loaded with freshmen 59-54 for the Cardinals' first NCAA National Championship. This time in Indy, will UofL beat the freshmen again, or will that blue and white Dodge Dart keep rolling on to Texas?

QUOTES

No matter if you are bigger, slower or quicker than me, a basketball player always sees themselves as having an advantage. That's the way I am.

UofL GUARD RUSS SMITH
BY SAM UPSHAW JR./The C-J

If I force turnovers who cares about their length?

UofL GUARD CHRIS JONES
BY JOSH GREER LOUISVILLE COURIER-JOURNAL

He's calmer; I wouldn't say he's gentler. He's calmer because we're playing better.
UK GUARD JON HOOD (Commenting on Coach John Calipari)
BY JOHN CLAY LEXINGTON HERALD-LEADER

I was born to hate Louisville. (Said with a big smile)
UK GUARD JARROD POLSON
BY JERRY TIPTON tipton@herald-leader.com

PROBABLE STARTERS

Louisville

POS.	PLAYER	HT.	WT.	CLS.	PT.
F/G	LUKE HANCOCK	6-6	200	SR.	12.1
F	MONTREZL HARRELL	6-8	235	SO.	14.0
F	STEPHEN VAN TREESE	6-9	245	SR.	2.9
G	RUSS SMITH	6-1	165	SR.	18.1
G	CHRIS JONES	5-10	175	JR.	10.4

Kentucky

POS.	PLAYER	HT.	WT.	CLS.	PT.
G	ANDREW HARRISON	6-6	215	FR.	11.0
G	AARON HARRISON	6-6	218	FR.	14.1
G	JAMES YOUNG	6-6	215	FR.	14.3
F	JULIUS RANDLE	6-9	250	FR.	15.1
C	DAKARI JOHNSON	7-0	265	FR.	4.7

KENTUCKY 74, LOUISVILLE 69
WILDCATS TOPPLE CARDS IN WILD FINISH
LEXINGTON HERALD-LEADER

FROM OUT OF THE BLUE
LOUISVILLE COURIER-JOURNAL

Back on December 28th UofL scored the first eight points of the game, but in less than four minutes, UK had rallied and taken an 11-10 lead. In the Sweet Sixteen in Indianapolis, UK launched five three-pointers in the first five minutes of the game, connecting on none, finding themselves down 8-4 when Coach Calipari called a timeout with 16:11 on the clock. But a key play occurred 57 seconds later when Luke Hancock was called for his second foul, sending him to the bench with Louisville leading 10-4.

The next three-minute fifteen-second span would spell trouble for UofL even though as a Cardinal fan, you had to feel good about the game as it was developing. UK did almost nothing. The Cats were 0/3 from the field, 1/2 from the foul line and had committed three turnovers. But the Cards were hitting only 3/8 from the field and were 1/2 on free throws, and when the TV timeout was taken, Louisville led 18-5 with 11:53 remaining in the first-half.

Exhorting his Cats, Calipari's players were rejuvenated mentally and started an uphill struggle to get back in the game. Pitino's troops outscored UK 22-12 in the paint, but left the proverbial door open by making only six of 15 fouls shots in the first-half. The poor free throw shooting was compounded by Montrezl Harrell picking-up his second and third personal fouls in just 13 seconds in the waning minutes of the half.

UofL led by just three points, 34-31 at the intermission. With those three fouls, Harrell didn't start the second-half and remained on the bench for about three minutes, but UK, who lost Willie Cauley-Stein to an ankle injury after only four minutes of action in the first-half, couldn't take advantage of Harrell's absence. However, when Dakari Johnson make a jumper with 13:05 left in the game, the Cats trailed by just two, 44-42. But Russ Smith's layup and Harrell's dunk pushed the Cardinal lead to 48-42. The UofL lead fluctuated between two and six points until Hancock's three-point shot gave Louisville a 59-52 lead with 7:13 to go in the game.

UK's Johnson made an old-fashioned three-point play cutting UofL's lead to four at 59-55, but Luke Hancock answered with a three and two free throws to put the Cardinals out in front 64-57 with 5:32 left. Then, the 41,000 plus inside the Lucas Oil Stadium witnessed a thrilling completion of play. Aaron Harrison made two free throws for the Cats, but Luke Hancock returned the favor keeping UofL on top, 66-59. Andrew Harrison found Alex Poythress inside for a dunk----66-61. However, Poythress wasn't finished for the night. He followed his dunk with a block and Randle made a layup----66-63.

With 2:12 left in the game, Mangok Mathiang blocked Randle's shot, but Poythress grabbed the offensive rebound, scored and was fouled. His free throw tied the game at 66-all. Aaron Harrison missed a layup for Kentucky and Harrell grabbed the rebound, but Russ Smith turned it over and Harrell committed his fifth foul sending Poythress to the charity stripe. He missed the first, made the second giving UK a 67-66 lead with 2:12 remaining. But Russ Smith countered with a jump shot and the lead was right back in UofL's favor, 68-67.

Thirty-seconds later Aaron Harrison made the biggest shot of the game. Julius Randle was heading down main street towards the basket when instead of continuing his dribble drive, he found Harrison in the left-corner for a three-point shot which put UK on top, 70-68. Hancock missed a shot, but the Cards got the rebound and Wayne Blackshear was fouled. In the second-half, the Cardinals had reversed their free throw shooting woes connecting on 6/6. Blackshear, was shooting 74.4% from the line on the year, managed to hit the second attempt after missing the first and UK still had the advantage at 70-69. UK, who had lost so many games this season struggling from the foul line won tonight's game in large part, by making 22 of 27 attempts. Randle made two more, Smith missed a three-point attempt for UofL to tie the game, and Aaron Harrison made two more foul shots making the final score, UK 74-UofL 69.

STATS

Louisville

	Min	FG	FG A	3PT FG	3 PT FGA	FT	FT A	Reb	PF	Ast	St	BS	TO	Pts
Luke Hancock	25	6	9	3	5	4	4	0	2	2	1	0	3	19
Montrezl Harrell	33	7	9	0	0	1	3	8	5	2	0	0	3	15

	Min	FG	FG A	3PT FG	3 PT FGA	FT	FT A	Reb	PF	Ast	St	BS	TO	Pts
Stephan Van Treese	25	0	0	0	0	0	0	4	5	2	0	1	1	0
Russ Smith	34	9	20	1	7	4	10	2	3	3	1	0	2	23
Chris Jones	28	2	5	0	1	2	2	2	3	0	0	0	1	6
Terry Rozier	17	0	3	0	0	0	0	4	3	0	1	0	0	0
Anton Gill	2	0	0	0	0	0	0	0	0	0	0	0	0	0
Mangok Mathiang	17	1	3	0	0	1	2	4	3	1	2	2	0	3
Wayne Blackshear	17	1	4	0	2	1	2	1	0	1	1	0	0	3
Akoy Agau	2	0	0	0	0	0	0	0	0	0	0	0	0	0
Team								4						
Totals	**200**	**26**	**53**	**4**	**15**	**13**	**23**	**29**	**24**	**11**	**6**	**3**	**10**	**69**

Kentucky

	Min	FG	FG A	3PT FG	3 PT FGA	FT	FT A	Reb	PF	Ast	St	BS	TO	Pts
James Young	22	3	8	0	2	3	4	1	5	0	0	1	2	9
Julius Randle	35	5	11	0	1	5	6	12	2	1	1	0	4	15
Dakari Johnson	31	7	10	0	0	1	2	6	2	0	0	0	1	15
Aaron Harrison	38	3	13	3	7	6	6	3	1	0	3	0	1	15
Andrew Harrison	38	4	11	1	4	5	6	5	3	7	0	0	2	14
Marcus Lee	1	0	0	0	0	0	0	0	1	0	0	0	0	0
Jared Polson	2	0	0	0	0	0	0	0	0	0	0	0	1	0
Willie Cauley-Stein	4	0	0	0	0	0	0	1	1	0	0	0	0	0
Alex Poythress	14	2	2	0	0	2	3	4	1	0	1	1	1	6
Dominique Hawkins	15	0	0	0	0	0	0	0	3	0	0	0	0	0
Team								5						
Totals	**200**	**24**	**55**	**4**	**14**	**22**	**27**	**37**	**19**	**8**	**5**	**2**	**12**	**74**

POINTS AFTER

You can't miss as many free throws as we missed. If you take that away, we played really almost a near-perfect game in a lot of areas.
UofL COACH RICK PITINO
BY JEFF GREER LOUISVILLE COURIER-JOURNAL

I empathize with the fans. I wish I could've given them the win.
UofL GUARD RUSS SMITH
BY JEFF GREER LOUISVILLE COURIER-JOURNAL

I was looking to attack. The dude kind of cut me off so I spun back. I saw (Aaron's) man kind of cheating in. I went up to shoot, but I saw Aaron was wide open. I had all the confidence in the world that he was going to make the shot, and he did.
UK FORWARD JULIUS RANDLE
BY BEN ROBERTS LEXINGTON HERALD-LEADER.

Alex Poythress won the game for us.
UK COACH JOHN CALIPARI
BY KYLE TUCKER LOUISVILLE COURIER-JOURNAL

I thought this was an exciting game. I've said all along that this rivalry takes no backseat to any other tandem matchup in college basketball. And CBS announcer Jim Nantz agrees: ". . .No rivalries compare with Kentucky-Louisville and North Carolina-Duke. What makes Kentucky and Louisville a little sweeter, maybe, is you get it once a year, except for this year." (and 2012, and 1984) Quote from Courier-Journal's Jonathan Lintner.

Shooting percentage is vital to determining the winner in championship play, but if one of the other two categories, 3-point shooting and/or free throw accuracy is badly out-of-balance, you are in serious trouble. The Cardinals shot 49.1 percent from the field compared to UK's 43.6 percent. So far, so good for Cardinal fans. Both teams were horrendous from 3-point land. UK was 4 out of 14 for 28.6 percent, and UofL was 4 out of 15 for 26.7 percent.

Now the free throw percentage tells the tale. Louisville was 13 of 23 for 56.5 percent and UK 22 of 27 for 81.5 percent. If you make two free throws equal one field goal, the Cats made 35 two-point baskets out of 68.5 attempts for 51.1 percent, and the Cards made 32.5 baskets out of 64.5 attempts for 50.4 percent. Close in percentage, but the Cats made almost three more field goals.

The Cardinals scored six more points off turnovers, but the Wildcats had an eight point advantage on second chance points. UofL scored 44 points in the paint to UK's 34, but after a 22-12 Red and Black margin in the first-half, it was even 22-22 in the second. Coach Pitino said the free shooting made the difference, but wasn't the shoe on the other foot at the YUM Center on 12-29-2012 when the Cats were 11 for 23 and the Cards 17 for 25 from the free throw stripe with Louisville winning 80-77?

Randle made a great assist to Aaron Harrison who buried a three-pointer to give the Cats a 70-68 lead with 40 seconds left in the game. Coach Pitino said his defensive player missed the play allowing Harrison to come off a curl and get open. That happened in Rupp back on December 28,

2013 when UK's James Young got open, made a three and stretched the Wildcat lead to 63-56. Missed assignment again.

Here's a much larger question or strategy I would like answered. Why take Hancock out with two personal fouls and 15:08 remaining in the first-half and never put him back in that half when you needed a lift? Hancock still has three fouls to give. Chuck Hayes for UK in 2005 didn't foul out, but was re-inserted too late to beat Michigan State.

Josh Harrellson hasn't any college eligibility left, but he still has two fouls to give from the 2011 Final Four battle against Connecticut. Coach Calipari was being ripped by the talk show hosts. He couldn't coach. I made some comments myself, but in postseason play, this team has made a marvelous transformation.

Cal's critics said he would never win a championship using "One and Dones." When he did in 2012, the same critics claimed he would never win another. The Cats have beaten a No. 1, No. 4 and No. 2 seed to reach their 16th Final Four. If they don't go all the way for their ninth title, will those critics pile on with: "I told you so"?

These same people claim it means nothing that Cal leads Rick 5-1, now 6-1 in the series. Sure it means something, but no one is writing that Cal owns the series. The "worst" conference in the nation according to those same critics is 11-1 in 2014 tournament play, and two of its three teams are in the Final Four on a a collision course to meet in the championship game.

But I still would like to see non-UK fans pulling or least prepared to give the Wildcats their due if they win-it-all. I would be pulling for Louisville if they had beaten Kentucky. I want this rivalry to continue to dominate.

Five times in the last four years, either the Cards or the Cats have been in the Final Four. Each has won a national championship in that same time period and Kentucky has the opportunity to win again. Surely for the rivalry's sake, the non-Cat fans don't want Florida, Wisconsin or Connecticut to win it? With the win in Game 47 74-69, UK now leads the series in games won 32-15.

When they play each other enjoy the battle. When one advances further than the other in tournament play, pull for the rivalry to maintain College Basketball's No. 1 status. Congratulations to Louisville's Russ Smith who with this Sweet Sixteen appearance, becomes the first rivalry player since the "Dream Game" on March 26th, 1983 to play in six games. His 23 points in this game gives him a grand total of 102 points scored versus the Wildcats.

And Russ's best scoring performance, next to his contribution in the 2013 NCAA Final Four won by the Cardinals, was the class he showed after UofL's 74-69 loss to UK in the Sweet Sixteen. He went inside the Kentucky locker room and shook all the players' hands and told them to go on and win the national championship. He said in an interview that we shouldn't hate anybody.

Monday morning, March 31st, 2014 many of the fans calling the talk shows took the "classy" road. UofL fans are certainly disappointed, but not vindictive. Cat fans are happy, and many are not rubbing it in. Some may still take the distasteful approach, but that's another reason why UK vs. UofL is College Basketball's No. 1 Rivalry; hate is not its strong point----Enough Said!